# Lecture Notes in Computer Science 2011

Edited by G. Goos, J. Hartmanis and J. van Leeuwen

T0232838

# Springer

*Berlin*
*Heidelberg*
*New York*
*Barcelona*
*Hong Kong*
*London*
*Milan*
*Paris*
*Singapore*
*Tokyo*

Markus Mohnen  Pieter Koopman (Eds.)

# Implementation of Functional Languages

12th International Workshop, IFL 2000
Aachen, Germany, September 4-7, 2000
Selected Papers

Springer

Series Editors

Gerhard Goos, Karlsruhe University, Germany
Juris Hartmanis, Cornell University, NY, USA
Jan van Leeuwen, Utrecht University, The Netherlands

Volume Editors

Markus Mohnen
RWTH Aachen, Lehrstuhl für Informatik II
Ahornstr. 55, 52056 Aachen, Germany
E-mail: mohnen@informatik.rwth-aachen.de

Pieter Koopman
KUN Nijmegen
Toernooiveld 1, 6525 ED Nijmegen, The Netherlands
E-mail: pieter@cs.kun.nl

Cataloging-in-Publication Data applied for

Die Deutsche Bibliothek - CIP-Einheitsaufnahme

Implementation of functional languages : 12th international workshop ;
selected papers  IFL 2000, Aachen, Germany, September 4 - 7, 2001.
Markus Mohnen ; Pieter Koopman (ed.). - Berlin ; Heidelberg ; New York ;
Barcelona ; Hong Kong ; London ; Milan ; Paris ; Singapore ; Tokyo :
Springer, 2001
    (Lecture notes in computer science ; Vol. 2011)
    ISBN 3-540-41919-5

CR Subject Classification (1998): D.3, D.1.1, F.3

ISSN 0302-9743
ISBN 3-540-41919-5 Springer-Verlag Berlin Heidelberg New York

Springer-Verlag Berlin Heidelberg New York
a member of BertelsmannSpringer Science+Business Media GmbH

http://www.springer.de

© Springer-Verlag Berlin Heidelberg 2001

Typesetting: Camera-ready by author, data conversion by Olgun Computergrafik, Heidelberg
Printed on acid-free paper      SPIN 10782109      06/3142      5 4 3 2 1 0

# Preface

The International Workshops on Implementation of Functional Languages (IFL) are a tradition that has lasted for over a decade. The aim of these workshops is to bring together researchers to discuss new results and new directions of research related primarily but not exclusively to the implementation of functional or function–based languages. A not necessarily exhaustive list of topics includes: language concepts, type checking, compilation techniques, (abstract) interpretation, automatic program generation, (abstract) machine architectures, array processing, concurrent/parallel programming and program execution, heap management, runtime profiling and performance measurements, debugging and tracing, tools and programming techniques.

IFL 2000 was held at Schloß Rahc, an 18th century castle in Aachen, Germany, during the first week of September 2000. It attracted 49 researchers from the international functional language community, presenting 33 contributions during the four days of the workshop. The contributions covered all topics mentioned above.

In addition, a special session organised by Thomas Arts from the Ericsson Computer Science Laboratory in Stockholm, Sweden, attracted several practitioners from industry who reported on their experiences using the functional language Erlang. The Erlang session was sponsored by Ericsson Computer Science Laboratory.

This year, the workshop was sponsored by local industry (Ericsson Eurolab Deutschland GmbH and debis Systemhaus Aachen), which indicates the growing importance of functional language concepts in commercial spheres. We thank our sponsors for their generous contributions.

With this volume, we follow the lead of the last four IFL workshops in publishing a high-quality subset of the contributions presented at the workshop in the Springer Lecture Notes in Computer Science series. All speakers attending the workshop were invited to submit a paper afterwards. Each of the 33 submissions was reviewed by three or four PC members and thoroughly discussed by the PC. We selected 15 papers for publication in this volume.

The overall balance of the papers is representative, both in scope and technical substance, of the contributions made to the Aachen workshop as well as to those that preceded it. Publication in the LNCS series is not only intended to make these contributions more widely known in the computer science community but also to encourage researchers in the field to participate in future workshops, of which the next one will be held in Stockholm, Sweden in September 2001 (see http://www.ericsson.se/cslab/ifl2001/ for further details).

January 2001                                        Markus Mohnen and Pieter Koopman

## Program Committee

Markus Mohnen      (RWTH Aachen, Germany)
Pieter Koopman     (KUN Nijmegen, The Netherlands)
Marko van Eekelen  (KUN Nijmegen, The Netherlands)
Sven-Bodo Scholz   (University of Kiel, Germany)
Thomas Arts        (Ericsson Computer Science Laboratory, Sweden)
Phil Trinder       (Heriot-Watt University, UK)
John Peterson      (Yale University, USA)
John O'Donnell     (University of Glasgow, UK)
John Glauert       (University of East Anglia, UK)
Colin Runciman     (University of York, UK)

## Referees

Peter Achten         Greg Michaelson           Sjaak Smetsers
Maarten de Mol       Rinus Plasmeijer          John van Groningen
Frank Huch           R.F. Pointon
Martin Leucker       Thomas Richert
H-W. Loidl           Ronny Wichers Schreur

## Sponsors

Ericsson Eurolab
Deutschland GmbH

Services by DaimlerChrysler

debis Systemhaus Aachen

# Table of Contents

# Non-determinism Analysis
# in a Parallel-Functional Language*

Ricardo Peña and Clara Segura

Universidad Complutense de Madrid, Spain
{ricardo,csegura}@sip.ucm.es

**Abstract.** The paper presents several analyses to detect non-deterministic expressions in the parallel-functional language Eden. First, the need for the analysis is motivated, and then each one is presented. The first one is type-based, while the other two are based on abstract interpretation. Their power and efficiency is discussed, and an example is used to illustrate the differences. Two interesting functions to adapt abstract values to types appear, and they happen to be a Galois insertion.

## 1 Introduction

The paper presents several analyses to determine when an Eden [BLOP98] expression is sure to be deterministic, and when it may be non-deterministic.

The parallel-functional language Eden extends the lazy functional language Haskell by constructs to explicitly define and communicate processes. The three main new concepts are *process abstractions*, *process instantiations* and the non-deterministic process abstraction `merge`. Process abstractions of type `Process a b` can be compared to functions of type `a -> b`, and process instantiations can be compared to function applications. An instantiation is achieved by using the predefined infix operator `(#)` :: `Process a b -> a -> b`. Each time an expression `e1 # e2` is evaluated, a new parallel process is created to evaluate (`e1 e2`).

Non-determinism is introduced in Eden by means of a predefined process abstraction `merge` :: `Process [[a]] [a]` which *fairly* interleaves a set of input lists, to produce a single non-deterministic list. Its implementation immediately copies to the output list any value appearing at any of the input lists. So, `merge` can profitably be used to quickly react to requests coming in an unpredictable order from a set of processes. This feature is essential in reactive systems and very useful in some deterministic parallel algorithms [KPR00]. Eden is aimed at both types of applications.

Eden has been implemented by modifying the *Glasgow Haskell Compiler* (GHC) [PHH+93]. GHC translates Haskell into a minimal functional language called Core where a lot of optimizations [San95,PS98] are performed. Some of them are incorrect in a non-deterministic environment. So, a non-determinism analysis is carried out at Core level and, as a result, variables are annotated as

---

* Work partially supported by the Spanish-British Acción Integrada HB 1999-0102 and Spanish projects TIC 97-0672 and TIC 2000-0738.

M. Mohnen and P. Koopman (Eds.): IFL 2000, LNCS 2011, pp. 1–18, 2001.

deterministic or (possibly) non-deterministic. After that, the dangerous transformations are disallowed if non-determinism is present.

The plan of the paper is as follows: In Section 2, we review some approaches to non-determinism in functional languages and in particular in Eden. We further motivate the need for a non-determinism analysis. Section 3 presents a first simple analysis by using a type inference system. Section 4 provides a second view of this analysis as an abstract interpretation with no functional domains. The analysis is efficient and powerful enough for most purposes, but it loses precision in function applications and in process instantiations. A non-trivial example is also given. In Section 5, a new abstract interpretation is developed, in which functions and process abstractions are interpreted as abstract functions. The previous example is used to illustrate the differences between both analyses, being the second one more powerful but less efficient. Section 6 presents some related work in type based and abstract interpretation based analyses. Finally, Section 7 concludes and gives some guidelines on future work.

## 2    Non-determinism in Eden

The introduction of non-determinism in functional languages has a long tradition and has been a source of strong controversy. John McCarthy [McC63] introduced the operator `amb :: a -> a -> a` which non-deterministically chooses between two values. Henderson [Hen82] introduced instead `merge :: [a] -> [a] -> [a]` which non-deterministically interleaves two lists into a single list. Both operators violate referential transparency in the sense that it is no longer possible to replace equals by equals. For instance, `let x = amb 0 1 in x + x ≠ amb 0 1 + amb 0 1` as the first expression may only evaluate to 0 or to 2, while the second one may also evaluate to 1.

Hughes and O'Donnell proposed in [HO90] a functional language in which non-determinism is compatible with referential transparency. The idea is the introduction of the type `Set a` of sets of values to denote the result of non-deterministic expressions. The programmer explicitly uses this type whenever an expression may return one value chosen from a set of possible values. The implementation represents a set by a single value belonging to the set. Once a set is created, the programmer cannot come back to single values. So, if a deterministic function `f` is applied to a non-deterministic value (a set `S`), this must be expressed as `f * S` where `(*) :: (a -> b) -> Set a -> Set b` is the `map` function for sets. A limited number of set operations are allowed. The most important one is ∪ (set union) that allows the creation of non-deterministic sets and can be used to simulate `amb`. Other, such as `choose :: Set a -> a` or ∩ (set intersection) are disallowed either because they violate referential transparency or because they cannot be correctly implemented by 'remembering' one value per set. In the paper, a denotational semantics based on Hoare powerdomains is given for the language and a number of useful equational laws are presented so that the programmer can formally reason about the (partial) correctness of programs.

But the controversy goes further. In [SS90,SS92], the authors claim that what is really missing is an appropriate definition of *referential transparency*. They show that several apparently equivalent definitions (replacing equals by equals, unfoldability of definitions, absence of side effects, definiteness of variables, determinism, and others) have been around in different contexts and that they are not in fact equivalent in the presence of non-determinism. To situate Eden in perspective, we reproduce here their main concepts:

**Referential transparency.** Expression $e$ is purely referential in position $p$ iff $\forall e_1, e_2.[\![e_1]\!] \; \rho = [\![e_2]\!] \; \rho \Rightarrow [\![e[e_1/p]]\!] \; \rho = [\![e[e_2/p]]\!] \; \rho$. Operator $op :: t_1 \rightarrow \cdots$ $t_n \rightarrow t$ is referentially transparent if for all expressions $e \overset{\text{def}}{=} op \; e_1 \cdots e_n$, whenever expression $e_i, 1 \leq i \leq n$ is purely referential in position $p$, expression $e$ is purely referential in position $i.p$. A language is referentially transparent if all of its operators are.

**Definiteness.** Definiteness property holds if a variable denotes the same single value in all its occurrences. For instance, if variables are definite, the expression $(\lambda x.x - x)(amb \; 0 \; 1)$ evaluates always to 0. If they are not, it may also evaluate to 1 and $-1$.

**Unfoldability.** Unfoldability property holds if $[\![(\lambda x.e) \; e']\!] \; \rho = [\![e[e'/x]]\!] \; \rho$ for all $e, e'$. In presence of non-determinism, unfoldability is not compatible with definiteness. For instance, if variables are definite $[\![(\lambda x.x - x)(amb \; 0 \; 1)]\!] \; \rho \neq [\![(amb \; 0 \; 1) - (amb \; 0 \; 1)]\!] \; \rho$.

In the above definitions, the semantics of an expression is a set of values in the appropriate powerdomain. However, the environment $\rho$ maps a variable into a single value in the case variables are definite (also called *singular semantics*), and to a set of values in the case they are indefinite (also called *plural semantics*).

In Eden, the only source of non-determinism is the predefined process `merge`. When instantiating a new process by evaluating the expression `e1 # e2`, closure `e1`, together with the closures of all the free variables referenced there, are copied (possibly unevaluated) to another processor where the new process is instantiated. However, within the same processor, a variable is evaluated at most once and its value is shared thereafter. We are still developing a denotational semantics for the language but, for the purpose of this discussion, we will assume that the denotation of an expression of type a is a (downwards and limit closed) set of values of type a representing the set of possible values returned by the expression. If the expression is deterministic, its denotation is a singleton.

Under these premises, we can characterize Eden as referentially transparent. The only difference with respect to Haskell is that now, in a given environment $\rho$, an expression denotes a set of values instead of a single one. Inside an expression, a non-deterministic subexpression can always be replaced by its denotation without affecting the resulting set of values.

Variables are definite within the same process and are not definite within different processes. When an unevaluated non-deterministic free variable is duplicated in two different processes, it may happen that the actual value computed by each process is different. However, denotationally both variables represent the same set of values, so the semantics of the enclosing expressions will not change by the fact that the variable is evaluated twice.

In general, in Eden we do not have the unfoldability property except in the case that the unfolded expression is deterministic. This is a consequence of having definite variables within a process. The motivation for a non-determinism analysis in Eden comes from the following two facts:

- In future, Eden's programmers may wish to have definite variables in all situations. It is sensible to think of having a compiler flag to select this semantic option. In this case, the analysis will detect the (possibly) non-deterministic variables and the compiler will force their evaluation to normal form before being copied to a different processor.
- At present, some transformations carried out by the compiler in the optimization phases are semantically incorrect for non-deterministic expressions. The most important one is *full laziness* [JPS96]. The compiler will detect the non-deterministic bindings and disallow the floating of a let out of a lambda in these situations. Other dangerous transformations are the *static argument transformation* [San95] and the *specialization* (see [PPRS00] for more details). The general reason for all of them is the increasing of closure sharing: Before the transformation, several evaluation of a non-deterministic expression can produce several different values; after the transformation, a shared non-deterministic expression is once evaluated, yielding a unique value.

To justify the last item, let us consider the following two bindings:

```
f = λy.let x = e1          f' = let x = e1
in x + y                     in λy. x + y
```

If e1 is non-deterministic, the semantics of $f$ is a non-deterministic function. Then, $[\![f\ 5 - f\ 5]\!]\ \rho$ will deliver a non-single set of values as x is evaluated each time $f$ is applied. The semantics of the expression bound to $f'$ is instead a set of deterministic functions and, due to the definiteness of variables x and f', $[\![f'\ 5 - f'\ 5]\!]\ \rho$ evaluates always to $\{0\}$. So, the semantics has changed.

## 3   A Type-Based Analysis

**The Language.** As Eden is implemented by modifying GHC, the language being analysed is an extension of Core. This is a simple functional language with second-order polymorphism, so the language includes type abstraction and type application. In Figure 1 the syntax of the language and of the type expressions is shown. There, $v$ denotes a variable, $k$ denotes a literal and $x$ denotes an atom (a variable or a literal). A program is a list of possibly recursive bindings from variables to expressions. Such expressions include variables, lambda abstractions, applications of a functional expression to an atom, constructor applications, primitive operators applications, and also *case* and *let* expressions. Constructor

$$
\begin{array}{lll}
prog \rightarrow & bind_1; \ldots; bind_m & \\
bind \rightarrow & v = expr & \{\text{non-recursive binding}\} \\
& |\ \mathbf{rec}\ v_1 = expr_1; \ldots; v_m = expr_m & \{\text{recursive binding}\} \\
expr \rightarrow & expr\ x & \{\text{application to an atom}\} \\
& |\ \lambda v.expr & \{\text{lambda abstraction}\} \\
& |\ \mathbf{case}\ expr\ \mathbf{of}\ alts & \{case\ \text{expression}\} \\
& |\ \mathbf{let}\ bind\ \mathbf{in}\ expr & \{let\ \text{expression}\} \\
& |\ C\ x_1 \ldots x_m & \{\text{saturated constructor application}\} \\
& |\ op\ x_1 \ldots x_m & \{\text{saturated primitive operator application}\} \\
& |\ x & \{\text{atom}\} \\
& |\ \Lambda\alpha.expr & \{\text{type abstraction}\} \\
& |\ expr\ type & \{\text{type application}\} \\
& |\ v\ \#\ x & \{\text{process instantiation}\} \\
& |\ \mathbf{process}\ v \rightarrow expr & \{\text{process abstraction}\} \\
alts \rightarrow & Calt_1; \ldots; Calt_m; [Deft] \quad m \geq 0 & \\
& |\ Lalt_1; \ldots; Lalt_m; [Deft] \quad m \geq 0 & \\
Calt \rightarrow & C\ v_1 \ldots v_m \rightarrow expr \quad\quad m \geq 0 & \{\text{algebraic alternative}\} \\
Lalt \rightarrow & k \rightarrow expr & \{\text{primitive alternative}\} \\
Deft \rightarrow & v \rightarrow expr & \{\text{default alternative}\} \\
type \rightarrow & K & \{\text{basic types: Integers, characters}\} \\
& |\ \alpha & \{\text{type variables}\} \\
& |\ T\ type_1 \ldots type_m & \{\text{type constructor application}\} \\
& |\ type_1 \rightarrow type_2 & \{\text{function type}\} \\
& |\ Process\ type_1\ type_2 & \{\text{process type}\} \\
& |\ \forall\alpha.type & \{\text{polymorphic type}\}
\end{array}
$$

**Fig. 1.** Language definition and type expressions

and primitive operators applications are saturated. The variables contain type information, so we will not write it explicitly in the expressions.

The new Eden expressions are a process abstraction **process** $v \rightarrow e$, and a process instantiation $v \# x$. There is also a new type $Process\ t_1\ t_2$, see Figure 1, representing the type of a process abstraction **process** $v \rightarrow e$ where $v$ has type $t_1$ and $e$ has type $t_2$. Frequently $t_1$ and $t_2$ are tuple types, where each tuple element represents an input or an output channel of the process.

**The Annotations.** As type information is already available in the language, we just need to annotate types. The analysis attaches non-determinism annotations to types. These are basic annotations $n$ or $d$, or tuples of basic annotations. A basic annotation $d$ in the type of an expression means that such expression is sure to be deterministic. For example, an integer constant is deterministic. A basic annotation $n$ means that the expression may be non-deterministic.

Tuples of basic annotations correspond to expressions of tuple type (or processes/functions returning tuples, see below) where each component carries its own annotation. The tuple type is treated in a special way; the rest of data types just carry a basic annotation. Processes usually have several input/output

$$b \rightarrow n$$
$$| \ d$$
$$a \rightarrow b$$
$$| \ (b_1, \ldots, b_m)$$

$$(b_1, \ldots, b_m)_t = (b_1, \ldots, b_m)$$
$$b_{(t_1, \ldots, t_m)} = (\overset{1}{b}, \ldots, \overset{m}{b})$$
$$b_{t_1 \rightarrow t_2} = b_{Process \ t_1 \ t_2} = b_{t_2}$$
$$b_{\forall \alpha.t} = b_t$$
$$b_t = b \ \text{if} \ t = K, \alpha, T \ t_1 \ldots t_m$$

**Fig. 2.** Annotations and adaptation function definition

channels, and this fact is represented by using tuples. In the implementation, an independent concurrent thread is provided for every output channel of a process. We would like to express which ones are deterministic and which ones may be non-deterministic. For example, in the following process abstraction

```
process v →  case v of (v1,v2) →  let y1 = v1 in
let y2 = merge # v2 in (y1,y2)
```

we say that the first output is deterministic and that the second one may be non-deterministic. The same happens to functions returning tuples. As the internal tuples do not represent output channels only one level of tupling is maintained.

**Some Notation.** In the following, $b$ is used to denote a basic annotation and $a$ to denote a basic annotation or a tuple of basic annotations, see Figure 2. Regarding the types, $t$ is used to denote the unannotated ones, see Figure 1, and $\tau$ or $t^a$ to denote the annotated ones. In the type environments $A + [v :: t^a]$ denotes the extension of environment $A$ with the annotated typing for $v$. In the typing rules of Figure 3, $i$ ranges from 1 to $m$ and $j$ from $\overline{1 \ \text{to} \ l_i}$. Overlining is used to indicate an indexed sequence. For example, $A + \overline{[v_i :: \tau_i]}$ represents the extension of $A$ with new typings for the variables $v_1, \ldots, v_m$.

An ordering between the annotations is established, $d \sqsubseteq n$ (naturally extended to tuples). Several least upper bound (lub) operators can be defined, as well as an operator to flatten the internal tuples so that nested tuples do not appear; all of them are shown in Figure 3. In the rules shown there it is necessary to adapt an annotation $a$ of type $t'$ to a type $t$ in some places. This adaptation function, see Figure 2, is represented as $a_t$: If $a$ is basic and $t$ is a tuple type, it replicates $a$ to construct a tuple of the corresponding size; if it is already a tuple, it behaves as the identity.

**The Type System.** In Figure 3 the type system is shown. Rule [$VAR$] is trivial. Rule [$LIT$] specifies that constants of basic types are deterministic. There are two rules for constructors: One for tuples [$TUP$] and another one [$CONS$] for the rest. In the first case, we obtain the annotation of each component, flatten them (if they are tuples, nesting must be eliminated) and give back the resulting tuple. In the second case, we also obtain the components' annotations, flatten them and finally apply the lub operator, so that a basic annotation is obtained. This implies that, if any component of the construction may be non-deterministic,

$$\frac{}{A + [v :: \tau] \vdash v :: \tau} \; VAR \qquad\qquad \frac{}{A \vdash k :: K^d} \; LIT$$

$$\frac{\textbf{data} \; T \; \overline{\alpha_k} = \overline{C_i \; \overline{t_{ij}}} \quad A \vdash x_j :: [t_{ij}[\alpha_k := t_k]]^{a_j}}{A \vdash C_i \; \overline{x_j} :: (T \; \overline{t_k})^{\;\bigsqcup(\widehat{\bigsqcup}a_j)} \; j} \; CONS \qquad \frac{op :: t_1 \to (t_2 \to \dots (t_m \to t)) \quad A \vdash x_i :: t_i^{\;a_i}}{A \vdash op \; x_1 \dots x_m :: t^{\;(\bigsqcup(\widehat{\bigsqcup}a_i))_t} \; i} \; PRIM$$

$$\frac{A \vdash x_i :: t_i^{\;a_i}}{A \vdash (x_1, \dots, x_m) :: (t_1, \dots, t_m)^{(\widehat{\bigsqcup}a_1, \dots, \widehat{\bigsqcup}a_m)}} \; TUP \qquad \frac{A \vdash e :: t_1 \xrightarrow{a_1} t_2 \quad A \vdash x :: t_1^{\;a_2}}{A \vdash (e \; x) :: t_2^{\;(\widehat{\bigsqcup}a_2) \sqcup a_1}} \; APPLY$$

$$\frac{A + [v :: t^{dt}] \vdash e :: t'^{\;a}}{A \vdash (\lambda v.e) :: t \xrightarrow{a} t'} \; ABS \qquad \frac{A + [v :: t^{dt}] \vdash e :: t'^{\;a}}{A \vdash \textbf{process} \; v \to e :: Process^a \; t \; t'} \; PABS$$

$$\frac{A \vdash e_1 :: \tau_1 \quad A + [v :: \tau_1] \vdash e :: \tau_2}{A \vdash \textbf{let} \; v = e_1 \; \textbf{in} \; e :: \tau_2} \; LETNONREC$$

$$\frac{A + \overline{[v_i :: \tau_i]} \vdash e_i :: \tau_i \quad A + \overline{[v_i :: \tau_i]} \vdash e :: \tau'}{A \vdash \textbf{let rec} \; \overline{v_i = e_i} \; \textbf{in} \; e :: \tau'} \; LETREC$$

$$\frac{A \vdash p :: Process^a \; t \; t' \quad A \vdash x :: t^{a'}}{A \vdash p\#x :: t'^{\;b \sqcup a} \; \text{where} \; b = \widehat{\bigsqcup}a'} \; PINST \qquad \frac{}{A \vdash \textbf{merge} :: (Process \; [[\alpha]] \; [\alpha])^n} \; MERGE$$

$$\frac{A \vdash e :: (t_1, \dots, t_m)^{(b_1, \dots, b_m)} \quad A + \overline{[v_i :: t_i^{\;b_i}t_i]} \vdash e' :: \tau'}{A \vdash \textbf{case} \; e \; \textbf{of} \; (v_1, \dots, v_m) \to e' :: \tau'} \; CASETUP$$

$$\frac{\textbf{data} \; T \; \overline{\alpha_k} = \overline{C_i \; \overline{t_{ij}}} \quad A \vdash e :: (T \; \overline{t_k})^b \quad A + A_i \vdash e_i :: t^{a_i} \; \text{where} \; A_i = \overline{[v_{ij} :: tv_{ij}^{\;b}tv_{ij}]}, \; tv_{ij} = t_{ij} \; \overline{[\alpha_k := t_k]}}{A \vdash \textbf{case} \; e \; \textbf{of} \; \overline{C_i \; \overline{v_{ij}} \to e_i} :: t^{\;b \sqcup (\bigsqcup a_i)} \; i} \; CASEALG$$

$$\frac{A \vdash e :: K^b \quad A \vdash e_i :: t^{a_i}}{A \vdash \textbf{case} \; e \; \textbf{of} \; \overline{k_i \to e_i} :: t^{\;b \sqcup (\bigsqcup a_i)} \; i} \; CASEPRIM$$

$$\frac{A, \alpha \vdash e :: t^a}{A \vdash \Lambda\alpha.e :: (\forall\alpha.t)^a} \; TYABS \qquad \frac{A \vdash e :: (\forall\alpha.t)^a}{A \vdash (e \; t') :: tinst^{a\;tinst} \; \text{where} \; tinst = t[\alpha := t']} \; TYAPP$$

$$n \sqcup b = n$$
$$d \sqcup b = b$$
$$b \sqcup (b_1, \dots, b_m) = (b_1 \sqcup b, \dots, b_m \sqcup b)$$
$$(b_1, \dots, b_m) \sqcup (b'_1, \dots, b'_m) = (b_1 \sqcup b'_1, \dots, b_m \sqcup b'_m)$$
$$\widehat{\bigsqcup}b = b$$
$$\widehat{\bigsqcup}(b_1, \dots, b_m) = \bigsqcup_i b_i$$

**Fig. 3.** Types annotation system

the whole expression will be considered as possibly non-deterministic; the information about the components is lost.

Rules [*ABS*] and [*PABS*] need some explanation. What is a deterministic function/process? As merge process is the only source of non-determinism, we will say that an expression may be non-deterministic when it 'contains' any instantiation of this process. So we will consider that a function/process is deterministic if it does not generate non-deterministic results from deterministic arguments. This means that we are only interested in the result of the function when it is applied to a deterministic argument. So, in the rule [*ABS*] the annotation attached to the function is the one obtained for the body when in the environment the argument is assigned a deterministic annotation. If the body gets a deterministic annotation, the function is deterministic; but if the body may be non-deterministic then the function may be non-deterministic. The deterministic annotation given to the argument is an adaptation of the basic annotation $d$ to the type of the argument, see Figure 2. For example, if it is a $n$-tuple, the annotation should be an $n$-tuple $(d, \ldots, d)$. If the argument were non-deterministic we are always assuming that the result may be non-deterministic. This means that we are not expressing how the output depends on the input. In Section 5 we will see that this leads to some limitations of the analysis. The lack of such information is reflected in the [*APPLY*] rule. The result of the application may be non-deterministic either the function is annotated as non-deterministic or the argument is annotated as non-deterministic. This is expressed by using a lub operator. If the argument's annotation is a tuple, then we have to previously flatten it as we cannot use the information that its components provide. Such information (independent annotations) is used when the components are separately used in different parts of the program, and this is what usually happens with processes: Each output channel feeds a different process.

Rules [*PABS*] and [*PINST*] are analogous to [*ABS*] and [*APPLY*]. In [*PRIM*] rule, primitive operators are considered as deterministic, so we just flatten the annotations of the arguments and apply a lub operator to them. Finally, the annotation is adapted to the type of the result. The [*MERGE*] rule specifies that merge may be a non-deterministic process (in fact, it is the source of non-determinism). The [*LETNONREC*] and [*LETREC*] rules are the expected ones: The binders are added to the environment with the annotations of the right hand sides of their bindings.

An algebraic *case* expression may be non-deterministic if either the discriminant expression (the choice between the alternatives could be non-deterministic) or any of the expressions in the alternatives may be non-deterministic. This is expressed in the [*CASEALG*] rule. However if the discriminant is a tuple, there is no non-deterministic choice between the alternatives. This information is just passed to the right hand side of the alternative, so that only if the non-deterministic variables are used there, the result will be annotated as non-deterministic. This is reflected in the [*CASETUP*] rule. In general, the same applies to those types with only one constructor, so it could be extended to all such types. In these two *case* rules, the annotation obtained from the discrimi-

$$Basic = \{d, n\} \text{ where } d \sqsubseteq n$$
$$D_K = D_\alpha = D_{T \ t_1 \ldots t_m} = Basic$$
$$D_{(t_1, \ldots, t_m)} = \{(b_1, \ldots, b_m) \mid b_i \in Basic\}$$
$$D_{t_1 \rightarrow t_2} = D_{Process \ t_1 \ t_2} = D_{t_2}$$
$$D_{\forall \alpha.t} = D_t$$

**Fig. 4.** Abstract domains

nant has to be adapted to the types of the variables in the left hand side of the alternatives. In the $[CASEALG]$ rule the discriminant annotation is just a basic annotation that represents the whole structure. If it is deterministic, then we can say that each of the components of the value is deterministic; and in case it is non-deterministic, we have to say that each component is non-deterministic, as we have lost information when annotating the discriminant. In the $[CASETUP]$ rule each component has its own annotation, so we don't lose so much information, but, as there are no nested tuples, we still have to adapt each annotation to the component's type. The optional default alternative has not been included in the figure for clarity but it is easy to do.

We have type polymorphism but not annotation polymorphism. In $[TYABS]$ rule $A, \alpha$ means that $\alpha$ is a type variable not free in $A$. When the instantiation of a polymorphic type takes place, it is necessary to adapt the annotation of the polymorphic type to the instantiated type. This is necessary when new structure arises from the instantiation. For example if we apply the identity process $\Lambda\alpha.process \ v \rightarrow v$, with annotated type $(\forall\alpha.Process \ \alpha \ \alpha)^d$, to $(Int, Int)$ we need to adapt $d$ to $Process \ (Int, Int) \ (Int, Int)$, which produces $(d, d)$, see Figure 2. If the external structure was already a tuple, the annotation is maintained. For example, in $\Lambda\alpha.process \ v \rightarrow (v, v)$, with annotated type $(\forall\alpha.Process \ \alpha \ (\alpha, \alpha))^{(d,d)}$, the adaptation gives back the same annotation $(d, d)$.

# 4   Abstract Interpretation

The analysis of the previous section has several limitations, explained in Section 5. In this section an abstract interpretation version of the analysis is presented. This version will lead us to develop a more powerful analysis, also abstract interpretation based, in which we will be able to overcome these limitations. Such extension does not seem so evident in the type annotation system.

**The Abstract Domains.** The type system is directly related to an abstract interpretation where the domains corresponding to functions/processes are identified with their range domains. This means there are no functional domains, so the fixpoint calculation is less expensive. Figure 4 shows the abstract domains.

There is a basic domain $Basic$ that corresponds to the annotations $d$ and $n$ in the previous section, with the same ordering. This is the abstract domain corresponding to basic types and algebraic types (except tuples). Tuples are again specially treated, as tuples of basic abstract values. The abstract domain

$\llbracket v \rrbracket \ \rho = \rho \ v$

$\llbracket k \rrbracket \ \rho = d$

$\llbracket (x_1, \ldots, x_m) \rrbracket \ \rho = (\widehat{\sqcup}(\llbracket x_1 \rrbracket \ \rho), \ldots, \widehat{\sqcup}(\llbracket x_m \rrbracket \ \rho))$

$\llbracket C \ x_1 \ldots x_m \rrbracket \ \rho = \bigsqcup_i \widehat{\sqcup}(\llbracket x_i \rrbracket \ \rho)$

$\llbracket e \ x \rrbracket \ \rho = (\widehat{\sqcup}(\llbracket x \rrbracket \ \rho)) \sqcup \llbracket e \rrbracket \ \rho$

$\llbracket op \ x_1 \ldots x_m \rrbracket \ \rho = (\bigsqcup_i \widehat{\sqcup}(\llbracket x_i \rrbracket \ \rho))_t \ \text{where} \ op :: t_1 \to (t_2 \to \ldots (t_m \to t))$

$\llbracket p \# x \rrbracket \ \rho = \widehat{\sqcup}(\llbracket x \rrbracket \ \rho) \sqcup \llbracket p \rrbracket \ \rho$

$\llbracket \lambda v.e \rrbracket \ \rho = \llbracket e \rrbracket \ \rho \ [v \mapsto d_t] \ \text{where} \ v :: t$

$\llbracket \mathbf{process} \ v \to e \rrbracket \ \rho = \llbracket e \rrbracket \ \rho \ [v \mapsto d_t] \ \text{where} \ v :: t$

$\llbracket merge \rrbracket \ \rho = n$

$\llbracket \mathbf{let} \ v = e \ \mathbf{in} \ e' \rrbracket \ \rho = \llbracket e' \rrbracket \ \rho \ [v \mapsto \llbracket e \rrbracket \ \rho]$

$\llbracket \mathbf{let \ rec} \ \overline{\{v_i = e_i\}} \ \mathbf{in} \ e' \rrbracket \ \rho = \llbracket e' \rrbracket \ (\textit{fix} \ (\lambda \rho'.\rho \ \overline{[v_i \mapsto \llbracket e_i \rrbracket \ \rho']}))$

$\llbracket \mathbf{case} \ e \ \mathbf{of} \ (v_1, \ldots, v_m) \to e' \rrbracket \ \rho = \llbracket e' \rrbracket \ \rho \ \overline{[v_i \mapsto \pi_i(\llbracket e \rrbracket \ \rho)_{t_i}]} \ \text{where} \ v_i :: t_i$

$\llbracket \mathbf{case} \ e \ \mathbf{of} \ \overline{C_i \ \overline{v_{ij}} \to e_i} \rrbracket \ \rho = b \sqcup (\bigsqcup_i \llbracket e_i \rrbracket \ \rho_i)$

$$\text{where} \ b = \llbracket e \rrbracket \ \rho$$
$$\rho_i = \rho \ \overline{[v_{ij} \mapsto b_{t_{ij}}]}, v_{ij} :: t_{ij}$$

$\llbracket \mathbf{case} \ e \ \mathbf{of} \ \overline{k_i \to e_i} \rrbracket \ \rho = \llbracket e \rrbracket \ \rho \sqcup (\bigsqcup_i \llbracket e_i \rrbracket \ \rho)$

$\llbracket \Lambda \alpha.e \rrbracket \ \rho = \llbracket e \rrbracket \ \rho$

$\llbracket e \ t \rrbracket \ \rho = (\llbracket e \rrbracket \ \rho)_{tinst} \ \text{where} \ (e \ t) :: tinst$

**Fig. 5.** Abstract interpretation

corresponding to functions and processes is the abstract domain corresponding to the type of the result. The abstract domain of a polymorphic type is that of its smallest instance, i.e. that one in which $K$ is substituted for the type variable. So the domain corresponding to a type variable is *Basic*.

**The Abstract Interpretation.** In Figure 5 the abstract interpretation is shown. It is very similar to the type annotation system, so we just outline some specific details. In the recursive *let* we have to calculate a fixpoint, which can be obtained by using the Kleene's ascending chain:

$$\llbracket \mathbf{let \ rec} \ \overline{\{v_i = e_i\}} \ \mathbf{in} \ e' \rrbracket \ \rho = \llbracket e' \rrbracket \ (\bigsqcup_{n \in \mathbb{N}} (\lambda \rho'.\rho \ \overline{[v_i \mapsto \llbracket e_i \rrbracket \ \rho']})^n (\rho_0))$$

where $\rho_0$ is an environment in which all variables have as abstract value the infimum $\perp_t$ of its corresponding abstract domain. At each iteration, the abstract values of bindings' right hand sides are computed and the environment is updated until no changes are found. Termination is assured, as the abstract domains corresponding to each type are finite. The number of iterations is $O(N)$, where $N$ is the total number of 'components' in the bindings. We consider a non-tuple variable as a single component, and a tuple variable $v :: (t_1, \ldots, t_m)$ as $m$ components.

From the abstract interpretation we have obtained an algorithm that annotates each subexpression with its abstract value. This algorithm has been imple-

```
rw = λ worker.λ ts.
      let rec
        t = (ts, is)
        ys = manager # t
        y1 = case ys of (z1,z2,z3) → z1
        y2 = case ys of (u1,u2,u3) → u2
        y3 = case ys of (v1,v2,v3) → v3
        o1 = worker # y1
        o2 = worker # y2
        os = [o1, o2]
        is = merge # os
      in y3

manager = process ts → case ts of
            (t1, t2) → (g t1 t2,h t1 t2,r t1)
```

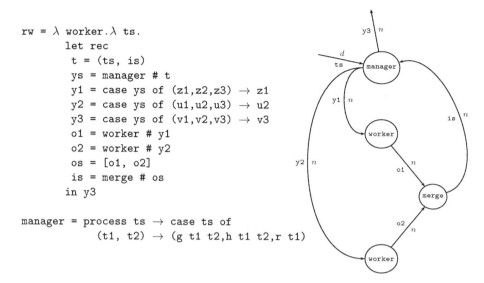

**Fig. 6.** Replicated workers process structure where $n = 2$

mented in Haskell, and we have executed it with some examples, one of which is shown below. This algorithm uses syntax-driven recursive calls that accumulate variables in the environment as necessary. This is equivalent to a bottom-to-top pass in the type annotation rules where only the type environments are built. When recursive calls finish, lub operations are carried out. This is equivalent to the application of the types annotation rules from top to bottom, once we have the appropriate environment.

**An Example: Replicated Workers.** This example shows a simplified version of a replicated workers topology [KPR00]. We have a manager process and $n$ worker processes. The manager provides the workers with tasks. When any of the workers finishes its task, it sends a message to the manager including the obtained results and asking for a new task. In order to enable the manager to assign new tasks to idle processes inmediately, even though the answers may be received from the workers in any order, a **merge** process is needed. The function **rw** representing this scheme when $n = 2$ is shown in Figure 6, where **worker** is the worker process and **ts** is an initial list of tasks to be done by the workers. The output of the manager process **manager** usually depends on both input lists, the initial one **ts** and that produced by the workers **os**. However, in order to compare the power of this analysis with that one presented in Section 5 we are assuming that **manager** is defined as shown in Figure 6, where **g**, **h** and **r** are deterministic functions (i.e they have as abstract value $d$). So, **manager**'s abstract value is $(d, d, d)$. With this definition, the third component of the process output only depends on the first input list. This means that the final result of the function **rw** only depends on the initial tasks list. In Figure 6 the process topology with the annotations in each channel is shown. As there are mutually recursive definitions, all of them get the $n$ annotation. However, we know that that when `ts` is deterministic, the result of the function is also deterministic, as it only depends on that initial list, and not on the one coming from the `merge` process. The analysis answer is safe but just approximate. In Section 5 a more powerful analysis is presented. There the results are more accurate.

In the real applications of this scheme, although the manager receives the results from the workers in any order, it sorts them and the output of the whole structure is deterministic. However this cannot be detected with the analysis and the result still produces an $n$ annotation.

## 5    Limitations and Refinement

**Limitations.** As we have previously said, there are no functional abstract domains in this analysis. This means that the fixpoint calculation is not expensive, but it also imposes some limitations to the analysis. For instance, we cannot express the dependency of the result with respect to the argument. As we have said before, in a function application or process instantiation, we cannot fully use the information provided by the argument.

This happens, for example, when the function does not depend on any of its arguments. For example, if we define the function $f\ v = 5$, the analysis tells us that the function is deterministic, but when we apply $f$ to a possibly non-deterministic value, the result of the application is established as possibly non-deterministic. This is not true, as we will always obtain the same unique value. Of course this a safe approximation, but not a very accurate one. The function $g\ v = v$ would have the same abstract behaviour. Both $f$ and $g$ are deterministic functions, but they have different levels of determinism: $f$ does not depend on its argument, but $g$ does. If functions and processes were interpreted as functions, this limitation would be over. The abstract function $f^{\#}$ corresponding to $f$ would be $f^{\#} = \lambda z.d$, while that of $g$, $g^{\#}$, would be $\lambda z.z$. Now, if we applied $f^{\#}$ to $n$, we would obtain $d$, but $n$ in the case of $g^{\#}$. The same happens when tuples are involved. The abstract value of

$$h\ v_1\ v_2\ v_3 = \textbf{let}\ u = merge\ \#\ v_3\ \textbf{in}\ (v_1, v_2, u)$$

is $(d, d, n)$. But when we apply it, if any of the arguments has $n$ as abstract value, the result will be $(n, n, n)$. If the abstract value were $h^{\#} = \lambda z_1.\lambda z_2.\lambda z_3.(z_1, z_2, n)$ then we would not lose so much information, for example $h^{\#}\ d\ n\ d = (d, n, n)$.

So the solution seems to be to interpret the functions and processes as abstract functions, and this is what we do in what follows.

**The Second Abstract Interpretation.** We will denote everything related to this analysis with the underscript 2 to distinguish it from the previous one. In Figure 7 the abstract domains are shown. There are two differences. The abstract domain corresponding to a function/process is the domain of continuous functions between the abstract domains of the argument and the result. The tuple type now is interpreted as the cartesian product of the corresponding abstract domains. So nested tuples are allowed. This is important as now

$$Basic = \{d, n\} \text{ where } d \sqsubseteq n$$
$$D_{2\,K} = D_{2\,T\ t_1 \ldots t_m} = D_{2\beta} = Basic$$
$$D_{2\,(t_1, \ldots, t_m)} = D_{2\,t_1} \times \ldots \times D_{2\,t_m}$$
$$D_{2\,t_1 \to t_2} = D_{2\,Process\ t_1\ t_2} = [D_{2\,t_1} \to D_{2\,t_2}]$$
$$D_{2\,\forall\beta.t} = D_{2\,t}$$

**Fig. 7.** Abstract domains for the refined analysis

$[\![v]\!]_2\ \rho_2 = \rho_2(v)$

$[\![k]\!]_2\ \rho_2 = d$

$[\![(x_1, \ldots, x_m)]\!]_2\ \rho_2 = ([\![x_1]\!]_2\ \rho_2, \ldots, [\![x_m]\!]_2\ \rho_2)$

$[\![C\ x_1 \ldots x_m]\!]_2\ \rho_2 = \bigsqcup_i \alpha_{t_i}([\![x_i]\!]_2\ \rho_2) \text{ where } x_i :: t_i$

$[\![e\ x]\!]_2\ \rho_2 = ([\![e]\!]_2\ \rho_2)\ ([\![x]\!]_2\ \rho_2)$

$[\![op\ x_1 \ldots x_m]\!]_2\ \rho_2 = (\gamma_{t_{op}}(d))\ ([\![x_1]\!]_2\ \rho_2) \ldots ([\![x_m]\!]_2\ \rho_2) \text{ where } op :: t_{op}$

$[\![p\#x]\!]_2\ \rho_2 = ([\![p]\!]_2\ \rho_2)\ ([\![x]\!]_2\ \rho_2)$

$[\![\lambda v.e]\!]_2\ \rho_2 = \lambda z \in D_{2\,t_v}.[\![e]\!]_2\ \rho_2\ [v \mapsto z] \text{ where } v :: t_v$

$[\![\textbf{process}\ v \to e]\!]_2\ \rho_2 = \lambda z \in D_{2\,t_v}.[\![e]\!]_2\ \rho_2\ [v \mapsto z] \text{ where } v :: t_v$

$[\![merge]\!]_2\ \rho_2 = \lambda z \in Basic.n$

$[\![\textbf{let}\ v = e\ \textbf{in}\ e']\!]_2\ \rho_2 = [\![e']\!]_2\ \rho_2\ [v \mapsto [\![e]\!]_2\ \rho_2]$

$[\![\textbf{let rec}\ \overline{\{v_i = e_i\}}\ \textbf{in}\ e']\!]_2\ \rho_2 = [\![e']\!]_2\ (fix\ (\lambda \rho'_2.\rho_2\ \overline{[v_i \mapsto [\![e_i]\!]_2\ \rho'_2]}))$

$[\![\textbf{case}\ e\ \textbf{of}\ (v_1, \ldots, v_m) \to e']\!]_2\ \rho_2 = [\![e']\!]_2\ \rho_2\ \overline{[v_i \mapsto \pi_i([\![e]\!]_2\ \rho_2)]}$

$$[\![\textbf{case}\ e\ \textbf{of}\ \overline{C_i\ \overline{v_{ij}} \to e_i}]\!]_2\ \rho_2 = \begin{cases} \gamma_t(n) \text{ if } [\![e]\!]_2\ \rho_2 = n \\ \bigsqcup_i [\![e_i]\!]_2\ \rho_{2i} \text{ otherwise} \end{cases}$$

$$\text{where } \rho_{2i} = \rho_2\ \overline{[v_{ij} \mapsto \gamma_{t_{ij}}(d)]}, v_{ij} :: t_{ij}, e_i :: t$$

$$[\![\textbf{case}\ e\ \textbf{of}\ \overline{k_i \to e_i}]\!]_2\ \rho_2 = \begin{cases} \gamma_t(n) \text{ if } [\![e]\!]_2\ \rho_2 = n \\ \bigsqcup_i [\![e_i]\!]_2\ \rho_2 \text{ otherwise} \end{cases}$$

$$\text{where } e_i :: t$$

**Fig. 8.** The refined analysis

functions/processes are interpreted as abstract functions. If a process has several output channels and any of them returns a function/process, we would like to maintain the information provided, so we don't apply the flattening. In Figure 8 the new abstract interpretation is shown.

Now the interpretation of a tuple is the tuple of abstract values of the components. The interpretation of a function is an abstract function that takes an abstract argument[1] and returns the abstract value of the body. So application is interpreted as function application. In the recursive *let* the fixpoint can be computed by using the Kleene's ascending chain, starting with an initial environment where all the variables have $\perp_{2t}$ as abstract value.

---

[1] In the examples, we will not write explicitly the domain of the argument when it is clear from the type of the function.

$$\alpha_t : D_{2t} \to Basic$$

$$\alpha_K = \alpha_T\ t_1 \ldots t_m = id_{Basic}$$

$$\alpha_{(t_1,\ldots,t_m)}(e_1,\ldots,e_m) = \bigsqcup_i \alpha_{t_i}(e_i)$$

$$\alpha_{Process\ t_1\ t_2}(f) = \alpha_{t_1 \to t_2}(f)$$

$$\alpha_{t_1 \to t_2}(f) = \alpha_{t_2}(f(\gamma_{t_1}(d)))$$

$$\gamma_t : Basic \to D_{2t}$$

$$\gamma_K = \gamma_T\ t_1 \ldots t_m = id_{Basic}$$

$$\gamma_{(t_1,\ldots,t_m)}(b) = (\gamma_{t_1}(b),\ldots,\gamma_{t_m}(b))$$

$$\gamma_{Process\ t_1\ t_2}(b) = \gamma_{t_1 \to t_2}(b)$$

$$\gamma_{t_1 \to t_2}(b) = \begin{cases} \lambda z \in D_{2t_1}.\gamma_{t_2}(n) & \text{if } b = n \\ \lambda z \in D_{2t_1}.\gamma_{t_2}(\alpha_{t_1}(z)) & \text{if } b = d \end{cases}$$

**Fig. 9.** Abstraction and concretisation functions definition

In this new analysis we need two functions conceptually similar to the flattening operator and to the adaptation of an abstract value to a type. These functions are $\alpha_t$, called the *abstraction function*, and $\gamma_t$, called the *concretisation* function, both defined in Figure 9. They are respectively used in constructor applications and in *case* expressions.

Given a type $t$, the abstraction function takes an abstract value in $D_{2t}$ and *flattens* it to a value in *Basic*. This is necessary in constructor applications as a single basic abstract value represents the whole structure.

Given a type $t$, the function $\gamma_t$ *unflattens* a basic abstract value and produces an abstract value in $D_{2t}$. This function is used in an algebraic *case* expression. The discriminant has a basic abstract value, as we have flattened all the values of the components. We have to recover the values of the components in order to analyse the right hand sides. But we have lost the information, so the only thing we can do is to give a safe approximation of those values. This is what $\gamma_t$ does: given a basic value, it gives a safe approximation to any abstract value that the component could have had, considering how the flattening has been done.

The functions are mutually recursive. The idea of the abstraction function is to flatten the tuples and apply the functions to the unflattening of $d$ for the argument's type. The abstraction function loses information. As an example, if $t = Int \to Int$, $\alpha_t(\lambda z.z) = \alpha_t(\lambda z.d) = d$. In Figure 10 we show the abstraction function for the type $(Int \to Int) \to Int \to Int$.

The idea of the concretisation function is to obtain the best safe approximation to determinism and non-determinism. It tries to recover the information that the abstraction function lost. The function type needs explanation, the rest of them are inmediate. As we have said before, a function is deterministic if it produces deterministic results from deterministic arguments. If the argument is non-deterministic, the safer we can produce is a non-deterministic result: It is like an 'identity' function. So, the unflattening of $d$ for a function type is a function that takes an argument, flattens it to see whether it is deterministic or not and again applies the concretisation function with the type of the result. As an example, if $t = Int \to Int$, $\gamma_t(d) = \lambda z.z$. In Figure 10 we show the concretisation function for the type $(Int \to Int) \to Int \to Int$. The unflattening of $n$ for a function type is the function that returns a non-deterministic result independently of the argument (it is the top of the abstract domain). For example, if $t = Int \to Int$, $\gamma_t(n) = \lambda z.n$.

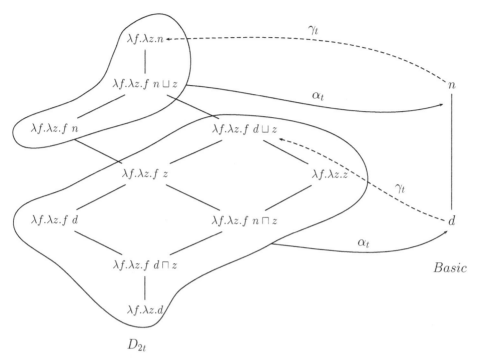

**Fig. 10.** Abstraction and concretisation functions for $t = (Int \rightarrow Int) \rightarrow Int \rightarrow Int$

We have proven that these functions are monotone and continuous and that they are a Galois insertion [NNH99], i.e. $\alpha_t \cdot \gamma_t = id_{Basic}$ and $\gamma_t \cdot \alpha_t \sqsupseteq id_{D_{2t}}$. This means that given a basic abstract value $b$ and a type $t$, $\gamma_t(b)$ gives the best safe approximation to those abstract values that abstracted to $b$. So, the abstract values below $\gamma_t(d)$ are deterministic.

In the primitive operator application we have considered, as we did before, that the primitive operators are deterministic, choosing as abstract value the best safe approximation corresponding to the type of the operator $\gamma_{t_{op}}(d)$. Another, more accurate, option would have been to include in an initial environment the abstract values of all the primitive operators.

Using this analysis in the example of Figure 6 we obtain more accurate information than in the first analysis. We have assumed that $g$, $h$ and $r$ are deterministic functions. But now we have to provide abstract functions as their abstract values. We assume that their abstract values are: $g^{\#} = h^{\#} = \lambda t.\lambda s.t \sqcup s$ and $r^{\#} = \lambda t.t$. These are $\gamma_{Int \rightarrow Int \rightarrow Int}(d)$ and $\gamma_{Int \rightarrow Int}(d)$, that is, the 'biggest' deterministic functions of the corresponding types. Then, the abstract value of $\texttt{manager}$ is $manager^{\#} = \lambda t.(\pi_1(t) \sqcup \pi_2(t), \pi_1(t) \sqcup \pi_2(t), \pi_1(t))$. This means that $\texttt{ys}$ has as abstract value $ys^{\#} = (n, n, l)$ where $l$ is the abstract value of the argument $\texttt{ts}$. So the abstract value of $\texttt{rw}$ is $rw^{\#} = \lambda w.\lambda l.l$. This result tells us that the abstract value of the $\texttt{worker}$ process is ignored and that if $\texttt{ts}$ is deterministic ($l = d$), then the result of the function is deterministic as well.

# 6   Related Work

The first analysis presented in this paper has been expressed using first a type annotation system and afterwards an abstract intepretation easily extensible to a more powerful analysis. In recent years typed based analyses have been widely used for several reasons such as their better efficiency and their adequacy when the information being looked for is preserved across transformations. For example in [TWM95] a type based analysis is developed to detect values that are accessed at most once. In [WJ99] type polymorphism and user-defined data types are added. The language being analysed is a second order polymorphic $\lambda$-calculus extended with some Core constructions. The analysis annotates the types with usage information.

In [BFGJ00] C. Baker-Finch, K. Glynn and S. Peyton Jones present their *constructed product result* (CPR) analysis. The analysis pretends to determine which functions can return multiple results in registers, that is, which functions return an explicitly-constructed tuple. It is an abstract interpretation based analysis where the abstract domain corresponding to a function type $t_1 \rightarrow t_2$ is not the corresponding functional domain, but it is instead isomorphic to the abstract domain of the result's type $t_2$. Product types are interpreted as cartesian product of a basic abstract domain, so nested tuples are not allowed. Our first analysis, expressed as an abstract interpretation, follows the same ideas but for different reasons that have been already explained in the paper.

The second analysis is a typical abstract interpretation in the style of [BHA86], where functions are interpreted as abstract functions. There, a strictness analysis is presented where the basic abstract domain is also a two-point domain ($\bot \sqsubseteq \top$). However, the analyses are rather different. As an example, let $f :: (Int \rightarrow Int) \rightarrow Int$ be a function whose abstract interpretations in the strictness analysis and in the non-determinism analysis are respectively $f^s$ and $f^n$. To find out if such function is strict in its argument we apply $f^s$ to $\bot_{Int \rightarrow Int}$, that is, to $\lambda z.\bot$: If the result is $\bot$, then it is strict in its argument; otherwise it may be non-strict. On the other hand, if we want to know whether it is is deterministic or not, we apply $f^n$ to $\gamma_{Int \rightarrow Int}(d)$, that is, to $\lambda z.z$: If the result is less than or equal to $\gamma_{Int}(d)$ (that is, it is equal to $d$) then it is deterministic; otherwise it may be non-deterministic. For example, $\lambda g.g \ (head(merge\#[[0],[1]]))$ is strict in its argument but it may be non-deterministic, i.e. $f^s \ (\lambda z.\bot) = \bot$ but $f^n \ (\lambda z.z) = n$. Also, the abstract interpretation of primitive operators, constructors and *case* expressions is different in each analysis.

# 7   Conclusions and Future Work

We have seen that non-determinism affects the definiteness of variables in the programs written in Eden: If a non-deterministic expression is evaluated in different processes, the variable it is bound to will denote possibly different values. It would be desirable to warn the programmer about this situation, or to force the evaluation of such an expression so that all the occurrences of the variable have the same value. Additionally there exist sequential transformations that are incorrect when non-determinism is involved. Such transformations should be applied only to those parts of the program that are sure to be deterministic.

In this paper several analyses of different efficiency and power have been presented. They detect when an expression is sure to be deterministic, and when it may be non-deterministic. The first one, both expressed as a type based analysis and as an abstract interpretation based one, is efficient (linear) but less accurate. The second one, an abstract interpretation based analysis, is more powerful but less efficient (exponential). One example has been given to compare their accuracy. The details regarding polymorphism are not explained in the refined abstract interpretation, but the idea is the same as in the first analysis: To represent a polymorphic type by its smallest instance and afterwards to adapt the abstract value to the particular instance. This can be achieved by using functions similar to the abstraction and concretisation functions.

Correctness of the analyses has not been proved, as still there is not a formal semantics for Eden. However a simplified version where some details are abstracted could be used to prove the correctness. Another interesting question is the relation between the two analyses presented. Intuitively, the first analysis is a safe approximation to the second one. It can be proved that it is in fact an approximation to a widening [CC92] of the second analysis. Both the introduction of polymorphism and the relation between the analyses will be presented in a forthcoming paper.

We have already said that the first analysis has linear complexity, while the second one has a exponential one, as functions are involved. However the second analysis is more powerful than the first one. Following the ideas in [PP93] an intermediate analysis could be developed so that it is more powerful than the first one but less expensive than the second one. The idea is to use a probing to obtain a signature for the function. Such signature is easily comparable and represents a widening of the function. This speeds up the fixpoint calculation, as the chain of widened approximations is shorter. The first analysis is in fact a particular case of probing, where all the arguments are set to 'd'. The idea is to probe also the combinations of arguments where 'n' occupies each position. For example, in a function with three integer arguments, the additional probings would be $(n, d, d)$, $(d, n, d)$ and $(d, d, n)$.

Another alternative to improve efficiency in the second analysis could be to extend the type based analysis in the style of [GS00] so that it mimicked the powerful abstract interpretation with less cost.

# References

BFGJ00.   C. Baker-Finch, K. Glynn, and S. L. Peyton Jones. Constructed Product Result Analysis for Haskell. 2000. Submitted to *International Conference on Functional Programming, ICFP'00*.

BHA86.    G. L. Burn, C. L. Hankin, and S. Abramsky. The Theory of Strictness Analysis for Higher Order Functions. In *Programs as Data Objects*, volume 217 of *LNCS*, pages 42–62. Springer-Verlag, Oct. 1986.

BLOP98.   S. Breitinger, R. Loogen, Y. Ortega Mallén, and R. Peña. Eden: Language
          Definition and Operational Semantics. Technical Report, Bericht 96-10.
          Revised version 1.998, Philipps-Universität Marburg, Germany, 1998.
CC92.     P. Cousot and R. Cousot. Abstract interpretation frameworks. *Journal of
          Logic and Computation*, 2(4):511–547, Aug. 1992.
GS00.     J. Gustavsson and J. Svenningsson. A usage analysis with bounded usage
          polymorphism and subtyping. In *Proceedings of the 12th International
          Workshop on Implementation of Functional Languages*, pages 279–294,
          2000. Also in this volume.
Hen82.    P. Henderson. Purely Functional Operating Systems. In *Functional Pro-
          gramming and its Applications: An Advanced Course*, pages 177–191. Cam-
          bridge University Press, 1982.
HO90.     R. J. M. Hughes and J. O'Donnell. Expressing and Reasoning About Non-
          Deterministic Functional Programs. In *Functional Programming: Proceed-
          ings of the 1989 Glasgow Workshop, 21-23 Aug. 1989*, pages 308–328, Lon-
          don, UK, 1990. Springer-Verlag.
JPS96.    S. L. Peyton Jones, W. Partain, and A. L. M. Santos. Let-floating: moving
          bindings to give faster programs. *International Conference on Functional
          Programming ICFP'96*, May 1996.
KPR00.    U. Klusik, R. Peña, and F. Rubio. Replicated Workers in Eden. 2nd In-
          ternational Workshop on Constructive Methods for Parallel Programming
          (CMPP 2000). To be published by Nova Science, 2000.
McC63.    J. McCarthy. Towards a Mathematical Theory of Computation. In *Proc.
          IFIP Congress 62*, pages 21–28, Amsterdam, 1963. North-Holland.
NNH99.    F. Nielson, H. R. Nielson, and C. Hankin. *Principles of Program Analysis*.
          Springer-Verlag, 1999.
PHH+93.   S. L. Peyton Jones, C. V. Hall, K. Hammond, W. D. Partain, and P. L.
          Wadler. The Glasgow Haskell Compiler: A Technical Overview. In *Joint
          Framework for Inf. Technology, Keele, DTI/SERC*, pages 249–257, 1993.
PP93.     S. L. Peyton Jones and W. Partain. Measuring the effectiveness of a sim-
          ple strictness analyser. In *Glasgow Workshop on Functional Programming
          1993*, Workshops in Computing, pages 201–220. Springer-Verlag, 1993.
PPRS00.   C. Pareja, R. Peña, F. Rubio, and C. Segura. Optimizing Eden by Trans-
          formation. In *Trends in Functional Programming (Volume 2). Proceedings
          of 2nd Scottish Functional Programming Workshop, SFP'00*, pages 13–26.
          Intellect, 2000.
PS98.     S. L. Peyton Jones and A. L. M. Santos. A Transformation-based Optimiser
          for Haskell. *Science of Computer Programming 32(1-3):3-47*, Sept. 1998.
San95.    A. L. M. Santos. *Compilation by Transformation in Non-Strict Functional
          Languages*. PhD thesis, Department of Computing Science. University of
          Glasgow, 1995.
SS90.     H. Søndergaard and P. Sestoft. Referential Transparency, Definiteness and
          Unfoldability. *Acta Informatica*, 27(6):505–517, May 1990.
SS92.     H. Søndergaard and P. Sestoft. Non-Determinism in Functional Languages.
          *Computer Journal*, 35(5):514–523, Oct 1992.
TWM95.    D. N. Turner, P. L. Wadler, and C. Mossin. Once Upon a Type. In *1995
          Conf. on Functional Programming and Computer Architecture*, pages 1–11,
          1995.
WJ99.     K. Wansbrough and S. L. Peyton Jones. Once upon a polymorphic type.
          In *The Twenty-sixth ACM SIGPLAN-SIGACT Symposium on Principles
          of Programming Languages*, San Antonio, Texas, Jan. 1999.

# Exploiting Implicit Parallelism
# in Functional Programs with SLAM*

John Sargeant, Chris Kirkham, and Ian Watson

Department of Computer Science
University of Manchester
Manchester M13 9PL, UK
{js,cck,iw}@cs.man.ac.uk

**Abstract.** An effective execution model is a vital component of any general-purpose implicitly parallel programming system. We introduce SLAM (Spreading Load with Active Messages), an execution model which overcomes many of the problems with previous approaches. SLAM is efficient enough to operate at low granularity without hardware support, and has other necessary properties. Compiling for SLAM presents an unusual set of problems, and we describe how this is done from UFO-Lite, a simplified version of the United Functions and Objects programming language. Linear speedups are obtained for a program with irregular, fine-grain, parallelism on stock hardware.

## 1  Introduction

Despite many years of research, the space between instruction-level parallelism and fully distributed computation remains sparsely occupied. Compilers can parallelise suitable loops automatically, and highly skilled programmers can exploit process-level parallelism, but these approaches only work in restricted application domains. The main problem is the difficulty of programming parallel machines for complex tasks, especially ones whose dynamic behaviour is irregular and unpredictable.

The situation would change dramatically if an ordinary application programmer could write, in a suitable high-level language, a program with parallelism in a very abstract sense, and have the system automatically produce an efficient parallel program for the target machine. This goal of *implicit parallelism* has proved very elusive. It is helpful to start with a programming language which does not over-specify sequencing. Both functional and parallel-object-oriented languages are good candidates, and our work is based on the United Functions and Objects (UFO) language [1,2], which combines these two paradigms. The techniques described in this paper could, in principle, be applied to more conventional languages, although this would present additional engineering problems, some of which are indicated below.

---

* The work described in this paper was funded by EPSRC grant GR/M10861

M. Mohnen and P. Koopman (Eds.): IFL 2000, LNCS 2011, pp. 19–36, 2001.

The gap between the programming language and the machine is usually considered too large to bridge directly. Various intermediate forms have been proposed, variously called "computational models", "abstract machines", and "bridging models". Some intermediate forms are close to the semantics of the programming language, and need further mapping to reflect the properties of an actual parallel machine. Others have a straightforward implementation on a real machine; we will refer to these as *execution models* (EMs).

Our experience has shown that getting the EM right is the most important prerequisite for practical implicit parallelism. Whether a higher-level intermediate form is also necessary is a secondary issue. In fact, in our recent work we have abandoned our high-level intermediate form, Uflow [3], as the extra complexity it introduced proved largely unnecessary. The current compiler operates on a standard AST data structure instead.

The rest of the paper is structured as follows. In the next section we review the properties which a successful EM requires, and briefly highlight some of the problems which need to be overcome. We then introduce the SLAM (Spreading Load with Active Messages) model, and show how it overcomes many of these problems. We then discuss the way in which SLAM code is compiled from the UFO-Lite programming language, and present some encouraging performance results.

## 2   Review of Execution Models

### 2.1   Ground Rules

Firstly, we assume that our target applications are general-purpose, with unpredictable flow of control, and unpredictable amounts of parallelism at irregular, potentially fine, granularity. The benchmark used to obtain the results in this paper is a purely functional program, although the techniques used should also be applicable to parallel object-oriented programs.

Secondly, we assume that the target hardware is a conventional parallel processor. We do not assume shared (or virtual-shared) memory, but we do assume high bandwidth, low latency interconnection between the processors. In other words, we are interested in exploiting parallelism "within one box", not distributed computing. The results presented below are for shared-memory machines, although SLAM is designed to be equally suitable for distributed-memory architectures.

There has, of course, been considerable work on alternative parallel architectures such as dataflow; see for example the survey in [4]. However, the cost of building novel machines is very high compared to machines built from commodity processors. Few commercially available multiprocessors have arisen from this work. Our execution model requires minimal hardware support. It is also designed to work in a practical environment where exclusive access to processors is not guaranteed.

## 2.2   Properties Required of an EM

In order to work properly, an EM needs to have a number of critical, interrelated properties.

**Ability to exploit parallelism revealed at runtime.** We wish to deal with applications which cannot be statically partitioned into parallel processes. The compiler can detect *potential* parallelism, but the actual parallelism available is known only at runtime.

**Low overhead, even at fine granularity.** Without special hardware, inherently fine-grain models such as dataflow or packet-based graph reduction are expensive. Models which rely on conventional "lightweight" threads can be expensive if granularity is low because of the costs of creating and switching between such threads.

**Effective load balancing.** Under high parallelism the load balancing system must avoid unnecessary idle time by spreading work quickly. Under low parallelism it should avoid trying to use more processors than necessary. In both cases it should avoid sending excessive numbers of messages between processors. Coarse-grain, thread-based models tend to have problems in the former case, and fine-grain models in the latter.

**Locality.** The model should preserve, as far as possible, the locality present in serial code. As well as preserving good cache hit-rates etc., the model should try to ensure that related data is held in the same memory as often as possible so that the number of remote data accesses (RDAs) is reasonable. Fine-grain models often have poor locality properties, and if fine-grain tasks are processed in a FIFO order, poor locality and excessive resource usage result [5,6].

**Ability to hide remote data access latency.** We do not want to be limited to machines with shared memory, or where remote data access latency can be neglected. Remote data access is a problem in thread-based models, because doing a full thread switch to cover an RDA is expensive.

**Ability to combine load balancing and data-following.** It should be possible to take the computation to the data where appropriate. For instance, in an object-oriented language, it should be possible to execute a method on an object in the processor where the object is. This is difficult in coarse-grain models because many method calls on different objects are contained within the same thread.

An important alternative to the SLAM model is a coarse-grain stack-based evaluation model. Such models are relatively easy to compile for, and there is essentially no overhead if there is no parallelism - normal sequential execution occurs. Lazy task creation (LTC) [7] is an essential feature of such models. In LTC, at each point where a task can be spawned, if the machine is busy at the time, a packet representing a *potential* task is created. This can be called upon if the activity level subsequently drops. LTC reduces idle time and improves granularity, because on average larger tasks are selected (by taking them from as far down the stack as possible).

A number of LTC-style models have been investigated at Manchester, e.g. [8,9], but the results were never totally convincing. The dynamics of such systems are complex, the overheads are significant when granularity is low, and it is difficult to take the computation to the data where this is desirable. Nevertheless, an LTC-based approach is probably the only viable alternative to SLAM, at least on conventional hardware.

# 3   SLAM

## 3.1   Overview

SLAM (Spreading Load with Active Messages) requires no special hardware support, and should be efficient on a range of parallel machines. It is based on *active messages* [10], which basically consist of a code pointer and some data. The distinctive feature of active messages is not what they are, but the way they are used. The requirement on the hardware is that when an active message arrives at a processor, it should be possible to execute it directly, in user mode, by simply jumping to the code with no operating system intervention. If this criterion is met (trivial for shared memory; [10] discusses distributed-memory implementations), construction and execution of active messages is very cheap. The basic properties of SLAM are:

- Everything - real computation, load balancing, housekeeping and (if necessary) remote data access is done with active messages.
- Each physical processor holds a stack of active messages (the SLAM stack) and repeatedly executes the active message on the top of this stack. There is exactly one thread running in each processor; we refer to the activation stack of this thread as the "C stack", since the runtime system is implemented in C.

The use of a stack avoids heap management overhead and controls parallelism. Note that we do not create a separate thread with its own stack when we execute an active message; we simply execute code using the existing C stack. This means that the "lifecycle cost" of an AM is very small, and so we can exploit parallelism at a much lower granularity than a thread-based model. The downside is that *an active message cannot be suspended* (since there is no stack to maintain its state on) - once it starts it must run to completion. Situations which would be dealt with by suspension in a thread-based model can be handled by creating further AMs to execute the code required after the suspension, but this is messy to compile for, and we try to avoid such situations where possible.

## 3.2   Details of the Model

An active message is implemented as a packet consisting of a code pointer, a return address, arguments, and a header which includes the size of the packet and a count of the number of results it is waiting for; if this count is zero the packet is active. This "header" is actually at the bottom end of the packet, for reasons explained shortly.

A packet can be in one of three states: executing, active (ready to execute) and waiting (for results from other packets). Note that there is no suspended state; once a packet starts executing it runs to completion.

Each processor executes the following driver loop:

```
while (not terminated)
  { if (message buffer not empty) put message on TOS;
    if (packet at TOS is active) execute it;
    else try to steal work from other processors
  }
```

At the bottom of each stack there is a packet which contains code to look for work if the processor is idle. This means that there is always a packet on the stack, and the driver loop merely has to check whether it is active.

There are several possible variations. For instance, if the packet at TOS is not active (because it is waiting for results from other processors), this implementation tries to steal work from elsewhere, and if it fails it busy-waits. An alternative is to search down the SLAM stack for an active packet, haul it up to the top, and execute it. Early experiments using hand-generated code indicated that the extra complexity and resultant loss of locality was not worthwhile.

It is even possible to eliminate the explicit driver loop altogether, and have the execution of each packet end with a jump to the next. In fact, the original SLAM model (as conceived by the third author) worked this way. These issues are discussed in [11], which also describes the interface to which generated SLAM code conforms, and other details.

When work is exported from one processor to another, the active packet *nearest the bottom* of the SLAM stack is taken. Hence execution within a processor is LIFO, but distribution of parallelism across processors is FIFO. This improves both locality and the probability that an exported packet will represent a significant amount of work (because it is nearer to the root of the execution tree). This local-LIFO-global-FIFO execution order is extremely important [6]. The header is at the bottom of the packet for the benefit of this mechanism, which otherwise could not interpret the contents of the stack. Each exported packet is replaced with a no-op, so that the SLAM stack can safely unwind back past it.

### 3.3   Load Balancing

Load balancing is implemented via active messages, but the details of the algorithm used are independent of SLAM. The current implementation uses a receiver-initiated work-stealing scheme. Such schemes tend to behave poorly under low parallelism, because they generate traffic to look for work which is not there, and handling these messages distracts the processors which do have work. This can be a significant problem even for programs with good overall parallelism; they often have sequential tails (e.g. simply producing the results) which cause the load balancing to become unstable enough to seriously damage the overall performance.

We compensate for this by adopting a conservative notion of when a processor is "busy" enough to be asked for work, namely that it must execute a prescribed number of consecutive tasks without an idle cycle or a load balancing message intervening. (This is cheaper to track than the natural measure of activity for SLAM, i.e. the number of active packets on the stack.) Resetting the count when a load balancing message is processed prevents the busy processor from being flooded with requests. Effectively we have a control system with feedback and we are adding hysteresis to stabilise it.

An alternative is to use an adaptive symmetric load balancing scheme [12], which is specifically designed to work well in both high-parallelism and low-parallelism situations. It appears that the extra complexity of such a scheme is unnecessary, since the results below suggest that the current scheme is adequate. All the evidence available suggests that, for purely functional code, the load balancing strategy is application independent. However this needs to be re-examined when stateful objects are considered.

## 3.4  Other Issues

Garbage collection is not currently implemented, but is obviously essential to a "real" implementation. We intend to use one of the schemes designed elsewhere, since we are not specifically interested in parallel garbage collection. Active messages can of course be used to implement the necessary communication between processors.

There are a number of possible ways of dealing with remote data access in SLAM. For instance, in an object-oriented setting, a packet represents a method call on an object and can be sent to the processor where that object is. Conversely, active messages provide an efficient way of fetching copies of remote data. There are a number of issues to resolve, and the tradeoffs between approaches are architecture-specific. This is an area of future research, and is not discussed further here.

The results presented below are for shared-memory machines. Explicit message passing between processors is only used for load balancing; RDA and returning of results is done using the shared memory. Implementing a message-passing system on top of shared memory hardware may seem a little odd. One advantage is that the system can cope with very fine-grain parallelism, as exhibited by the test program described below. Also, when mutable objects are involved, taking the computation to the data, even on shared memory, avoids both consistency and performance problems. Pragmatically, using shared memory provides us with a test-bed for most aspects of SLAM, without the extra complexity of dealing with RDA.

The primary consideration in the shared-memory case is to make best use of the cache hardware. In particular, unnecessary sharing (real or false) leads to disastrous loss of performance. The processors each allocate from separate areas of store, and the runtime system is carefully tuned. For instance, data structures which are always written to and read by the same processor are carefully aligned with the (L2) cache lines.

# 4    Compiling for SLAM

## 4.1    Overview

Compiling for SLAM presents no fundamental theoretical problems, but is very complex in practice. "Real world" requirements such as separate compilation and dynamic linking would present significant additional problems, and we have simplified the task in two major ways:

1. The source language, UFO-Lite, is a hybrid functional/object-oriented language with semantics which make detecting parallelism easy. UFO-Lite is a greatly simplified version of UFO, with many features omitted. Like UFO, UFO-Lite is strongly typed and the functional part is strict but, for instance, UFO-Lite does not have higher-order functions - they are simulated using objects when necessary. It is intended as a vehicle for exploring implicit parallelism, not as a programming language for real applications.
2. Compilation takes place under a strong closed-world assumption that the complete source code for a program is available to the compiler throughout. (Cf. Java, where the ability to load classes at runtime presents fearsome challenges for optimisers etc.)

The compilation process will be illustrated using a naive quicksort function. This has little useful parallelism in practice (except perhaps for extremely large data sets) and the results presented later are for a more substantial program with more usable parallelism.

UFO-Lite source is as follows:

```
quicksort(input: List[String]) : List[String] is
if input.length <2 then input
else {
pivot = input.head;
// filter is a sequential function which does the comparisons
(left, right) =
  filter(input.tail, pivot, []: List[String], []: List[String]);
return
  quicksort(left) ++ [pivot] ++ quicksort(right)
}
fi
```

Clearly UFO-Lite is a rather primitive language, and features such as collection comprehensions and type inference would reduce the function to a couple of lines. However, this is just a matter of syntactic sugar[1] and having everything

---

[1] Apart from type inference, which we consider inappropriate for a hybrid language, for reasons discussed elsewhere [1].

explicit makes it easier to correlate the source with the output (and intermediate versions) produced by the compiler.

The above code uses only the built-in classes List, String and Tuple2. A simple example of a user-defined class (used in the test program described below) is:

```
class Domino(front, back: String)

toString: String is front ++ "|" ++ back

// The constructor is implicit and there is no 'new' keyword.
reverse: Domino is Domino(back, front)

matches(other: Domino): Bool is this.back.equals(other.front)
end // Domino
```

UFO-Lite also has (single) inheritance and dynamic binding. All examples discussed in this paper are purely functional, but UFO-Lite, like earlier version of UFO, also has "stateful objects" which allow explicit state to be manipulated in a disciplined way.

The compiler operates on a simple AST representation of the program. It consists of the following phases:

**Parsing.** The AST is built by a conventional parser generated using the JavaCC tool.

**Semantic checking.** The program is checked for type correctness and other semantic constraints, so subsequent phases can assume that the program is well-formed.

**Optimisation.** Very little is currently done in this phase at present; minor optimisations are performed on blocks of value definitions, because this simplifies the SLAM partitioning process. A wide variety of optimisations were implemented for a previous version of UFO [13] and could therefore be applied here. However, optimisation is not really relevant to our current purposes.

**Property determination.** The main purpose of this phase is to gather statistics on the estimated runtime costs of each part of the program, as described below. Other properties can also be determined; for instance it is useful to identify functions which do not create any objects, since this simplifies tracking of roots for GC. The syntax tree is annotated with properties as appropriate. [2]

**Call graph building.** A separate data structure representing the call graph of the program is built from the AST, and compressed so that it shows only the basic recursive structure of the program.

**Execution mode determination.** (EMD) The compressed call graph is used to determine the SLAM execution mode (inline, active, or waiting) for each function call. This information is then mapped back onto the main AST.

---

[2] This phase and the optimisation phase could be iterated, but while they are only done once each, the properties determined need to be those of the optimised program.

**SLAM partitioning.** The AST is transformed to include various SLAM-related operations, according to execution mode information.

**Code generation.** The target code is ANSI C, including calls to SLAM library functions. Rather than output text directly, we generate an intermediate data structure called Abstract Imperative Code. This contains abstractions for the basic constructs of an imperative language, such as assignments, conditionals etc. and related utilities. The rest of the compiler knows almost nothing about the form of the output. This decoupling makes it easier to produce correct output, and also allows for the possibility of different output forms, such as Java or JVM code in the future.

If ordinary sequential C code is required, the SLAM-related phases are simply omitted. The phases relevant to SLAM are discussed in more detail in the following sections.

## 4.2   Property Determination

The primary purpose of this phase is to gather statistics about the expected execution times of various parts of the program. Our conjecture, supported by results so far, is that a crude static estimate of execution time, supported by a simplistic cost model, provides sufficient information for the following Execution Mode Determination phase to make sensible decisions about where we should and should not attempt to exploit parallelism.

In principle, given any expression of the form $f(e_1, \ldots, e_n)$, each of the $e_i$ expressions can be evaluated in parallel as a separate packet. However, in many cases the expressions will be trivial, and parallel evaluation is only appropriate if at least two of them involve significant computation. It is therefore clear that any sort of plausible partitioning requires at least some idea of the sizes of computations.

It is, of course, impossible to know how long a computation will take, except for trivial cases, because of conditionals. In UFO-Lite, we have both explicit conditionals and dynamic binding.

However, in both cases we can obtain upper and lower *bounds* on the amount of computation involved (for recursive computation the upper bound will be infinite). The upper bound (**U**) is the maximum of the upper bounds for the different possibilities and the lower bound (**L**) is the minimum of the alternative lower bounds. For a dynamically bound function, the bounds are calculated over all the alternative implementations. (This is possible because of our closed-world assumption.)

Since the cost of a call depends on the cost of the function called, in the presence of recursion the statistics gathering process has to be iterated to a fixedpoint.

Clearly this is extremely crude, but it does enable us to identify some important special cases, for instance trivial computations with small upper bounds, and "banker" computations with large lower bounds. For most interesting cases, the lower bound is low and the upper bound is very high (often infinite). Better information could be obtained by using runtime monitoring, along the lines suggested in [14]. However, it is interesting to see how well we can do with purely static information. Since SLAM is inherently very efficient, very crude information may be good enough.

We therefore simply guess the expected cost, **E**, of a computation as some function of **L** and **U**. The guess currently used is

```
if U < infinity then (L+U)/2
else L * infinityfactor
```

where `infinityfactor` is an arbitrarily chosen constant.

This enables us to distinguish trivial from non-trivial computations, but we also need to distinguish parallel ones from sequential ones. The sums above return approximately the same values from `f(g(h(x)))` and `f(g(x),h(x))` and clearly the difference is important.

In addition to the statistical information, it is also necessary to analyse the underlying structure of the program.

### 4.3    Call Graph Building

The call graph is a cyclic graph with the following types of nodes:

**Leaf** nodes represent computations deemed trivial, such as constants or calls to primitives.

**Seq** nodes represent computations which have to be done in sequence, e.g. data-dependent local definitions.

**Par** nodes represent computations which can potentially be executed in parallel. For instance, a binary operator is mapped onto a Par node.

**Alt** nodes represent alternative computations, due either to explicit conditionals or to dynamic binding.

**Call** nodes represent calls, which in turn refer to the function being called.

The call graph is built from the AST and then recursively compressed until all leaf nodes are eliminated. What is left is a "bare-bones" view of the recursive structure of the program (plus any non-recursive components deemed large enough to be interesting). For instance, the call graph for the quicksort function reduces to
`Seq(Call:filter, Par(Call:quicksort, Call:quicksort))`.
The uncompressed graph has an `Alt` node representing the conditional, but this disappears because the condition and one alternative are leaves.

The call graph is not theoretically necessary, as it contains no "new" information. However, building it has several practical advantages:

- It makes the EMD phase much simpler, since this operates on a graph with the four relevant node types, rather than the 30 or so in the main AST.
- It makes it easier to see what is going on, both in the current research and potentially as the basis for a visualisation tool for end-users.

- It potentially provides the basis for other forms of analysis of the program. For instance, in a binary recursion such as the quicksort function, the base case must occur half the time. The call graph provides a good data structure for spotting such patterns, which can in turn be used to make a more "educated" guess about expected costs.[3]

## 4.4    Execution Mode Determination

The execution mode is one of:

**Inline.** The node will be translated to ordinary sequential C.

**Active.** The node will be translated to an active SLAM packet.

**Waiting (k).** The node will (in principle) be translated to a packet waiting for the results of k other packets.

The active parts of a graph are dependent only on the inline nodes while the waiting part is in general dependent on both the active nodes and further inline nodes.

In the current scheme, active nodes are always call nodes in the graph. These may or may not correspond directly to calls in the source program, depending on the optimisations performed earlier.

EMD is first performed on the compressed call graph, annotating it as required. For instance, in the quicksort example, the two recursive calls to quicksort are marked as active, and the Par node which combines them as waiting for two results.

The execution modes of the key call nodes in the compressed call graph are then mapped back onto the main AST, and a sweep across this fills in the execution modes of the rest.

The combination of statistical and structural information guarantees that no attempt is made to parallelise expressions with no real parallelism.

## 4.5    SLAM Partitioning

This is the key stage, and the most complex. Only a brief outline is given here. The code resulting from partitioning the quicksort function is shown in outline here:

```
{
Unpack stack pointer(SP), return address(RA) and argument(input)
if length of input < 2 {
  return value of input to RA
}
else {
  Sequential code to get pivot and call filter;   (1)
```

---

[3] Although this requires a less compressed graph than that shown, since we would need to preserve the Alt node representing the conditional.

```
Construct waiting packet to append the results together
   and return the answer; (2)
Construct active packets for the two recursive quicksorts,
   returning to slots in the waiting packet; (3)
}
return new value of SP;
}
```

The corresponding C code appears in appendix A.

The code segments (1) - (3) correspond to the inline, waiting, and active parts of the graph. Note that the waiting packet appears before the active packets, because they must return values to it; this part of the code is effectively reversed from its normal ordering.

A naive partitioning would create two waiting packets for the expression

`quicksort(left) ++ [pivot] ++ quicksort(right)`

– one for each append. The overhead of this is unacceptable, and instead all the waiting code is gathered together in a single auxiliary function, so there is only ever one waiting packet corresponding to a set of active packets.

Conditional computations typically create packets in some branches and not others. The partitioning process preserves the branching structure of the original code. Branches which do not create packets return their results directly. Ones which do are recursively partitioned, so that each such branch contains some active packets and a waiting packet.

## 5   Results

### 5.1   An Example Application

Finding suitable benchmarks is problematic. The traditional toy programs give the usual good speedups but lack credibility. Translating "real" programs into UFO-Lite would be a substantial effort and the results would be hard to interpret. Existing benchmark sets are intended for other purposes (e.g. assessing the performance of sequential lazy FL implementations) or require features such as arrays which UFO-Lite does not have.

We chose to invent our own benchmark, one which is relatively simple but which provides significant challenges to the compiler and the runtime system, and has yielded a lot of useful information.

We define a *domino* to be an object containing two strings. Two dominos match if the "front" string of one equals the "back" string of the other. Dominos can be reversed, except for "doubles" whose front and back are the same. The program, given a collection of dominos, returns all chains of matching dominos which use the complete collection. For instance, for the set:

`one|two three|two  two|two`

there are two solutions:

```
one|two two|two two|three
three|two two|two two|one
```

The data used to obtain the results below follows the same pattern up to fifteen.

The program operates by exhaustive, brute-force search, implemented by recursions along lists of dominos, and is certainly not the most efficient solution to the problem. However, it is large enough (around 50 lines of UFO-Lite) to show some interesting behaviour, but small enough for that behaviour to be understandable. The program presents a significant challenge to any scheme of implicit parallelism because:

1. As well as being dynamic and irregular, the parallelism in this application is at a very fine grain; most branches of the search tree terminate immediately because most pairs of dominos don't match.[4] In fact, it is not a priori obvious that the program has much usable parallelism at all.
2. It is very store-intensive; lists of dominos are created and discarded at a very high rate.

The system must therefore be efficient at fine granularity and at the same time preserve locality, so that most data is read by the processor which wrote it.

The results presented below are for two slightly different versions of the program. The first (the S-version) represents the strings as standard UFO Strings. This means that comparisons between them cost almost nothing (they are calls to the C strcmp() function). This is arguably unrepresentative of more realistic applications, where we would expect a higher proportion of "real work" to store allocation (e.g. matching molecular structures or evaluating game positions rather than comparing strings). The second (the L-version) represents the strings as list of characters, and so does rather more work in the comparisons, although it is still very fine-grain.

Results were obtained on a 4 processor SGI Challenge shared memory multiprocessor and on a 16 processor SGI Origin 2000 virtual-shared-memory machine. All code was compiled using the SGI C compiler at its highest optimisation level (-O3). Times are user times in seconds as reported by /bin/time. Stopwatch times and internal timings from the C library clock() function gave very similar results; the user times are slightly less affected by other activity in the machine. All numbers reported are the mean values derived from at least 3 runs.

## 5.2  Shared Memory Results

Table 1 shows the results obtained on the Challenge. The execution times for the ordinary sequential versions are given in the top row. The table gives times for the SLAM versions on different numbers of PEs, and the relative speedup

---

[4] For data where this is not the case, the number of solutions is very large, and the program becomes I/O bound.

**Table 1.** Performance results on a 4 processor SGI Challenge

| PEs | S version (37.4) | | | L version (63.9) | | |
|---|---|---|---|---|---|---|
| | Time | S (rel) | S (true) | Time | S (rel) | S (true) |
| 1 | 52.9 | 1.00 | 0.71 | 84.7 | 1.00 | 0.75 |
| 2 | 26.4 | 2.00 | 1.41 | 41.6 | 2.04 | 1.54 |
| 4 | 13.2 | 4.01 | 2.83 | 21.0 | 4.03 | 3.04 |

(compared to SLAM on one PE) and true speedup (compared to the ordinary sequential version) in each case. The sequential versions are compiled with garbage collection and all associated overheads disabled, since the SLAM versions do not have GC. Clearly the program does have useful amount of parallelism, something which is far from immediately obvious. The relative speedups are linear, or even slightly superlinear. On this machine the performance of the caches dominates performance. Having N times as much cache available by using N processors negates much of the cost of parallel execution. This of course excludes the overhead which is paid for SLAM even on one PE. This overhead can probably be reduced by further tuning, but in any case we are observing real speedups of around 3 on 4 processors.

**Table 2.** Statistics for a 4 PE execution

| PE | Cycles | Packets | Messages | Store |
|---|---|---|---|---|
| 0 | 984418 | 984213 | 108 | 4929705 |
| 1 | 814913 | 814286 | 133 | 5059410 |
| 2 | 1007754 | 1006863 | 231 | 6193026 |
| 3 | 1046719 | 1045827 | 160 | 6364242 |

A sample 4 PE run (of the S-version) gives the information in Table 2. The number of SLAM packets executed is very close to the total number of cycles of the driver loop, indicating very little idle time. By contrast the number of messages between processors is very small, showing that the load balancing is very stable. The final column shows the amount of store (in 32 bit words) allocated by each PE, illustrating how store-intensive the program is. In particular, note that the total memory use considerably exceeds the cache size.

There is some variation between PEs, indicating that there was some other activity due to other users on the machine at the time. However, the system copes with this smoothly.

## 5.3   Virtual Shared Memory Results

The results in Table 3 were obtained on a moderately-loaded 16 processor SGI Origin 2000 virtual shared memory multiprocessor. The code was identical to that for the Challenge, except for the values of two constants used to fine-tune

**Table 3.** Results on a 16 processor SGI Origin 2000

| PEs | S version (9.25) | | | L version (16.4) | | |
|---|---|---|---|---|---|---|
| | Time | S (rel) | S (true) | Time | S (rel) | S (true) |
| 1 | 12.55 | 1.0 | 0.75 | 20.1 | 1.0 | 0.8 |
| 2 | 6.3 | 2.0 | 1.5 | 10.0 | 2.0 | 1.6 |
| 4 | 3.2 | 3.9 | 2.9 | 5.1 | 3.9 | 3.2 |
| 8 | 1.8 | 7.0 | 5.1 | 2.8 | 7.2 | 5.9 |
| 10 | 1.75 | 7.2 | 5.3 | 2.4 | 8.4 | 6.8 |

cache behaviour. Other activity on the machine limited the available resources to 10 PEs. The individual processors are much faster than on the Challenge, as the sequential times show. The results are very similar to the shared-memory case up to 4 PEs, and further speedups are obtained up to 10. The drop-off in speedup for 8 and 10 PEs may be due to limited parallelism in the application, overly conservative load balancing or other implementation artifacts, competition from other users, or some combination. Further investigation is needed to determine how much each of these factors apply.

### 5.4   Lessons Learned

For a long period, speedups such as those shown above were unobtainable, even though the basic SLAM mechanism were working correctly. We learned two important lessons from this:

1. Slight instabilities in the load balancing system are rapidly magnified as the number of processors increases, even from 2 to 4. Decent speedups were only obtained once the very conservative scheme described in section 3.3 was adopted.
2. On these machines, every unnecessary instance of sharing (real or false) must be ruthlessly eliminated. There were numerous instances of this: the final bottleneck was a single shared counter, left over from the sequential List library, where it was used for monitoring purposes. One of the potential benefits of implicit parallelism is that the number of programmers who need to worry about such things is much reduced.

### 5.5   Improvements and Extensions

Obviously it is necessary to investigate larger and more realistic programs, in particular ones with dynamic binding, and also ones using stateful objects, where it will be necessary to ensure that the computation goes to the data rather than vice versa. We also hope to obtain results for larger numbers of processors, and in the long run different types of machines.

The overhead of SLAM execution can be reduced further. A realistic target may be "breakeven" (real speedup on 2 processors) at a granularity of 100 machine instructions, and it appears that the compiler can certainly guarantee this granularity.

Many improvements can be made to the compiler, for instance inlining to increase granularity. Garbage collection needs to be incorporated, and may be beneficial in improving locality.

## 6    Conclusions

We have shown that SLAM meets many of the requirements for an effective execution model for implicit parallelism. The UFO-Lite to SLAM compiler is able to expose parallelism in irregular recursive programs, and avoids generating trivial tasks by using simple static estimates of the costs of partial computations. Although the cost modelling is very imprecise, it appears to be good enough, because the underlying SLAM model can cope with relatively small granularities. We have demonstrated linear relative speedups and significant real speedups, on a program with complex dynamic behaviour. It must be admitted, however, that the results quoted are for just this single program, and that a wider spread of applications is needed to be fully convincing. However we have demonstrated, in principle at least, that implicit parallelism can be made to work on conventional parallel machines.

## A    SLAM C Code for the Quicksort Function

```
// SLAM functions take and return stack pointer values.
SPTR _SLAM_quicksort(SPTR _sptr){
SPTR _block3;
{
SPTR _sp;
RA _ra;
Oid _input;
_sp = _sptr;

// Unpack the stack pointer, return address and argument from the
// SLAM stack.
_unpack_2_1(_sp, _ra, _input);

// If length(input) < 2...
if (( _ListP_length(_input) < 2 ))
{
// Return the value of input to the return address
_retval(_input, _ra);
}
else {

// Inline call to filter etc.  _dollar_lhs_dummy3 is an internally
// generated identifier for the (left, right) tuple.
Oid _pivot;
Oid _dollar_lhs_dummy3;
```

```
Oid _temp__10;
SPTR _temp_waiting_11;
_pivot = _ListP_head(_input);
_dollar_lhs_dummy3 = _List_String_filter(_ListP_tail(_input),
                                         _pivot, null_ListP, null_ListP);
_temp__10 = _ListP_cons(_pivot, null_ListP);

// Set up a waiting packet to call the auxiliary function below.
// LOCAL means the packet will not be exported to another processor
// once it becomes active (in order to maintain locality).
// The EMPTY slots are where the results will go.
_sp = _pack_5_1(_sp, _SLAM_aux_quicksort_4, 2, LOCAL, _ra,
                                     _input, EMPTY, _temp__10, EMPTY);
_temp_waiting_11 = _sp;

// Active packets for the recursive calls to quicksort.
// FREE means these can be exported to other processors.
// _mk_RA constructs appropriate return addresses.
// INDEX_Oid accesses components of objects (in this case of tuples)
_sp = _pack_2_1(_sp, _SLAM_quicksort, 0, FREE,
        _mk_RA(_temp_waiting_11, 2),  INDEX_Oid(_dollar_lhs_dummy3, 2));
_sp = _pack_2_1(_sp, _SLAM_quicksort, 0, FREE,
        _mk_RA(_temp_waiting_11, 4),  INDEX_Oid(_dollar_lhs_dummy3, 3));
}
_block3 = _sp;
}
// Always return the stack pointer. The C compiler tidies up the
// extra identifiers etc.
return _block3;
}

// Auxiliary function to append the results together.
SPTR _SLAM_aux_quicksort_4(SPTR _sptr){
SPTR _block8;
{
SPTR _sp;
RA _ra;
Oid _input;
Oid _rval_quicksort_6;
Oid _temp__10;
Oid _rval_quicksort_7;
_sp = _sptr;
// Unpack the results..
_unpack_5_1(_sp, _ra, _input, _rval_quicksort_6, _temp__10,
                                            _rval_quicksort_7);
_pivot = _ListP_head(_input);
// And return the result of appending them.
_retval(_ListP_append(_ListP_append(_rval_quicksort_6, _temp__10),
                                    _rval_quicksort_7), _ra);
_block8 = _sp;
```

```
}
return _block8;
}
```

# References

1. J. Sargeant: **Uniting Functional and Object-Oriented Programming**, International Symposium on Object Technologies for Advanced Software, volume 742 of LNCS, pages 1-26. Springer-Verlag, 1993,
2. **UFO home page**, http://www.cs.man.ac.uk/arch/projects/ufo.html
3. J. Sargeant, C.C. Kirkham, S. Anderson: **Towards a Computational Model for UFO** proc. PACT94, Montreal, Canada, IFIP transactions A-50, North Holland, August 1994
4. J-L. Gaudiot & L. Bic (editors):**Advanced Topics in Data Flow Computing**, published by Prentice-Hall, 1991.
5. Arvind & D.E. Culler: **Managing Resources in a Parallel Machine**, Fifth Generation Computer Architectures, J.V. Woods ed., pages 103-121, North Holland 1986.
6. C.A. Ruggiero & J. Sargeant, **Control of Parallelism in the Manchester Dataflow Machine**, in Proc. 1987 Conference on Functional Programming Languages and Computer Architecture, volume 274 of LNCS 274, pages 1-15, Springer-Verlag, 1987.
7. E. Mohr, A. Kranz, R.H. Halstead: **Lazy Task Creation: A Technique for Increasing the Granularity of Parallel Programs** ACM Conference on Lisp and Functional Programming, Nice, France, June 1990.
8. P.S. Wong: **Parallel Evaluation of Functional Programs**. PhD thesis, Department of Computer Science, University of Manchester 1993.
9. S. Hwang: **Dynamic Control of Parallel Task Granularity** PhD thesis, Department of Computer Science, University of Manchester 1996.
10. T. von Eicken, D.E. Culler, S.C.Goldstein & K.E. Schauser: **Active Messages: a Mechanism for Integrated Communication and Computation**. proc 19th International Symposium on Computer Architecture, pages 256-266, 1992.
11. J. Sargeant: **The SLAM Report**, draft technical report, department of Computer Science, University of Manchester, 1997. Linked from the UFO home page, [2].
12. N.G. Shivaratri & P. Krueger: **Two Adaptive Location Policies for Global Scheduling Algorithms** 10th International Conference on Distributed Computing Systems, June 1990.
13. J. R. Seward, J. Sargeant, S.J. Hooton, C.C. Kirkham & I. Watson: **Optimised Compilation of UFO** Proceedings of RWC97, Tokyo, Japan, 1997.
14. J. Sargeant: **Improving Compilation of Implicit Parallel Programs by Using Runtime Information**, Proc. Workshop on Compilation of Symbolic Languages for Parallel Computers, San Diego, 1991, Argonne National Laboratory tech. report ANL-91/34, pages 129-148.

# Verifying Generic Erlang Client–Server Implementations

Thomas Arts[1] and Thomas Noll[2]

[1] Ericsson, Computer Science Lab,
Box 1505, S-12525 Älvsjö, Sweden, thomas@cslab.ericsson.se
[2] Department of Teleinformatics, Royal Institute of Technology (KTH),
S-16440 Kista, Sweden, noll@it.kth.se

**Abstract.** The Erlang Verification Tool is an interactive theorem prover tailored to verify properties of distributed systems implemented in Erlang. It is being developed by the Swedish Institute of Computer Science in collaboration with Ericsson.

In this paper we present an extension of this tool which allows to reason about the Erlang code on an architectural level. We present a verification method for client–server systems designed using the generic server implementation of the Open Telecom Platform. For this purpose, we specify a set of transition rules which characterize the abstract behaviour of the generic server functions. By this means we can reason in a partitioned way about any client–server application without having to consider the concrete implementation details of the generic part, which simplifies proofs dramatically.

The generic server architecture is just an example, and the technique extends to many other generic components. Moreover, the idea of considering standard components to reason on the architectural level of a concrete implementation can also be explored when using other verifications tools for Erlang or in the context of another language.

## 1 Introduction

The high quality demands on software for telecommunication applications may partly be ensured by the use of formal methods in the design and development. By the high degree of concurrency in those applications, *testing* is often not sufficient to guarantee correctness to a satisfactory degree. *Verification*, namely formally proving that a system has the desired properties, is therefore becoming a more and more widespread practice (see [CW96] for an overview).

Although a complete formal specification of an application would probably be one of the best ways to ensure its correctness, in practice the descriptions are rather informal, written in natural language in combination with some fragments of, for example, the Standard Description Language SDL [SDL93]. Reasons for the absence of a complete formal specification can be found in the fact that the specification changes several times during development, triggered by experiments with a release or by changed requirements. It is felt too time consuming to modify both the formal specification and the code. Even the informal specification tends

M. Mohnen and P. Koopman (Eds.): IFL 2000, LNCS 2011, pp. 37–52, 2001.
© Springer-Verlag Berlin Heidelberg 2001

to run out of phase with the actual implementation and is often only updated after a release of the product.

Towards the end of a project, it is the running code that represents the best 'specification' of the implementation. Questions about its correctness are therefore best formulated in terms of this code: 'is there a possibility that this finite–state machine implementation deadlocks?', 'does this server implementation correctly respond to all possible requests?'.

In order to find answers for these questions, one might abstract from the code (having the informal specification helping in this) and check the questions in an obtained model [CGL94,Huc99]. If one takes this realistically, the verification is used for finding errors, more than for proving correctness. If the model does *not* fulfill a certain property, then this might indicate an error in the code. It is common practice to analyze the given trace that leads to the detected error and to check whether this is also a valid trace in the actual code. The latter need not be, since a model (which is an abstraction) neglects some, potentially essential, details.

In general the constructed model depends on the property one wants to prove. Often one does not directly construct the final model, but many models are built, which are refinements of an initial rough model. The model is refined until either a detected error can be identified as a real error, or until one has enough confidence in the detailedness of the model to believe that the code is error–free. In this analysis method, finding a trace to an error can efficiently and automatically be performed by a model checker. The construction of a model and its refinements, including checking the trace in the real code, can often only be done by hand or with some minor computer assistance.

Given that the code is the only available formal description of the software, as an alternative to building the models and checking the traces one can use a theorem prover to reason about the code directly. An interactive proof assistant for the purpose of verifying properties of programs written in the functional programming language Erlang [AVWW96] has been developed by the Swedish Institute of Computer Science (SICS) in collaboration with Ericsson. This Erlang Verification Tool (EVT; [ADFG98]) can be regarded as a tableau–based prover with proof rules for first–order modal logic in Gentzen–style, extended by rules that reflect the semantics of Erlang, rules for decomposing proofs about compound systems to proofs about the components, and rules for induction and co–induction [DFG98].[1] The disadvantage that proofs have to be provided by hand should be put against the advantages of obtaining certainty that a property holds for the code and of the possibility to reason about unbounded data structures, unbounded message queues, and dynamic creation of processes. Moreover, bugs are detected by the fact that proofs cannot be provided, and the attempt to prove the property usually clearly indicates a trace in the code which can be used as a counterexample.

In this paper we present an addition to this verification tool which allows to reason about the Erlang code on an architectural level. In this way we provide

---

[1] EVT is available at `ftp://ftp.sics.se/pub/fdt/evt/index.html`.

a general abstraction, obtained automatically from the code, that is detailed enough to prove many different properties of the program.

Many applications that we consider consist of several servers that communicate with their clients. These servers are all implemented in a predefined, generic way. The generic implementation takes care of starting the server, receiving synchronous and asynchronous messages, and providing debug and log information for maintenance purposes. We added the specification of the functions of this generic server as proof rules to the verification tool. More precise: based on the transition–system semantics of Erlang as presented in [Fre], we provide rules which describe the possible transitions that any Erlang process evaluating the respective function can take, restricted by the shape of the environment if necessary. Thus, we abstract from the actual implementation of the server and concentrate on its specific behaviour instead, such that we can argue about any client–server application without having to consider the source code of the generic part. In this way we support a relativized style of reasoning which is based on the assumption that the concrete implementation of the generic module follows its specification. This abstraction is property–independent and can hence be used for all properties we are interested in, whereas we gain that we may skip many details, leading to much smaller proofs.

The remainder of this paper is organized as follows. Sect. 2 describes the class of systems addressed by our approach, namely, client–server systems implemented in Erlang using the gen_server module. In Sect. 3 we give the abstract representation of some of the gen_server functions (the complete specification can be found in [AN00]). Their implementation in EVT is discussed in Sect. 4. In Sect. 5 we address the correctness of our approach and conclude with some comparative remarks.

## 2   Generic Client–Server Implementations

Large software applications are built using a software architecture. Elements of such architectures are: databases, device drivers, finite–state machines, supervisors, monitors, servers, and many more. After putting the architecture together, the actual implementation of the components may start. Software engineering practice has taught that having all servers implemented in some general way is an advantage, both for development and for maintenance. Even better, when parts of the server software are already written and are used as the basis for all specific servers, it serves the correctness of the whole application, since the generic part is well developed and tested. Therefore, the Open Telecom Platform (OTP; [OTP]), the set of libraries and design principles that comes along with Erlang, supports a standard, generic implementation of a server by providing the gen_server module. This module implements several interface functions providing synchronous and asynchronous communication, debugging support, error and timeout handling, and other administrative tasks. In order to obtain the required specific server functionality the programmer provides an instantiation for this generic server. This instantiation consists of a separate module, the so–called *callback module*, which contains (*callback*) functions that are invoked by the generic part of the server. Thanks to this software engineering practice we are able to easily abstract from the actual server implementation in the code.

The typical flow of control in a gen_server–based client–server application is as follows. When a client process wants to synchronously communicate with the server, it uses the standard gen_server:call function with a certain message as an argument. The generic part sends the message to the server process and blocks the client. In the server process, another function of the generic part receives the message and forwards it to the application–specific part by calling a function in the callback module. This callback function should return the response and the new server state. The new state is stored in the server process, and the reply is returned to the client by the generic part of the server, completing therewith the synchronous event.

In greater detail, the following single steps are taken.

- To start the server process the gen_server:start function is called. This function creates a new process, the *server process*, in which a function is started that implements the server. The first thing this function does is computing its initial state by calling the init function in the callback module. After that, the process waits for a request from a client process.
- The client uses the gen_server:call function to send a synchronous request to the server. The request is handled by the handle_call function in the callback module while the client is being suspended, waiting for the response. The current state of the server is passed as an argument to the callback function, which on its turn returns both a reply message and a new state. The reply message is sent to the suspended process.
- Alternatively, gen_server:cast can be used to send asynchronous requests to the server. Here only the internal state of the server is changed according to the result of the handle_cast function in the callback module.
- Both handle_call and handle_cast can return a value indicating that the server should terminate. In this case, gen_server invokes the terminate function in the callback module to clean up before the process terminates.

Clearly the flow of control as described above may look different when error situations occur, such as a server that cannot be started or a call that cannot be handled. In those cases some standard error handling is performed by the generic server. In addition several options can be provided to the standard calls in order to have them behave slightly different.

The following example of a simple locker server implements a scheduler that arbiters the access to a single resource. It can be used by several clients at a time, communicating synchronously by executing function calls of the form gen_server:call(Server, request) and gen_server:call(Server, release) to request a lock and release it thereafter, respectively.

The example is classical and the properties of interest are likewise (formulated for a server with arbitrary many clients), such as: no deadlock, no starvation, mutual exclusion.

For details on the syntax and semantics of Erlang see [AVWW96]. It is a concurrent programming language with processes that execute functions. Erlang is an eager, dynamically typed language with only a few data types. In this paper we use atoms (constants) which are denoted by lowercase symbols, tuples, and lists. Variables start with an uppercase character, except for the special variable '_' which matches any value without getting bound to it (i.e., it is always a free variable).

The client function is trivially implemented in a module called client by a function with the same name that takes the process identifier of the server as a parameter (to establish communication).

```erlang
-module(client).

client(Server) ->
  gen_server:call(Server,request),
  access_the_resource(),
  gen_server:call(Server,release).
```

The state of the server consists of a list of pending clients. More exactly, the client that currently has access to the resource is stored in the head, and all waiting clients are kept in the tail of this list. We start the server by evaluating gen_server:start([]) to initialize it with an empty list of pending processes.

```erlang
-module(locker).
-behaviour(gen_server).

init(Requests) ->
  {ok, Requests}.

handle_call(request, From, Requests) ->
  case Requests of
       [] ->
          {reply, ok, [From]};
       _ ->
          {noreply, Requests++[From]}
  end;
handle_call(release, From, [_|Waiting]) ->
  case Waiting of
       [] ->
          {reply, done, Waiting};
       _ ->
          gen_server:reply(hd(Waiting), ok),
          {reply, done, Waiting}
  end;
handle_call(stop, From, Requests) ->
  {stop, normal, ok, Requests}.
```

```
terminate(Reason, Requests) ->
  ok.
```

The gen_server:call function in the client causes the handle_call function in the callback module to be executed. Note that the return value (either ok or done) is ignored by the client process, i.e., no check is performed to see if the value really is the expected one. The return of a value is a synchronization mechanism which in this case is independent of the actual value. In this particular example we could have restricted us to asychrounous communication for releasing by using gen_server:cast instead of gen_server:call, but for readability we aim to concentrate on only one communication primitive. Also note that the server expects the clients to stick to the locking protocol. In other words, in this simple version we left out any effort to program defensively. For example, misbehaving programmers can crash the locker by sending a release without a previous request or by sending a message that is not recognized by the locker at all.

On the level of the actual execution, Erlang supports only one way of communicating messages, which is asynchronous. However, the gen_server implementation ensures a synchronized behaviour: the gen_server:start function will not return before the init function has returned a state, and the gen_server:call function only returns if the handle_call function returns a reply to the callee. In the gen_server module this synchronous communication is implemented by using the asynchronous primitives: a message is sent and a receive statement directly succeeds this output operation, waiting for the response. The main goal of the technique we present in this paper is to be able to abstract from the implementation of the synchronous communication. The fact that the message is read from the message queue in a certain way, that a timeout primitive is supported and all that, need not be of our concern.

In this abstract setting, the given server implementing the locker can be described as a server that stores a list of clients which claim access to the resource. The number of clients is arbitrary and in properties or proofs we want to make no assumptions about an upper bound. Access is granted to the first client in this list, the other clients are suspended. Only after a release by the client that currently accesses the resource the client that is next in line gets access to it. The suspension of clients is implemented by not providing the reply immediately (returning {noreply,...}), but sending it later (gen_server:reply(..., ok)).

## 3   The Verification Approach

Already without our addition, the Erlang Verification Tool can be used to verify the Erlang code of an application which makes use of the generic server implementation[2]. When establishing such a proof, one has to follow the simulation of the synchronous communication by the underlying asynchronous implementation. By the nature of the Erlang semantics this means that one should also

---

[2] Although the EVT tool lacks support for modules at the moment, one can combine the callback, the gen_server and, if present, some client module into one bigger module by little effort.

prove some properties about the message queues of the client(s) and of the server, which seems irrelevant given the knowledge how the server works. In particular, when many clients are involved, a lot of nondeterminism can be introduced in the proof by observationally equivalent traces. As such, the number of proof goals may be much larger than it seems strictly necessary.

Another disadvantage in such a proof is that one gets confronted with details such as debug features implemented in the **gen_server** module. Although the verification is performed in a context where debug facilities are assumed to be disabled, one still generates an extra proof goal for testing the debug flag. This test is not atomic, and since we work in a concurrent setting, even those few steps cause duplication of work, since another action may be chosen in another process at that same time.

In our approach we simplify the verification task by ignoring the concrete implementation of the **gen_server** module. We specify its abstract behaviour by making its syntactic constructs recognizable as keywords by EVT, and by adding appropriate transition rules to the proof system. Since these transition rules are of a general nature, they can also be used for implementing our approach in other tools supporting Erlang. The actual implementation of the rules in EVT is described in Sect. 4.

## 3.1   Extending the Erlang Verification Tool

An Erlang system is specified by a composition of *processes*, each represented as $\langle e, pid, q \rangle$, where $e$ is the Erlang *expression* being evaluated, $pid$ is the uniquely defined *process identifier*, and $q$ is the *mailbox queue* in which incoming messages are stored. In order to have the tool recognize a generic server function call, we add these as special syntactic constructs to the set of expressions:

$$e ::= \ldots \mid \texttt{gen\_server:start}(e_1, e_2, e_3) \mid \texttt{gen\_server:call}(e_1, e_2) \mid$$
$$\texttt{gen\_server:reply}(e_1, e_2) \mid \texttt{gen\_server:wait}(e) \mid$$
$$\texttt{gen\_server:ready}(e) \mid \texttt{gen\_server:busy}(e_1, e_2) \mid$$
$$\texttt{gen\_server:down}(e_1, e_2, e_3) \mid \ldots$$

In this way, those function calls can be treated in a different way than the other function calls. The standard method is to search for a definition of the function, to substitute the arguments, and to continue with evaluating the body of the definition. The way the special function calls are treated is defined by an extension of the operational semantics which is defined by labeled transition rules (in the style of [Fre]).

A *reduction context* is an Erlang expression $r[\cdot]$ with a 'hole' $\cdot$ in it, which identifies the position of $r$ where the next evaluation step takes place. In this way, the rules for the actual expression evaluation have to be given only for exceptional cases, namely, when all parameters of an expression construct are *values*, i.e., have been fully evaluated.

For example, process creation is formally described by the following rule[3]:

$$\langle r[\mathtt{spawn}(f, [v_1, \ldots, v_n])], pid, q \rangle \\ \xrightarrow{\tau} \langle r[pid'], pid, q \rangle \parallel \langle f(v_1, \ldots, v_n), pid', \varepsilon \rangle \tag{1}$$

Here, $f$ is a (function) atom, $v_1, \ldots, v_n$ are values, $q$ is an arbitrary mailbox and $\varepsilon$ denotes the empty mailbox. Thus, a process evaluating a spawn function call has a transition to a system of two processes ($\parallel$ denotes parallel composition) which have to evaluate the expressions $r[pid']$ ($pid'$ is the return value of spawn) and $f(v_1, \ldots, v_n)$, respectively. For the process identifiers $pid$ and $pid'$ we require $pid' \neq pid$.

Assuming now that the set of reduction contexts has been extended accordingly to cope with the new syntactic constructs, we can formalize the intuitive meaning of the gen_server functions as described in the previous section as follows. Here we describe the starting of a server process and the handling of a server call; the complete specification is given in [AN00].

Starting a server is similar to spawning a process, but the continuation of the process depends on the evaluation of the init callback function. This is the reason for adding the special gen_server:wait construct:

$$\langle r[\mathtt{gen\_server:start}(mod, arg, opt)], pid, q \rangle \\ \xrightarrow{\tau} \langle r[\mathtt{gen\_server:wait}(spid)], pid, q \rangle \parallel \langle \mathtt{init}(arg), spid, \varepsilon \rangle \tag{2}$$

Here, $spid$ denotes a fresh (server) pid, and the server is created with an empty mailbox. The term gen_server:wait($spid$) should not be treated as a normal form, since then reductions in the context $r[\cdot]$ would be allowed, but rather as a construct from which currently no transitions are possible (similar to a receive statement with an empty mailbox).

According to the generic server description, the result of evaluating the init function should be a tuple with the initial server state as its second component. This state should be kept as part of the looping server (looping over: receiving a request, computing the answer and the next state, and responding).

$$\langle r[\mathtt{gen\_server:wait}(spid)], pid, q \rangle \parallel \langle \{\mathtt{ok}, state\}, spid, sq \rangle \\ \xrightarrow{\tau} \langle r[\{\mathtt{ok}, spid\}], pid, q \rangle \parallel \langle \mathtt{gen\_server:ready}(state), spid, sq \rangle \tag{3}$$

Note that the identifier of the process that started the server is not known to the server in this specification. Since pids of newly created processes are unique, this causes no problem in our setting. The starting process 'remembers' which server it has started (by the obtained process identifier $spid$).

A call by a client can be handled by the server if it is in an idle state, denoted by the gen_server:ready construct. In this case, the server process invokes the handle_call callback function, and the client process is put into a waiting state

---

[3] Actually, in the definition of the semantics a two–layer scheme is employed which separates expression–level from process–level steps. We will consider this distinction in Sect. 4 in greater detail.

until the request has been answered. Now, however, the server needs to store the pid of the calling client in order to be able to distinguish clients if several of them are waiting for the same server:

$$
\begin{aligned}
&\langle r[\texttt{gen\_server:call}(spid, req)], pid, q\rangle \parallel \\
&\quad \langle \texttt{gen\_server:ready}(state), spid, sq\rangle \\
&\xrightarrow{\tau} \langle r[\texttt{gen\_server:wait}(spid)], pid, q\rangle \parallel \\
&\quad \langle \texttt{gen\_server:busy}(\texttt{handle\_call}(req, pid, state), pid), spid, sq\rangle
\end{aligned}
\tag{4}
$$

If the handle_call function yields a triple of the form {reply, *answer*, *state*}, then this *answer* is immediately returned to the waiting client, and the server changes into the idle state again:

$$
\begin{aligned}
&\langle r[\texttt{gen\_server:wait}(spid)], pid, q\rangle \parallel \\
&\quad \langle \texttt{gen\_server:busy}(\{\texttt{reply}, answer, state\}, pid), spid, sq\rangle \\
&\xrightarrow{\tau} \langle r[answer], pid, q\rangle \parallel \\
&\quad \langle \texttt{gen\_server:ready}(state), spid, sq\rangle
\end{aligned}
\tag{5}
$$

The fact that the process identifier is stored in the second argument in the server expression guarantees that the reply is received by the right waiting client.

As can be seen in our locker example, the handle_call may also return a tuple of the form {noreply, *state*}. In this case the client process remains in the waiting state (and does not have to be considered therefore), whereas the server becomes idle again:

$$
\begin{aligned}
&\langle \texttt{gen\_server:busy}(\{\texttt{noreply}, state\}, pid), spid, sq\rangle \\
&\xrightarrow{\tau} \langle \texttt{gen\_server:ready}(state), spid, sq\rangle
\end{aligned}
\tag{6}
$$

Note that when we have two clients, one suspended and one calling the server, then both clients are in the waiting state, but only one client can be activated by the return of the handle_call, viz. the process which called. The other process must be activated by explicitly using the gen_server:reply function:

$$
\begin{aligned}
&\langle r[\texttt{gen\_server:wait}(spid)], pid, q\rangle \parallel \\
&\quad \langle r'[\texttt{gen\_server:reply}(pid, answer)], spid, sq\rangle \\
&\xrightarrow{\tau} \langle r[answer], pid, q\rangle \parallel \langle r'[\texttt{true}], spid, sq\rangle
\end{aligned}
\tag{7}
$$

In this way semantical rules can be used to accurately describe the given example of the locker server. As can be seen, the asynchronous communication actions that are used in the gen_server module to implement synchronous message passing are abstractly represented by simple handshaking operations which do not consider the message queues of the client nor of the server.

Asynchronous communication, not on the level of Erlang, but on the level of gen_server is also supported. This is implemented via the gen_server:cast and handle_cast functions. The gen_server:cast mechanism is formalized similar to the gen_server:call mechanism. The only difference is that the client immediately proceeds without waiting for a server response. Having evaluated the `handle_cast` function (which is indicated by a `noreply` result tuple), the server just changes into the `gen_server:ready` state, modifying its local data according to the result.

Apart from the `reply` and `noreply` values, `handle_call` (and `handle_cast`) can instead return a result that indicates that the server has to terminate. If so, the `terminate` function in the callback module is invoked. In this situation, the response is stored on the server side until `terminate` has finished:

$$\begin{aligned}
&\langle \texttt{gen\_server:busy}(\{\texttt{stop}, reason, answer, state\}, pid), spid, sq\rangle \\
&\xrightarrow{\tau} \langle \texttt{gen\_server:down}(\texttt{terminate}(reason, state), pid, answer), spid, sq\rangle
\end{aligned} \quad (8)$$

The `terminate` function is supposed to return the value `ok` and after that, the client is released and the server process is removed:

$$\begin{aligned}
&\langle r[\texttt{gen\_server:wait}(spid)], pid, q\rangle \parallel \\
&\langle \texttt{gen\_server:down}(\texttt{ok}, pid, answer), spid, sq\rangle \\
&\xrightarrow{\tau} \langle r[answer], pid, q\rangle
\end{aligned} \quad (9)$$

Note that the callback functions such as `init` and `handle_call` are specified in the callback module. We use the rules provided by the system to reason about their behaviour. Thus, abstraction by means of the semantical rules is only provided for the generic part of the server.

# 4  Implementation

As mentioned in the introduction, our `gen_server` verification approach has been implemented using the Erlang Verification Tool. Some minor additions had to be made to the tool itself, basically the recognition of the special constructs whose handling is left to the user. Thus, whenever a special construct occurs, the tool is aware of the fact that this is not a normal form, but that transitions may arise from the respective term. It leaves it to the user to check which transitions are possible. We, as a user, provided tactics to analyze the term and to apply the corresponding transition rule. These tactics are combinations of proof rules that are applied to the proof goal. Hence, we specified the transition rules given in Sect. 3 as logical formulae.

Specifying the transition rules as logical formulae rather than integrating them as an extension of the original Erlang semantics into the EVT source code has two advantages: first of all, the reasoning within the tool remains sound with respect to the abstract `gen_server` semantics. By using an abstract model of a server one introduces a potential unsoundness. If the property that one wants to prove depends on the actual implementation of the server, one might be able to falsely prove it for the abstraction, whereas it does not hold for the real program (this point is discussed in the conclusions). By using logical rules for the transitions, one explicitly states in the assumptions how one expects the server to behave. Since the reasoning that involves these assumptions is based on the (sound) EVT proof system, soundness is guaranteed under the premise that the (low–level) implementation of the **gen_server** module behaves as described by the (high–level) specification.

Second, one obtains a greater flexibility for experimenting. It is easier to change a logical expression and a tactic than to modify the implementation of EVT itself. Moreover, several different specifications of the server may exist at the same time, all using the same tool.

In the following we give the logical representation of the transition rules which describe the starting of a server process. As mentioned earlier, the formal semantics of Erlang is given by a two–layer scheme [Fre], which is also used in the EVT implementation. First the Erlang expressions are provided with a semantics on the expression level. The actions here are a functional computation step, an output, a receiving of a message, and a call of a builtin function (like **spawn** for process creation) with side effects on the process–level state. Second, the transition behaviour of Erlang systems (that is, concurrent processes evaluating expressions in the context of a unique process identifier and a mailbox of incoming messages) is captured through a set of transition rules which lift the expression actions to the process level, and which describe the interleaving of concurrent actions. Here, possible process actions are computation steps, input, and output actions.

In this setting, (1) is decomposed into an expression–level rule which indicates the spawning action, and a process–level rule which models the actual process creation:

$$\texttt{spawn}(f, [v_1, \ldots, v_n]) \xrightarrow{\texttt{spawn}(f, [v_1, \ldots, v_n]) \to pid'} pid'$$

$$\frac{e \xrightarrow{\texttt{spawn}(f, [v_1, \ldots, v_n]) \to pid'} e' \quad pid' \neq pid}{\langle e, pid, q \rangle \xrightarrow{\tau} \langle e', pid, q \rangle \parallel \langle f(v_1, \ldots, v_n), pid', \varepsilon \rangle}$$

These transition rules in the tool automatically generate possible next states of an Erlang system when we want to prove that something holds in some successor state or in all successor states (diamond or box modality, respectively). Thus, given a **spawn** call in the program, we can reason about the state in which a new process is created, among the other possible next states that the tool computes for us. For the generic server behaviour we want to obtain a similar level of comfort. However, now we specify the transitions as logical formulae. For example, (2) gives rise to the following logical formula which describes the starting of a server.

$\forall mod : \texttt{Atom}. \ \forall arg : \texttt{Value}. \ \forall opt : \texttt{List}.$

$\left( \begin{array}{l} \forall spid : \texttt{Pid}. \\ \texttt{gen\_server:start}(mod, arg, opt) \xrightarrow{\texttt{spawn}(\texttt{init}, [arg]) \to spid} \texttt{gen\_server:wait}(spid) \end{array} \right)$

$\wedge$

$\left( \begin{array}{l} \forall a : \texttt{Action}. \ \forall e : \texttt{Expr}. \ \texttt{gen\_server:start}(mod, arg, opt) \xrightarrow{a} e \Rightarrow \\ \exists spid : \texttt{Pid}. \ a = \texttt{spawn}(\texttt{init}, [arg]) \to spid \wedge e = \texttt{gen\_server:wait}(spid) \end{array} \right)$

By associating a **spawn** action with the **gen_server:start** function call, we employ the process–level rule for **spawn** as given above for computing the next state. The server starts evaluating the `init` function[4], which may involve some standard reasoning with the tool.

However, since we now specify the transition as a logical rule, we also need to state that no other transition is possible from this point, as expressed by the second subformula of the conjunction. The implementation of our generic server primitives in the tool is such that it presents all known actions at every point where one of these primitives may enable a transition. We manually have to prove that a certain transition is possible and that the others are not. The information needed for this proof is provided in the assumptions by means of a logical formula as presented above.

Since we try to achieve a high degree of automation in our proofs, we provided tactics for automatically showing that a certain action can take place and that the others are not enabled. For example, when proving a diamond property for an expression where a server is started, the tactics scan in the assumptions of the goal for a property named `start_dia`, and this property is used to automatically prove that after the `gen_server:start` call a new process is created evaluating the `init` function.

Rule (3) expresses that, after the successful initialization, the server pid is returned to the spawning process. Since it makes a provision on the syntactic structure of the two expressions computed by the processes, we have to give four formulae in the EVT specification. The first two specify the local effects of sending/receiving a message by/from the server, respectively.

$$\forall state : \textsf{Value}.$$
$$\begin{pmatrix} \forall spid : \textsf{Pid}. \ \forall pid : \textsf{Pid}. \\ \{\textsf{ok}, state\} \xrightarrow{\textsf{server}(spid,pid)\rightarrow\{\textsf{ok},spid\}} \textsf{gen\_server:ready}(state) \end{pmatrix} \wedge$$
$$\begin{pmatrix} \forall a : \textsf{Action}. \ \forall e : \textsf{Expr}. \ \{\textsf{ok}, state\} \xrightarrow{a} e \Rightarrow \exists spid : \textsf{Pid}. \ \exists pid : \textsf{Pid}. \\ a = \textsf{server}(spid, pid) \rightarrow \{\textsf{ok}, spid\} \wedge e = \textsf{gen\_server:ready}(state) \end{pmatrix}$$

$$\forall spid : \textsf{Pid}.$$
$$\begin{pmatrix} \forall v : \textsf{Value}. \ \textsf{gen\_server:wait}(spid) \xrightarrow{\textsf{client}(spid)\rightarrow v} v \end{pmatrix} \wedge$$
$$\begin{pmatrix} \forall a : \textsf{Action}. \ \forall e : \textsf{Expr}. \ \textsf{gen\_server:wait}(spid) \xrightarrow{a} e \Rightarrow \\ \exists v : \textsf{Value}. \ a = \textsf{client}(spid) \rightarrow v \wedge e = v \end{pmatrix}$$

Furthermore the expression–level synchronization actions have to be lifted to the process level. We only give the formula for the server side; the dual one (defining corresponding input actions of the form $spid?\textsf{sync}(pid, v)$) is of a similar shape.

$$\forall e : \textsf{Expr}. \ \forall e' : \textsf{Expr}. \ \forall spid : \textsf{Pid}. \ \forall pid : \textsf{Pid}. \ \forall v : \textsf{Value}. \ \forall sq : \textsf{Queue}.$$
$$\begin{pmatrix} e \xrightarrow{\textsf{server}(spid,pid)\rightarrow v} e' \Rightarrow \langle e, spid, sq \rangle \xrightarrow{spid!\textsf{sync}(pid,v)} \langle e', spid, sq \rangle \end{pmatrix} \wedge$$
$$\begin{pmatrix} \langle e, spid, sq \rangle \xrightarrow{spid!\textsf{sync}(pid,v)} \langle e', spid, sq \rangle \Rightarrow e \xrightarrow{\textsf{server}(spid,pid)\rightarrow v} e' \end{pmatrix}$$

---

[4] To be precise the function $mod{:}\textsf{init}$ is called, but the tool, at the moment, lacks support for function calls in remote modules, such that we have to localize all calls.

Now the standard synchronization mechanism implemented in EVT is used to model the actual communication between the two **sync** events. Note that both the client and the server pid is used to match the synchronization actions.

Similar formulae are obtained for (4) to (9) describing the synchronous **gen_server:call** mechanism and the termination of a server process, and for the remaining **gen_server** constructs. All single properties are collected in a big conjunction named **gen_server**, which completely specifies the abstract behaviour of **gen_server** systems, and which can be found in [AN00].

By implementing the transition rules as logical formulae we gain a flexible and easily adaptable extension of the tool. However, by the fact that we also need the 'negative' information that a certain transition is the only possible, we have some overhead in disproving extra generated subgoals for all other types of transitions. These subgoals are, however, relatively easy to reject and we implemented tactics to deal with them automatically.

For example it is possible to establish the mutual exclusion property of the locker protocol as defined in Sect. 2. Let us assume that the **access_the_resource** function, which implements the client's activity in the critical section, is given by

```
access_the_resource() ->
  self()!access.
```

Hence the fact that within a given process system S a client with pid **Client** has entered its critical section can be expressed by the formula

```
in_cs: erlangPid -> erlang_system -> prop =
  \Client: erlangPid.
  \S: erlang_system.
  (S: <Client!message(access)>tt).
```

In the simplest case of a system with two clients using one locker, the mutual exclusion property can be characterized by the following safety formula, asserting for every reachable state of the system that not both clients are in their critical sections at the same time:

```
mutex: erlangPid -> erlangPid -> erlang_system -> prop =>
  \Client1: erlangPid.
  \Client2: erlangPid.
  \S: erlang_system.
  ( not (S: (in_cs Client1) /\ (in_cs Client2))
    /\
    (S: [tau](mutex Client1 Client2))
  ).
```

We have experimented with our implementation of the generic server specifications applying it to some small examples like the above. Indeed the proofs are easier and shorter than without using this extension. On larger examples this benefit can only become more significant.

# 5    Conclusions and Future Work

In this article we presented an addition to the Erlang Verification Tool that enables us to reason on a higher level about the code implementing a client–server architecture using the generic server paradigm. The addition drastically reduces the amount of details one needs to consider when proving a property of an Erlang application that uses this client–server architecture, therefore resulting in shorter proofs.

We formalized the operational semantics of the generic server behaviour similar to the way in which the operational semantics of more primitive Erlang functions is specified. For implementing this formalization we defined it in terms of logical formulae such that the only change in the tool that we required was the extension of the list of recognizable keywords by the gen_server–specific function names. It turned out that, in comparison to proofs based on the concrete implementation, the logical formulae support a more effective reasoning about client–server systems. The efficiency of this reasoning has been increased by adding tactics that automatically prove subgoals about impossible alternative transitions.

By specifying only the 'essential' behaviour of any reasonable gen_server implementation, we introduce a certain unsoundness in the proofs. That is, if employing our approach we succeed to prove a certain property of an Erlang program that contains servers implemented by the gen_server module, then it depends on the property whether it really holds for the actual code. This, however, is a consequence of abstraction and not at all a problem in practice. First of all we are not so much interested in proving correctness but rather in finding errors in the program. If we find an error with respect to this abstraction, it is most likely an error in the real code as well. Second, if the property is independent of the specification of the generic server, then the property should hold for the actual code. Since we abstract several server steps into one handshake operation in our semantics, the property should be at least $\tau$–insensitive, i.e., its validity should not depend on the number of internal actions the system evaluates. The $\tau$–insensitivity is a minimal requirement of the property, but insufficient, since there are several other issues involved as well that make it very hard to formalize the exact independence criteria. For example, the property should be independent of: the number of messages in the mailbox of a server, the priority used to read messages from a mailbox, the debug and fault tolerance additions not specified by us, etc.

Pragmatically, our concern is to provide a framework in which we can prove properties of the code in an abstract setting, where we use one abstraction for all possible properties. This abstraction is very close to the real implementation, but there will always exist properties for which it turns out to be too general. However, if we can prove a certain property about the abstraction, then we increased the level of confidence in the code; if we find that a certain property does not hold by reasoning in this abstracted setting, then, most likely, this corresponds to an error in the real program. For that part, our technique is therefore rather close to the model–checking approach. Here, however, we only need one abstraction for arbitrary properties and we do not have to abstract over unbounded data structures, dynamic process spawning, or dynamic network creation. Our approach obtains the abstraction automatically, but needs human assistance in non–trivial proofs, whereas the latter can often automatically be handled when using a model checker.

In order to compare efforts, we experiment with using the same formalization of the behaviour of the generic server and its callback module with model–checking tools (such as TRUTH/SLC [LLNT99]). Since one possible source of infinite state spaces, the unbounded message queue of an Erlang process, is abstracted away in our model, this approach should potentially be more successful than for arbitrary Erlang programs. However, we can still apply those tools only to examples where the state space is finite; in particular, the number of processes must be bounded.

The Open Telecom Platform contains several additional generic architectures, such as generic finite–state machines, generic event handlers, generic supervision trees, etc. Those concepts can be formalized and added to EVT along the same lines. A major part of the tactics that we have already written will directly be usable for those other generic concepts. In this way, with only little extra effort, the verification of even more realistic large applications can be simplified.

### Acknowledgement

We thank Lars–åke Fredlund for his support in making the necessary changes in the tool and explaining and helping us with the implementation of the tactics.

### References

ADFG98.     T. Arts, M. Dam, L.–å. Fredlund, and D. Gurov. System description: Verification of distributed Erlang programs. In *Proc. CADE'98*, volume 1421, pages 38–41. Springer–Verlag, 1998.

AN00.       T. Arts and T. Noll. Verifying generic Erlang client–server implementations. Technical Report 00–08, Aachen University of Technology, Aachen, Germany, 2000.
            `ftp://ftp.informatik.rwth-aachen.de/pub/reports/2000/00-08.ps.gz`.

AVWW96.     J.L. Armstrong, S.R. Virding, M.C. Williams, and C. Wikström. *Concurrent Programming in Erlang*. Prentice Hall International, 2nd edition, 1996.

CGL94.      E.M. Clarke, O. Grumberg, and D.E. Long. Model checking and abstraction. *ACM Transactions on Programming Languages and Systems*, 16(5):1512–1542, 1994.

CW96.       E.M. Clarke and J.M. Wing. Formal methods: State of the art and future directions. Technical Report CMU–CS–96–178, Carnegie Mellon University, Pittsburg, USA, 1996.

DFG98.      M. Dam, L.–å. Fredlund, and D. Gurov. Toward parametric verification of open distributed systems. In *Compositionality: the Significant Difference*, volume 1536 of *Lecture Notes in Computer Science*, pages 150–185. Springer–Verlag, 1998.

Fre.       L.-å. Fredlund. Towards a semantics for Erlang. Unpublished manuscript.
           Swedish Institute of Computer Science.
Huc99.     F. Huch. Verification of Erlang programs using abstract interpretation
           and model checking. *ACM SIGPLAN Notices*, 34(9):261–272, 1999. Pro-
           ceedings of the ACM SIGPLAN International Conference on Functional
           Programming (ICFP '99).
LLNT99.    M. Lange, M. Leucker, T. Noll, and S. Tobies. Truth – a verification
           platform for concurrent systems. In *Tool Support for System Specifi-
           cation, Development, and Verification*, Advances in Computing Science.
           Springer–Verlag Wien New York, 1999.
OTP.       Open Telecom Platform (OTP). Ericsson Utvecklings AB,
           `http://www.erlang.org/documentation/doc/index.html`.
SDL93.     CCITT Specification and Description Language (SDL). Technical Report
           03/93, International Telecommunication Union, 1993.
           `http://www.itu.int/`.

# The Design and Implementation
# of Glasgow Distributed Haskell⋆

R.F. Pointon, P.W. Trinder, and H.-W. Loidl

Department of Computing and Electrical Engineering,
Heriot-Watt University,
Edinburgh, EH14 4AS, UK
{RPointon,Trinder,HWLoidl}@cee.hw.ac.uk

**Abstract.** This paper presents the design and implementation of Glasgow distributed Haskell (GdH), a non-strict distributed functional language. The language is intended for constructing scalable, reliable distributed applications, and is Haskell'98 compliant, being a superset of both Concurrent Haskell and Glasgow parallel Haskell (GpH).
GdH distributes both pure and impure threads across multiple Processing Elements (PEs), each location is made explicit so a program can use resources unique to PE, and objects including threads can be created on a named PE. The location that uniquely owns a resource is identified by a method of a new **Immobile** type class. Impure threads communicate and synchronise explicitly to co-ordinate actions on the distributed state, but both pure and impure threads synchronise and communicate implicitly to share data. Limited support for fault tolerant programming is provided by distributed exception handling. The language constructs are illustrated by example, and two demonstration programs give a flavour of GdH programming.
Although many distributed functional languages have been designed, relatively few have robust implementations. The GdH implementation fuses and extends two mature implementation technologies: the GUM runtime system (RTS) of GpH and the RTS for Concurrent Haskell. The fused RTS is extended with a small number of primitives from which more sophisticated constructs can be constructed, and libraries are adapted to the distributed context.

## 1 Introduction

Distributed languages are used for a number of reasons. Many applications, particularly those with multiple users, are most naturally structured as a collection of processes distributed over a number of machines, e.g. multi-user games, or software development environments. Applications distributed over a network of machines can be made more *reliable* because there is greater hardware and software redundancy: a failed hardware or software component can be replaced by

---

⋆ Supported by research grant GR/M 55633 from UK's EPSRC and APART fellowship 624 from the Austrian Academy of Sciences.

M. Mohnen and P. Koopman (Eds.): IFL 2000, LNCS 2011, pp. 53–70, 2001.

another. Distributed architectures are more *scalable* than centralised architectures: additional resources can be added as system usage grows.

We distinguish between large-scale and small-scale distribution. Large-scale distributed applications are supported by standard interfaces like CORBA [Sie97] or Microsoft DCOM [Mer96] and may have components written in multiple languages, supplied by several vendors, execute on a heterogeneous collection of platforms, and have elaborate failure mechanisms. In contrast, small-scale distributed programs entails components written in a single language, typically constructed by a single vendor, and is often restricted to an homogeneous network of machines, with a simple model of failures. Small-scale distributed applications are typically constructed in a distributed programming language, e.g. Java with Remote Method Invocation (RMI) [DSMS98]. A distributed language allows the system to be developed in a single, homogeneous, framework, and makes the distribution more transparent to the programmer.

Functional languages potentially offer benefits for small-scale distributed programming, and several have been developed, e.g. Kali Scheme [CJK95], Facile Antigua [TLP+93], OZ[HVS97], Concurrent Clean[PV98], and Pict [PT97]. They allow high level distributed programming, e.g. capturing common patterns of distribution as higher-order functions. Functional languages provide type safety within the constraints of a sophisticated, e.g. higher-order and polymorphic, type system. Several benefits accrue if significant components of the application are *pure*, i.e. without side-effects. Such components are easy to reason about, e.g. to optimise, derive or prove properties. Pure components can be evaluated in arbitrary order, e.g. lazily or in parallel. It also may be easier to implement fault tolerance for pure computations because a failed computation can be safely restarted [TPL00].

We have designed and implemented a language based on (non-strict) distributed graph reduction, in the anticipation of the following benefits that we seek to demonstrate in future work. Not all synchronisation and communication between threads need be explicit, in particular the shared graph model means that a thread has implicit (read-only) access to variables shared with other threads. Moreover, all data transfer between threads is lazy and dynamic. The cost of laziness is an additional message from the recipient requesting the data, but there are several specific benefits. Lazy transfer is useful if part of a large (or infinite) data structure is to be exchanged. Logically the entire data structure is exchanged, but the receiving thread will only demand as much of the data structure as is needed. Lazy transfer automatically avoids the problem of a fast producer flooding a slow consumer's memory. Dynamic transfer is useful if the amount of data to be sent is hard to determine *a priori*, or varies between program execution.

Section 2 outlines distributed architecture and language concepts. Section 3 describes GpH and Concurrent Haskell. Section 4 presents the design of GdH, discussing the motivation. Section 5 describes the implementation of GdH. Section 6 presents and discusses two small GdH demonstration programs. Section 7 compares our approach to some other distributed functional languages before section 8 discusses future work and section 9 concludes.

## 2  Distributed Language Concepts

To provide a framework in which to present our design, we define both distributed architecture and language concepts. Distributed languages execute on multiple processors connected by some network. A *Processing Element* is a processor with associated resources such as memory, disk, and screen. A *Thread* is an independent stream of execution within a program. In functional languages we distinguish between *Pure threads* that have no side-effects, e.g. perform no I/O, and *Impure threads* which may manipulate state, e.g. by performing I/O. A *Process* is a set of threads executing a program and sharing a common address space and resources such as files.

A distributed language may or may not make architectural entities explicit, e.g. threads are explicit in many languages, but implicit in others. More often the language provides abstractions of the architecture level entities, e.g. naming a PE. There are several important concepts for distributed languages.

*Locations.* A location is a set of resources, e.g. files, memory, etc. A location is an abstraction of a PE and its resources. A process may be considered to be a location with threads. A language is *location independent* if locations are implicit. A language is *location aware* if locations are explicit, enabling the programmer to utilise the resources of a location, e.g. forking a new thread into a named location.

*Communication and Synchronisation.* Communication involves the exchange of data and synchronisation is the co-ordination of control between threads. The two are closely related as having one allows the implementation of the other. Non-determinism naturally results from communication when messages come from multiple threads. In languages with *implicit communication/synchronisation* threads typically communicate and synchronise using shared data, freeing the programmer from describing the communication/synchronisation. For example Java threads may share a class of objects and communicate using synchronised methods. In languages with *explicit communication/synchronisation* threads within a process typically communicate/synchronise using a shared resources of the location, e.g. a semaphore. If the threads belong to different processes then communication/synchronisation may either address the thread or some other common location like a channel or port.

*Centralised/Decentralised.* There is no reason why communicating threads must belong to the same program, and often large systems consist of multiple co-operating programs. *Centralised* languages are a single program, and this approach has the advantage that the program and the inter-thread communication/synchronisation can be statically typed. *Decentralised* languages allow multiple programs to interact using a predefined protocol, e.g. a client-server model. This requires some language support to initialise communication. Such languages support dynamic systems that can be extended by adding PEs and new programs. However, the communication between such a dynamic set of programs cannot be statically typed.

*Fault Tolerance* is the ability of a program to detect, recover and continue after encountering faults. Faults may either be internal to the program, e.g. divide by zero, or external, e.g. disk failure.

Distributed languages support explicit communication/synchronisation between multiple threads on multiple PEs. A distributed language may be centralised or decentralised, and typically provide some support for fault tolerance. Functional languages often attempt to relieve the programmer of the burden of managing distribution, that is, they often provide implicit communication/synchronisation, and a degree of location independence.

## 3    GpH and Concurrent Haskell

Haskell'98 is sequential and programs execute as a single impure thread, termed an *I/O Thread*, that is executed by one PE. Two well-developed parallel extensions to sequential Haskell are GpH and Concurrent Haskell. GpH targets parallel transformational programming [Loo99], i.e. the program takes some input, performs some parallel calculation and produces an output. In contrast Concurrent Haskell is aimed at reactive systems, i.e. the program constantly interacts with its environment, not necessarily terminating.

### 3.1    GpH

GpH[THM+96] is a small extension to Haskell'98 that executes on multiple PEs. The program still has one main I/O thread, but may introduce many pure threads to evaluate sub-parts of the heap in parallel. *Pure Threads* are advisory, i.e. they may or may not be created and scheduled depending on the parallel machine state. The `par` function is used to suggest that an expression may be evaluated in parallel with another by a new thread. Pure threads are anonymous in that they cannot be manipulated by the programmer once created. Parallelism can be further co-ordinated using `seq` to specify a sequence of evaluation - that one expression is evaluated before another. Higher-level co-ordination of parallel computations is provided by abstracting over `par` and `seq` in lazy, higher-order, polymorphic functions, called *evaluation strategies* [THLP98].

### 3.2    Concurrent Haskell

Concurrent Haskell[PHA+97] adds several extensions to Haskell'98. The program consists of one main I/O thread, but now the programmer has explicit control over the generation of more I/O threads and the communication between them.

*I/O Threads* are created explicitly by the monadic command, `forkIO`. A new I/O thread is mandatory, i.e. it is created and must be scheduled by the RTS. Once created it can be addressed by its *threadId* to further manipulate their operation, e.g. to terminate it:

$$forkIO \quad :: \ IO \ () \to IO \ ThreadId$$
$$myThreadId :: \ IO \ ThreadId$$

*Synchronisation and Communication.* Implicit inter-thread synchronisation occurs within the shared heap, as threads block upon entering shared closures that are under evaluation by other threads. Explicit thread synchronisation and communication occurs within the monadic I/O system by the use of polymorphic semaphores - *MVar*. An MVar is created by `newEmptyMVar`, and is a container that has a state of either empty or full. Using `takeMVar` returns and empties the container contents if it was full, otherwise it blocks the thread that is attempting to take. A `putMVar` fills the container giving an error if it was already full. Multiple threads may share an MVar, in which case operations on it may be non-deterministic:

$$newEmptyMVar :: \ IO \ (MVar \ a)$$
$$takeMVar \qquad :: \ MVar \ a \to IO \ a$$
$$putMVar \qquad :: \ MVar \ a \to a \to IO \ ()$$
$$isEmptyMVar \ :: \ MVar \ a \to IO \ Bool$$

These primitives can then be abstracted over to give buffers, FIFO channels, merging, etc [PHA$^+$97].

*Fault Tolerance* is supported by exceptions which allow the flexible handling of exceptional, or error situations by changing the flow of control within a thread. Synchronous exceptions occur within a threads execution, e.g. divide by zero. Asynchronous exceptions occur outside of the thread, somehow affecting it, e.g. an interrupt generated when the user hits <ctrl> −C:

$$raiseInThread :: \ ThreadId \to Exception \to a$$
$$throw \qquad \quad :: \ Exception \to a$$
$$catchAllIO \quad :: \ IO \ a \to (Exception \to IO \ a) \to IO \ a$$

## 4   Design of GdH

GdH provides the following facilities to support distributed programming:

- *Location Awareness* – through new language constructs enabling the manipulation of the specific resources at each location. For example to interact with the GUI of a specific user at a machine.
- *Explicit Synchronisation/Communication* – enabling the co-ordination of distributed impure threads. For example to synchronise multiple users who are sharing a resource like a gameboard.
- *Location Independence* – to maintain backward compatibility with Concurrent Haskell and GpH. This allows program behaviour to remain the same even when a program is distributed.
- *Fault Tolerance* – has some support in GdH so that robust programs may be constructed.
- *A Centralised* – approach is adopted, although future versions of GdH may be decentralised. A decentralised distributed Haskell is described in Section 7.

A more complete description of the design of GdH can be found in [Poi01].

## 4.1  Location Awareness

A GdH program executes at a set of locations. Each location is labelled with a value of a new abstract data type PEId. A PEId cannot be constructed by the programmer, instead it must be obtained by querying the program state. Locations are part of the global state of the program, therefore GdH primitives to interrogate this state must be monadic commands rather than pure functions.

A GdH program is centralised with a distinguished main location which represent where the program was started from, this location consists of the main I/O thread and provides the environment with stdin, stdout, etc.

To support location awareness the program must be able to obtain four vital pieces of information: Where is this location, where are other locations, where is an object located, and what is located here? Then to utilise the resources and attributes of a location it is necessary to have some primitive to specify a remote operation.

*Where is this location?* This is a request for the current location which is provided by the function myPEId:

$$myPEId \; :: \; IO \; PEId$$

*Where are other locations?* The set of all PEIds must be provided, which is returned conveniently as a list. In recognising that a GdH program will be a centralised program with a distinguished main location, the further decision is made that the head of the list returned by allPEId should always be the main location:

$$allPEId \; :: \; IO \; [PEId]$$

*Where is an object located?* Objects, i.e. items representing part of the world state such as: MVars, threads, files, etc, are made stationary at one location and only one copy of them ever exists. An object is constructed at a particular location because that is where the current thread is executing and often an object must be associated with a particular location because it is immobilised at that location, e.g. files and foreign objects.

A new Haskell class, Immobile, groups stateful objects together, and has a method owningPE which returns the location of the specified object:

$$\textbf{class} \; Immobile \; a \; \textbf{where}$$
$$owningPE \; :: \; a \rightarrow IO \; PEId$$

$$\textbf{instance} \; Immobile \; PEId$$
$$\textbf{instance} \; Immobile \; (MVar \; a)$$
$$\textbf{instance} \; Immobile \; ThreadId$$

*What is located here?* Each location has access to its local environment and existing Haskell interrogation commands, e.g. on files, environment variables, function appropriately.

*A Remote Operation* is executed by a remote impure I/O thread to manipulate state. Remote operation also allows the creation of process networks spanning multiple locations.

A new command, `revalIO`, is provided in the I/O monad. Calling `revalIO` job p causes the calling thread to block until the execution of `job` at the location p completes and returns a result, i.e. it has the effect of temporarily changing the location of the current thread. Conceptually `revalIO` is very similar to Java RMI:

$$revalIO \;::\; IO\ a \rightarrow PEId \rightarrow IO\ a$$

The command `revalIO` represents the current thread temporarily changing location, and so preserves all location independent properties of that thread. This has an advantages for fault tolerance as the error handling capabilities of the thread are location independent, i.e. an exception raised in a thread that is within an `revalIO` will propagate back until an exception handler is found. The exception handler may be within the job at a remote location, or in the original thread.

Object placement can be accomplished by `revalIO`, this allows the creation of an object at a specific location, for example to create a distributed version of the Concurrent Haskell `forkIO` command that places a thread:

$$rforkIO \;::\; IO\ () \rightarrow PEId \rightarrow IO\ ThreadId$$

An example of usage of these location aware functions is shown in Figure 1. The program show that regardless of where a thread executes it consistently determines that a resource is at a particular location. The output of the program is a list of pairs showing thread location and resource location. Firstly the resource, an MVar, is created by `newEmptyMVar` and the list of of available locations is obtained via `allPEId`. A function, `work`, is defined that uses `myPEId` to determine the thread location and then utilises `owningPE` to determine the location of the MVar, the result is returned as a pair of PEIds. The monadic map operation, `mapM`, is used to call this new function, `work`, for each location. The result of the monadic map is a list of pair of PEIds that is shown by the `putStrLn`.

```
main =  do
           ps <- allPEId
           m  <- newEmptyMVar              -- create the MVar on the main PE
           let work = do
                   i <- myPEId
                   o <- owningPE m                 -- where's the MVar?
                   return (i,o)
           rs <- mapM (\p ->(revalIO work p)) ps -- map work across all PEs
           putStrLn (show rs)

-- Output: [(262215,262215),(524319,262215),(393218,262215)]
```

**Fig. 1.** Using the location aware primitives

## 4.2  Location Independence

In a functional language the majority of the data is non-mutable, some data represents suspended computation and thus is mutable once, while the remainder of the data is objects that are mutable many times. When data is distributed over multiple locations then some form of synchronisation is necessary so that the data remains consistent.

Suspended computations synchronise implicitly using the same approach as GpH and Concurrent Haskell, where the first thread that enters the suspension will perform the evaluation and other threads that enter then block until the evaluation completes.

Location independence of objects requires that the language supports some means for manipulating an object regardless of its location. The design decision was made to rewrite the relevant libraries, i.e. for MVars, threads, etc, to encapsulate and hide the location dependent properties. To do this the mechanisms of location awareness can be used by allowing a remote operation via `revalIO` on the object once its location has been determined by `owningPE`.

## 4.3  Fault Tolerance

Exceptions are a useful construct for supporting fault tolerance. The synchronous and asynchronous exceptions supported by Concurrent Haskell are extended so that they operate in a location independent manner, that is, exceptions can be raised at one location and handled at a remote location.

The only source of synchronous exceptions between locations in GdH occurs within the `revalIO` mechanism when a thread has temporarily migrated to another location as discussed earlier. Asynchronous exceptions between locations are possible when a `raiseInThread` function is applied to a thread which resides at a remote location. The semantics are extended for location independent operation, but no new language constructs are required.

New exceptions may be raised in response to a failure of a PE or connection to a PE. The detection of this class of errors is difficult as often the system cannot distinguish between the loss of a PE, or the loss of a message, from a message being delayed. The handling of these errors is also problematic as the loss of any part of the virtual shared heap can result in dangling heap references and therefore corrupt data and code. Handling these errors is critical for the construction of robust system and we have made an initial study [TPL00] but not yet implemented our design.

# 5  Implementation

To implement GdH the following steps were necessary. The GpH and Concurrent Haskell runtime systems had to be merged into a new RTS. The new language primitives (`myPEId`, `allPEId`, `owningPE`, and `revalIO`) for location awareness need to be provided in a new Haskell module for the programmer, and require

|              | Haskell'98 | Concurrent Haskell | GpH         | GdH                 |
|--------------|------------|--------------------|-------------|---------------------|
| PEs          | One        | One                | Many        | Many                |
| Location     | N/A        | N/A                | Independent | Aware               |
| Centralisation | N/A      | N/A                | Centralised | Centralised         |
| Threads      | One        | Many impure        | Many pure   | Many pure & impure  |
| Communication | N/A       | Implicit & explicit | Implicit   | Implicit & explicit |
| Fault Tolerance | None    | Exceptions         | None        | Exceptions          |

**Fig. 2.** The relationship between Haskell'98, the extensions GpH and Concurrent Haskell, and the new extension GdH

implementation in the merged RTS. Finally the existing libraries need to be extended to operate safely in a location independent manner. Each of these steps is discussed below, and more detailed information may be found in [Poi01].

### 5.1   Merge Runtime Systems

GdH fuses and extends the runtime systems used by the Glasgow Haskell Compiler (GHC) [PHH+93]. GHC supports not only Haskell'98 but the extensions for Concurrent Haskell and GpH. The standard GHC RTS has extensions for concurrency and exceptions for use in Concurrent Haskell. GpH is implemented by using a second RTS, GUM, that uses PVM for low-level location communication, adds support for parallelism and a virtual shared heap.

The GdH RTS, Sticky GUM[1], is an extended fusion of GUM and the GHC RTS. The two original runtime systems share significant amounts of code, yet were not primarily designed to coexist. The overlap of the different RTS extensions and the languages they support can be seen in Figure 3. One of the major differences in the GHC RTS and GUM, is what requires synchronisation: the GHC RTS requires additional synchronisation for the implementation of MVars, thread delays, and exceptions; where GUM requires additional synchronisation for the portions of the heap that are shared across multiple locations.

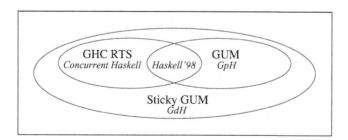

**Fig. 3.** Relationship of each Haskell extensions and RTS

---

[1] The RTS is *sticky* in that immobile objects adhere to a particular location.

## 5.2  New Language Primitives

The language design identified the following new language primitives: myPEId, allPEId, owningPE, and revalIO. These primitives form part of the new Haskell module *Distributed* shown in Figure 4.

```
data PEId                        -- abstract

myPEId      :: IO PEId           -- the current location
allPEId     :: IO [PEId]         -- list of all locations

class Immobile a where
  owningPE :: a -> IO PEId       -- the location of an object
  revalIO  :: IO b -> a -> IO b  -- remote evaluation to an object
  revalIO job xx = do
       p <- owningPE xx
       doRevalIO job p

instance Immobile PEId           -- a location is immobile
```

**Fig. 4.** Interface to the new Haskell module *Distributed*

The current location is returned by myPEId. This result corresponds directly to the unique taskId from the underlying PVM system. It is straightforward to call a C function, through the Haskell foreign language interface via a callc, to fetch this value.

The list of available locations is returned by allPEId. GUM already stores a table of all locations for use by the garbage collector and global addressing subsystems. The allPEId function accesses the RTS via a callc to build a list from this table.

The Immobile class contains both owningPE and revalIO as with practical usage of the language it quickly became apparent that one of the most common uses of the result of owningPE is to then immediately call revalIO, thus sending a specific piece of work to where the resource is located. Therefore revalIO can now operate on any member of the Immobile class, automatically calling owningPE and then the underlying primitive doRevalIO which uses values of type PEId only. If the programmer still wishes to reference the location of an object explicitly then they may do so since PEId is a member of the Immobile class.

*Implementing Immobile Objects.* Sticky GUM maintains information about which types are immobile and the Haskell programmer cannot alter this. When immobile objects are communicated between locations by the RTS, they are first converted into a new closure type, REMOTEREF. Hence there only ever exists one copy of the object and multiple REMOTEREF closures that refer back to it. The RTS assigns a unique global address to closures communicated between locations. The REMOTEREF has a global address which includes the original PEId that is accessed by owningPE via a callc.

*Implementing Remote Evaluation.* A new PVM message REVAL is defined that carries the information necessary for the generation of the remote thread. When the remote location receives an REVAL, it creates a mandatory thread and immediately begins executing it. Upon termination of this remote thread, the result is sent back to the original thread via the existing GUM `RESUME` message, as depicted in Figure 5.

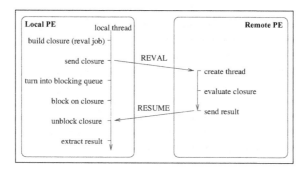

**Fig. 5.** The remote evaluation process

The execution of a `doRevalIO` is outlined in Figure 6, and proceeds as follows. It tests if the destination location is the same as the current location and if so then performs the optimisation of doing the work locally. For the cases involving a remote location, an exception handler is installed around the piece of work, `job`, which is wrapped up in a constructed type, `Status`, so that a valid result value is always returned. The primitive `unsafePerformIO` is used to write the result to a single closure, `result`, this closure is where the synchronisation of waiting for the remote result takes place.

```
data Status a = Okay a | Fail Exception

doRevalIO :: IO a -> PEId -> IO a
doRevalIO job p = do
  i <- myPEId
  if i==p
    then job                    -- do it locally if you can.
    else do
      _ccall_ cRevalIO result p  -- send the work off.
      case result of             -- check the result.
        Okay r  -> return r
        Fail e  -> throw e
  where
    tryjob = do                  -- construct an 'Okay' result.
      r <- job
      return (Okay r)
    caughtjob = catchAllIO tryjob (\e -> return (Fail e))
    result = unsafePerformIO caughtjob
```

**Fig. 6.** Blocking and error handling of `doRevalIO`

The synchronisation mechanism used by Sticky GUM to block the original thread while the remote evaluation takes place is almost identical to that used in GUM. In Figure 5 the root of the work to be sent is a closure, so when the doRevalIO function calls a `callc` to create the REVAL message it also changes the closure into a blocking queue that has an initial state of blocked. A blocking queue is used to synchronise activities such as waiting on an MVar, or for evaluation to complete.

Finally doRevalIO enters the closure in a case statement to check if the result should raise an exception or not. By entering the closure it automatically blocks the local thread until the RESUME message arrives with the result.

### 5.3    Extend Existing Libraries

Many of the libraries need to be made location aware. The design identified that many useful constructs could be built from the four distribution primitives and much of the implementation to do so required rewriting existing libraries rather than providing totally new constructs. There are two types of extensions needed, the first to provide a location independent means for accessing objects, and the second to provide a method for specifying object placement.

To illustrate the process we provide an example for threads. First threadId is made an instance of the Immobile class so that location independent access routines can be defined, i.e. for killThread and raiseInThread. Finally new object placement functions can be added, i.e. rforkIO. Some functions may require no change, for example forkIO, Eq, and myThreadId:

```
instance Immobile ThreadId
killThread th       = revalIO (Concurrent.killThread th) th
raiseInThread th ex = revalIO (Concurrent.raiseInThread th ex) th
rforkIO job p       = revalIO (forkIO job) p
```

## 6    Demonstrators

We present two small demonstration programs to illustrate the new constructs provided by GdH; these programs make almost exclusive use of explicit communication. In contrast to these examples we intend GdH to be used for larger applications where the majority of the communication can be implicit, e.g. a game where multiple player can implicitly share a large environment, dynamically fetching the parts of the environment on demand.

### 6.1    Ping

A very simple distributed program is our UNIX ping-like utility that gives an indication of location-to-location communication cost by timing the use of revalIO to perform a simple operation remotely.

The code in Figure 7 obtains the list of available locations using allPEId. Then mapM is used to map loop across the locations. Within loop we use timeit to measure how long the revalIO remote operation takes on that location.

The results are given for a group of linux x86 PCs on our local network. The first result is approximately zero since the work is being executed locally. GdH

```
main = do
        pes <- allPEId
        putStrLn ("PEs = "++show pes)
        mapM loop pes
      where
        loop pe = do
                putStr ("Pinging "++show pe++" ... ")
                (name,ms) <- timeit (revalIO remote pe)
                putStrLn ("at "++name++" time="++show ms++"ms")
        remote = getEnv "HOST"

-- Output: PEs = [262344,524389,786442,1048586,1310730]
--         Pinging 262344 ... at ushas time=0ms
--         Pinging 524389 ... at bartok time=3ms
--         Pinging 786442 ... at brahms time=3ms
--         Pinging 1048586 ... at selu time=2ms
--         Pinging 1310730 ... at kama time=2ms
```

**Fig. 7.** GdH Ping program

use PVM for communication and the times returned are comparable to the PVM
**timings** program which returned round trip times of 1.1 - 2.7ms.

## 6.2  Co-operative Editor

A more sophisticated distributed program is a co-operative text editor that supports multiple text editor windows, on different machines, allowing users to communicate through them and share files. Such an editor allows the sharing of files
that are only accessable locally on a particular machine. An interface library in
Haskell for the Tcl/Tk libraries, TclHaskell [SD99], is used to create multiple
instances of Tcl/Tk running a simple text editor (ted). A new menu within the
editors is used to manage the distributed interaction. The menu enables an editor to **send** its current buffer contents to all other editors, or for it to **fetch**
messages sent to it from any other editor.

The communication mechanism is a FIFO channel implemented via multiple
MVars as provided in the standard libraries of Concurrent Haskell. The channels
are used for two purposes:

*Termination Control* – There is one global channel, named **fin** in Figure 8,
and upon GUI quit or failure each GUI sends a message along this channel,
which is then used by the startup thread to detect when every GUI thread
in the program has terminated. The auxiliary functions **newWait**, **rforkWait**,
and **untilWait** co-ordinate this behaviour, where **rforkWait** encapsulates the
**rforkIO** and additional exception handling.

*Data Exchange* – Each GUI has its own channel, which is a FIFO buffer. By
reading or writing to each channel it is possible to co-ordinate the data exchange
between editors. Note, however, the data is transferred lazily, i.e. only when the
receiving editor displays it.

Initialisation is shown in Figure 8, where all the channels, the list **ports**, are
generated by the first **mapM**. It uses **reval** to ensure that all channels are created
separately on each location for efficiency. Later the **pick** function chooses the
appropriate channels for each editor instance. The second **mapM** is used create

```
main = do
        pes <- allPEId
        putStr("PEs = "++(show pes)++"\n")
        fin <- newWait
        ports <- mapM (\p -> revalIO newChan p) pes
        let remote p = do
                let startGUI = do
                        name <- getEnv "HOST"
                        primPutEnv ("DISPLAY="++name++":0.0")
                        start $ (ted (pick ports p) )
                rforkWait fin startGUI p
        mapM remote pes
        untilWait fin
```

**Fig. 8.** Initialisation of the editor

separate instances of the TclHaskell GUI running the editor (`ted`) on each location. Finally the termination control mechanism of `untilWait` causes the main
thread to wait until all the GUIs have finished.

```
buffer_menu :: Context -> GUI ()
buffer_menu ctx@(Ctx w mp e rf) =
    do m <- menu w [tearoff False]                        -- define the menu layout
        cascade mp m [wgt_label "Buffer"]
        mbutton m    [wgt_label "Fetch", command doFetch]
        mbutton m    [wgt_label "Send" , command doSend ]
        mbutton m    [wgt_label "List" , command doList ]
    where
        doFetch =
            do FES c _ _ _ <- readState rf               -- get input channel
                empty <- proc $ (isEmptyChan c)
                if empty
                    then return ()
                    else do (f,s) <- proc $ (readChan c)
                        resetEdit e s                    -- show text in the editor
                        change_fn ctx f                  -- show source as filename
        doSend =
            do FES _ cs fn _ <- readState rf             -- get output chans&filename
                s <- getEdit e                           -- get text in editor
                host <- proc $ (getEnv "HOST")
                proc $ (mapM (\c -> writeChan c ((fn++"(from@"++host++")"),s)) cs)
        doList =
            do FES c _ _ _ <- readState rf               -- get input channel
                vs <- proc $ (snapChan c)
                resetEdit e (unlines (map (\(f,_) -> f) vs)) -- show text in the editor
                change_fn ctx "(message list)"           -- show "(m..." as  filename
```

**Fig. 9.** Buffer communication for the editor

Buffer Communication is handled within the new menu in the editor. The
menu's TclHaskell code is shown in Figure 9. It defines a new menu named
`buffer` with three options `Fetch`, `Send`, and `List`, and associates appropriate
functions with each option. The function `doFetch` handles the receiving of the
data with `isEmptyChan` being used to check if any message exists, and if so then
`readChan` extracts the first message. Each message consists of two strings: the
name of the buffer and the buffer contents. The second function `doSend` appends
the name of the host machine to the file name and then uses `writeChan` mapped
across all the other channels to send it's buffer contents to all the other editors.
The final function `doList` uses `snapChan` to take a snap-shot of the entire channel

contents and then maps a function across it to list all the names of the messages in the buffer.

In the screenshot Figure 10 the bottom two windows are instances of the editor, redirected via X to the same host, the other windows show PVM running and the console output.

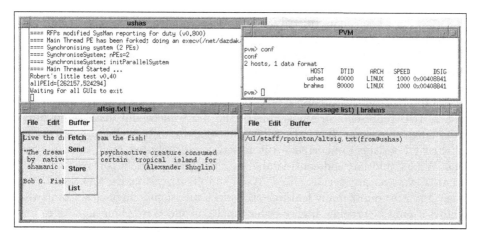

**Fig. 10.** Editor screenshot

# 7 Related Work

Conventional distributed languages like Java or C-Split [DSMS98] provide high-level support for communication and synchronisation, e.g. remote procedure calls and synchronised methods. They typically have explicit, static task and data partitioning, although some recent languages now support dynamic task and data placement, for example the object-orientated, functional, constraint based language Oz [HVS97]. Every value communicated between processes is sent explicitly, and in many languages must be fully evaluated prior to transmission. Hence values transmitted must be first order, i.e. functions and infinite data structures cannot be transmitted. Programs are non-deterministic and the programmer is responsible for avoiding problems of deadlock and starvation.

Like other distributed functional languages, GdH supports a more dynamic approach to distribution than conventional distributed languages. For example in GdH pure and I/O threads can be dynamically created, with pure threads dynamically allocated to PEs. Also data is dynamically communicated between locations on demand and it allows the transmission of higher order values. Like other distributed functional languages, GdH supports more implicit distribution, for example threads communicate and synchronise implicitly on shared data values. Using I/O threads a GdH programmer can construct programs equally as expressive as conventional distributed languages, including programs that are non-deterministic or deadlock.

While many distributed languages opt for the flexibility of a decentralised approach, GdH's centralised approach makes verification easier: all of the interacting threads are part of a single program and both threads and communication can be statically typed. In the former approach, there is no common analysis of the co-operating programs.

There have been many distributed functional language designs and implementations, e.g. Facile Antigua [TLP+93], Goffin Distributed Haskell [CGK98], OZ[HVS97], Kali Scheme [CJK95], Concurrent Clean[PV98], and Pict [PT97]. Some are only paper designs, and others have only been supported by short-lived implementations. There are relatively few robust long-lived implementations, and we discuss some of the more recent and most closely-related to GdH.

ERLANG represents arguably one of the most successful distributed functional languages so far. It was developed specifically in the telecommunications industry for writing concurrent, soft real-time, distributed fault tolerant systems [Wik94] and has had considerable success in this area.In contrast to GdH, ERLANG systems are decentralised. As a simple strict impure functional language, ERLANG omits many features of modern functional languages. Compared to GdH it omits: currying, higher-order functions and lazy evaluation. More importantly, coming from a logic programming background it is untyped which allows many programmer errors to go unnoticed at compile time. ERLANG supports a number of extremely useful features, especially useful for large complex applications, which are not available in GdH. These include hot loading of new code into running applications, explicit time manipulation to support soft real time systems, and message authentication.

*Haskell with Ports* [HN00] is a new library for Haskell that adds the benefits of ERLANG style communication using ports, thus allowing inter-process communication and fault tolerance. Use of the library allows decentralised systems to be constructed that communicate with each other over ports using a predefined protocol with dynamic typing of the communication. Unlike GdH it only allows explicit communication and only first order values (including ports) to be transmitted through the ports. Communication of higher-order values is mentioned as possible future work.

*Brisk* [Spi99] is a derivative of Haskell (currently partially implemented) which makes use of lazy evaluation to give deterministic concurrencyin a multiple demand driven approach. A deterministic form of communications based on merging with hierarchical timestamps is also introduced to extend the expressiveness of the basic deterministic concurrency. Other useful features include the sharing of binary code between machines. Compared to GdH, Brisk uses a more powerful *pure* functional approach without resorting to monadic style I/O, yet is closest in terms of the implicit and lazy communication. Brisk's deterministic concurrency model is much more restrictive and prevents the expressing of many inherently non-deterministic programs, e.g. the dining philosophers problem.

# 8    Future Work

Some minor work is still required to make the GdH implementation more robust. Once this is complete we plan to consider the following issues:

*Use and Evaluation of GdH* – in comparison to conventional distributed languages like Java. In particular we have constructed a GdH version of an existing distributed factory simulation [Kit92], and are constructing a larger application - a multiuser game with map navigation that utilises implicit communication.

*Fault Tolerance.* – The RTS can distinguishes between pure and impure computations: impure computations must be recovered using conventional exception-based techniques, but the RTS could attempt implicit recovery of pure computations [TPL00].

*Decentralised* – systems would require GdH to provide connection/disconnection language constructs. Sticky GUM would require further extensions to allow dynamic typing of communication and a robust virtual shared heap that allows PEs and their heap to disconnect.

# 9    Discussion

The design objectives and concepts underlying the distributed functional language GdH have been presented. GdH provides explicit threads, with explicit mapping onto PEs. Communication between threads is achieved via virtual shared memory, implemented as a shared heap in our graph reduction machine. Special features of our language are the implicit communication of, and synchronisation on, shared data, and the lazy dynamic communication of the data between locations.

The implementation of GdH combines two mature runtime systems, and adds a small set of new primitives. The main modifications necessary to support the requirements of a distributed language affect remote thread creation, and the treatment of immobile objects. By basing our system on GHC we utilise mature compiler technology including: sophisticated sequential code optimisations, a foreign language interface, libraries for graphical user interfaces, etc.

We plan to evaluate GdH on larger examples and to make it freely and publicly available as part of the GHC distribution.

# References

CGK98.    M. Chakravarty, Y. Guo, and M. Köhler. Distributed Haskell: Goffin on the Internet. In *Third Fuji International Symposium on Functional and Logic Programming*, pages 80–97, 1998.

CJK95.    H. Cejtin, S. Jagganathan, and R. Kelsey. Higher-order distributed objects. *ACM Trans. On Programming Languages and Systems (TOPLAS)*, 17(1), September 1995.

DSMS98.    M.C. Daconta, A. Saganich, E. Monk, and M. Snyder. *Java 1.2 and JavaScript for C and C++ Programmers*. John Wiley & Sons, New York, 1998.

HN00.    F. Huch and U. Norbisrath. Distributed Programming in Haskell with Ports. In *12th International Workshop on Implementation of Functional Languages (IFL'00)*, Aachen, Germany, September 2000.

HVS97.    S. Haridi, P. Van Roy, and G. Smolka. An Overview of the Design of Distributed Oz. In *2nd Intl. Symposium on Parallel Symbolic Computation (PASCO 97)*, New York, USA, 1997.

Kit92.    P. Kiteck. Analysis of Component Interaction in a Distribution Facility using Simulation. In *EUROSIM*, 1992.

Loo99.    R. Loogen. Programming Language Constructs. In K. Hammond and G. Michaelson, editors, *Research Directions in Parallel Functional Programming*, pages 63–91. Springer, 1999.

Mer96.    L. Merrick. DCOM Technical Overview. Technical report, Microsoft White Paper, 1996.

PHA+97.    J. Peterson, K. Hammond, L. Augustsson, B. Boutel, W. Burton, J. Fasel, A.D. Gordon, J. Hughes, P. Hudak, T. Johnsson, M. Jones, E. Meijer, S. Peyton Jones, A. Reid, and P. Wadler. *Report on the Programming Language Haskell (Version 1.4)*, April 1997.

PHH+93.    S. Peyton Jones, C. Hall, K. Hammond, W. Partain, and P. Wadler. The Glasgow Haskell Compiler: a technical overview. In *The UK Joint Framework for Information Technology*, pages 249–257, Keele, 1993.

Poi01.    R. Pointon. *The Design, Implementation, and Use of a Distributed Functional Language*. PhD thesis, Department of Computing and Electrical Engineering, Heriot-Watt University, 2001. In Preparation.

PT97.    B. Pierce and D. Turner. Pict: A Programming Language Based on the Pi-Calculus. Technical report, Indiana University, 1997.

PV98.    R. Plasmeijer and M. Van Eekelen. *Concurrent Clean - Language Report*. High Level Software Tools B.V. and University of Nijmegen, version 1.3 edition, 1998.

SD99.    M. Sage and C. Dornan. *TclHaskell - users manual*, Aug 1999.

Sie97.    J. Siegel. *CORBA Fundamentals and Programming*. John Wiley and Sons, New York, 1997.

Spi99.    E. Spiliopoulou. *Concurrent and Distributed Functional Systems*. PhD thesis, Department of Computer Science, University of Bristol, 1999.

THLP98.    P. Trinder, K. Hammond, H.-W. Loidl, and S. Peyton Jones. Algorithm + Strategy = Parallelism. *Journal of Functional Programming*, 8(1):23–60, January 1998.

THM+96.    P. Trinder, K. Hammond, J. Mattson, A. Partridge, and S. Peyton Jones. GUM: A portable implementation of Haskell. In *Proceedings of Programming Language Design and Implementation (PLDI'96)*, Philadelphia, USA, May 1996.

TLP+93.    B. Thomsen, L. Leth, S. Prasad, T-M. Kuo, A. Krammer, F. Knabe, and A. Giacalone. Facile Antigua Release Programming Guide. Technical report, European Computer-Industry Centre , Germany, 1993.

TPL00.    P. Trinder, R. Pointon, and H.-W. Loidl. Runtime System Level Fault Tolerance for a Distributed Functional Language. In *2nd Scotish Function Programming Workshop (SFP'00)*, University of St Andrews, Scotland, July 2000.

Wik94.    C. Wikstrom. Distributed programming in Erlang. In *1st International Symposium on Parallel Symbolic Computation (PASCO'94)*, Linz, September 1994.

# Implementation Skeletons in Eden: Low-Effort Parallel Programming[*]

Ulrike Klusik[1], Rita Loogen[1], Steffen Priebe[1], and Fernando Rubio[2]

[1] Philipps-Universität Marburg, Fachbereich Mathematik und Informatik
Hans Meerwein Straße, D-35032 Marburg, Germany
{klusik,loogen,priebe}@mathematik.uni-marburg.de
[2] Universidad Complutense de Madrid, Departamento de Sistemas Informáticos y
Programación, Facultad de Ciencias Matemáticas, E-28040 Madrid, Spain
fernando@sip.ucm.es

**Abstract.** *Algorithmic skeletons* define general patterns of computation which are useful for exposing the computational structure of a program. Being general structures they qualify as a target for parallelisation, which is most often carried out by providing specialised, non-portable, low-level parallel implementations (*architectural skeletons*) of each algorithmic skeleton for different platforms. In the paper we introduce an intermediate layer of *implementation skeletons* for the parallel functional language Eden. These are portable high-level skeletons which simplify the design of parallel programs substantially. Runtime experiments on a network of workstations and on a Beowulf cluster have shown that even on such *high-latency* parallel platforms good speedups can be obtained.

## 1 Introduction

The inherent parallelism of functional programs often leads to many fine-grained tasks, while, due to costly communication and fast processors, conventional parallel machines depend on coarse-grained tasks to deliver speedups. A parallel functional language has to bridge that gap, either in an implicit or explicit way. Ideally, the programmer should not be bothered with the low-level details of parallel execution. But often speedups can only be achieved when one is able to control the costs introduced by processes, communication, and data distribution. Therefore it is necessary to find a level of abstraction which gives programmers enough control to implement their parallel algorithms efficiently (including granularity issues) and at the same time frees them from the low-level details of process management.

The parallel functional language Eden[1] [3,4] provides such a level of abstraction. Eden is explicit about processes and their input and output data, but abstracts from the communication of data between processes and the synchronisation required. The Eden implementation is a freely available[1] distributed

---

[*] Work supported by the DAAD (Deutscher Akademischer Austauschdienst), by the spanish project CICYT-TIC97-0672, and by the Acción Integrada HB 1999-0102
[1] URL: http://www.mathematik.uni-marburg.de/inf/eden

M. Mohnen and P. Koopman (Eds.): IFL 2000, LNCS 2011, pp. 71–88, 2001.

implementation that maps process structures directly to the underlying architecture giving the programmer more control over work and data distribution.

In this paper we show methods to support the construction of efficient parallel programs in Eden. This is a first step towards a programming methodology for Eden programmers which shows how to use the language effectively. Our approach is based on the concept of *skeletons* [5]. A skeleton is a high-level parallel programming construct (often a polymorphic higher-order function) which represents a common parallel computation pattern. Associated with a skeleton are usually specialised, efficient low-level implementations for various parallel machines called *architectural skeletons*. We propose to consider an intermediate layer of *implementation skeletons* between the high-level algorithmic skeletons and the low-level architectural skeletons. As a case study we introduce various parallel Eden implementation skeletons for the well-known algorithmic skeleton map. Being able to define the abstract specification of a skeleton as well as its parallel implementations in the same declarative language gives a solid basis for proving the correctness and other properties of skeleton implementations. We present runtime results of several realistic benchmark programs which have been parallelised using the implementation skeletons on a network of workstations and on a Beowulf cluster. These architectures are examples of extremely high-latency, low-bandwidth parallel machines, favouring coarse-grained computation with minimal communication. Our test cases have been a ray tracer, a computer algebra algorithm for solving linear equation systems and the calculation of Mandelbrot sets. Although it is difficult to achieve speedups in the presence of high communication costs, Eden provides enough control to cope with this obstacle.

The main contributions of this paper are the introduction of parallel implementation skeletons which enable parallel programming with low effort in Eden (and in every other language in which such skeletons can be expressed) and the presentation of runtime results which reveal reasonable absolute speedups on high-latency systems for the non-trivial benchmark programs mentioned above.

The next section introduces the key features of Eden which are necessary to understand the implementation skeletons defined in Section 3. Section 4 presents the results of our experiments. The paper finishes with a discussion of related work and conclusions.

## 2  Eden

Eden [3] extends the lazy functional language Haskell [18] with syntactic constructs for *explicitly* defining processes [4]. Eden's process model provides direct control over process granularity, data distribution and communication topology.

**Defining Processes.** An Eden process maps inputs in_1, ..., in_m to outputs out_1, ..., out_n. Its behaviour is specified by a *process abstraction* with Process being a newly defined type constructor:

```
p :: Process (it_1,...,it_m) (ot_1,...,ot_n)
```

```
p =  process (in_1,...,in_m) -> (out_1,...,out_n)
     where equation_1 ... equation_r
```

*Example 1.* A function `f :: a -> b` can be embedded into a process abstraction via the function `mkProc`:

```
mkProc   :: (a -> b) -> Process a b
mkProc f =  process x -> f x
```

The function argument will be communicated to a process generated using `mkProc f`.                                                                            ◁

Processes are dynamically created using process instantiations. A *process instantiation* provides a process abstraction with actual input parameters. Its evaluation leads to the creation of a process together with its interconnecting communication channels. Processes communicate via *unidirectional channels* which connect one writer to exactly one reader. We use the operator

```
# :: (Transmissible a, Transmissible b) =>
     Process a b -> a -> b
```

for process instantiation. The context `Transmissible a` ensures that functions for the transmission of values of type `a` are available. In the equation

```
(out_1,..., out_n) = p # (inexp_1,..., inexp_m)
```

a process abstraction `p` is instantiated with a tuple of input expressions, yielding a tuple of outputs.

*Example 2.* The higher-order function `map`

```
map      :: (a -> b) -> [a] -> [b]
map f xs =  [f x | x <- xs]
```

can be lifted to a parallel setting by using a process abstraction instead of a function as first parameter. This process abstraction is instantiated with each element of the list of input data yielding a list of results:

```
parMap      :: (Transmissible a, Transmissible b) =>
               Process a b -> [a] -> [b]
parMap p xs =  [p # x | x <- xs]
```

The function `parMap` can be combined with `mkProc` to construct a parallel map which has (apart from the type context) the same type as `map`:

```
map_par :: (Transmissible a, Transmissible b) =>
           (a -> b) -> [a] -> [b]
map_par =  parMap . mkProc
```

Preserving the original type of `map` makes it easy to parallelise sequential programs by replacing appropriate occurrences of `map` by `map_par`.                ◁

A predefined nondeterministic process `merge` is provided for *many-to-one communication* in process systems. The `merge` process takes a list of input streams and merges the incoming values in the order in which they arrive into a single output stream.

**Evaluating Processes.** Each Eden process evaluates its output expressions to normal form and sends the results on the corresponding communication channels. Lists are transmitted as streams. This means that in two respects additional demand is introduced in favour of parallelism:

1. Evaluation to normal form is used for process outputs instead of evaluation to weak head normal form (WHNF).
2. Communication is not demand-driven. Values are sent to the receiver process without that the latter has to request for them. In general terms, Eden employs pushing instead of pulling of information.

To achieve an early instantiation of a process system it is necessary to impose an appropriate demand on the expression describing the process system [13]. This can be achieved by using *evaluation strategies* [21]. A `parMap` version which eagerly creates all its processes when evaluated to WHNF uses the strategy `spine` to force the evaluation of the result list's spine:

```
parMap      :: (Transmissible a, Transmissible b) =>
               Process a b -> [a] -> [b]
parMap p xs = [p # x | x <- xs] 'using' spine
```

## 3   Implementation Skeletons

Often a given algorithm can be parallelised in many ways. The most suitable parallelisation depends heavily on the kind of inherent parallelism (granularity) and the characteristics of the parallel machine executing the program. In this section we identify three alternative parallelisations of the higher-order function `map`. The parallelisations are defined in a machine-independent way as *implementation skeletons*, a new concept we introduce in the following.

An *algorithmic skeleton* is a higher-order scheme that abstracts from the details of a (parallel) algorithm and defines the general pattern of a (parallel) computation [5]. Well-known skeletons are e.g. the divide-and-conquer scheme and the data-parallel process farm. In skeletal programming one often distinguishes between three aspects of skeletons [9]:

- the higher-order function defining a general computation scheme with inherent parallelism (the proper algorithmic skeleton)
- different parallel implementations for different target architectures (architectural skeletons)
- a cost (performance) model to estimate the execution time.

In this paper we concentrate on the first two aspects. In our context different parallel implementations are not related to different architectures. Therefore the notion of architectural skeleton is inappropriate and we introduce the term implementation skeleton instead. An *implementation skeleton* is an architecture-independent scheme that describes a parallel implementation of an algorithmic skeleton on a higher level of abstraction than an architectural skeleton, the latter usually being optimized for a special target architecture. Often parallel implementations of an algorithmic skeleton are only described informally and hidden from the user of the skeleton (see e.g. [7,17]). In Eden, it is possible to describe the algorithmic skeleton and its parallel implementations in the same language context. This constitutes a good basis for formal reasoning and correctness proofs, although this is not further elaborated in this paper.

In most parallel implementations of `map` the input list is seen as a task queue that can be processed using several processor elements (PEs). We have already seen a straightforward parallelisation of `map`, `parMap`, in Section 2. `parMap` creates a new process for each task. This simple approach is not always well suited, especially in the presence of fine-grained or irregular tasks. Alternative parallelisations of `map` found in the literature use a fixed number of worker processes which process a subset of tasks each. They differ in the way the tasks are distributed among the worker processes:

- *static task distribution*
  `farm`: an equal number of tasks is sent to each worker
  `direct mapping`: each worker computes the task list, and selects part of it
- *dynamic task distribution* (distribution on demand)
  `workpool`: send a new task to a worker only when it has finished a task.

A visualisation of the parallelisations `parMap`, `farm` and `direct mapping` is given in Fig. 1. These schemes can be used for regular problems with equally complex subtasks while the workpool scheme is better suited for problems where the task granularity is irregular and load balancing problems can occur.

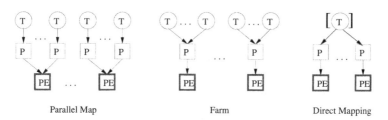

Parallel Map                    Farm                    Direct Mapping

**Fig. 1.** Implementation skeletons for problems with regular task granularity

In the following we define implementation skeletons for these different methods of parallelising the map function. Note that the simple skeleton `map_par` has already been defined in Section 2. The original type interface of `map` is always retained, although this is not essential for implementation skeletons. It has, however, the advantage that the parallelisation of calls to `map` simply consists of replacing `map` by one of the implementation skeletons.

### 3.1 Static Task Distribution: Farm

While the simple `parMap` defined in Section 2 creates a new process for each task, the *farm* scheme creates only a finite number `np` of processes and assigns every process *more than one* task. It uses parameter functions `distribute` and `combine` to distribute the tasks to the processes and to combine the results. The following Eden function defines the farm scheme:

```
farm :: (Transmissible a,Transmissible b) =>
        Int -> (Int->[a]->[[a]]) -> ([[b]]->[b]) ->
        Process [a] [b] -> [a] -> [b]

farm np distribute combine proc tasks
    = combine (parMap proc (distribute np tasks))
```

This definition is very general as it takes the number of processes and functions for distributing the tasks and combining the results as parameters. The process creation is done using `parMap`. A round robin task distribution is defined by the function `unshuffle` which on $n$ PEs, assigns every $n$-th task (starting with offset $i$) to the $i$-th process (see Fig. 2). Assuming regular task granularities or at least a random distribution of task granularities, and assuming that the number of tasks is much larger than the number of processes, every process gets a representative set of tasks and an unequal work distribution is avoided. Note that `unshuffle` is incremental in the sense that it supplies every process with at least a part of its input as soon as possible and its definition allows for a parallel access to the sublists. The function `shuffle` in Fig. 2 is a counterpart of the function `unshuffle` which collects the results and restores the original order. It also works incrementally. When the order of the list elements need not be maintained, one can apply *faster* merging functions or even Eden's nondeterministic fair `merge` process.

```
unshuffle        :: Int -> [a] -> [[a]]
unshuffle n  xs  =  [ takeEach n (drop i xs) | i <- [0..n-1] ]
   where takeEach :: Int -> [a] -> [a]
         takeEach n []     = []
         takeEach n (x:xs) = x : takeEach n (drop (n-1) xs)

shuffle      :: [[a]] -> [a]
shuffle []   =  []
shuffle xxs  =  (map head xxs) ++ shuffle (map tail xxs)
```

**Fig. 2.** Distribution and Composition Functions

Another implementation skeleton for `map` can now be defined using the `farm` scheme and the round robin task distribution defined by `unshuffle`. The `farm` scheme is applied to the number `noPE` of processor elements available, where `noPE` is a constant provided by the Eden runtime system. The process placement in the Eden system will place one process on every processor element.

```
map_farm :: (Transmissible a,Transmissible b) =>
            (a -> b) -> [a] -> [b]
map_farm =  (farm noPE unshuffle shuffle) . (mkProc . map)
```

There are two differences to the simple parallelisation shown in Section 2: Firstly, the total number of processes is fixed and set to the number noPE of processor elements. By bundling tasks this scheme increases the granularity and creates less processes than the *parMap* approach, saving process creation and communication costs. Secondly, *farm* can save memory compared to the simple parallelisation. If there are data structures which are used by all tasks, then *parMap* will have multiple copies of the data per PE[2], while in the *farm* approach there will only be a single copy on each PE.

In the following we discuss the possibility of replacing the communication of tasks by the recomputation of the task list in each process. We call this scheme *direct mapping*, because the original computation is simply divided into as many parts as there are PEs and the parts are directly mapped onto the PEs.

## 3.2  Static Task Distribution: Direct Mapping

Like farm, the direct mapping scheme creates one process per PE each working on a subpart of the task list. But each process lazily evaluates the whole task list and selects its own subpart of it. This local task list evaluation and selection saves a considerable amount of communication. The price one has to pay is the partial recomputation of the task list by each process. But especially on systems with high communication costs, this putative overhead pays off. Replacing communication by recomputation is a well-known parallel programming technique. The direct mapping scheme makes this technique available to parallel functional programmers in an easy to handle way.

The trick is to pass the task list to the processes not as input but as a parameter. Each process can then compute the part of the task list determined by its unique process identifier pid and the total number of processes np:

```
dm :: (Transmissible b) =>
      Int -> (Int->[a]->[[a]]) -> ([[b]]->[b]) ->
      ([a]->Process () [b]) -> [a] -> [b]

dm np distribute combine proc tasks
   = combine [ proc (extract pid np tasks) # ()
             | pid <- [0..np-1] ] 'using' spine
   where extract i np ts = (distribute np ts) !! i
```

A corresponding direct mapping implementation skeleton for map which uses the functions unshuffle and shuffle for distributing tasks and combining results is defined by:

---

[2] Sometimes this copying can be avoided by declaring the data at top level. In this special case the compiler, as an extension of the Glasgow Haskell Compiler (GHC), will keep only one copy of the data in each PE.

```
map_dm  :: (Transmissible b) =>
           (a -> b) -> [a] -> [b]
map_dm  = (dm noPE unshuffle shuffle) . (rfi . map)

rfi     :: (Transmissible b) =>
           (a -> b) -> a -> Process () b
rfi f x = process () -> (f x)
```

Similar to mkProc, the function rfi (*remote function invocation*) maps a function to a process abstraction. The function argument is however not communicated as in mkProc but passed as a parameter to the process abstraction. As in the farm scheme the tasks have to be of equal complexity to avoid a load imbalance. Tasks of different complexity can be dealt with by employing a workpool which is described next.

### 3.3   Dynamic Task Distribution: Workpool

For so called *irregular parallelism*, i.e. tasks of different granularity, we need an approach different to the ones presented before, which were static in the sense that every process was working on a predefined subset of tasks. To cope with extremely variable task granularities one usually employs a *workpool* with a set of tasks which are dynamically assigned to free worker processes. In our version, every PE hosts one worker process, which iteratively 1) receives a task from the workpool, 2) computes the result and 3) sends back the result. The results are interpreted as new requests for work and composed to produce the overall result. The flow of data together with their types is shown in Fig. 3.

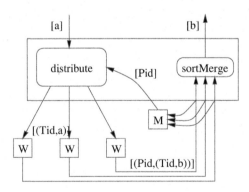

**Fig. 3.** The workpool scheme

The Eden program which implements the workpool is shown in Fig. 4. The **tasks** are spread across the worker processes using the **distribute** function defined in Fig. 5. The distribution depends on which workers have delivered the result of their previous computation. Initial requests **initialReqs** are generated depending on the **prefetch** argument to avoid workers from being idle while waiting

```
type Pid = Int   -- Process Ids
type Tid = Int   -- Task Ids
workpool :: (Transmissible a, Transmissible b) =>
            Int -> Int -> (Pid -> Process [(Tid,a)] [(Pid,(Tid,b))])
            -> [a] -> [b]
workpool np prefetch proc tasks
    = sortMerge (map (map (\ (pid,res) -> res)) fromWorkers)
      where fromWorkers    = [ proc pid # ts | (pid,ts) <- toWorkers]
            toWorkers      = zip [0..np-1] taskQueues
            taskQueues     = distribute np requests numberedtasks
            numberedtasks  = zip [0..] tasks
            requests       = initialReqs ++ newReqs
            initialReqs    = concat (replicate prefetch [0..np-1])
            newReqs        = merge # (map (map (\ (pid,res) -> pid))
                                                        fromWorkers)
```

**Fig. 4.** Workpool

to receive a new task. For the programs measured to date, a prefetch argument of 2 has been sufficient. More elaborate versions for this workpool scheme with dynamic task creation and termination detection have been presented in [14]. Using the workpool process scheme of Fig. 4 one can define the following implementation skeleton for map:

```
map_wp  :: (Transmissible a,Transmissible b) =>
           (a -> b) -> [a] -> [b]
map_wp  = (workpool noPE 2) . workerProc

workerProc  :: (a -> b) -> Int -> Process [(Int,a)] [(Int,(Int,b))]
workerProc f pid
    = process numberedTasks -> map solveTask numberedTasks
      where solveTask (nr,t) = (pid, (nr, f t))
```

Note that the workpool scheme is not only worthwhile for irregular problems but also when working on non-uniform systems with processors of different speed. For our measurements we used however only uniform systems with equally equipped processors.

## 3.4 Increasing Task Granularity

A well-known technique to increase the granularity in fine-grained problems is to put several tasks together to form *chunks* of tasks or *macro-tasks*. Working with coarse-grained macro-tasks instead of fine-grained tasks reduces the communication overhead substantially and thus improves the runtime behaviour on high-latency distributed systems. The following function embeds implementation skeletons into ones with increased task granularity.

```
distribute                     :: Int -> [Int] -> [a] -> [[a]]
distribute np rs      []     = replicate np []
distribute np []      ts     = unshuffle np ts
distribute np (r:rs) (t:ts) = (take r tqs) ++
                               ((t:(tqs!!r)) : (drop (r+1) tqs))
                               where tqs =  distribute np rs ts

sortMerge      :: [[(Int,a)]] -> [a]
sortMerge xss =  sm (\ x y -> (fst x) < (fst y)) (sortMerge odds)
                                                 (sortMerge evens)
  where [odds,evens]          = unshuffle 2 xss
        sm                    :: (a->a->Bool) -> [a] -> [a] -> [a]
        sm  p []      ys     = ys
        sm  p xs      []     = xs
        sm  p (x:xs) (y:ys) = if (p x y) then (x : sm p xs (y:ys))
                               else (y : sm p (x:xs) ys)
```

**Fig. 5.** Auxiliary functions for the workpool

```
macro :: Int -> (Int -> [a] -> [[a]]) -> ([[b]] -> b)
             -> (([a] -> [b]) -> [[a]] -> [[b]])
             -> (a -> b) -> [a] -> [b]
macro size decompose compose mapscheme f xs
    = compose (mapscheme (map f) (decompose size xs))
```

The parameter function decompose is meant to divide the input list into subparts of a given size. The parameter function compose should be the counterpart of decompose, i.e. the equation compose (chunk size xs) == xs should be valid for finite lists xs. Especially the parMap scheme can take profit from macro-tasks as the number of processes is reduced to the number of macro-tasks:

```
map_par_macro = macro size chunk concat map_par
  where chunk :: Int -> [a] -> [[a]]
        chunk k [] = []
        chunk k xs = (take k xs) : chunk k (drop k xs)
```

For an input list with length $k$ this scheme will produce $\lceil k/\text{size} \rceil$ processes where size should be defined globally. Using unshuffle for chunking, although unshuffle will not produce chunks of the given size but size chunks, and shuffle for combining will make the macro task version of parMap identical to the farm scheme:

```
                macro noPE unshuffle shuffle map_par = map_farm.
```

## 4    Experimental Results

Eden has been implemented by extending the Glasgow Haskell Compiler, version 3.02. The Eden runtime system consists of a set of multi-threaded abstract machines, each of which is mapped to a separate processor element (PE) on a multi-computer system [2]. The system can be used with the message passing libraries MPI (Message Passing Interface) [20] or PVM (Parallel Virtual Machine) [8]. A special Eden prelude module has been constructed which implements much of Eden's functionality in Eden itself.

In the following we will explore the implementation skeletons in the context of several examples on a network of workstations (NOW) and discuss their efficiency. Afterwards we show a few additional measurements on a Beowulf cluster[3] located at the University of St. Andrews. The two systems, which both represent low-cost high-performance parallel computing platforms, have the following characteristics:

| System | CPU (MHz) | OS | Mem | #Nodes | Ethernet | Latency |
|--------|-----------|-----|-----|--------|----------|---------|
| NOW | UltraSparc IIi (300) | Solaris 2.6 | 128MB | 6 | 10MBit | $282\mu s$ |
| Beowulf | Pentium II (450) | Linux RH 6.2 | 384MB | 64 | 100MBit | $142\mu s$ |

The latency on both systems is relatively high, favouring coarser grained parallel programs. All experiments (including determination of the latencies) were done under PVM 3.4.2. To rule out speedup gains due to the usage of more memory in the parallel setting (less garbage collections compared to the sequential version), we used only 40 MB on each processor node. This keeps the time for garbage collection under 5% of the sequential runtime.

The examples have been compiled with full optimization (flag -O2). We show the runtimes of different parallelisations and give the *absolute speedups*, i.e. comparing parallel runtimes with the runtime of the corresponding purely sequential programs containing no parallel machinery. The runtimes are given as the average over five runs to rule out erroneous measurements due to temporary network traffic caused by other services. We compare the effectiveness of the implementation skeletons for tasks with equal or varying granularity. A more complete presentation of the experiments described in this section will be contained in the forthcoming thesis [12].

## 4.1   Regular Tasks: A Simple Ray Tracer

Given a scene consisting of 3D objects and a camera, a ray tracer calculates a 2D image of the scene. For every pixel of the output image, the ray tracer shoots a ray into the scene and tests whether it impacts with any object of the scene. In this simple version object properties like reflection and transparency are neglected. Therefore a pixel gets the color of the object its corresponding ray hits first; if it hits none at all, it gets the color of the background. The scene itself is maintained as an unordered list of objects, so that the effort to compute the nearest impact with the objects is nearly the same for all rays. The main function of the ray tracer is top:

```
top :: ScreenSize -> CPos -> [Objects] -> [Impact]
top detail cameraPos scene
```

---

[3] EPSRC Research Grant No. GR/M 32351

```
= map (firstImpact scene) allRays
  where allRays = generateRays detail cameraPos
```

This simple algorithm contains fine-grained parallelism with tasks of the same time complexity and depends only on medium-sized globally shared data (the scene). The top level parallelism is inherent in the call of the function `map` which can be parallelised using the four implementation skeletons introduced in the previous sections.

**Results.** For the runtime measurements we used a screen of $400 \times 400$ pixels with a scene consisting of 17 objects, so the shared data was relatively small. From the runtimes and absolute speedups (shown in Fig. 6) we see that the *direct mapping scheme* performs best. The reason is that for this version only half of the communication is needed, as the rays for each process are given in a compact format.

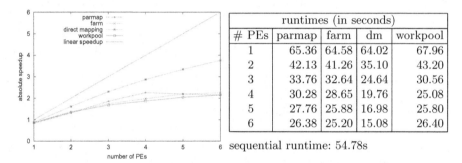

| runtimes (in seconds) | | | |
|---|---|---|---|
| # PEs | parmap | farm | dm | workpool |
| 1 | 65.36 | 64.58 | 64.02 | 67.96 |
| 2 | 42.13 | 41.26 | 35.10 | 43.20 |
| 3 | 33.76 | 32.64 | 24.64 | 30.56 |
| 4 | 30.28 | 28.65 | 19.76 | 25.08 |
| 5 | 27.76 | 25.88 | 16.98 | 25.80 |
| 6 | 26.38 | 25.20 | 15.08 | 26.40 |

sequential runtime: 54.78s

**Fig. 6.** Absolute speedups and runtimes of ray tracer on the NOW

All the other schemes take nearly the same time. *parMap* performs worst, as for each task we have to copy the scene within the process abstraction. The difference is not big, as the scene is still small. The *workpool* (with prefetch 2) on one PE is slower than the other schemes due to additional computations caused by the sequence numbers added to the tasks to be able to reconstruct them in the correct order. Moreover, more work for the task distribution is done in this scheme.

## 4.2    Irregular Tasks: An Exact Linear System Solver

The algorithm LinSolv discussed in this section finds an exact solution of a linear system of equations of the form $Ax = b$ where $A \in \mathbb{Z}^{n \times n}, b \in \mathbb{Z}^n$. LinSolv uses a *multiple homomorphic images* approach which consists of the following three stages: map the input data into several homomorphic images; compute the solution in each of these images; and combine the results of all images to a result in the original domain ('lifting'). The original `LinSolv` program was written by Hans-Wolfgang Loidl [15].

The advantage of this approach is that calculations over arbitrary precision integers are quite expensive, thus the main computation can be performed cheaper in the smaller domains $\mathbb{Z}_p$ ($\mathbb{Z}$ modulo $p$), where it is possible to work with the standard integers. Each $\mathbb{Z}_p$ is determined by a different prime number $p$. The computations on these domains can be performed in parallel and be expressed in a map-like fashion. Cramer's Rule was chosen as the basic linear system solver as it computes the exact solution and provides again a high potential for parallelism. The solution is computed by

$$x_{pj} = \det A'_{pj} / \det A_p, \quad j = 1, \ldots, n$$

where the matrix $A'_{pj}$ is $A_p$ ($A$ modulo $p$) with the $j$-th column replaced by vector $b_p$ ($b$ modulo $p$). Each of the determinants can be computed independently. In the algorithm we have to take care that we do not take prime numbers for which $\det A_p$ is zero. We need to filter out these *unlucky* prime numbers after computing the determinant in the homomorphic image. This results in tasks with two different granularities: small ones, only computing $\det A_p$, and big ones, computing $n$ determinants more.

**Results.** The measurements were taken for linear systems of various sizes, with elements not greater than 2000. As an example we show the results for a linear system with dimension 8. For this system we get only few tasks as 21 lucky primes are sufficient to find the exact solution. If there are more PEs than tasks it would be necessary to also parallelise the computation of the homomorphic solutions, e.g. by computing the determinants in parallel. The runtimes and speedups are given in Fig. 7.

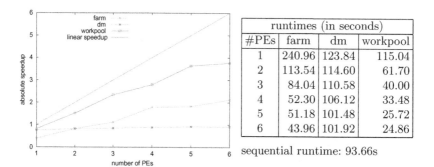

| runtimes (in seconds) | | | |
|---|---|---|---|
| #PEs | farm | dm | workpool |
| 1 | 240.96 | 123.84 | 115.04 |
| 2 | 113.54 | 114.60 | 61.70 |
| 3 | 84.04 | 110.58 | 40.00 |
| 4 | 52.30 | 106.12 | 33.48 |
| 5 | 51.18 | 101.48 | 25.72 |
| 6 | 43.96 | 101.92 | 24.86 |

sequential runtime: 93.66s

**Fig. 7.** Absolute speedups and runtimes of LinSolv on the NOW

Although there are only few tasks, the *workpool* version delivers the best results. This has two reasons: first of all because the load can be balanced better, and what is probably more significant is that not too many primes are generated without real demand. The runtimes of the *farm* on one processor are unusually high, because the main process produces prime numbers without demand, and this thread gets the same amount of time as the local process solving the equations and the thread computing the final lifting phase. The problem of the *direct mapping* version is the recomputation of the prime list in each worker process.

### 4.3   Compensating Irregularity: Mandelbrot Sets

Mandelbrot sets can be used to generate fractal graphics. For each pixel of the screen, it is necessary to compute its color (in fact, its distance to the Mandelbrot set), which depends on the coordinates of the pixel. This computation is performed for each pixel by iterating a function until a good approximation is obtained, or until a maximum number of iterations has been reached. For some pixels it is sufficient to compute a few iterations, while for others the maximum number of iterations is needed. Therefore the problem's inherent pixel-wise parallelism is of irregular granularity.

```
mandel :: Int -> Int -> [Int] -- Using a (sizeX x sizeY) screen
mandel sizeX sizeY = map calcPix (range (0,0) (sizeX-1,sizeY-1))

range  :: (Int,Int) -> (Int,Int) -> [(Int,Int)]
range (x1,y1) (x2,y2) = [(x,y) | x <- [x1..x2], y <- [y1..y2]]

calcPix       :: (Int,Int) -> Int
calcPix (x,y) = loop (firstApprox (x,y)) 0
```

The much too fine granularity has to be coarsened by grouping pixels into larger tasks. Time-consuming pixels may be clustered with this approach, which bears the risk of a serious load imbalance.

**Results.** We have generated Mandelbrot sets for a $1024 \times 1024$ screen, using 1000 as maximum number of iterations. Fig. 8 shows the results on the NOW.

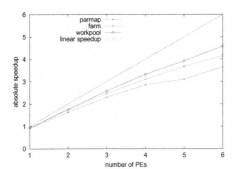

| \# PEs | parmap | farm | workpool |
| --- | --- | --- | --- |
| 1 | 235.00 | 231.10 | 227.92 |
| 2 | 131.94 | 123.74 | 121.92 |
| 3 | 93.42 | 87.13 | 83.44 |
| 4 | 75.44 | 69.20 | 64.70 |
| 5 | 69.22 | 58.54 | 54.83 |
| 6 | 58.80 | 51.82 | 46.88 |

runtimes (in seconds)

sequential runtime: 215.06s

**Fig. 8.** Absolute speedups and runtimes of Mandelbrot on the NOW

As expected, even when using a row-wise partitioning the *workpool* scheme is the best suited for the original inherently irregular problem. But *parMap* and *farm* can also produce good speedups if we use a different partitioning. When rows are combined with `unshuffle` these schemes can be nearly as good as *workpool*. The reason is that the round robin distribution with `unshuffle` often compensates the irregularity of the rows. There is a big difference in the computation needed for different rows, but neighbouring rows usually need similar times. Hence, unshuffling the tasks leads to bigger tasks of a more regular granularity, giving *workpool* only a small advantage over the other schemes.

## 4.4    Measurements on a Beowulf Cluster

We had the opportunity to repeat some of our measurements on the St. Andrews Beowulf cluster. As can be seen from the absolute speedups achieved on up to ten PEs for the ray tracer with the same input parameters as before (see Fig. 9) and for the LinSolv example with the $8 \times 8$ input matrix on up to 25 PEs (see Fig. 10), the implementation skeletons show the same relative performance in comparison to each other. The direct mapping scheme performs best for the regular tasks of the ray tracer, while the workpool scheme copes best with the irregularity within the LinSolv program.

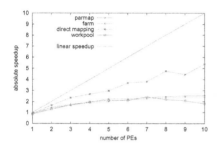

**Fig. 9.** Absolute speedups of the simple ray tracer on the Beowulf cluster

**Fig. 10.** Absolute speedups of LinSolv with $8 \times 8$ input matrix on the Beowulf cluster

## 4.5    Summary

In this section we have considered examples with inherent data parallelism. The problems can be distinguished by the number of tasks and their granularity. We had two problems with fine-grained parallelism: the ray tracer and the Mandelbrot sets. LinSolv is coarse-grained as there are only a few expensive tasks. To observe the impact of load balancing we had two problems with varying task granularity: In Mandelbrot between 0 and 1000 iterations are needed per pixel, whereas in LinSolv there are two different complexities. The complete characterization is shown in Table 1.

**Table 1.** Characterization of the problems

| problem | granularity | decomposition | best scheme |
|---------|-------------|---------------|-------------|
| mandelbrot | fine | irregular | workpool |
| raytracer | fine | regular | direct mapping |
| linsolv | coarse | irregular | workpool |

The *workpool* is the best choice if the task granularity is varying, although the maintenance of the *workpool* is not for free. If all tasks have the same granularity the *direct mapping* yields the best results, because we can save communications by implicitly passing the task description as a parameter. As a consequence of increasing the task granularity by the use of macro-tasks in `parMap`, the *parMap* and *farm* schemes show a very similar behaviour. The results obtained on the Beowulf cluster show that the direct mapping and the workpool scheme behave equally well on large numbers of processor elements.

### 4.6   Further Measurements on the Beowulf Cluster

Additional measurements on the St. Andrews Beowulf cluster with up to 61 processor nodes have shown that Eden achieves a good scalability for complex problems. We have studied a more complex ray tracer for spheres and the LinSolv program explained before. The spheres ray tracer differs from the ray tracer · described in Subsection 4.1 in that it is restricted to spherical objects, but takes into account reflection and light conditions. The original version of this algorithm has been ported from the Impala suite of implicitly parallel programs[4].

**Spheres Ray Tracer Results.** Fig. 11 shows the speedups obtained for the ray tracer program with a direct mapping parallelisation for screens with dimension 350 (sequential runtime: 213.42s) and 500 pixels (sequential runtime: 435.01s). The largest speedup is 27 on 37 PEs for the larger screen size. The speedup increases almost linearly until about 40 processor elements. Then a dramatic decrease is observed which is due to an increase of the startup time of the Eden system on the Beowulf cluster. The startup problems on more than 40 processors have not been solved yet. Nevertheless these results are very promising for what is a relatively immature implementation.

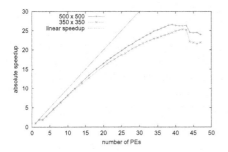

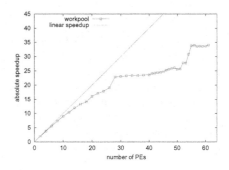

**Fig. 11.** Absolute speedups of spheres ray tracer on the Beowulf cluster

**Fig. 12.** Absolute speedups of LinSolv with $14 \times 14$ input matrix on the Beowulf cluster

**LinSolv Results.** Fig. 12 shows the speedups obtained for the LinSolv algorithm described in Subsection 4.2. The measurements used a sparse matrix with dimension 14 (sequential runtime: 552.59s) and a workpool parallelisation. Measurements were taken for up to 61 PEs and show good performance: The largest speedup is 35 on 61 PEs.

---

[4] URL: `http://www.csg.lcs.mit.edu/impala/`

# 5 Related Work

In the last decade a great variety of different approaches to the combination of functional programming and parallelism has evolved. A comprehensive collection of introductory chapters and surveys of current research projects has been published by Hammond and Michaelson [10]. Besides many other approaches to efficient parallel functional programming the concept of *algorithmic skeletons* [5] has received a lot of attention. For efficiency, skeletons are often implemented in a low-level language different from the language in which they are used. Therefore skeleton implementations tend to be a "black box" for the programmer, which can make them hard to use in an efficient way. Well-known approaches to introduce skeletons in a parallel language include: *Darlington et al.* [6], $P^3L$ [17], *Skil* [1], and others. As Eden, Skil allows to design new skeletons in the language itself, the main difference being that Skil is based on the imperative host language C [19]. More closely related to our work are the following approaches:

In *GAPML* [9] Michaelson, Hamdam et al. extend an ML compiler by machinery which automatically searches the given program for higher-order functions which are suitable for parallelisation. During compilation these are replaced by efficient low-level implementations written in C and MPI. In *HaskSkel* [11], Hammond and Rebón Portillo combine the evaluation strategies of *GpH* [21] with Okasaki's Edison library [16] (which provides efficient implementations of data structures) to implement parallel skeletons directly in GpH.

# 6 Conclusion

We have introduced four implementation skeletons for the higher-order function map which are based on the schemes *parMap*, *farm*, *direct mapping*, and *workpool*. Depending on problem characteristics like degree and granularity of inherent parallelism, static or dynamic evolution of parallelism etc. the programmer can choose the appropriate skeleton to obtain an efficient parallel program. The schemes have proven to be helpful during program construction and efficient during program execution.

This is supported by runtime results measured with the Eden system on two different high-latency parallel machines. The current implementation contains the basic functionality without optimisations, but it is already mature enough to deliver reasonable speedups with several examples on a conventional network of workstations and on a Beowulf cluster.

### Acknowledgements

The authors thank Ricardo Peña, Kevin Hammond, Hans-Wolfgang Loidl, Phil Trinder and Robert Pointon for their collaboration and helpful comments on previous versions of this paper. Special thanks go to Kevin Hammond and Álvaro Rebón Portillo for giving us the opportunity to work with the St. Andrews Beowulf Cluster.

# References

1. G. H. Botorog and H. Kuchen. Efficient Parallel Programming with Algorithmic Skeletons. In *Europ. Conf. on Par. Proc. (Euro-Par)*, LNCS 1123. Springer, 1996.
2. S. Breitinger, U. Klusik, and R. Loogen. From (sequential) Haskell to (parallel) Eden: An Implementation Point of View. In *Principles of Declarative Programming, PLILP'98*, LNCS 1490. Springer, 1998.
3. S. Breitinger, R. Loogen, Y. Ortega-Mallén, and R. Peña. Eden — Language Definition and Operational Semantics. TR 96-10, Philipps-Univ. Marburg, 1996.
4. S. Breitinger, R. Loogen, Y. Ortega-Mallén, and R. Peña. The Eden Coordination Model for Distributed Memory Systems. In *High-Level Parallel Progr. Models and Supportive Env. (HIPS)*. IEEE Press, 1997.
5. M. Cole. *Algorithmic Skeletons: Structure Management of Parallel Computations*. MIT Press, 1989. Research Monographs in Parallel and Distributed Computing.
6. J. Darlington, A. Field, P. Harrison, P. Kelly, D. Sharp, Q. Wu, and R. While. Parallel Programming Using Skeleton Functions. In *Parallel Architectures and Languages Europe*. Springer, 1993.
7. J. Darlington, Y.-K. Guo, H. To, and J. Yang. Functional Skeletons for Parallel Coordination. In *Euro-Par*, LNCS 966. Springer, 1995.
8. A. Geist, A. Beguelin, J. Dongarra, and W. Jiang. *PVM: Parallel Virtual Machine*. MIT Press, 1994.
9. M. Hamdan. *A Combinatorial Framework for Parallel Programming Using Algorithmic Skeletons*. PhD thesis, Heriot-Watt Univ. Edinburgh, 2000.
10. K. Hammond and G. Michaelson. *Research Directions in Parallel Functional Programming*. Springer-Verlag, 1999.
11. K. Hammond and Á. R. Portillo. HaskSkel: Algorithmic Skeletons in Haskell. In *Impl. of Functional Languages (IFL'99)*, LNCS 1868. Springer-Verlag, 2000.
12. U. Klusik. *An Efficient Implementation of the Parallel Functional Language Eden on Distributed-Memory System*. PhD thesis, University of Marburg, 2001. In prep.
13. U. Klusik, R. Loogen, and S. Priebe. Controlling Parallelism and Data Distribution in Eden. In *Trends in Functional Programming, Vol. 2, (SFP 2000)*. Intellect, 2001.
14. U. Klusik, R. Peña, and F. Rubio. Replicated Workers in Eden. *Workshop on Constructive Methods for Par. Progr. (CMPP)*. TR-MIP-0007, Passau Univ., 2000.
15. H. W. Loidl. *Granularity in Large-Scale Parallel Functional Programming*. PhD thesis, Dept. of Computing Science, University of Glasgow, 1997. TR-1998-7.
16. C. Okasaki. An Overview of Edison. In *ICFP 2000 (Haskell Workshop)*, 2000.
17. S. Pelagatti. *Structured Development of Parallel Programs*. Taylor & Francis, 1998.
18. J. Peterson and K. Hammond (eds.). Report on the programming language Haskell: a non-strict, purely functional language, version 1.4. TR YALEU/DCS/RR-1106, Yale Univ., 1997.
19. T. Richert. Skil: Programming with Algorithmic Skeletons — A Practical Point of View. In *Proc. of the 12th Int. Workshop on Impl. of Funct. Lang. (IFL'00)*, Aachener Informatik-Berichte 00-7, RWTH Aachen, 2000.
20. The MPI Forum. MPI: A Message-Passing Interface Standard. TR, Univ. of Tennessee, Knoxville, 1994.
21. P. W. Trinder, K. Hammond, H. W. Loidl, and S. L. Peyton Jones. Algorithm + Strategy = Parallelism. *Journal of Functional Programming*, 8(1), 1998.

# ObjectCurry: An Object-Oriented Extension of the Declarative Multi-Paradigm Language Curry

Michael Hanus[1,*], Frank Huch[2], and Philipp Niederau[2]

[1] Institut für Informatik, Christian-Albrechts-Universität zu Kiel, Germany,
mh@informatik.uni-kiel.de
[2] Lehrstuhl für Informatik II, RWTH Aachen, Germany
hutch@i2.informatik.rwth-aachen.de phn@navigium.de

**Abstract.** Curry combines the concepts of functional, logic and concurrent programming languages. Concurrent programming with ports allows the modeling of objects in Curry similar to object-oriented programming languages. In this paper, we present ObjectCurry, a conservative extension of Curry. ObjectCurry allows the direct definition of templates which play the role of classes in conventional object-oriented languages. Objects are instances of a template. An object owns a state and reacts when it receives a message—usually by sending messages to other objects or a transformation of its state. ObjectCurry also provides inheritance between templates. Furthermore, we show how programs can be translated from ObjectCurry into Curry by exploiting the concurrency and distribution features of Curry. To implement inheritance, we extend the type system of Curry, which is based on parametric polymorphism, to include subtyping for objects and messages.

## 1 Introduction

Curry [4,6] is a multi-paradigm declarative language which integrates functional, logic, and concurrent programming paradigms (see [3] for a survey on integrated functional logic languages). The syntax of Curry is similar to Haskell [15], e.g., functions are defined by rules of the form "$f\, t_1 \ldots t_n\ = e$" where $f$ is the function to be defined, $t_1, \ldots, t_n$ are the pattern arguments, and $e$ is an expression which replaces a function call matching the left-hand side. In addition to Haskell, local names introduced in `let` and `where` clauses can be declared as "`free`" which means that their value is unknown. Such *free* or *logical variables* in expressions supports logic programming features like partial data structures and search for solutions. Furthermore, functions in Curry can be defined by conditional equations "$l\ \mid c\ = r$" where the condition $c$ is a *constraint* (an expression of the predefined type `Success`) which must be solved in order to apply the equation. Basic constraints are "`success`" (the always satisfiable constraint) and equational constraints of the form "$e_1\ \texttt{=:=}\ e_2$" which are satisfied if both sides $e_1$

---

\* This research has been partially supported by the German Research Council (DFG) under grant Ha 2457/1-2 and by the DAAD under the PROCOPE programme.

M. Mohnen and P. Koopman (Eds.): IFL 2000, LNCS 2011, pp. 89–106, 2001.

and $e_2$ are reducible to the same value (data term). More complex constraints can be constructed with the concurrent conjunction operator &. A non-primitive constraint like "$c_1$ & $c_2$" is solved by solving both constraints $c_1$ and $c_2$ concurrently. Finally, "$c_1$ &> $c_2$ denotes the sequential conjunction of two constraints, i.e., first the constraint $c_1$ is solved and, if this was successful, the constraint $c_2$ is evaluated.

Using both functional and logic features of Curry, it is possible to model objects with states (see Section 2) at a very low level. Therefore, we propose an extension of Curry, called ObjectCurry, which provides all standard features of object-oriented programming, like (concurrent and distributed) objects with state that can be defined by class templates and inheritance between templates.

This paper is structured as follows. In the next section, we review the modeling of concurrent objects in Curry as proposed in [5]. We present ObjectCurry in the subsequent section and show the translation of ObjectCurry programs into Curry in Sect. 4. Section 5 describes an extended type system for ObjectCurry in order to detect type errors related to inheritance at compile time before we discuss related work in Sect. 6 and conclude in Sect. 7.

## 2   Implementing Objects in Curry

It is well known from concurrent logic programming [16] that objects can be easily implemented as predicates processing a stream of incoming messages. The internal state of the object can be implemented as a parameter which may change in recursive calls when the message stream is processed. Since constraints play the role of predicates in Curry, we consider objects as functions with result type Success. These functions take the current state of the object and a stream of incoming messages as arguments. If the stream is not empty, the "object" function calls itself recursively with a new state, depending on the first element of the message stream. Thus,

$$o :: State \rightarrow [MessageType] \rightarrow \texttt{Success}$$

is the general type of an object where $State$ is the type of the internal state of the object and $MessageType$ is the type of messages. Usually, we define a new algebraic data type for the messages.

The following example shows a counter which understands the messages Inc, Set s, and Get v. Thus, we define the data type

```
data CounterMessage = Inc | Set Int | Get Int
```

The counter has an integer value as an internal state. Receiving Inc increments the internal state and Set s assigns it to a new value s. To get the current state of the counter as an answer, we send the message Get v to the object where v is a free logical variable. In this case the counter object binds this variable to its current state:

```
counter :: Int -> [CounterMessage] -> Success
```

```
counter eval rigid
counter x (Inc   : ms) = counter (x+1) ms
counter _ (Set s : ms) = counter s     ms
counter x (Get v : ms) = v =:= x  &  counter x ms
counter _ []           = success
```

The evaluation of the constraint "counter 42 s" creates a new counter object with initial value 42. Messages are sent by instantiating the variable s. The object terminates if the stream of incoming messages is empty. In this case the constraint is reduced to the trivial constraint success. For instance, the constraint

```
let s free in counter 41 s & s=:=[Inc, Get x]
```

is successfully evaluated where x is bound to the value 42. The annotation

```
counter eval rigid
```

marks counter as a rigid function. This means that an expression "counter x s" can be reduced only if s is bound.[1]

If there is more than one process sending messages to the same counter object, it is necessary to merge the message streams from different processes into a single message stream. Doing that with a merger function causes a set of problems as discussed in [5,8]. Therefore, Janson et al. [8] proposed the use of ports for the concurrent logic language AKL which are generalized in [5] to support distributed programming in Curry. In principle, a *port* is a constraint between a multiset and a stream which is satisfied if the multiset and the stream contain the same elements. In Curry a port is created by a constraint "openPort p s" where p and s are free logical variables. This constraint creates a multiset and a stream and combines them over a port. Elements can be inserted into the multiset by sending them to p. When a message is sent to p, it will automatically be added to the stream s in order to satisfy the port constraint. For sending a message, there is a constraint "send m p" where m is the message and p is a port created by openPort.

Using ports, we can rewrite the counter example as follows

```
openPort p s &>  counter 0 s & (send Inc p &> send (Get x) p)
```

## 3   ObjectCurry, an Object-Oriented Extension of Curry

Using the technique presented above is troublesome and error-prone, in particular, if the state consists of many variables, because the programmer has to

---

[1] In contrast to rigid functions, Curry also provides flexible functions which nondeterministically instantiate their arguments in order to allow the reduction of function calls, which provides for goal solving like in logic programming. As a default (which can be changed by eval annotations), constraints are flexible and all other functions are rigid.

repeat the whole state in the recursive calls. This motivated us to introduce some special syntax for defining *templates*. Templates play the role of classes in conventional object-oriented programming languages. We use the word "template" instead of class to avoid confusion between classes in an object-oriented meaning and Haskell's type classes. For instance, a *template for counter objects* can be defined in ObjectCurry as follows:

```
template Counter =
constructor
  counter init = x := init
methods
  Inc    = x := x + 1
  Set s  = x := s
  Get v  = v =:= x
```

A template definition starts with the reserved keyword `template` followed by the name of the template. Similar to a data type declaration, the name of the template is its own type. The *constructor* is a function which we use to instantiate new objects. The left-hand side is constructed as in conventional function declarations. The right-hand side is a set of assignments describing the *attributes* of the object and their initial values. The assignments are consecutively written using the offside rule.

The messages which are understood by the object and the reactions to these messages are defined by *methods*. Messages are defined similarly as the constructor. The left-hand side of a method declaration consists of the name of the method followed by a list of patterns as in a function declaration and describes the signature of a message with the same name as the method. The right-hand side describes the behavior of the object in response to receiving a message. A reaction can be a transformation of the internal state of the object. The transformation of a state can be expressed by a set $A$ of assignments of the form "$v := e$". If the tuple $(v'_1, \ldots, v'_n)$ is the current state of the object where the template has the attributes $v_1, \ldots, v_n$, $A$ specifies the state transformation $(v'_1, \ldots, v'_n) \mapsto (v''_1, \ldots, v''_n)$ defined by

$$v''_i = \begin{cases} e_i & \text{if } v_i := e_i \in A \\ v'_i & \text{otherwise} \end{cases}$$

Additionally, the right-hand side of a method can also include constraints, i.e., expressions of the type `Success`, because constraints offer further possibilities to express reactions, e.g., equational constraints are used to yield an answer by binding a logical variable, or messages are sent to other objects by the `send` constraint.

The assignments and constraints in the right-hand side of a method are treated as a set (where for each component of the state at most one assignment is allowed), i.e., they can be placed in any order: an assignment has no side effect to another assignment in the same method.

A template definition introduces the type of the template, the constructor function and the messages at the top level of the Curry program. If $T$ is the type of the template and the constructor function has $n$ arguments $\tau_1, \ldots, \tau_n$, the type of the constructor function is

$$\tau_1 \to \ldots \to \tau_n \to \texttt{Constructor } T$$

In a similar manner, a method has the type

$$\tau_1 \to \ldots \to \tau_n \to \texttt{Message } T$$

if it takes $n$ arguments. Additionally, each object understands the predefined message `Stop` which terminates the object.

To instantiate a template, there is a constraint

```
new :: Constructor α → Object α → Success .
```

`new` takes a constructor function and a free logical variable and binds the variable to a new instance of the template $\alpha$. Messages can be sent to such an object using the constraint `send :: Message α → Object α → Success`. For instance, the evaluation of the following expression binds the variable v to the value 42:

```
new (counter 41) o
& (send Inc o &>  send (Get v) o &>  send Stop o)
```

To give an object the possibility to send a message to itself, there is a predefined identifier `self`. `self` is visible in the right-hand side of each method and bound to the current object. Note that sending a message to `self` has no immediate side effect to the attributes of the object because the objects can only react to this message after the evaluation of the current method is finished.

As a true extension to the modeling of objects in Curry as described in Sect. 2, ObjectCurry also provides inheritance. A template can inherit attributes and methods from another template, which we call *parent*, where inherited methods can be redefined or new attributes and methods can be added. A *supertemplate* of a template $T$ is $T$ or one of its ancestors w.r.t. the parent relation. *Subtemplates* are analogously defined.

For instance, we define a new template `maxCounter` which inherits the attribute x and the methods `Inc`, `Set`, and `Get` from `counter`. It also introduces a new attribute `max` which represents an upper bound for incrementing the counter. The method `Inc` will be redefined to avoid incrementing x to a value greater than `max`. Additionally, we define a new method `SetMax v` to set the upper bound:

```
template MaxCounter extends Counter =
constructor
  maxCounter init maxInit = counter init
                            max := maxInit
methods
  Inc             = x   := (if x < max then x+1 else x)
  SetMax newMax   = max := newMax
                    x   := (if x<max then x else max)
```

The reserved keyword **extends** followed by the name of the parent specifies that the template inherits the attributes and methods from Counter.

The first expression in the right-hand side of the constructor of a subtemplate must be the function call of the constructor of the parent. In this way the initial values of the inherited attributes are determined.

Methods can be redefined by defining a method with the same name in the subtemplate. All methods which are not redefined will be inherited.

## 4   Translating ObjectCurry into Curry

To translate ObjectCurry programs into Curry, we basically use the technique presented in Sect. 2. An abstract data type `Msg` contains data constructors for each message defined in all templates and the additional message `Stop`. We decided to use only one data type for all messages to obtain a maximum of flexibility. Of course, ObjectCurry programs translated in this way are not type safe in a sense that messages can be sent to objects which cannot understand these messages. We will discuss this issue and propose a solution for this in Sect. 5.

For our counter example, we generate one data type for all messages:

```
data Msg = Inc | Set Int | Get Int | SetMax Int | Stop
```

Next we define a function which defines the initial state of a new object. If the state of the object consists of more than one attribute, the state is implemented as a tuple.

```
counterInitState init = init
```

The initialization function of a subtemplate uses the initialization function of its parent to obtain the initial values for the inherited attributes:

```
maxCounterInitState (init,maxInit) =
  let r_x = counterInitState init
  in (r_x,maxInit)
```

Given a state and a message, the following action function computes the next state defined by the corresponding method.

```
counterAction x self Inc                = State (x+1)
counterAction x self (Set s)            = State s
counterAction x self (Get v) | v =:= x  = State x
counterAction x self Stop               = Final
```

We use the abstract data type "data State a = State a | Final" to distinguish normal states and the final state.

In a subtemplate, redefined and new methods are similarly translated:

```
maxCounterAction (x,max) self Inc
  = State (if x < max then x + 1 else x, max)
```

```
maxCounterAction (x,max) self (SetMax newMax)
  = State (if x < max then x else max, newMax)
```

The action function of a subtemplate also contains an equation for each inherited method. Such an equation calls the action function of the parent of the template for receiving the next state:

```
maxCounterAction (x,max) self (Get v)
  = let State r_x = counterAction x self (Get v)
    in State (r_x,max)
maxCounterAction (x,max) self Stop = Final
```

To create a new object, we use the constructor function and the **new** constraint. The constructor function determines the initial state of the object using the translated function for the initialization defined above and transfers the initial state and the action function of the object to a generic function `loop` which handles the recursive calls until the final state is reached:

```
counter init self =
  loop (counterInitState init) counterAction self
```

For each template the same function `loop` is used which is defined by:

```
loop eval rigid
loop state action self (m:ms) = continuation nextState self ms
  where
    nextState = action state self m
    continuation (State ns) self ms = loop ns action self ms
    continuation Final      _    _  = success
```

The function **new** has a constructor function and a free logical variable as arguments. It creates a port to which the logical variable is bound and passes a stream associated with the port to the constructor function. Additionally, it passes the port to the constructor as the value for the identifier `self`:

```
new constructor port =
  let stream free in
    openPort port stream &> constructor port stream
```

In the transformation, each message has the type `Msg`. Objects are represented by ports, so an object has the type `Port Msg` instead of `Object Template`.

We have implemented a compiler for ObjectCurry which translates a program from ObjectCurry to Curry following the ideas sketched in this section. The compiler is written in Curry itself.

## 5   Type Safeness

The presented translation into Curry programs is not type safe in the sense that messages can be sent to objects which cannot understand these messages.

To detect such a kind of type errors without restricting the use of objects and messages, it is necessary to define a new type system and implement a new type checker which supports subtyping.

## 5.1   Subtyping

We introduce a new type system which uses subtype constraints for expressing the types of objects, messages and functions which have such argument types or deliver objects or messages as their results.

First we take a look at the type of constructor functions, objects, messages and the predefined functions send and new. In a first step, we define three new predefined type constructors named Constructor, Object and Message with arity one. An object as an instance of a template $T$ has type Object $T$. A message has type $\tau_1 \to \cdots \to \tau_n \to$ Message $T$, where $\tau_1, \ldots, \tau_n$ are the types of the arguments of this message and $T$ is the template which defines this message. A constructor of a template $T$ has type $\tau_1 \to \cdots \to \tau_n \to$ Constructor $T$, where again $\tau_1, \ldots, \tau_n$ are the types of the arguments of this constructor. For example, an instance of the template Counter has type Object Counter, the message Get has type Int $\to$ Message Counter and the constructor function counter has type Int $\to$ Constructor Counter. With these types the function send must have the type

$$\text{send :: Message } \alpha \to \text{Object } \alpha \to \text{Success}$$

and new has the type

$$\text{new :: Constructor } \alpha \to \text{Object } \alpha \to \text{Success}$$

These types do not allow subtyping w.r.t. a Hindley/Milner-like type system [2] as used in Curry. Therefore, we need subtyping in three cases in order to support object-oriented programming techniques and to combine them with the advantages of parametric polymorphism:

1. We want to send messages defined in a template $T$ to instances of subtemplates of $T$.
2. It should be possible to keep objects of different templates in a polymorphic data structure, e.g., in a list: If these objects have a common supertemplate, there are common messages which all of these objects understand.
3. We also want to store messages defined in different templates in a polymorphic data structure if these templates have a common subtemplate.

Therefore, we introduce subtype constraints and constrained types. We use them to define new types of objects and messages which supports subtyping in the three described cases. Note that, in contrast to other approaches to subtyping or order-sorted types, we consider only subtype relations between templates and not subtyping of standard data types, like numbers or functions, since this is sufficient for our purposes.

**Definition 1.** *A* subtype constraint *is an expression* $\tau_1 \leq \tau_2$ *where* $\tau_i$ *$(i = 1, 2)$ is a type variable or the name of a template.*

**Definition 2.** *A* constrained type *is a pair* $\tau | C$ *consisting of a type expression $\tau$ and a set $C$ of subtype constraints. A* constrained type scheme *has the form* $\forall \alpha_1 \ldots \alpha_n.\tau | C.$

Intuitively, a constraint of the form $\tau_1 \leq \tau_2$ expresses that $\tau_1$ must be a subtemplate of $\tau_2$. To allow keeping instances of different templates in one polymorphic data structure, an object gets the type `Object` $\alpha \,|\, \{T \leq \alpha\}$. For example, an instance of `Counter` gets the type `Object` $\alpha \,|\, \{$`Counter` $\leq \alpha\}$ and an instance of `MaxCounter` gets the type `Object` $\alpha \,|\, \{$`MaxCounter` $\leq \alpha\}$. We can keep both objects in a list where this list has the type `[Object` $\alpha]\,|\,\{$`Counter` $\leq \alpha,$ `MaxCounter` $\leq \alpha\}$. The type of the list is inferred by using standard typing rules but additionally collecting all subtype constraints in one set.

Intuitively, this constraint set can be satisfied because there exists a template $T$ which is a supertemplate of `Counter` and a supertemplate of `MaxCounter`: `Counter` is a supertemplate of both `Counter` and `MaxCounter` . If we mix objects which do not have a common supertemplate, the constraint set cannot be satisfied. This makes sense because these objects do not have a common message and so there is no reason to store them in one data structure. We will formally define the satisfiability of a constraint set later.

Using this type for an object, we must also modify the type of **new** as follows:

$$\text{\bf new} :: \text{Constructor } \alpha \rightarrow \text{Object } \beta \rightarrow \text{Success} \mid \{\alpha \leq \beta\}$$

A similar modification of the type of a message allows to mix messages of different types in a common data structure: A message gets the type

$$\tau_1 \rightarrow \cdots \rightarrow \tau_n \rightarrow \text{Message } \alpha \mid \{\alpha \leq T\}$$

where $\tau_1, \ldots, \tau_n$ are the types of the arguments of this message.

With these definitions it is possible to send a message defined in a template $T$ to an instance of a subtemplate of $T$: The resulting constraint set can be satisfied iff the object understands the message. For instance, if we send the message `Inc` to an object of the instance `MaxCounter`, we get the typed expression

$$\text{send Inc maxCounterObject} :: \text{Success} \mid \{\alpha \leq \text{Counter}, \text{MaxCounter} \leq \alpha\}$$

Unfortunately, we must also modify the type of **send**. Consider the following example:

```
f m1 m2 o1 o2 = send m1 o1 & send m2 o2 & send m1 o2
```

`f` has two messages and two objects as arguments. It sends the first message to the first object, the second message to the second object, and also the first message to the second object. With the type of **send** defined above, we get the type

$$\text{f} :: \text{Message } \alpha \rightarrow \text{Message } \alpha \rightarrow \text{Object } \alpha \rightarrow \text{Object } \alpha \rightarrow \text{Success}$$

For our running example, we assume:

$$
\begin{array}{ll}
\texttt{Inc} & \texttt{:: Message } \alpha \;\mid\; \{\alpha \leq \texttt{Counter}\} \\
\texttt{(SetMax 42)} & \texttt{:: Message } \alpha \;\mid\; \{\alpha \leq \texttt{MaxCounter}\} \\
\texttt{counterObject} & \texttt{:: Object } \alpha \;\mid\; \{\texttt{Counter} \leq \alpha\} \\
\texttt{maxCounterObject} & \texttt{:: Object } \alpha \;\mid\; \{\texttt{MaxCounter} \leq \alpha\}
\end{array}
$$

Thus, the application of $f$ to these arguments would yield the type

$$
\begin{aligned}
&\texttt{f Inc (SetMax 42) counterObject maxCounterObject ::} \\
&\texttt{Success } \mid, \{\alpha \leq \texttt{Counter}, \alpha \leq \texttt{MaxCounter}, \texttt{Counter} \leq \alpha, \texttt{MaxCounter} \leq \alpha\}
\end{aligned}
$$

The set of constraints of this type is not satisfiable because there is no substitution for $\alpha$ such that all constraints are elements of the inheritance hierarchy. This does not match our intuition because it is possible to send `Inc` to `counterObject` and `maxCounterObject` and `(SetMax 42)` to `maxCounterObject`.

The problem can be easily solved if we modify the type of `send`:

$$
\texttt{send :: Message } \alpha \rightarrow \texttt{Object } \beta \rightarrow \texttt{Success } \mid \{\beta \leq \alpha\}
$$

This type corresponds to the intuition that a message defined in template $\alpha$ can be send to all instances of template $\beta$ provided that $\beta$ is a subtemplate of $\alpha$. Now the type of $f$ is

$$
\begin{aligned}
\texttt{Message } \alpha \rightarrow \texttt{Message } \beta \rightarrow \;&\texttt{Object } \gamma \rightarrow \texttt{Object } \delta \rightarrow \texttt{Success} \\
&\mid \{\gamma \leq \alpha, \delta \leq \beta, \delta \leq \alpha\}
\end{aligned}
$$

and "`f Inc (SetMax 42) counterObject maxCounterObject`" has type

$$
\begin{aligned}
\texttt{Success } \mid \{&\gamma \leq \alpha, \delta \leq \beta, \delta \leq \alpha, \alpha \leq \texttt{Counter}, \beta \leq \texttt{MaxCounter}, \\
&\texttt{Counter} \leq \gamma, \texttt{MaxCounter} \leq \delta\}
\end{aligned}
$$

These subtype constraints are satisfiable by the following substitution $\sigma$:

$$
\sigma(\alpha) = \texttt{Counter}, \sigma(\beta) = \texttt{MaxCounter}, \sigma(\gamma) = \texttt{Counter}, \sigma(\delta) = \texttt{MaxCounter}
$$

## 5.2    Core ObjectCurry

In order to define the type system of ObjectCurry, we introduce a simplified core language to provide a more compact representation of ObjectCurry's typing rules. The expressions and templates of the core language are defined in Fig. 1.

An expression $E$ of the core language is either a variable, a lambda abstraction, an application of two expressions, an expression combined with the declaration of free variables, or a conditional expression. A template $T$ consists of an initial assignment $I$, which defines the attributes and initial values of the template, and a set of methods. A template can also be defined as a subtemplate of another template by an **extends** clause. $I'$ contains additionally to the initial assignments of the subtemplate a call to the constructor function of its supertemplate. This ensures that each inherited attribute gets an initial value.

$$
\begin{array}{lll}
E & ::= x & \text{variable} \\
& |\ \lambda x.E & \text{abstraction} \\
& |\ E_1\,E_2 & \text{application} \\
& |\ \texttt{let}\ x\ \texttt{free}\ \texttt{in}\ E & \text{free variable} \\
& |\ \texttt{if}\ E_1\ \texttt{then}\ E_2\ \texttt{else}\ E_3 & \text{conditional} \\
\\
T & ::= \texttt{Template}\ name\ I\ M^* & \text{template} \\
& |\ \texttt{Template}\ name_1 & \\
& \quad\quad \texttt{extends}\ name_2\ I'\ M^* & \text{subtemplate} \\
\\
A & ::= (x := E)^* & \text{assignment} \\
\\
I & ::= A & \text{initial assignment} \\
& |\ \lambda x.I & \text{abstraction} \\
\\
I' & ::= E, A & \text{initial assignment of subtemplates} \\
& |\ \lambda x.I' & \text{abstraction} \\
\\
M & ::= E \Rightarrow A & \text{body} \\
& |\ \lambda x.M & \text{abstraction}
\end{array}
$$

**Fig. 1.** A core language for ObjectCurry

A block of assignments $A$ consists of assignments of the form $x := E$ where $E$ is any expression. Due to the fact that a constructor function of ObjectCurry can have some arguments, we allow lambda abstraction on initial assignments.

A method $M$ is defined by an expression $E$ and a block of assignments $A$. $E$ has to be a constraint (a function with the result type **Success**) which has to be solved when the method is called. The assignments define the transformation of the current state of the object.

A *program* of Core ObjectCurry is a set of definitions of functions and templates. The definition of a function has the form *functionName* $= E$ (where $E$ is usually a lambda abstraction) and the definition of a template is written as

$$(constrName, methodName_1, \ldots, methodName_n) = T \ .$$

Such a program contains no local definitions, i.e., all identifiers are introduced on top level (thus, local declarations in ObjectCurry programs are globalized in Core ObjectCurry by lambda lifting).

As an example, our original **Counter** and **MaxCounter** template definitions are transformed into the core language as follows:

$$
\begin{array}{ll}
(\texttt{counter}, \texttt{Inc}, \texttt{Set}, \texttt{Get}) = \texttt{Template Counter} & \\
\quad\quad\quad\quad \lambda i\,.\ \texttt{x} := i & \text{(body of } \texttt{counter}) \\
\quad\quad\quad\quad \texttt{success} \Rightarrow \texttt{x} := \texttt{x+1} & \text{(body of } \texttt{Inc}) \\
\quad\quad\quad\quad \lambda s\,.\ \texttt{success} \Rightarrow \texttt{x} := s & \text{(body of } \texttt{Set}) \\
\quad\quad\quad\quad \lambda v\,.\ (v =:= \texttt{x}) \Rightarrow \epsilon & \text{(body of } \texttt{Get})
\end{array}
$$

```
(maxCounter, Inc, SetMax) = Template MaxCounter extends Counter
                    λi . λmi . counter i, max := mi
                    success ⇒ x := if x<max then x+1 else x
                    λv . success ⇒ max := v,
                                x := if x<max then x else max
```

## 5.3   A Type System for ObjectCurry

Before we present a type system for this core language, we define the satisfiability of a set of constraints.

**Definition 3.** *A (type) substitution $\sigma$ is a mapping from type variables to types such that $\sigma(\alpha) \neq \alpha$ only for finitely many type variables $\alpha$. We write a substitution as follows: $\sigma = [x_1/\tau_1, \ldots, x_n/\tau_n]$ if $\sigma(x_i) = \tau_i$ for all $i = 1, \ldots, n$ and $\sigma(y) = y$ for all $y \notin \{x_1, \ldots, x_n\}$. The extension of a substitution to types and constraint sets is obvious.*

In the following we assume that $P$ is a Core ObjectCurry program.

**Definition 4.** *Let $\mathcal{H}$ be the relation of subtemplates of $P$ defined by its* extend *clauses. The reflexive and transitive closure of $\mathcal{H}$ is denoted by $\mathcal{H}^*$, also called* inheritance hierarchy.

**Definition 5.** *A substitution $\sigma$ satisfies a subtype constraint $\tau_1 \leq \tau_2$ w.r.t. the inheritance hierarchy $\mathcal{H}^*$, denoted $\sigma \models_{\mathcal{H}^*} \tau_1 \leq \tau_2$, if there is a substitution $\sigma$ with $(\sigma\tau_1, \sigma\tau_2) \in \mathcal{H}^*$.*

   *A substitution $\sigma$ satisfies a set $C$ of subtype constraints ($\sigma \models_{\mathcal{H}^*} C$) if for all $c \in C$: $\sigma \models_{\mathcal{H}^*} c$.*

   *A set $C$ of subtype constraints is satisfiable w.r.t. the inheritance hierarchy $\mathcal{H}^*$, denoted $\models_{\mathcal{H}^*} C$, if there is a substitution $\sigma$ with $\sigma \models_{\mathcal{H}^*} C$.*

Type environments collect the type information for named entities in a program:

**Definition 6.** *A type environment $\Gamma$ is a mapping from names to constrained type schemes. In the following we denote by TE the set of all type environments.*

The union of two type environments $\Gamma_1$ and $\Gamma_2$ with non-overlapping domains is defined as follows:

$$(\Gamma_1 \cup \Gamma_2)(\alpha) = \begin{cases} \Gamma_2(\alpha), & \text{if } \Gamma_1(\alpha) \text{ is undefined} \\ \Gamma_1(\alpha), & \text{if } \Gamma_2(\alpha) \text{ is undefined} \end{cases}$$

Additionally, we define another concatenation of two type environments $\Gamma_1$ and $\Gamma_2$ which gives preference to $\Gamma_2$ if an identifier is a member of the domains of both environments. We need this operation in order to extend the global type environment with the attributes of a template.

$$(\Gamma_1 \oplus \Gamma_2)(\alpha) = \begin{cases} \Gamma_2(\alpha), & \text{if } \Gamma_2(\alpha) \text{ is defined} \\ \Gamma_1(\alpha), & \text{otherwise} \end{cases}$$

Generic instances of constrained type schemes are defined as usual:

**Definition 7.** *A constrained type $\tau'|C'$ is a* generic instance *of a constrained type scheme* $\forall \alpha_1 \ldots \alpha_n.\tau|C$ *if there is a substitution* $\sigma$ *with* $\sigma \tau \mid \sigma C = \tau' \mid C'$ *and* $\sigma(\beta) = \beta$ *for all* $\beta \notin \{\alpha_1, \ldots, \alpha_n\}$.

An attribute which is defined in a template $T$ is also visible in the subtemplates of $T$ with the same type. To specify the visibility of attributes in the methods of all subtemplates, we introduce attribute type environments:

**Definition 8.** *An* attribute type environment $\Theta : Templates \to TE$ *maps the name of a template to a type environment. This type environment contains the types of the attributes defined in this template.*

Now we are able to define the well-typedness of Core ObjectCurry programs:

**Definition 9.** *A function definition* $f = \lambda x_1 \ldots \lambda x_n.e$ *is well-typed w.r.t. a type environment* $\Gamma$, *an attribute type environment* $\Theta$, *and an inheritance hierarchy* $\mathcal{H}^*$, *if the following conditions are satisfied:*

- $\Gamma(f) = \forall \alpha_1 \ldots \alpha_m.\tau|C$
- $\Gamma, \Theta, \mathcal{H}^* \vdash \lambda x_1 \ldots \lambda x_n.e : \tau|C$ *can be deduced by the rules of Fig. 2 and 3*
- $\models_{\mathcal{H}^*} C$

*A template definition* $(c, m_1, \ldots, m_n) = e$ *is well-typed w.r.t. a type environment* $\Gamma$, *an attribute type environment* $\Theta$, *and an inheritance hierarchy* $\mathcal{H}^*$, *if*

- $\Gamma(c) = \tau_0|C_0$, $\Gamma(m_i) = \forall \alpha_i.\tau_i|C_i$    *for* $i = 1, \ldots, n$,
- $\Gamma, \Theta, \mathcal{H}^* \vdash e : (\tau_0|C_0, \tau_1|C_1, \ldots, \tau_n|C_n)$ *can be deduced by the rules of Fig. 2 and 3*
- $\models_{\mathcal{H}^*} C_0 \cup C_1 \cup \ldots \cup C_n$

*A Core ObjectCurry program is well-typed if there exist a type environment* $\Gamma$, *an attribute type environment* $\Theta$ *and an inheritance hierarchy* $\mathcal{H}^*$ *such that all function and template definitions are well-typed w.r.t. these environments and*

$$\Gamma(send) = \forall \tau_1, \tau_2 . \texttt{Message } \tau_1 \to \texttt{Object } \tau_2 \to \texttt{Success} \mid \{\tau_2 \leq \tau_1\}$$
$$\Gamma(new) = \forall \tau_1, \tau_2 . \texttt{Constructor } \tau_1 \to \texttt{Object } \tau_2 \to \texttt{Success} \mid \{\tau_1 \leq \tau_2\}$$

In the inference rules of Fig. 2 and 3, we use the auxiliary functions *super* and *templates* which yield all supertemplates of a template (including the template itself) and all templates of a program, respectively.

In order to check the well-typedness of a program by the rules of Fig. 2 and 3, the type environment $\Gamma$ must contain the types of each defined function and template. The attribute type environment $\Theta$ maps the name of each template to a new type environment which contains the types of the attributes defined in that template. The inheritance hierarchy consists of the subtype relations between all templates which are defined in the program.

The inference rules [Axiom], [Abstraction], [Existential], and [Application] are defined in the usual way, compare the Curry Report [6]. The only modification is the collection of all constraints of all subexpressions into one set of constraints. The satisfiability of this constraint set is checked outside the typing

[Axiom]       $$\frac{}{\Gamma, \Theta, \mathcal{H}^* \vdash x : \tau | C} \quad \text{if } \tau | C \text{ generic instance of } \Gamma(x)$$

[Abstraction]     $$\frac{\Gamma[x/\tau|C], \Theta, \mathcal{H}^* \vdash E : \tau'|C'}{\Gamma, \Theta, \mathcal{H}^* \vdash \lambda x.E : \tau \to \tau'|C'}$$

[Existential]     $$\frac{\Gamma[x/\tau|C], \Theta, \mathcal{H}^* \vdash E : \tau'|C'}{\Gamma, \Theta, \mathcal{H}^* \vdash \texttt{let } x \texttt{ free in } E : \tau'|C \cup C'}$$

[Application]     $$\frac{\Gamma, \Theta, \mathcal{H}^* \vdash E_1 : \tau_1 \to \tau_2|C_1 \qquad \Gamma, \Theta, \mathcal{H}^* \vdash E_2 : \tau_1|C_2}{\Gamma, \Theta, \mathcal{H}^* \vdash E_1\, E_2 : \tau_2|C_1 \cup C_2}$$

[Template]

$$name \in templates(\mathcal{H}^*)$$
$$(name, x) \notin \mathcal{H}^* \text{ for all } x \in templates(\mathcal{H}^*) \text{ with } x \neq name$$
$$\Gamma' = \Gamma \oplus \Theta(name)$$
$$\frac{\Gamma', \Theta, \mathcal{H}^* \vdash_I^{name} I : \tau_0|C_0 \quad \Gamma', \Theta, \mathcal{H}^* \vdash_M^{name} M_i : \tau_i|C_i \ (i = 1, \ldots, m)}{\Gamma, \Theta, \mathcal{H}^* \vdash \texttt{Template } name\ I\ M_1\ \ldots\ M_m\ : (\tau_0|C_0, \tau_1|C_1, \ldots, \tau_m|C_m)}$$

[Subtemplate]

$$(name_1, name_2) \in \mathcal{H}^*, (name_2, name_1) \notin \mathcal{H}^*$$
$$\Gamma' = \Gamma \oplus \bigcup_{p \in super(\mathcal{H}^*, name_1)} \Theta(p)$$
$$p_i \in super(\mathcal{H}^*, name_1) \quad (i = 1, \ldots, m)$$
$$\frac{\Gamma', \Theta, \mathcal{H}^* \vdash_{I'}^{\substack{name_1 \\ name_2}} I' : \tau_0|C_0 \quad \Gamma', \Theta, \mathcal{H}^* \vdash_M^{p_i} M_i : \tau_i|C_i \ (i = 1, \ldots, m)}{\Gamma, \Theta, \mathcal{H}^* \vdash \texttt{Template } name_1 \texttt{ extends } name_2\ I'\ M_1\ \ldots\ M_m}$$
$$: (\tau_0|C_0, \tau_1|C_1, \ldots, \tau_m|C_m)$$

**Fig. 2.** Typing rules for ObjectCurry programs (1)

rules in the definition of a well-typed program (see Def. 9). In the rule [Abstraction] we do not have to collect the constraints $C$ of the type of the variable $x$: If $E$ contains an occurrence of $x$, the constraints of the type of $x$ are collected into the set of constraints of $E$ by the other rules. Otherwise, $x$ is never used and its constraints can be ignored.

In addition to Curry's type system, we introduce new rules [Template] and [Subtemplate] for checking the types of templates and subtemplates. In the rule [Template], which is applicable if there is no true supertemplate in $\mathcal{H}^*$, we extend the type environment $\Gamma$ by the type assumptions for the attributes of the template in order to make the attribute types visible in the type checking of the methods. Note that the global type environment $\Gamma$ contains the types of all identifiers defined in the program (including the method identifiers) so that we can use the methods of the template also inside the template and we do not need a special rule for recursion.

$$[\text{Assignment}_1] \quad \frac{\Gamma,\Theta,\mathcal{H}^* \vdash x : \tau|C_1 \qquad \Gamma,\Theta,\mathcal{H}^* \vdash E : \tau|C_2 \qquad \Gamma,\Theta,\mathcal{H}^* \vdash_A A : C_A}{\Gamma,\Theta,\mathcal{H}^* \vdash_A x := E, A : C_1 \cup C_2 \cup C_A}$$

$$[\text{Assignment}_2] \quad \frac{}{\Gamma,\Theta,\mathcal{H}^* \vdash_A \epsilon : \emptyset}$$

$$[\text{Init}] \quad \frac{\Gamma,\Theta,\mathcal{H}^* \vdash_A A : C}{\Gamma,\Theta,\mathcal{H}^* \vdash_I^{name} A : \texttt{Constructor } name|C}$$

$$[\text{Init}'] \quad \frac{\Gamma,\Theta,\mathcal{H}^* \vdash E : \texttt{Constructor } name_2|\epsilon \qquad \Gamma,\Theta,\mathcal{H}^* \vdash_A A : C}{\Gamma,\Theta,\mathcal{H}^* \vdash_{I'}^{name_2} E, A : \texttt{Constructor } name_1|C}$$

$$[\text{Method}] \quad \frac{\Gamma,\Theta,\mathcal{H}^* \vdash E : \texttt{Success}|C \quad \Gamma,\Theta,\mathcal{H}^* \vdash_A A : C' \quad v \text{ new type variable}}{\Gamma,\Theta,\mathcal{H}^* \vdash_M^{name} E \Rightarrow A : \texttt{Message } v|\{v \leq name\} \cup C \cup C'}$$

$$[\text{Abstraction}_{\mathcal{X}}] \quad \frac{\Gamma[x/\tau|C],\Theta,\mathcal{H}^* \vdash_{\mathcal{X}}^n X : \tau'|C'}{\Gamma,\Theta,\mathcal{H}^* \vdash_{\mathcal{X}}^n \lambda x.X : \tau \to \tau'|C'} \qquad \mathcal{X} \in \{I, I', M\}$$

**Fig. 3.** Typing rules for ObjectCurry programs (2)

The rule [Subtemplate] is similar to [Template] except for the following differences:

- The type environment $\Gamma'$ also contains the type assumptions of the inherited attributes, i.e., the attributes of the current template and all its supertemplates.
- $I'$ contains a call to the constructor function of the parent. It must be checked that this has the type $\texttt{Constructor } name_2$ where $name_2$ is the name of the parent. This is ensured by using $\vdash_{I'}$ instead of $\vdash_I$.
- Furthermore, we have to ensure that $(name_1, name_2)$ is an element of the type hierarchy $\mathcal{H}^*$ and $(name_2, name_1)$ must not be in $\mathcal{H}^*$. Due to the fact that $\mathcal{H}^*$ is transitive and reflexive, it also contains $(name_2, name_2)$, $(name_1, name_1)$, and $(name_1, p)$ for all supertemplates $p$ of $name_1$.
- For checking the types of the methods, we also allow that a method $M_i$ is assigned to some supertemplate $p_i$ (note that $p_i$ is the current template $name_1$ or one of its supertemplates). This is necessary if the method is redefined. Note, however, that methods redefined in subtemplates must have the same type as in supertemplates. This is reasonable since, due to the logic features of Curry, arguments of a method can be used as value parameters as well as result parameters so that a contra- or covariance restriction on arguments cannot be clearly required.

[Template] and [Subtemplate] use the rules of Fig. 3 which we discuss next. The rule [Assignment$_1$] ensures that in an assignment of the form $x := E$ the type of $x$ is the same as the type of the expression $E$. [Assignment$_2$] handles the special case of an empty list of assignments. The rule [Init] checks the type of a constructor function where the name of the template must be provided as an extra argument. [Init'] additionally checks if $E$ is a valid call of the constructor function of the parent. For this purpose, we also need the name of the parent ($name_2$). The rule [Method] types a method with subtyping the result type as discussed in Sect. 5.1. It checks whether the expression $E$ of a method $E \Rightarrow A$ is a constraint (with the type Success) and collects the resulting constraints.

Due to the fact that we need lambda abstraction over initial assignments $I$ or $I'$ and methods $M$, we introduce a generic rule [Abstraction$_X$]. $X$ can be $I$, $I'$ or $M$. The rule is similar to the common rule for abstraction.

## 5.4   Type Inference

We have also developed a type inferencer for our modified type system. Due to lack of space we can not present it here but refer to [12] which contains the complete description of the type inferencer and its implementation. The algorithm is based on the algorithm $\mathcal{D}$ of Kaes [10]. However, our inference algorithm is simpler because we allow subtyping only for objects and messages. The algorithm unifies type expressions in the same way as standard type inference algorithms [2] but additionally collects the subtype constraints. The resulting set of subtype constraints is then checked for satisfiability with a simple test procedure.

Our implementation of the type checker for ObjectCurry is based on Mark Jones' "Typing Haskell in Haskell" [9] which we adapted to Curry. The implementation of the ObjectCurry compiler together with the type inferencer is freely available from the authors.

## 6   Related Work

In this section we compare ObjectCurry with some other approaches for the object-oriented extension of functional (logic) languages.

Oz [17] is a concurrent constraint programming language with a particular syntax for object-oriented programming, thus, offering similar features as ObjectCurry. The main differences between ObjectCurry and Oz are the type system and the operational semantics. Oz is untyped and supports no detection of type errors at compile time in contrast to ObjectCurry. Furthermore, the operational model of ObjectCurry is based on Curry's computation model [4] which combines an optimal lazy evaluation strategy [1] for the functional (logic) parts of a program with the concurrent evaluation of constraints. In particular, we consider objects as functions consuming the stream of incoming messages where the state is passed as an argument between the different function calls. In contrast, Oz evaluates functions in an eager manner and implement stateful objects via a specific cell store.

Haskell++ [7] extends Haskell's type classes to object classes. It provides a limited form of multiple inheritance and virtual methods but does not provide subtype polymorphism. For instance, it is not possible to create a list with elements of different instances of one object class. The main goal in the development of Haskell++ was a minimal extension to Haskell which supports the inheritance of functions. Objects in Haskell++ contain only methods but no states. On the other hand, ObjectCurry provides real objects with states in the sense of object-oriented programming. It combines the flexibility of conventional object-oriented languages with the features of functional logic programming.

O'Haskell [13,14] provides an extension for full object-oriented programming with states and subtype polymorphism. It uses monads for the implementation of concurrent objects and states. The main advantage of our implementation, which uses the concurrent and logical features of Curry, is the opportunity to combine this with Curry's port concept [5] for distributed programming. In contrast to O'Haskell, objects in ObjectCurry can also be executed in a distributed setting. This is supported by a function `newNamedObject` which is similar to `new` but makes the new object accessible from other machines in the network with a unique port identifier (see [5] for more details). The implementation of objects remains unchanged. Furthermore, the logical variables in Curry can be exploited as answer channels since the receiver of a message can bind the logical variables in the message to send answers back to the sender.

Finally, Objective Caml [11] is an object-oriented extension of ML. Objective Caml inherits the strict evaluation strategy of ML and subtype polymorphism can only be programmed with explicit coercions in contrast to ObjectCurry which is lazy and provides subtype polymorphism without any annotations since all types can be automatically inferred.

## 7  Conclusions

We presented the language ObjectCurry as an extension of Curry to allow a convenient definition of objects via templates. Templates play the role of classes in conventional object-oriented languages. A template defines the attributes and methods of an object. Methods are used to determine the reactions to incoming messages where reactions can be the change of the object's state or a constraint to send messages to other objects. Assignments are used to express a transformation on the local state of an object. Templates can also inherit attributes and methods from other templates and inherited methods can be redefined.

We proposed a direct translation of templates into pure Curry but translated target programs using more than one template are not type safe in the sense of traditional typed object-oriented languages. Therefore, we developed a new type system which uses subtype constraints in the types of objects, messages and functions which use objects or messages. We implemented a compiler which translates ObjectCurry programs into Curry and a type checker which also infers types of expressions without explicit type annotations.

### Acknowledgements

The authors are grateful to the anonymous referees for their helpful remarks to improve the final version of this paper.

# References

1. S. Antoy, R. Echahed, and M. Hanus. A Needed Narrowing Strategy. *Journal of the ACM*, Vol. 47, No. 4, pp. 776–822, 2000.
2. L. Damas and R. Milner. Principal type-schemes for functional programs. In *Proc. 9th Annual Symposium on Principles of Programming Languages*, pages 207–212, 1982.
3. M. Hanus. The integration of functions into logic programming: From theory to practice. *Journal of Logic Programming*, 19&20:583–628, 1994.
4. M. Hanus. A unified computation model for functional and logic programming. In *Proc. 24th ACM Symp. Principles of Programming Languages*, pages 80–93, 1997.
5. M. Hanus. Distributed programming in a multi-paradigm declarative language. In *Proc. of the International Conference on Principles and Practice of Declarative Programming (PPDP'99)*, pages 376–395. Springer LNCS 1702, 1999.
6. M. Hanus. Curry: An Integrated Functional Logic Language, 2000.
   `http://www.informatik.uni-kiel.de/~curry/`
7. J. Hughes and J. Sparud. Haskell++: An object-oriented extension of Haskell. In *Proceedings of the Workshop on Haskell*, La Jolla, California, YALE Research Report DCS/RR-1075, 1995.
8. S. Janson, J. Montelius, and S. Haridi. Ports for objects in concurrent logic programs. In G. Agha, P. Wegner, and A. Yonezawa, editors, *Research Directions in Concurrent Object-Oriented Programming*, pages 211–231. MIT Press, London, 1993.
9. M.P. Jones. Typing Haskell in Haskell, 1999. In *Proceedings of the Workshop on Haskell*, Paris, France, Technical Report UU-CS-1999-28, University of Utrecht, 1999.
10. S. Kaes. Type inference in the presence of overloading, subtyping and recursive types. In *1992 ACM Conference on Lisp and Functional Programming*, pages 193–204. ACM, ACM, August 1992.
11. X. Leroy. The Objective Caml system. Technical report, 1996.
   `http://pauillac.inria.fr/ocaml/`.
12. P. Niederau. Object-oriented extension of a declarative language (in german). Master's thesis, RWTH Aachen, 2000.
13. J. Nordlander. Rationale for O'Haskell, August 1999.
   `http://www.cs.chalmers.se/~nordland/ohaskell/rationale.html`
14. J. Nordlander. *Reactive Objects and Functional Programming*. PhD thesis, Chalmers Göteborg University, May 1999.
15. J. Peterson et al. Haskell: A non-strict, purely functional language (version 1.4). Technical report, Yale University, Yale, 1997.
16. E. Shapiro and A. Takeuchi. Object oriented programming in Concurrent Prolog. *New Generation Computing*, 1:25–48, 1983.
17. G. Smolka. The Oz programming model. In J. van Leeuwen, editor, *Computer Science Today: Recent Trends and Developments*, pages 324–343. Springer LNCS 1000, 1995.

# Distributed Programming in Haskell with Ports

Frank Huch and Ulrich Norbisrath

Lehrstuhl für Informatik II, RWTH Aachen, 52056 Aachen, Germany
huch@i2.informatik.rwth-aachen.de
ulrich@norbisrath.de

**Abstract.** We present an extension of the lazy functional programming language Haskell for distributed programming. For the communication between processes we add a port concept. Ports behave like channels in Concurrent Haskell except that only the process which creates a port can read from it. Ports can also be sent through other ports. The receiver can then also write messages through the received port. This is independent of the location in a network. The programmer uses the same functions to write to local or remote ports. Communication between concurrent and distributed processes is programmed with the same functions. Concurrent processes can easily be distributed, for example to provide scalability of a system. In many distributed applications it is necessary that two independently started programs can connect at runtime. Therefore we provide the registration of ports. Other processes can look them up from anywhere in a network.

The implementation consists of a library which provides functions for creating new processes, communication between concurrent and distributed processes, and error handling with exceptions.

## 1 Distributed Programming

The development of software systems has changed in the last years. Many systems are distributed, because of the following reasons:

- **Parallelization:** Resources (e.g. speed or space) needed for an application are not sufficing on one computer.
- **Inherent distributed character:** The application itself is distributed. Examples are (mobile) telephones and a cash dispenser together with the bank server.
- **Reliability and fault tolerance:** To increase the reliability of a system it is possible to arrange for several computers to co-operate such that the failure of one or more computers does not effect the system behavior as a whole.
- **Access to special resources:** In a heterogeneous network, special resources, e.g. a scanner or printer can only be accessed from one computer.

With the boom of Networks and the Internet, the number of distributed applications increases. In particular more and more applications have an inherent distributed character. To provide convenient programming, modern programming

M. Mohnen and P. Koopman (Eds.): IFL 2000, LNCS 2011, pp. 107–121, 2001.

languages must support distributed programming. It is not sufficient to provide a library for communication via sockets. The language has to be extended with a high level concept for distribution and communication between processes. We want to extend the functional programming language Haskell [J+98] with features for elegant distributed programming.

The discussion of communication in distributed systems in Sect. 2 shows the advantages of a port concept, which is introduced in Sect. 3. We present the implementation in Sect. 4 and discuss related work in Sect. 5. Section 6 concludes and discusses future work.

## 2   Distributed Communication

There have been made some approaches for extending functional languages for concurrent or distributed programming. The most successful one is Erlang [AWV93], which was developed by Ericsson and has been used for the development of many telecommunication applications. Erlang is an eager functional programming language, which is extended with special features for concurrent and distributed programming. New processes can be created with **spawn** on a local or a remote computer. Every process has a process identifier (*pid*), which is used for the communication between processes. Other processes can send messages to this pid and messages can also contain pids to distribute pids in a network. If a message is sent to a process it is stored in a mailbox. The receiving process can conveniently access this mailbox with pattern matching. It need not extract messages in their chronological order. Only relevant messages can be fetched with pattern matching. The others can be left in the mailbox and processed later.

Another important point of Erlang is that communication between concurrent processes on the same computer does not distinguish from communication to remote processes in a network. The programmer uses the same programming techniques. Therefore a system developed in a concurrent setting can later be distributed easily. Scalability of the system is supported by the language.

For fault tolerant programming Erlang also provides a linking mechanism. Processes of the system can automatically be informed, if others die, for example because a computer crashes. Hence these processes can react on the failure and reorganize the system to a consistent state.

But for all that Erlang has a great disadvantages. It is untyped. Therefore it is more difficult to find program errors than in Haskell. There have been made two approaches for typing Erlang [MW97,AA98], but they only type sequential programming in Erlang. The communication stays untyped. But also here a type system is necessary. In Erlang already typing mistakes[1], like writing the atom **lookup** in the pattern of a receive statement and **lookUp** at the corresponding send statement does not yield a compile time or runtime error, but a deadlock. Finding these typing mistakes is very difficult.

---

[1] Here we do not mean type errors. An example for a typing mistake is 'Erlng'.

We want to extend Haskell with a similar communication mechanism, but in consideration of Haskells type system. This yields more safety in program development. Concurrent Haskell [JGF96] is state of the art for concurrent programming in Haskell. It provides functions to start and terminate threads inside an application and to synchronize them with mutable variables (*MVar*) in the IO monad. On top of these MVars it also provides semaphores and asynchronous channels for message passing. But there is no concept for distributed programming. Therefore we want to extend Haskell with a powerful mechanism for distributed programming.

In our first approach we extended Haskell with an Erlang-style communication mechanism [Huc99]. The main problem in this approach is to type the communication. Different processes can understand different messages but others can also understand the same messages. A type system with subtypes would be needed. But it is difficult to integrate subtyping into Haskells type system. Therefore we have implemented runtime type checking. But this is no good match to Haskells type system.

We now have decided to extend the concepts of Concurrent Haskell with communication via channels and MVars for distributed programming. But this leads into implementation problems. In Concurrent Haskell many processes may synchronize on a mutable variable (*MVar*) or a channel. Distributing some of these processes in a network leads to synchronization problems, because it is not clear where an MVar is located. Consider the following situation:

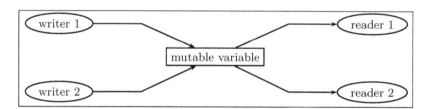

**Fig. 1.** Distribution of Concurrent Haskell Processes

Two processes can write a mutable variable and two other processes want to read it. In a distributed setting these processes could be located on four different computers in a network. But where can the mutable variable be located? It has to be located on one computer in the net, because it needs a state for the storage of a value, if no reader suspends on it and no reader wants to read the value. The possibilities for the location of the MVar are one of the four computers of the example or an independent computer. But all these locations have disadvantages for providing fault tolerance. It is necessary that parts of the system may terminate or even crash without effecting the rest of the system. If the computer the mutable variable is located on crashes, then the whole system cannot work anymore, although there is still a writer and a reader, which could communicate with each other from the logical structure of the system. The readers and the other writers hang-up and it is difficult to repair the system to a consistent state, where the other components can communicate with each other again.

Another problem is garbage collection. We do not know, when a mutable variable or channel is garbage. Other processes in the distributed setting communicate with each other and the MVar (a reference to it) can also be distributed to the whole network. So it will be almost impossible to check, if an MVar is still known somewhere in the net and an algorithm would be very expensive and produce much communication in the network. Especially, if some parts of the system have already crashed. Systems like Glasgow Parallel Haskell [THM+96] or Glasgow Distributed Haskell [PTL00] implement distributed garbage collection, but they do not provide the development of open systems, which is essential for the development of distributed applications. It is also not possible to implement fault tolerance in these systems, which is in our view a major requirement for a programming language for distributed system. It would be interesting to investigate, if distributed garbage collection can be efficiently implemented with the conditions of programming open and fault tolerant systems. We think that these algorithms are too complex and need too much communication, i.e. traffic in the network. Therefore we restrict communication to only one reader for each channel and can avoid these problems. Our practical experience showed, that this restriction is no disadvantage, as we will discuss later.

## 3   Distributed Haskell

In the discussion of distributing Concurrent Haskell, we have seen which problems appear with multiple readers and writers of an MVar. Our solution to this problem is a restriction to only one reader. With this restriction we can locate the MVar at the same place, where the reader is located. If the reader terminates or crashes, the MVar terminates too. No other readers can suspend on it. Therefore no processes are hanging. On the other side, there can still exist writers, that want to write to the MVar. Hence they are also in an inconsistent state. But they can recognize this, when they send a message to the MVar. A failed write operation can throw an exception. This can be caught and the writer can initialize a reorganization of the crashed components, for example on another computer.

Erlang also has this restriction, because a mailbox is associated with a single-ton process. Only this process can read from it. Transferring the Erlang model to Haskell leads to typing problems, because the Mailbox of a process needs a fixed type in Haskell. But consider two clients, which communicate with a database server, but handle different jobs in the rest of the system. Both will receive messages from the database, for example if they look up the value of a given key. Therefore there mailboxes must have the same type. But in other parts they communicate with different processes and exchange different data there. The result would be that all mailboxes of the system must have the same type. So type checking does not help to find errors. Another problem is that the system is not structured any more, because the messages a process may receive cannot be represented as one data type. But these messages are its communication interface and they have to be visible.

Another solution would be sub-typing for the messages. We have implemented this in [Huc99] by runtime type checking. But this concept is no good match to Haskells type system. Our way out of this problem is to allow multiple mailboxes for every process, like in Concurrent Haskell. We call these mailboxes *ports* and every port of a process may have another type. But we restrict these ports to one reader. This reader is the process which creates the port.

## 3.1    The Distributed Haskell Library

Ports are represented as a polymorphic data type

```
data Port a -- abstract
```

where the type variable a represents the type of the values, that can be sent to the port. A new port can be created with the function

```
newPort :: IO (Port a)
```

Like in Concurrent Haskell the operations for creating and sending have side-effects. Hence they belong to the IO monad in contrast to Eden [BLOMPM96] and Goffin [CGK98].

A value can be written to and read from a port with the functions

```
writePort :: Port a -> a -> IO ()
readPort :: Port a -> IO a
```

A port can be used in the same way, as a channel in Concurrent Haskell, except that only the process which creates the port can read from it.

To guarantee this by the type system we first wanted to distinguish read-write ports and write ports. Read-write ports can be converted into write ports and only write ports can be sent through other write ports. But sending a port to another process is not the only possibility for distributing ports in a process network. They can also be passed to other processes as parameters, when new processes are created with forkIO. Here we cannot avoid the distribution of read-write ports. Therefore we have renounced this distinction. A runtime checking is needed anyway. Hence, reading from a write port yields a runtime error.

A postulation we made above is that it is all the same, where a port is located in the net. Sending to it should stay the same. In the case of a remote computer the messages have to be coded binary. In this first implementation, as a library for the Glasgow Haskell Compiler [GHC], we send them as strings. Therefore the type of the messages, which can be sent with **writePort** must be an instance of the class **Show**. On the other hand a messages must be reconverted into the corresponding datatype, if a process reads from a port. Therefore the type of the messages, which can be received with **readPort** must be an instance of the class **Read**. This means the messages of a port need both instances. But this is no problem in Haskell, because they can be derived for algebraic data types. But this is a restriction, because no functions, infinite data structures, or mutable structures like MVars can be sent through ports.

On the first sight these functions seem to be enough for programming distributed systems. But consider the development of a chat. Designing a chat system one will program a chat server, which manages the clients taking part in the chat. New clients can join the chat and others can exit. But how can new clients connect to the chat server? For the connection of two independently started components we provide a global registration mechanism. With

```
registerPort :: Port a -> PortName -> IO ()
unregisterPort :: Port a -> IO ()
```

ports can globally be registered and unregistered on one computer. Other processes can then lookup a registered port with

```
lookupPort :: PortHost -> PortName -> IO (Port a)
```

from anywhere else in the net. In the actual implementation `PortHost` and `PortName` are just type synonyms for `String`. But in later implementations we will also extend PortHost to IP addresses and allow Haskell programs with names, as nodes in Erlang. Then `PortName` will also contain the name of the Haskell program and ports in different Haskell programs can be registered with the same name on one computer. This can for example be useful, because two servers which register themselves globally with the same name can still be executed on the same computer.

With these functions for registration and lookup of ports the chat server can register its in-port and the clients can lookup this port. Their first message to the chat server can contain a port, which the client has created and to which the server sends further messages.

But this example shows another problems. When a client has accessed a chat, it sends new text messages to the server and this server broadcasts them to the other clients. For the client process this means, that it has to read messages coming from the server and messages coming from the keyboard or another process managing the user interface. But there is no fixed order in which the client will receive these messages. Therefore it has to suspend on both. The easiest way would be, that the keyboard process and the chat server use the same port and the client process reads from it. But from the software engineering view this it not nice, because the chat server and the keyboard use messages of the same type to communicate with the client. Hence we need two different ports, the client can suspend on. Therefore Eden proposes a merge function which would in our setting have the type `merge :: Port a -> Port a -> IO (Port a)`. But this function would not solve the problem above, because still both ports must be of the same type. Therefore we provide a merge function, which allows a programmer to merge two ports of different types. We use Haskells `Either` type:

```
mergePort :: Port a -> Port b -> IO (Port (Either a b))
```

With this function the client can suspend on messages of different types from the chat server and the keyboard. It should also be possible, that the merged ports can afterwards also be used in there un-merged version, because the client wants to ignore messages from one of them. But the client is the only process that can read from these ports. Hence there can be no conflict, that two readers want to read from the ports and their merged version at the same time.

For the creation, termination and error handling of processes we use the same functions as Concurrent Haskell and the module `Exception`:

```
forkIO :: IO () -> IO ThreadID
myThreadId :: IO ThreadId
killThread :: ThreadID -> IO ()
raiseInThread :: ThreadId -> Exception -> IO ()
try :: IO a -> IO (Either Exception a)
```

Finally we provide a linking mechanism. With the function

```
linkAndKill :: Port a -> IO (Link)
```

a link between the executing process and a port is established. If the port does not exist anymore, the process is terminated by an exception. This can be caught and the process can initiate a reorganization of the whole system. A more convenient function for linking ports is the function

```
link :: Port a -> IO () -> IO (Link)
```

which takes an additional IO action as parameter. This action is performed, if the linked port does not exist anymore. With this function it is for example possible, to send a message if a port dies. If an established link is not needed anymore, it is possible to abolish links with the function

```
unlink :: Link -> IO ()
```

We have also added a fault tolerant version of `writePort`

```
writePortFail :: Port a -> a -> IO () -> IO ()
```

Similar to `link` the action in the third parameter is performed in the case of an erroneous sending.

## 3.2   A Chat Example

As an example we now present the implementation of a chat server. Its communication interface is given by the data type

```
data ServerMsg = Connect String (Port ClientChatMsg) |
                 Send String String |
                 Close String (Port ClientChatMsg)
          deriving (Read, Show)
```

The server creates a port for external communication in its initialization and registers this port as `ChatServer`.

```
main = do serverPort <- newPort
          registerPort serverPort "ChatServer"
          chatServer serverport []
```

After the initialization it proceeds in a loop, where it holds a list of the ports of all connected clients. This list changes in dependence of connecting or closing clients. A new chat message is broadcasted to all the other connected clients:

```
chatServer :: Port ServerMsg -> [Port ClientMsg]  -> IO ()
chatServer serverPort clientPorts = do
  msg <- readPort serverPort
  case msg of
    (Connect name clientPort) -> do
        mapM_ (\p -> writePort p (Login name)) newClientPorts
        chatServer serverPort (clientPort:clientPorts)
    (Close name clientPort) -> do
        let newClientPorts = filter (/= clientPort) clientPorts
        mapM_ (\p -> writePort p (Logout name)) newClientPorts
        chatServer serverPort newClientPorts
    (Send name str) -> do
        mapM_ (\p -> writePort p (Chat name str)) clientPorts
        chatServer serverPort clientPorts
```

A client process uses the interface

```
data ClientChatMsg = Chat String String | Login String |
                     Logout String
            deriving (Read, Show, Eq)
```

to receive messages from the chat server. The Chat message is used for new chat messages. The first string is the nickname of the user taking part in the chat and the second string is her chat message. The Logout message is sent, if a client leaves the chat. For the interface to the keyboard process we just use strings. First a client process initiates the connection to a chat server on host. Then its own read ports are created and a process for the input from the keyboard is forked.

```
main = do putStrLn "Host of chat server ? "
          host <- getLine
          putStrLn "Nickname? "
          name <- getLine
          chatserverPort <- lookupPort host "ChatServer"
          chatPort <- newPort
          writePort chatserverPort (Connect name chatPort)
          keyboardPort <- newPort
          forkIO (readKeyBoard keyboardport)
          inPort <- mergePort chatPort keyboardport
          client chatserverPort inPort chatPort
```

The two read ports are merged into one port and the process proceeds in a loop. Here messages from the server are displayed and messages from the keyboard are forwarded to the server.

```
client :: String -> Port ServerMsg -> Port (Either ServerMsg String)
          -> Port ClientChatMsg -> IO ()
client name serverPort inPort chatPort = do
  msg <- readPort inPort
  case msg of
    (Left serverMsg) -> do putStrLn (display serverMsg)
                           client name serverPort inPort chatPort
    (Right "") -> writePort serverPort (Close name chatPort)
    (Right str) -> do writePort serverPort (Send name str)
                      client name serverPort inPort chatPort
  where display :: ClientChatMsg -> String
        display (Chat name str) = name ++ " : " ++ str
        display (Login name)    = name ++ " logged in"
        display (Logout name)   = name ++ " logged out"
```

The process for reading from the keyboard is not presented here. It just reads strings from the keyboard, sends them to the client process and terminates itself, if the user inputs the empty string.

This chat application does not behave fault tolerant. If a client dies and the next chat message is broadcasted to all chat clients an exception is thrown and the chat server crashes, because the port of the dead client does not exist anymore. With the linking mechanism and the use of writePortFail instead of writePort we can easily guarantee fault-tolerance for our server. In the case of a failure we just close the port, which could not be written. Therefore we just add the following linking to the Connect case in the server process:

```
(Connect name clientPort) -> do
        link clientPort (writePort serverPort (Close clientPort))
        chatServer serverPort (clientPort:clientPorts)
```

and modify the writePort instruction in the broadcast of chat messages:

```
writePortFail p ... (writePort serverPort (Close p)) ...
```

The chat server just sends a Close message to itself if a port does not exist anymore.

The example shows, that it is easy to implement a client server architecture like a chat in Distributed Haskell. Our practical experience shows, that our communication model with only one reader per port is no real restriction in the development of arbitrary distributed systems. This is also confirmed by the success of Erlang, which has the same restriction.

As an example multiple readers seam to be useful for architectures like the producer/consumer problem. But this problem can easily be implemented in Distributed Haskell too. We add a process, which simulates the store for the products. The producers insert products by sending messages to the store process. The consumers request the store for new products and obtain them as messages from the store process. The system is divided into two client/server architectures. The opportunity of this implementation is that the processes can be linked to the ports of the store and we can detect if one of the components (e.g. the store) crashes. In this case we can replace the store by a new process. Some products may be lost, but the system still works. Another possibility would be the definition of a second store process, which is (with some delay) identical with the other store and can replace it if it crashes. This implementation of fault tolerance seems to be expensive in this case, but we think this cannot be avoided.

## 4    Implementation

The implementation is a library, which can be imported in any Haskell program. The whole library is written in Concurrent Haskell.

In our port based extension we have to handle two different kinds of communication through ports. For the internal communication inside a Haskell program, which consist of multiple concurrent processes, we want to use communication through channels from Concurrent Haskell. For the external communication between different Haskell programs, we want to use communication via TCP/IP. Therefore we use the GHC library `Socket`.

We also allow multiple Haskell programs on one computer. Hence distributed systems can also be developed on a single computer. No network of multiple computers is needed. Therefore on every computer an external post office is started. This external post office listens on a fixed socket. All started Distributed Haskell programs register themselves here and obtain a program number and a free socket number, they listen to for external messages. Global registrations of ports in the Distributed Haskell programs are recorded in this external post office and other processes can lookup the corresponding ports here.

The use of ports is supposed to be transparent, independent of the host a writing process is located on. Therefore the internal representation contains the IP-Address of the host, where the port is located and the program number of the Haskell program it is created in. Therefore messages that are written to the port from outside can be directed to the correct Haskell program. We want to guarantee, that only the process which creates a port can read from it. Hence a port also contains the `ThreadID` of its creating process. If another process tries to read from it, then a runtime exception is thrown.

For the internal communication through ports we use channels. This is efficient and even lazy. For external communication we cannot communicate through channels. The values which are sent through a port need a representation as a sequence of bytes. We use a string representation. Values can be converted from and into this representation with `read` and `show`. For algebraic data types, which do not contain function types, these functions can easily be derived in Haskell.

All external communication is sent through the external post office. Therefore all newly created processes are registered in the external post office. They also obtain a socket number, on which all messages from external processes arrive. When a new port is created a process is forked, which listens on this socket and forwards all incoming messages to the typed channel representing the port. When this process is created the type of the port is known. The conversion of incoming strings into typed values with `read` is fixed for the lifetime of the port and this process. So all messages which are sent to a port arrive in the typed channel, independently from their origin. The function `readPort` only tests, if the reading thread has created the port and then reads from this typed channel with `readChan`.

For communication via ports it is also necessary, that ports can be sent through external ports. This means that they also need a string representation and are an instance of the classes `Read` and `Show`. As long, as a port is just sent through the typed channel representing a port (internal communication) its representation stays unchanged. Only if it is sent through the net we lose the typed parts. The string representation only contains the threadID, the program identifier, the IP-address of the host, and the socket number. If a port is sent through the net and returns to the program where it is physically located, it is not possible to access its typed version again, because of the Haskell type system. We would need a data structure, which can contain ports of arbitrary types to get back the typed representation of the port. As an optimization we avoid communication via sockets in this case. For every port we have added a string channel, through which this kind of internal communication is executed. Again a special process forwards the messages from this string channel into the typed channel. This process is created in the function `newPort`. The string channel can be stored in a database. When a port returns to its origin, this string channel can be looked up in the database and added to its representation again. This lookup is a sideeffect. It is implemented with `unsafePerformIO`, but it behaves transparent to the application, because every port will only obtain one corresponding representation. The whole structure of a port and the internal and external communication is summarized in Figure 2.

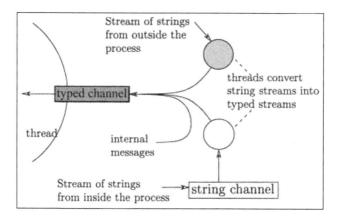

**Fig. 2.** Structure of a port and internal/external communication

The two conversion processes for each port, which convert the string messages into typed messages with `read` have a disadvantage. They impede garbage collection of a port. They always hold a reference to the string channel and the typed channel of a port. Therefore these port components never become garbage. As a solution we have implemented a function destroyPort :: Port t -> IO() which terminates the conversion processes and removes all entries of the port in the internal and external post office. If a new port is created we bind this function as a finalizer to the port. Hence if no reference to the exists anymore, then the conversion process is killed and all references to its channels are eliminated. So the channels become garbage too.

The last internal representation of a port is the merged port as read only port. Both merged ports are internally represented by channels. If a process wants to read from a merged port, two processes are created, which suspend on these two channels. If one of them receives a message, this message is extended with the constructor Left respectively Right and transfered to an MVar, representing the merged port. After that both processes are terminated and the original ports can be read again. The only problem here is that both processes can read their channels simultaneously. We have to guarantee mutual exclusion here, but this is impossible without busy waiting. Hence in this case we write one of the received messages back into the corresponding channel using the function unGetChan.

The function register registers the string channel component of the port at the external post office. With lookupPort this string channel can then be accessed from anywhere in the net.

For the process manipulation we just use the functions of Concurrent Haskell.

Finally we provide a polling mechanism for the linking of ports. All linked ports are stored in a database. A process in the background polls all registered ports in a fixed schedule. If one of these ports does not exist anymore, an exception is thrown (linkAndKill) or the specified IO action is performed (link, writePortFail). This could be programmed by hand from the programmer, but with the provided functions it is more convenient.

## 5    Related Work

There are many other approaches for the extension of functional programming languages. We compare the main ones with our approache:

– **Goffin** [CGK98] extends Haskell with concurrent constraint programming and a special port concept for internal and external communication. The ports are not integrated in the IO monad. Nondeterminism and input/output is not encapsulated in the IO monad anymore. Furthermore a user has to learn about concurrent constraint programming, another programming paradigm.

Goffin does not restrict the number of readers and writers of a port. As we described in Sect. 2 multiple readers of a port can yield problems implementing fault tolerant systems. An implementation of this concept seems difficult. This is confirmed by the fact, that an executable implementation of Goffin does not exist yet.

For reacting on multiple ports Goffin proposes a fair merge :: Port a -> Port a -> Port a for ports. With this function a process can wait for different messages of different ports and branch in dependence of the incoming message.

But both merged ports must have the same type. This restriction is a too strong, as we have seen in the chat example.

– **Eden** [BLOMPM96] is an extension of Haskell for concurrent and parallel programming. A process concept is added in which every process has a fixed number of input and output channels for communication with other processes. Communication is not integrated in the IO monad and with a fair `merge`, which is part of Eden, processes can behave nondeterministically. Like in Goffin this `merge` is restricted to channels of the same type.

Processes can suspend on their different input channels. Messages in other channels are buffered automatically. To react not only on one input channel, it is possible to merge channels, with the same restrictions as in Goffin. Furthermore in Eden a process can only read from or write to on a fixed number of channels. The connections between the processes cannot be changed dynamically.

Eden is developed for parallel programming where programs have a more hierarchical structure than in distributed programming and it is difficult to implement complex protocols in Eden. It is also not possible to connect two independently started processes in Eden. But this is needed for many distributed applications.

– **Curry** [Han99] is a functional-logic programming language, which extends Haskell with needed narrowing, residuation, and encapsulated search. For distributed programming Curry adds named ports, which guarantee, that all readers of one port are executed in the same Curry program. This is thought to eliminate the implementation problems with multiple readers. On the other hand a programmer can also send logical variables through ports, which is proposed as an easy answering mechanism. But with these logical variables channels can be programmed, which have multiple readers. This results in the same problems with multiple readers, which should be avoided by the introduction of ports. The problems are also reflected in the fact, that no actual Curry implementation provides unrestricted sending of logical variables through a net. Logical variables can only be used as comfortable answer variables. This is no restriction from the formal semantics, but from the implementation.

Communication in Curry is like in Goffin a constraint, which has to be solved. Only for the external communication the IO monad is used. Concurrent processes communicate via lazy streams. This can result in problems with laziness and strictness annotations have to be added sometimes. Another problem is that a concurrent application cannot easily be distributed to a network, because the processes have to be transfered into the IO Monad. This can yield problems with the scalability of a system.

– **Glasgow distributed Haskell** [PTL00] is an approach for the integration of Glasgow parallel Haskell [THM⁺96] and Concurrent Haskell. It is provides closed distributed systems and communication between processes like in Concurrent Haskell. The main idea is the distribution of a shared memory system. Communication between processes is not strict. Hence the programmer does not know when data is exchanged between the components of the network and can not estimate when and how much net traffic is produced. But this is necessary for the development of distributed applications.

Fault tolerance is restricted to error handling like in Concurrent Haskell. If one of the computers in the network crashes, then the whole system crashes too. But the greatest disadvantage of this approach is the restriction to closed systems, which makes it impossible to implement many distributed applications, like (mobile) telephony.

– **Facile** [TLK96] is an extension of Standard ML for distributed programming. It provides channels with multiple readers and writers in a network. It also provides open distributed systems and a registration mechanism similar to ours. But Facile does not provide a linking concept for fault tolerant programming, which is needed for the development of distributed applications. It is only possible to program with timeouts. Finally, Facile is a strict programming language and the communication is implemented as a side effect. We have integrated the communication in the IO monad and hence preserve referential transparency.

– Finally, we once again compare our approach with **Erlang** [AWV93]. The first advantage of Distributed Haskell is, that messages are statically typed. The type of the messages which can be sent through a port are the communication interface of the process which reads from the port. In Erlang such an interface does not exist. Furthermore this type system provides safety in program development. For example typing mistakes yield a compile-time error in Distributed Haskell, not a deadlock like in Erlang. Another opportunity is our linking mechanism, which is more powerful then linking in Erlang. We can add arbitrary IO actions to the links, which are performed, if the linked port dies. In Erlang it is only possible to receive a message, if another process dies. The process which receives this messages must interrupt its execution, react on this message, and afterwards resume its work. Performing different actions in case of different exceptions is much more difficult, then in our linking mechanism.

# 6    Conclusion and Future Work

We have extended Haskell for concurrent and distributed programming. With the example of a chat we have shown, how easy distributed systems can be developed using Distributed Haskell. The main concept of Distributed Haskell is the use of ports. Ports differ from channels in Concurrent Haskell in the fact that only the process, which created a port, can read from it. But this restriction is needed for the implementation, especially when we want to develop robust and fault tolerant systems. Another opportunity of this restriction is that ports, which are not used anymore are detected as garbage and get collected automatically. All described extensions are implemented using the Glasgow Haskell compiler [GHC] with the libraries `Concurrent` and `Socket` and built the library `Port`, which can be used together with the Glasgow Haskell Compiler [GHC].

In future work we want to implement lazy communication through the net. This means sending fragments of the heap instead of sending there string representation. With this extension we would also be able to send infinite data structures and functions. Furthermore we want to investigate if this is suggestive, because calculations can be duplicated. Therefore we want to inspect how good distributed programming and lazy evaluation match.

# References

AA98.        Thomas Arts and Joe Armstrong. A practical type system for Erlang. Technical report, Erlang User Conference, September 1998.

AWV93.       J. Armstrong, M. Williams, and R. Virding. *Concurrent Programming in Erlang*. Prentice-Hall, Englewood Cliffs, NJ, 1993.

BLOMPM96.    S. Breitinger, R. Loogen, Y. Ortega-Mallén, and R. Pena-Mari. Eden — the paradise of functional concurrent programming. *LNCS*, 1123:710ff., 1996.

CGK98.       Manuel M. T. Chakravarty, Yike Guo, and Martin Köhler. Distributed Haskell: Goffin on the Internet. In M. Sato and Y. Toyama, editors, *Proceedings of the Third Fuji International Symposium on Functional and Logic Programming*, pages 80–97. World Scientific Publishers, 1998.

GHC.         The Glasgow Haskell compiler. `http://www.haskell.org/ghc/`.

Han99.       M. Hanus. Distributed programming in a multi-paradigm declarative language. In *Proc. of the International Conference on Principles and Practice of Declarative Programming (PPDP'99)*. Springer LNCS (to appear), 1999.

Huc99.       Frank Huch. Erlang-style distributed haskell. In *Draft Proceedings of the 11th International Workshop on Implementation of Functional Languages*, September 7th – 10th 1999.

J⁺98.        Simon Peyton Jones et al. Haskell 98 report. Technical report, `http://www.haskell.org`, 1998.

JGF96.       Simon Peyton Jones, Andrew Gordon, and Sigbjorn Finne. Concurrent Haskell. In *Conference Record of POPL '96: The 23rd ACM SIGPLAN-SIGACT Symposium on Principles of Programming Languages*, pages 295–308, St. Petersburg Beach, Florida, 21–24 January 1996.

MW97.        Simon Marlow and Philip Wadler. A practical subtyping system for Erlang. In *Proceedings of the 1997 ACM SIGPLAN International Conference on Functional Programming*, pages 136–149, Amsterdam, The Netherlands, 9–11 June 1997.

PTL00.       R. Pointon, P. Trinder, and H-W. Loidl. The Design and Implementation of Glasgow distributed Haskell. In M. Mohnen and P. Koopman, editors, *Proceedings of the 12th International Workshop on Implementation of Functional Languages*, number AIB-00-7 in Aachener Informatik Berichte, pages 101–116. RWTH Aachen, 2000.

THM⁺96.      Philip W. Trinder, Kevin Hammond, James S. Mattson Jr., Andrew S. Partridge, and Simon L. Peyton Jones. GUM: a portable implementation of Haskell. In *Proceedings of Programming Language Design and Implementation*, Philadephia, USA, May 1996.

TLK96.       Bent Thomsen, Lone Leth, and Tsung-Min Kuo. A Facile tutorial. In Ugo Montanari and Vladimiro Sassone, editors, *CONCUR '96: Concurrency Theory, 7th International Conference*, volume 1119 of *Lecture Notes in Computer Science*, pages 278–298, Pisa, Italy, 26–29 August 1996. Springer-Verlag.

# The Dynamic Properties of Hume: A Functionally-Based Concurrent Language with Bounded Time and Space Behaviour

Kevin Hammond

School of Computer Science, University of St Andrews.
kh@dcs.st-and.ac.uk

**Abstract.** This paper provides a self-contained formal description of the dynamic properties of Hume, a novel functionally-based concurrent language that aims to target space- and time-critical systems such as safety-critical, embedded and real-time systems. The language is designed to support rigorous cost and space analyses, whilst providing a high level of abstraction including polymorphic type inference, automatic memory management, higher-order functions, exception-handling and a good range of primitive types.

## 1 Introduction

Hume (Higher-order Unified Meta-Environment) is a polymorphically typed functionally-based language for developing, proving and assessing concurrent, time- and space-critical systems, including embedded and real-time systems [3,4,10]. The language is intended to give strong guarantees of bounded time and space behaviour, whilst providing a relatively high level of expressive power through the use of functional language features. It has thus been designed to support the fundamental requirements of safety-critical software, as espoused by e.g. Leveson [8], whilst raising the level of abstraction at which that software can be implemented. Increased abstraction brings the usual advantages of faster development, reduced costs, and the complete elimination of certain kinds of error. In the safety-critical arena, however, such abstraction must be limited by the need for transparent implementation: high-level constructs must have obvious analogues in the low-level implementation, for example. This has traditionally been a weakness of functional language implementations.

A primary goal of the Hume design is to match sound formal program development practice by improving confidence in the correctness of implementation. Typical formal approaches to designing safety-critical systems progress rigorously from requirements specification to systems prototyping. Languages and notations for specification/prototyping provide good formalisms and proof support, but are often weak on essential support for programming abstractions, such as data structures and recursion. Implementation therefore usually proceeds less formally, or more tediously, using conventional languages and techniques. Hume is intended to simplify this process by allowing more direct implementation of

M. Mohnen and P. Koopman (Eds.): IFL 2000, LNCS 2011, pp. 122–139, 2001.

the abstractions provided by formal specification languages. Alternatively, in a less formal development process, it can be used to give a higher-level, more intuitive implementation of a real-time problem.

This paper provides a high-level formal description of the behaviour of concurrent Hume programs, incorporating a simple integrated model of time usage. This description is intended to formalise and explicate the language design, for the benefit of both users and implementors, but is not primarily intended to be used as a basis for direct proof.

## 2  The Hume Language

Hume has a 3-level structure: the *coordination layer*, based on communicating (parallel) processes, encompasses the inner, purely functional, *expression layer*. These two layers are enclosed in a static *declaration layer* which introduces type, function, value, exception etc. definitions that can be used in either or both dynamic layers. Exceptions may be raised in expressions, but are handled in the coordination layer. Strict cost mechanisms ensure that expressions produce results in bounded time and space, and that exception handling costs are also bounded.

### 2.1  The Hume Expression Layer

The Hume *expression layer* is a purely functional language with a strict semantics. It is intended to be used for the description of single, single-shot, non-reentrant processes. It is deterministic, and has statically bounded time and space behaviour. In order to ensure these strong properties, expressions whose time or space cost is not explicitly bounded must be restricted to a statically-checkable primitive recursive form [11].

### 2.2  The Hume Coordination Layer

The Hume *coordination layer* is a finite state language for the description of multiple, interacting, re-entrant processes built from the purely functional expression layer. The coordination layer is designed to have statically provable properties that include both *process equivalence* and *safety* properties such as the absence of deadlock, livelock or resource starvation.

The basic unit of coordination is the *box* (Figure 1), an abstract notion of a process that specifies the links between its input and output channels in terms of functional pattern matches, and which provides exception handling facilities including timeouts and system exceptions, with handlers defined as pattern matches on exception values. The coordination layer is responsible for interaction with external, imperative state through streams and ports that are ultimately connected to external devices. Our initial design allows the definition of simple, static process networks only using a static wiring notation (Figure 2). Only values with statically determined sizes may be communicated through wires.

```
<boxdecl> ::=           "box"    <boxid>
                        "in"     <in1>   ","  ...  ","  <inn>
                        "out"    <out1>  ","  ...  ","  <outn>
                        "match"  <matches>
                        [ "timeout" <expr> ]
                        [ "handle" <handlers> ]

<in>/<out> ::=          <varid> "::" <exprtype>

<matches> ::=           <match1> "|" ... "|" <matchn>          n >= 1

<match> ::=             <patt> "->" <expr>
```

**Fig. 1.** Syntax of boxes

```
<wiredecl> ::=          "wire" <boxid> <sources> <dests>

<sources>/<dests> ::=   "(" <link1> "," ... "," <linkn> ")"    n >= 0

<link> ::=              <boxid> "." <varid>  |  <streamid>
```

**Fig. 2.** Syntax of wires

## 2.3   Types

Hume is a polymorphically typed language in the spirit of ML [13] or Haskell [15]. It supports a wide range of scalar types, including booleans, characters, variable sized word values, fixed-precision integers (including natural numbers), floating-point values, and fixed-exponent real numbers. Precisely costed conversions are defined between values of those types and the sizes of all scalar types other than booleans must be specified precisely.

Hume also supports four kinds of structured type: vectors, lists, tuples and user-defined constructed types. Vector and tuple types are fixed size, whereas lists and user-defined types may be arbitrary sized. All elements of a single vector or list must have the same type.

## 2.4   Example: Railway Junction

As an example of a basic Hume program, we show a simple controller for a simple railway junction (Figure 3), comprising the junction of two tracks, $t1$ and $t2$ into the single track $t3$ through the point $p$. Each incoming track is controlled by a signal ($s1$ or $s2$) The controller avoids collisions by ensuring that at most one

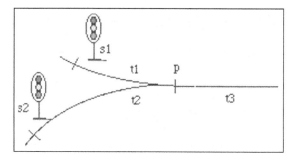

**Fig. 3.** Simple railway junction

signal is green and that both signals are red unless $t3$ is empty. The tracks and signals are modelled as Hume streams.

```
data Maybe a =   Just a | Nothing;
data Direction = Left   | Right;
data Signal =    Red    | Green;
type Point =     Maybe Direction;
type Speed =     Int;
type Train =     Maybe Speed;

left = (Green,Red,Just Left);
right = (Red,Green,Just Right);

box junction
in  (sense1, sense2, sense3 :: Train)
out (sig1, sig2 :: Signal, point :: Point)

match
  (_,_,Just _) -> (Red,Red,Nothing)
  (Just _,Nothing,Nothing) -> left
  (Just _,Nothing,Nothing) -> right
  (Just sp1,Just sp2,Nothing) -> if sp1 > sp2 then left else right;

wire junction (t1,t2,t3) (s1,s2,p);
```

## 3  Costing Hume Programs

This section gives a cost semantics for Hume programs, which will subsequently be integrated with a dynamic semantics in Section 4. The rules use a sequent style similar to that used for the semantics of Standard ML [13], but with a number of technical differences aimed at a more intuitive language description. For example, $E \overset{cost}{\vdash} exp \Rightarrow c$ means that under environment E, exp has cost $c$. The definitions of the cost domains and environments are given below. Cost environments (CostEnv) map variable identifiers to cost values. Arithmetic operations $+$, $max$ etc. are defined on cost expressions in the obvious way as for normal integers, with the addition of an infinite cost value $\infty$, which is treated as in normal integer arithmetic.

$E \in \text{Env} = \qquad \langle \text{VarEnv, CostEnv, SysEnv} \rangle$ Environments

$CE \in \text{CostEnv} = \{ \text{var} \mapsto \text{Cost} \}$ \qquad Cost Environments

$c, t \in \text{Cost} = \qquad 0, 1, \dots, \infty$ \qquad\qquad Cost Values $\quad$.

Figures 4–7 give rules to statically derive an upper bound on the time cost for Hume programs. The rules are a simple big-step operational semantics, with extensions to timeouts and exceptions. We have deliberately used a very simple cost semantics here rather than the more general form that we are developing as part of our work in parallel computation [9]. The latter is intended for arbitrary recursion and requires the use of a constraint solving engine, whereas Hume is restricted to function definitions that are either primitive recursive or which have explicit time and space constraints. The rules given here are also restricted to first-order functions. Although expressed in terms of time cost, it would be straightforward to modify these rules to cover space costs.

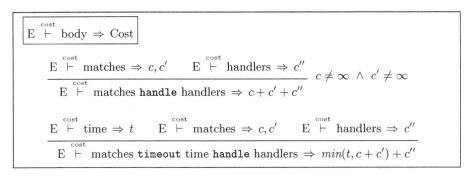

**Fig. 4.** Cost axioms for boxes

Figure 5 gives simplified cost rules for expressions taken from [3]. The cost of a function application is the cost of evaluating the body of the function plus the cost of each argument. The cost of building a new constructor value such as a tuple or a user-defined constructed type is the cost of evaluating the arguments to that constructor plus one for each argument (representing the cost of building each heap cell). An additional cost is added to user-defined constructor values to represent the cost of building a cell to hold the constructor tag. The cost of raising an exception is the cost of the enclosed expression plus one (representing the cost of actually throwing that exception). Finally the cost of an expression enclosed within a timeout is the minimum of the expression cost and the specified timeout (a static constant).

Figure 6 gives costs for pattern matches. Two values are returned from a match sequence, which are summed to give the overall cost of the match sequence. The first cost is the total cost of matching all the patterns in the match sequence. This places an upper bound on the match cost. The second cost is the cost of evaluating the most expensive right-hand-side. This places an upper

$$\boxed{\text{E} \ \vdash^{\text{cost}} \ \exp \ \Rightarrow \ \text{Cost}}$$

$$\frac{}{\text{E} \ \vdash^{\text{cost}} \ \text{var} \ \Rightarrow \ 1}$$

$$\frac{(\text{CE } \textit{of } \text{E}) \ (\text{var}) \ = \ c \qquad \forall i. \ 1 < i \le n, \ \text{E} \ \vdash^{\text{cost}} \ \exp_i \ \Rightarrow \ c_i}{\text{E} \ \vdash^{\text{cost}} \ \text{var} \ \exp_1 \ \ldots \ \exp_n \ \Rightarrow \ \sum_{i=1}^{n} c_i + c} \quad n > 0$$

$$\frac{\forall i. \ 1 < i \le n, \ \text{E} \ \vdash^{\text{cost}} \ \exp_i \ \Rightarrow \ c_i}{\text{E} \ \vdash^{\text{cost}} \ \text{con} \ \exp_1 \ \ldots \ \exp_n \ \Rightarrow \ \sum_{i=1}^{n} c_i + n + 1}$$

$$\frac{\text{E} \ \vdash^{\text{cost}} \ \exp_1 \ \Rightarrow \ c_1 \qquad \text{E} \ \vdash^{\text{cost}} \ \exp_2 \ \Rightarrow \ c_2 \qquad \text{E} \ \vdash^{\text{cost}} \ \exp_3 \ \Rightarrow \ c_3}{\text{E} \ \vdash^{\text{cost}} \ \textbf{if} \ \exp_1 \ \textbf{then} \ \exp_2 \ \textbf{else} \ \exp_3 \ \Rightarrow \ c_1 + max(c_2, c_3)}$$

$$\frac{\text{E} \vdash \text{decls} \Rightarrow \text{E'}, c \qquad \text{E} \ \overset{\rightarrow}{\oplus} \ \text{E'} \ \vdash^{\text{cost}} \ \exp \ \Rightarrow \ c'}{\text{E} \ \vdash^{\text{cost}} \ \textbf{let} \ \text{decls} \ \textbf{in} \ \exp \ \Rightarrow \ c + c'}$$

$$\frac{\text{E} \ \vdash^{\text{cost}} \ \exp \ \Rightarrow \ c}{\text{E} \ \vdash^{\text{cost}} \ \textbf{raise} \ \text{exnid} \ \exp \ \Rightarrow \ c + 1}$$

$$\frac{\text{E} \ \vdash^{\text{cost}} \ \exp_1 \ \Rightarrow \ c \qquad \text{E} \vdash \exp_2 \Rightarrow t}{\text{E} \ \vdash^{\text{cost}} \ \exp_1 \ \textbf{within} \ \exp_2 \ \Rightarrow \ min(c, t)}$$

**Fig. 5.** Cost axioms for expressions

bound on the expression cost. The cost of matching multiple patterns in a single match is the sum of matching each pattern. Wildcard patterns (_) cost nothing to match, whereas normal variables have a match cost (here specified as one). The cost of matching a constructor pattern is the cost of matching all subsidiary patterns plus one for the constructor itself.

Figure 7 gives the cost of matching exceptions. Since only one handler can ever be matched, the upper bound cost of a handler sequence is the greatest cost of any exception handler. The cost of an individual handler is the cost of the match plus 1 for returning the (fixed-cost) expression that is its right-hand-side.

### 3.1 Costing the Railway Junction Example

As an example of using the cost rules, we return to the railway junction example from Section 2.4. The cost of the junction box is defined as the sum of the

$$E \overset{\text{cost}}{\vdash} \text{matches} \Rightarrow \text{Cost}$$

$$\frac{E \overset{\text{cost}}{\vdash} \text{matches} \Rightarrow c, c'}{E \overset{\text{cost}}{\vdash} \text{matches} \Rightarrow c + c'}$$

$$E \overset{\text{cost}}{\vdash} \text{matches} \Rightarrow \text{Cost}, \text{Cost}$$

$$\frac{E \overset{\text{cost}}{\vdash} \text{match} \Rightarrow c, c' \qquad E \overset{\text{cost}}{\vdash} \text{matches} \Rightarrow c'', c'''}{E \overset{\text{cost}}{\vdash} \text{match} \mid \text{matches} \Rightarrow c + c'', max(c', c''')}$$

$$\frac{\forall i.\, 1 < i \le n,\ E \overset{\text{cost}}{\vdash} pat_i \Rightarrow c_i \qquad E \overset{\text{cost}}{\vdash} \text{exp} \Rightarrow c}{E \overset{\text{cost}}{\vdash} pat_1\ \ldots\ pat_n\ \rightarrow\ \text{exp} \Rightarrow \sum_{i=1}^{n} c_i, c}$$

$$E \overset{\text{cost}}{\vdash} \text{pat} \Rightarrow \text{Cost}$$

$$\frac{}{E \overset{\text{cost}}{\vdash}\ \_ \Rightarrow 0}$$

$$\frac{}{E \overset{\text{cost}}{\vdash} \text{var} \Rightarrow 1}$$

$$\frac{\forall i.\, 1 < i \le n,\ E \overset{\text{cost}}{\vdash} pat_i \Rightarrow c_i}{E \overset{\text{cost}}{\vdash} \text{con } pat_1\ \ldots\ pat_n \Rightarrow \sum_{i=1}^{n} c_i + 1}$$

**Fig. 6.** Cost axioms for pattern matches

$$E \overset{\text{cost}}{\vdash} \text{handlers} \Rightarrow \text{Cost}$$

$$\frac{E \overset{\text{cost}}{\vdash} \text{pat} \Rightarrow c \qquad E \overset{\text{cost}}{\vdash} \text{exp} \Rightarrow c'}{E \overset{\text{cost}}{\vdash} \{ \text{exnid pat} \rightarrow \text{exp} \} \Rightarrow c + 1} \quad c' \ne \infty$$

$$\frac{E \overset{\text{cost}}{\vdash} \text{handler} \Rightarrow c \qquad E \overset{\text{cost}}{\vdash} \text{handlers} \Rightarrow c'}{E \overset{\text{cost}}{\vdash} \text{handler} \mid \text{handlers} \Rightarrow max(c, c')}$$

**Fig. 7.** Cost axioms for exception handlers

costs of the left-hand-sides of the rules, plus the maximum cost of the right-hand-sides. The cost of each match can be derived using the match rules, as shown in the table below. For convenience, the costs for each match are split into their left-hand- and right-hand-side components.

| Rule | $\text{Cost}_{LHS}(cl)$ | $\text{Cost}_{RHS}(cr)$ |
|------|------|------|
| 1 | 2 | 7 |
| 2 | 4 | 9 |
| 3 | 4 | 9 |
| 4 | 6 | 13 |

The worst case cost is thus $\sum_{i=1}^{n} cl_i + max_{i=1}^{n} cr_i$. This is 16 + 13, or 29 time units.

# 4   Dynamic Semantics

This section gives a dynamic semantics for Hume, focusing on the coordination layer. We restrict our attention to a subset of the Hume declaration and expression layers, ignoring lists and vectors, for example. The full dynamic semantics is given in the language report [10].

The semantics is given in terms of the semantic domain of values *SemVal*, defined below. The notation $\langle \ldots \rangle$ is used for semantic tuples in the *SemVal* domain. The notation $D^*$ is the domain of all tuples of $D$: $\langle \rangle$, $\langle D \rangle$, $\langle D, D \rangle$, ... We use subscripts to select tuple components, e.g. $v_i$. For any tuple v, the notation *fst*(v) is equivalent to $v_1$ and *snd*(v) is equivalent to $v_2$.

$$
\begin{aligned}
\text{BasVal} &= \{\ \text{PrimPlusInt}, \text{PrimEqInt}, \ldots\ \} & &\text{Basic Values}\\
\text{BasCon} &= \{\ \text{True}, \text{False}, \ldots\ \} & &\text{Basic Constructors}\\
\text{Con} &= \text{BasCon} + \text{con} & & \\
v, vs \in \text{SemVal} &= \text{BasVal} + \text{Con SemVal}^* + & &\text{Semantic Values}\\
& \quad \text{SemVal}^* + \text{Exn} & & \\
x \in \text{Exn} &= \langle\ \text{var}, \text{SemVal}^*\ \rangle & &\text{Exceptions}
\end{aligned}
$$

Environments are unique maps from identifiers to values. An environment is applied to an identifier to give the the corresponding entry in the map. For example, if $E$ is the environment $\{\ \text{var} \mapsto v\ \}$, then $E$ (var) $=$ v. The operation $m_1 \oplus m_2$ updates an environment $m_1$ with the new mappings in $m_2$. The $m_1 \overset{\rightarrow}{\oplus} m_2$ operation is similar, but allows values in $m_1$ to be "shadowed" by those in $m_2$, for example, $\{\text{var} \mapsto v\} \overset{\rightarrow}{\oplus} \{\text{var} \mapsto \text{v'}\}$ is $\{\text{var} \mapsto \text{v'}\}$, whereas $\{\text{var} \mapsto v\} \oplus \{\text{var} \mapsto \text{v'}\}$ is an error. Where an environment comprises a number of sub-environments, we use the notation E *of* E' to select sub-environment E from E'. Similarly, E $\oplus_{VE}$ E' replaces the *VE* subenvironment of $E$ with $E'$ etc.

We define a number of different environments for use in the semantics. Variable environments (VarEnv) map identifiers to semantic values. System environments (SysEnv) map stream identifiers to the values that appear on the associated stream, plus a boolean indicating the availability of the value. Cost environments (Section 3) are also used in the dynamic semantics.

$$
\begin{array}{lll}
E \in & \text{Env} = & \langle \text{ VarEnv, CostEnv, SysEnv } \rangle & \text{Environments} \\
\text{IE, VE} \in & \text{VarEnv} = \{ \text{ var } \mapsto (\text{SemVal} + \text{matches}) \} & \text{Value Environments} \\
\text{SE} \in & \text{SysEnv} = \{ \text{ var } \mapsto \ < bool, \text{SemVal} >^* \ \} & \text{System Environment} \\
& bool = \ \ \{ \ true, false \ \} & \text{Booleans}
\end{array}
$$

Finally, a number of special values are used in the coordination semantics. Wiring environments (Wire) map box identifiers to their inputs and outputs. Process sets (Processes) are sets of processes. I, A, and P are used in the semantics to distinguish inactive, active and general process set, and a single process (Proc) comprises a box identifier, two tuples of identifiers representing its inputs and outputs, and an expression representing its body.

$$
\begin{array}{lll}
W \in & \text{Wire} = \ \ \{ \text{ var} \mapsto \langle \text{var}^*, \text{var}^* \ \rangle \ \} & \text{Wires} \\
\text{I, A, P} \in & \text{Process} = \{ \text{ Proc } \} & \text{Processes} \\
& \text{Proc} = \ \ \langle \text{ var, var}^*, \text{var}^*, \exp \ \rangle & \text{Process}
\end{array}
$$

We use three forms of rule. Values are determined by rules of the form $E \vdash exp \Rightarrow v$, which means that given the assumptions in environment $E$, the value $v$ can be determined for syntactic value $exp$. Costs are determined by rules of the form $E \overset{cost}{\vdash} exp \Rightarrow c$ (Section 3). Finally, results of pattern matches are determined by rules of the form $E, v \models match \Rightarrow v'$: under the assumptions in E, the result of matching v against the matches in $match$ is v'.

We use a sequent style for the rules whereby the consequence (below the line) holds wherever the premises hold, perhaps under some side-conditions. The rules are defined structurally for each syntactic case. Some syntactic forms may match more than one rule. In these cases, the premises and side-conditions for the two rules must be disjoint.

## 4.1   Dynamic Semantics: Declarations

Declaration sequences (Figure 8) are processed to generate an environment that contains a value environment and a cost environment, plus the cost of evaluating the declaration sequence. Only two forms of declaration are interesting. Variable declarations are evaluated at the start of a declaration block. They therefore have a fixed dynamic cost which is attributed to the declaration sequence, a constant value, and no entry in the cost environment (which is used to cost each dynamic function invocation). The cost of a function definition (*var matches*) is defined in Figure 6. In the simple cost semantics given here, recursive definitions are assigned infinite cost (a valid, though highly imprecise upper bound). We anticipate producing more refined cost functions for recursive definitions in the future.

Box and wire declarations are processed to give a set of processes and a wiring environment as shown in Figure 9. The set of processes and the wiring environment are used to define the semantics of Hume programs. The wiring environment maps the outputs of boxes or streams to the inputs of other boxes or streams. Every box input must be connected to some input stream or box output, while box outputs must be connected to some output stream or box input (in time, we intend to relax this restriction so that box outputs may be connected to multiple inputs). These restrictions are handled in the static semantics.

$$\boxed{E \vdash decls \Rightarrow E, Cost}$$

$$\forall i.\ 1 \le i \le n,\ E \oplus E' \vdash decl_i \Rightarrow VE_i, CE_i, c_i$$

$$E' = \langle\ (\bigoplus_{i=1}^{n} VE_i),\ (\bigoplus_{i=1}^{n} CE_i),\ \{\ \}\ \rangle$$

$$\overline{E \vdash decl_1\ ;\ \dots\ ;\ decl_n \Rightarrow E', \sum_{i=1}^{n} c_i}$$

$$\boxed{E \vdash decl \Rightarrow VE, CE, Cost}$$

$$\frac{E \vdash exp \Rightarrow v \qquad E \overset{cost}{\vdash} exp \Rightarrow c}{E \vdash var\ =\ exp \Rightarrow \{\ var \mapsto v\ \}, \{\ \}, c}$$

$$\frac{E \overset{\rightarrow}{\oplus}_{CE} \{var \mapsto \infty\} \overset{cost}{\vdash} matches \Rightarrow c}{E \vdash var\ matches \Rightarrow \{\ var \mapsto matches\ \}, \{\ var \mapsto c\ \}, 0}$$

**Fig. 8.** Dynamic semantics for declarations

$$\boxed{\vdash box \Rightarrow P}$$

$$\overline{\vdash \textbf{box}\ boxid\ \textbf{in}\ ins\ \textbf{out}\ outs\ \texttt{match}\ body \Rightarrow \{\ \langle\ boxid, ins, outs, body\ \rangle\ \}}$$

$$\boxed{\vdash wire \Rightarrow W}$$

$$\frac{W = \{\ boxid \mapsto \langle\ sources, dests\ \rangle\ \}}{\vdash \textbf{wire}\ boxid\ sources\ dests \Rightarrow W}$$

**Fig. 9.** Dynamic semantics for box and wire declarations

## 4.2   Dynamic Semantics: Expressions

The dynamic semantics of expressions (Figure 10) is analogous to that for Standard ML. The only interesting rules are those for time or space constraints. If the cost of evaluating an expression (given using the cost rules defined in Section 3) is greater than the specified timeout in a within-expression, then the Timeout exception is raised, otherwise the value of the within-expression is the same as the encapsulated expression. Similar rules apply to space constraints.

Exceptions are matched against each handler in a handler sequence as shown in Figure 11. Each exception that can be raised must be handled by precisely one handler in the sequence. The value contained within the exception is matched against the pattern in the handler using the normal pattern matching rules (also Figure 11). A syntactic pattern match sequence is matched against a concrete value. Each match in the sequence is tried in turn. If a match succeeds then the

$$\boxed{E \vdash exp \Rightarrow v}$$

$$\dfrac{E \vdash exp_2 \Rightarrow t \qquad E \overset{cost}{\vdash} exp_1 \Rightarrow t' \qquad t' < t}{E \vdash exp_1 \Rightarrow v}$$

$$E \vdash exp_1 \text{ within } exp_2 \Rightarrow v$$

$$\dfrac{E \vdash exp_2 \Rightarrow t \qquad E \overset{cost}{\vdash} exp_1 \Rightarrow t' \qquad t' \geq t}{E \vdash exp_1 \text{ within } exp_2 \Rightarrow \langle \text{ Timeout, } \langle \rangle \rangle}$$

**Fig. 10.** Dynamic semantics for within-expressions

result of the match is used as the value of the sequence. If a match fails, then the next match is tried. Precisely one match must succeed.

The individual pattern match rules given here consider only simple, unnested patterns which are either variables or constructors. It is straightforward to extend the rules to cover nested patterns or multiple patterns within a match (as for a function of multiple arguments) [10]. A variable pattern matches any value. The result of the match is the value of the expression in the environment extended with the binding of the variable to the value. A matching constructor binds each of its formal arguments to the corresponding actual parameter value.

### 4.3   Dynamic Semantics: Boxes

The dynamic semantics of a Hume program is given by repeatedly reducing each of its boxes in the context of the declarations and wirings. The result of a Hume program is a new environment reflecting the state of any new bindings in the system or value environments. Figure 12 shows this semantics. The set of processes defined in the program is split into two subsets: one of inactive processes, the other of active processes. These sets are reduced one step to give a new environment and new sets of inactive and active processes. This is repeated until the set of active processes becomes empty, at which point the result of the program is the current environment.

The set of processes is split into active (A) and inactive processes (I). A process is active if input is available on all its input channels, *or* if a timeout has been raised on any input channel. The auxiliary function *active* is used to determine whether a box should be active or not based on the current values on its inputs. It can be defined as follows:

$$active\ (E,\ \langle win_1\ \ldots\ win_n \rangle) = ready\ (E,\ \langle win_1\ \ldots\ win_n \rangle)$$
$$\lor\ timedout\ (E,\ \langle win_1\ \ldots\ win_n \rangle)$$

$$ready\ (E,\ \langle win_1\ \ldots\ win_n \rangle) = fst\ (E(win_1))\ =\ true\ \land$$
$$\ldots\ \land\ fst\ (E(win_n))\ =\ true$$

$$\boxed{E, v \models \text{handlers} \Rightarrow v}$$

$$\frac{E, v \models \text{handler} \Rightarrow v'}{E, v \models \text{handler} \mid \text{handlers} \Rightarrow v'}$$

$$\frac{E, v \models \text{handler} \Rightarrow FAIL \qquad E, v \models \text{handlers} \Rightarrow v'}{E, v \models \text{handler} \mid \text{handlers} \Rightarrow v'}$$

$$\boxed{E, v \models \text{handler} \Rightarrow v/FAIL}$$

$$\frac{v = \langle \text{exnid'}, v' \rangle \qquad E, v' \models \text{pat} \rightarrow \text{exp} \Rightarrow v''}{E, v \models \text{exnid pat} \rightarrow \text{exp} \Rightarrow v''} \quad \text{exnid} = \text{exnid'}$$

$$\frac{v = \langle \text{exnid'}, v' \rangle}{E, v \models \text{exnid pat} \rightarrow \text{exp} \Rightarrow FAIL} \quad \text{exnid} \neq \text{exnid'}$$

$$\boxed{E, v \models \text{matches} \Rightarrow v}$$

$$\frac{E, v \models \text{match} \Rightarrow v'}{E, v \models \text{match} \mid \text{matches} \Rightarrow v'}$$

$$\frac{E, v \models \text{match} \Rightarrow FAIL \qquad E, v \models \text{matches} \Rightarrow v'}{E, v \models \text{match} \mid \text{matches} \Rightarrow v'}$$

$$\boxed{E, v \models \text{match} \Rightarrow v/FAIL}$$

$$\frac{E \overset{\rightarrow}{\oplus} \{ \text{var} \mapsto v \} \vdash \text{exp} \Rightarrow v'}{E, v \models \text{var} \rightarrow \text{exp} \Rightarrow v'}$$

$$\frac{v = \text{con} < v_1, \ldots, v_n > \qquad E \overset{\rightarrow}{\oplus} \{ \forall i. \ 1 \leq i \leq n, \ \text{var}_i \mapsto v_i \} \vdash \text{exp} \Rightarrow v'}{E, v \models \text{con var}_1 \ldots \text{var}_n \rightarrow \text{exp} \Rightarrow v'}$$

$$\frac{v \neq \text{con} \langle v_1, \ldots, v_n \rangle}{E, v \models \text{con var}_1 \ldots \text{var}_n \rightarrow \text{exp} \Rightarrow FAIL}$$

**Fig. 11.** Dynamic semantics for exception handlers and pattern matches

$$\boxed{\mathrm{E,W} \vdash \mathrm{P} \Rightarrow \mathrm{E}}$$

$$\frac{\mathrm{E,W} \vdash \mathrm{P} \Rightarrow \mathrm{I,A} \qquad \mathrm{E,W} \vdash \mathrm{I,A} \Rightarrow \mathrm{E'}}{\mathrm{E,W} \vdash \mathrm{P} \Rightarrow \mathrm{E'}}$$

$$\boxed{\mathrm{E,W} \vdash \mathrm{P,P} \Rightarrow \mathrm{E}}$$

$$\frac{\mathrm{E,W} \vdash \mathrm{I,A} \Rightarrow \mathrm{E',I',A'} \qquad \mathrm{E',W} \vdash \mathrm{I',A'} \Rightarrow \mathrm{E''}}{\mathrm{E,W} \vdash \mathrm{I,A} \Rightarrow \mathrm{E'',I',A'}} \ \mathrm{A} \neq \{\,\}$$

$$\frac{}{\mathrm{E,W} \vdash \mathrm{I}, \{\,\} \Rightarrow \mathrm{E}}$$

$$\boxed{\mathrm{E,W} \vdash \mathrm{P} \Rightarrow \mathrm{P,P}}$$

$$\frac{\begin{array}{l} \forall i.\ 1 \leq i \leq n,\ \mathrm{E,W} \vdash \mathrm{P}_i \Rightarrow \mathrm{I}_i, \mathrm{A}_i \\ \quad \mathrm{I} = \bigcup_{i=1}^{n} \mathrm{I}_i \qquad \mathrm{A} = \bigcup_{i=1}^{n} \mathrm{A}_i \end{array}}{\mathrm{E,W} \vdash \{\ \mathrm{P}_1, \ldots, \mathrm{P}_n\ \} \Rightarrow \mathrm{I,A}}$$

$$\boxed{\mathrm{E,W} \vdash \mathrm{Proc} \Rightarrow \mathrm{P,P}}$$

$$\frac{\begin{array}{c} \mathrm{P} = \langle\ \mathrm{boxid, ins, outs, body}\ \rangle \qquad \mathrm{W\ (boxid)} = \langle\ \mathrm{wins, wouts}\ \rangle \\ \mathrm{I,A} = \mathit{if}\ \mathit{active}(\mathrm{E, wins})\ \mathit{then}\ \{\,\}, \{\ \mathrm{P}\ \}\ \mathit{else}\ \{\ \mathrm{P}\ \}, \{\,\} \end{array}}{\mathrm{E,W} \vdash \mathrm{P} \Rightarrow \mathrm{I,A}}$$

**Fig. 12.** Dynamic semantics for processes

$$\begin{array}{rl} \mathit{timedout}\ (\mathrm{E}, \langle \mathrm{win}_1\ \ldots\ \mathrm{win}_n \rangle) = \mathit{fst}(\mathit{snd}\ (\mathrm{E}(\mathrm{win}_1))) & = \langle\ \mathrm{Timeout}, \langle\ \rangle\ \rangle \\ & \vee\ \mathit{timedout}\ (\mathrm{E}, \langle \mathrm{win}_2\ \ldots\ \mathrm{win}_n \rangle) \end{array}$$

Having determined the set of currently active processes, each of these is executed for one step as shown in Figure 13. A process is executed by determining the value of each of its inputs, and then executing the body of the process in the context of those values. The new values of the inputs and outputs are used to update the stream and box input bindings in the system environment as appropriate.

The final set of coordination rules (Figure 14) define the semantics of executing a single box body. There are three cases, corresponding to normal execution, an exception or a timeout respectively.

$$\boxed{\mathrm{E, W} \vdash \mathrm{P, P} \Rightarrow \mathrm{E, P, P}}$$

$$\frac{\begin{array}{l}\forall i.\ 1 \le i \le card(\mathrm{A}),\ \mathrm{E, W} \vdash \mathrm{A}_i \Rightarrow \mathrm{outs}_i,\ \mathrm{E}_i^I, \mathrm{E}_i^O \\[1em] \mathrm{E'} = \bigcup_{i=1}^{card(\mathrm{A})} \mathrm{E}_i^I \ \vec{\oplus} \ \bigcup_{i=1}^{card(\mathrm{A})} \mathrm{E}_i^O \\[1em] \mathrm{E} \ \vec{\oplus} \ \mathrm{E', W} \vdash \mathrm{I} \cup \mathrm{A} \Rightarrow \mathrm{I', A'}\end{array}}{\mathrm{E, W} \vdash \mathrm{I, A} \Rightarrow (\mathrm{E} \ \vec{\oplus} \ \mathrm{E'}), \mathrm{I', A'}}$$

$$\boxed{\mathrm{E} \vdash \mathrm{P} \Rightarrow \mathrm{v, E, E}}$$

$$\frac{\begin{array}{l}\mathrm{W\ (boxid)} = \langle \mathrm{wins, wouts} \rangle \qquad n = card(\mathrm{wins}) \qquad \mathrm{SE} = \mathrm{SE}\ of\ \mathrm{E} \\ \mathrm{vs} = \langle\ snd(fst(\mathrm{SE\ (wins_1)})),\ \ldots,\ snd(fst(\mathrm{SE\ (wins}_n)))\ \rangle \\ \mathrm{E, vs} \vdash \mathrm{body} \Rightarrow \mathrm{vs'} \\ \mathrm{SE}^I = \{\ \forall i.\ 1 \le i \le n,\ \mathrm{wins}_i \mapsto snd(\mathrm{SE\ wins}_i)\} \\ \mathrm{SE}^O = \{\ \forall i.\ 1 \le i \le card(\mathrm{wouts}), \\ \qquad\qquad \mathrm{wouts}_i \mapsto \langle\ \langle true, \mathrm{vs'}_i \rangle\ ,\ \langle false, \langle\rangle \rangle\ \rangle\}\end{array}}{\mathrm{E, W} \vdash \langle\ \mathrm{boxid, ins, outs, body}\ \rangle \Rightarrow \mathrm{vs', SE}^I, \mathrm{SE}^O}$$

**Fig. 13.** Dynamic semantics for active processes

$$\boxed{\mathrm{E, v} \vdash \mathrm{body} \Rightarrow \mathrm{v}}$$

$$\frac{\begin{array}{c}\mathrm{E} \vdash \mathrm{time} \Rightarrow \mathrm{t} \qquad \mathrm{E} \overset{\mathrm{cost}}{\vdash} \mathrm{matches} \Rightarrow \mathrm{t'} \qquad \mathrm{t'} < \mathrm{t} \\ \mathrm{E, vs} \vdash \mathrm{matches} \Rightarrow \mathrm{v}\end{array}}{\mathrm{E, vs} \vdash \mathrm{matches}\ \mathtt{timeout}\ \mathrm{time}\ \mathtt{handle}\ \mathrm{handlers} \Rightarrow \mathrm{v}} \quad \mathrm{v} \notin \mathrm{Exn}$$

$$\frac{\begin{array}{c}\mathrm{E} \vdash \mathrm{time} \Rightarrow \mathrm{t} \qquad \mathrm{E} \overset{\mathrm{cost}}{\vdash} \mathrm{matches} \Rightarrow \mathrm{t'} \qquad \mathrm{t'} < \mathrm{t} \\ \mathrm{E, vs} \vdash \mathrm{matches} \Rightarrow \mathrm{v} \qquad \mathrm{E, v} \models \mathrm{handlers} \Rightarrow \mathrm{v'}\end{array}}{\mathrm{E, vs} \vdash \mathrm{matches}\ \mathtt{timeout}\ \mathrm{time}\ \mathtt{handle}\ \mathrm{handlers} \Rightarrow \mathrm{v'}} \quad \mathrm{v} \in \mathrm{Exn}$$

$$\frac{\begin{array}{c}\mathrm{E} \vdash \mathrm{time} \Rightarrow \mathrm{t} \qquad \mathrm{E} \overset{\mathrm{cost}}{\vdash} \mathrm{matches} \Rightarrow \mathrm{t'} \qquad \mathrm{t'} \ge \mathrm{t} \\ \mathrm{E}, \langle\ \mathrm{Timeout},\ \langle\ \rangle\ \rangle \models \mathrm{handlers} \Rightarrow \mathrm{v}\end{array}}{\mathrm{E, vs} \vdash \mathrm{matches}\ \mathtt{timeout}\ \mathrm{time}\ \mathtt{handle}\ \mathrm{handlers} \Rightarrow \mathrm{v}}$$

**Fig. 14.** Dynamic semantics for box bodies

## 5  Related Work

*Specification Languages.* Safety-critical systems have strong time-based correctness requirements, which can be expressed formally as properties of *safety, liveness* and *timeliness* [1]. Formal requirements specifications are expressed using notations such as temporal logics (e.g. MTL), non-temporal logics (e.g. RTL), or timed process algebras (e.g. LOTOS-T, Timed CCS or Timed CSP). Such notations are deliberately non-deterministic in order to allow alternative implementations, and may similarly leave some or all timing issues unspecified. It is essential to crystallise these factors amongst others when producing a working implementation.

*Non-Determinism.* Although non-determinism may be required in specification languages such as LOTOS, it is usually undesirable in implementation languages such as Hume, where predictable and repeatable behaviour is required [1]. Hume thus incorporates deterministic processes, but with the option of fair choice to allow the definition of alternative acceptable outcomes. Because of the emphasis on hard real-time, it is not possible to use the event synchronising approach based on *delayed timestamps* which has been adopted by e.g. the concurrent functional language BRISK [5]. The advantage of the BRISK approach is in ensuring strong determinism without requiring explicit specifications of time constraints as in Hume.

*Synchronicity.* *Synchronous* languages such as Signal, Lustre, Esterel or the visual formalism Statecharts obey the *synchrony hypothesis*: they assume that all events occur instantaneously, with no passage of time between the occurrence of consecutive events. In contrast, *asynchronous* languages, such as the extended finite state machine languages Estelle and SDL, make no such assumption. Hume uses an asynchronous approach, for reasons of both expressiveness and realism. Like Estelle and SDL, it also employs an asynchronous model of communication and supports asynchronous execution of concurrent processes.

*Summary Comparison.* As a vehicle for implementing safety-critical or hard real-time problems, Hume thus has advantages over widely-used existing language designs. Compared with Estelle or SDL, for example, it is formally defined, deterministic, and provably bounded in both space and time. These factors lead to a better match with formal requirements specifications and enhance confidence in the correctness of Hume programs. Hume has the advantage over Lustre and Esterel of providing asynchronicity, which is required for distributed systems. Finally, it has the advantage over LOTOS or other process algbras of being designed as an implementation rather than specification language: *inter alia* it supports normal program and data structuring constructs, allowing a rich programming environment.

## 5.1   Bounded Time/Space Models

Other than our own work, we are aware of three main studies of formally bounded time and space behaviour in a functional setting [2,7,20].

*Embedded ML.* In their recent proposal for Embedded ML, Hughes and Pareto [7] have combined the earlier *sized type system* [6] with the notion of *region types* [19] to give bounded space and termination for a first-order strict functional language [7]. Their language is more restricted than Hume in a number of ways: most notably in not supporting higher-order functions, and in requiring programmer-specified memory usage.

*Inductive Cases.* Burstall[2] proposed the use of an extended *ind case* notation in a functional context, to define inductive cases from inductively defined data types. Here, notation is introduced to constrain recursion to always act on a component of the "argument" to the *ind case* i.e. a component of the data type pattern on which a match is made. While *ind case* enables static confirmation of termination, Burstall's examples suggest that considerable ingenuity is required to recast terminating functions based on a laxer syntax.

*Elementary Strong Functional Programming.* Turner's *elementary strong functional programming* [20] has similarly explored issues of guaranteed termination in a purely functional programming language. Turner's approach separates finite data structures such as tuples from potentially infinite structures such as streams. This allows the definition of functions that are guaranteed to be primitive recursive. In contrast with the Hume expression layer, it is necessary to identify functions that may be more generally recursive. We will draw on Turner's experiences in developing our own termination analysis.

*Other work on Bounded Time/Space.* Also relevant to the problem of bounding time costs is recent work on *cost calculi* [16,17] and *cost modelling* [18], which has so far been primarily applied to parallel computing. In a slightly different context, *computer hardware description languages*, such as Hydra [14], also necessarily provide hard limits on time and space cost bounds, though in a framework that is less computationally based than Hume (the use of timeout exceptions to limit cost for potentially unbounded computation, and the provision of highly general forms of computation seem best suited to software rather than hardware implementation, for example). An especially interesting and relevant idea from the latter community is the use of polymorphic templates for communication channels (Hume wires), which can be specialised to monomorphic, bounded-size instances for implementation. A detailed comparison of language designs for hardware description with those for safety-critical systems should thus reveal interesting commonalities.

# 6    Conclusion

This paper has introduced the novel programming language Hume using a formal descriptive semantics. An unusual feature of this semantics is that it is integrated with a simple static time analysis for first-order programs. The semantics given here covers all essential features of the language including programs, the full coordination layer, unusual expression language features, exception handling and pattern-matching. Since the semantics is primarily intended to act as a formal *description* of Hume rather than a simple basis for a proof mechanism, we have not attempted to prove interesting properties of Hume programs. It should however, be possible to use this semantics to prove properties of the *language* such as guaranteed bounded time and space behaviour, and we have given a simple example of the use of our cost calculus to determine static bounds on program execution cost. In the longer term, we hope to be able to extend this work to deal with higher-order functions using techniques developed for costing parallel programs [9], and to provide better bounds for recursive function definitions [11]. Part of this work will involve constructing analyses to determine properties of primitive/nested recursion.

## Acknowledgements

This work has been generously supported by grants GR/L 93379, GR/M 32351 and GR/M 43272 from the UK's Engineering and Physical Science Research Council (EPSRC), and by grant 1097 from the British Council/DAAD. I am also grateful to the anonymous referees, who have made a number of useful comments and suggestions for improvement. Finally, in writing this paper, I am deeply indebted to my friend and colleague Greg Michaelson who initiated work on Hume and with whom I co-designed much of the Hume language.

## References

1. G. Blair, L. Blair, H. Bowman and A. Chetwynd, *Formal Specification of Distributed Multimedia Systems*, UCL Press, 1998.
2. R. Burstall, "Inductively Defined Functions in Functional Programming Languages", Dept. of Comp. Sci., Univ. of Edinburgh, ECS-LFCS-87-25, April, 1987.
3. K. Hammond and G.J. Michaelson, "Hume: a Functionally Inspired Language for Safety-Critical Systems", *Draft Proc. 2nd Scottish Funct. Prog. Workshop*, St Andrews, July 2000.
4. K. Hammond, "Hume: a Bounded Time Concurrent Language", *Proc. IEEE Conf. on Electronics and Control Systems (ICECS '2K)*, Kaslik, Lebanon, Dec. 2000.
5. I. Holyer and E. Spiliopoulou, "Concurrent Monadic Interfacing", *Proc. 10th. Intl. Workshop on Implementation of Functional Programming (IFL '98)*, Springer-Verlag, LNCS 1595, 1998, pp. 73–89.
6. R. Hughes, L. Pareto, and A. Sabry. "Proving the Correctness of Reactive Systems Using Sized Types", *Proc. POPL'96 — ACM Symp. on Principles of Programming Languages*, St. Petersburg Beach, FL, Jan. 1996.

7. R.J.M. Hughes and L. Pareto, "Recursion and Dynamic Data Structures in Bounded Space: Towards Embedded ML Programming", *Proc. 1999 ACM Intl. Conf. on Functional Programming (ICFP '99)*, 1999.
8. N.G. Leveson, *Safeware: System Safety and Computers*, Addison-Wesley, 1995.
9. H.-W. Loidl, A.J. Rebón Portillo and Kevin Hammond, "A Sized Time System for a Parallel Functional Language (Revised)", *Draft Proc. 2nd Scottish Funct. Prog. Workshop*, St Andrews, July 2000.
10. G.J. Michaelson and K.Hammond, "The Hume Language Definition and Report, Version 0.0", Heriot-Watt University and University of St Andrews, July 2000.
11. G.J. Michaelson, "Constraints on Recursion in the Hume Expression Language", *Draft Proc. International Workshop on Implementation of Functional Programming (IFL 2000)*, Aachen, Germany, RWTH Fachgruppe Informatik Research Report 00-7, M. Mohnen and P. Koopman (Eds.), September 2000, pp. 231–246.
12. A.J.R.G. Milner, J. Parrow and D. Walker, "A Calculus of Mobile Processes, Parts I and II", *Information and Computation*, **100**(1), 1992, pp. 1–77.
13. A.J.R.G. Milner, M. Tofte, R. Harper, and D. MacQueen, *The Definition of Standard ML (Revised)*, *MIT Press*, 1997.
14. J.T. O'Donnell, *personal communication*, September 2000.
15. *Report on the Non-Strict Functional Language, Haskell (Haskell98)* S.L. Peyton Jones (ed.), L. Augustsson, B. Boutel, F.W. Burton, J.H. Fasel, A.D. Gordon, K. Hammond, R.J.M. Hughes, P. Hudak, T. Johnsson, M.P. Jones, J.C. Peterson, A. Reid, and P.L. Wadler, Yale University, 1999.
16. B. Reistad and D.K. Gifford., "Static Dependent Costs for Estimating Execution Time", *Proc. 1994 ACM Conf. on Lisp and Functional Programming*, pp. 65–78, Orlando, Fl., June 27–29, June 1994.
17. D. Sands, "Complexity Analysis for a Lazy Higher-Order Language", *Proc. 1990 European Symp. on Prog. (ESOP '90)*, Springer-Verlag LNCS 432, May 1990.
18. D.B. Skillicorn, "Deriving Parallel Programs from Specifications using Cost Information", *Science of Computer Programming*, **20**(3), June 1993.
19. M. Tofte and J.-P. Talpin, "Region-based Memory Management", *Information and Control*, **132**(2), 1997, pp. 109–176.
20. D.A. Turner, "Elementary Strong Functional Programming", *Proc. Symp. on Funct. Prog. Langs. in Education — FPLE '95*, Springer-Verlag LNCS No. 1022, Dec. 1995.

# A Usage Analysis with Bounded Usage Polymorphism and Subtyping

Jörgen Gustavsson and Josef Svenningsson

Chalmers University of Technology and Göteborg University

**Abstract.** Usage analysis aims to predict the number of times a heap allocated closure is used. Previously proposed usage analyses have proved not to scale up well to large programs. In this paper we present a powerful and accurate type based analysis designed to scale up for large programs. The key features of the type system are usage subtyping and bounded usage polymorphism. Bounded polymorphism can lead to huge constraint sets so to express constraints compactly we introduce a new expressive form of constraints which allows constraints to be represented compactly through calls to *constraint abstractions*.

## 1 Introduction

In the implementation of a lazy functional language sharing of evaluation is performed by updating. For example, the (unoptimised) evaluation of

$$(\lambda x.x + x)\,(1 + 2)$$

proceeds as follows. First, a closure for $1 + 2$ is built in the heap and a reference to the closure is passed to the abstraction. Second, to evaluate $x + x$ the value of $x$ is required. Thus the closure is fetched from the heap and evaluated. Third, the closure is updated with the result so that when the value of $x$ is required again the expression needs not be recomputed.

Measurements by Marlow show that 70% of all closures are used at most once and that it is therefore unnecessary to update them. Usage information also enables a series of program transformations such as more aggressive inlining and let-floating [TWM95,WPJ99,GS99]. It is therefore no surprise that considerable effort has been put into static analyses that can discover if a closure is used at most once [Ses91,LGH+92,Mar93,TWM95,Fax95,BJ96,Mog97,Gus98,WPJ99]. This line of research has produced analyses with increasing accuracy, and benchmarks have shown that for small programs they discover a large portion of closures used at most once. However these analyses are monovariant and do not take the context where a function is called into account. When analysing large programs it is crucial to take the context into account – when Wansbrough and Peyton Jones implemented the recent analysis from [WPJ99] into the Glasgow Haskell Compiler they discovered that it was almost useless in practice since it did not scale up for large programs. [WPJ00].

M. Mohnen and P. Koopman (Eds.): IFL 2000, LNCS 2011, pp. 140–157, 2001.

In this paper we present a powerful and accurate type system which attempts to solve this problem. It takes the context where a function is called into account through bounded usage polymorphism. We designed our type system by putting together and extending the best ideas from previous work. The salient features of the type system are these:

- Our system has full-blown bounded usage polymorphism and supports usage polymorhic recursion.
- In [WPJ98] Wansbrough and Peyton Jones give an overview of the design space for how to treat data structures. We choose the most aggressive approach which corresponds to the hard-wired treatment of lists in [TWM95].
- Our system is based on subsumption between usage types. The use of subtyping in usage analysis goes back to Faxén [Fax95].
- We have a three-level type language which incorporates separate notions of usage of closures and usage of values which gives increased precision. To separate the usage of closures and values is an idea due to Faxén [Fax95].
- We have expressive update annotations which allow us to express more aggressive optimisations than previous analyses.

Having all these features is not very useful unless there is an efficient inference algorithm for the type system. Here bounded polymorphism presents a problem. See for example Mossin's thesis [Mos97] for an account of the problems with bounded flow polymorphism in type based flow analyses. The core of the problem is that the quantified variables in a type schema may be constrained by a huge number of constraints. In the naive inference algorithm first presented by Mossin the number of constraints may be exponential in the size of the program. Mossin refines the algorithm by adding a constraint simplification phase which renders an inference algorithm which is $O(n^7)$.

A novelty in our work is a new expressive form of constraints which allows constraints to be represented compactly through calls to *constraint abstractions*. To efficiently compute least solutions to constraints with constraint abstractions is an involved problem and is the subject of a companion paper [GS01]. There we show how to efficiently compute a least solution to constraints in a constraint language with constraint abstractions and inequality constraints over a lattice. Using these techniques we can obtain an inference algorithm for our usage analysis which is $O(n^3)$ where $n$ is the size of the explicitly typed program. We believe that constraint abstractions can be very useful for a range of program analyses which features bounded annotation polymorphism and in [GS01] we show how to apply the ideas to a flow analysis with bounded flow polymorphism. Other candidates may be effect analysis, e.g., [TJ94], binding time analysis, e.g., [DHM95], non determinism analysis, e.g., [PS00] and uniqueness type systems, e.g., [BS96].

## 1.1 Outline

This paper is organised as follows. Section 2 introduces the language and its semantics. Section 3 presents the type system. Section 4 describes related work. Section 5 concludes.

# 2  Language

In this section we will present our language and its semantics in the form of an abstract machine.

## 2.1  Syntax

The language we use is a lambda calculus extended with integers, lists, case-expressions and recursive let-expressions. We omit user defined data structures to simplify the presentation but it is a straightforward matter to add them [Sve00].

| Variables | $x, y, z$ |
|---|---|
| Values | $v ::= \lambda x.e \mid n \mid \mathtt{nil} \mid \mathtt{cons}\ x\ y$ |
| Expressions | $e ::= v^\kappa \mid x \mid e\ x \mid e_0 +^\kappa e_1 \mid \mathtt{let}\ b_1, \ldots, b_n\ \mathtt{in}\ e \mid \mathtt{case}\ e\ \mathtt{of}\ alts$ |
| Bindings | $b ::= x =^\kappa e$ |
| Alternatives $alts$ | $::= \{\mathtt{nil} \Rightarrow e_0; \mathtt{cons}\ x\ y \Rightarrow e_1\}$ |
| Annotations | $\kappa ::= 1 \mid \omega$ |

We annotate bindings, values and $+$ with usage annotations 1 and $\omega$ ranged over by $\kappa$. The intuitive meaning of 1 and $\omega$ is that the annotated binding (or value) may be used at most once and any number of times respectively.

A distinguishing feature of the syntax is that arguments (in applications of terms and constructors) are restricted to variables. We will occasionally use unrestricted application $e_0\ e_1$ as syntactic sugar for $\mathtt{let}\ x =^\omega e_1\ \mathtt{in}\ e_0\ x$ where $x$ is a fresh variable. The purpose of the restricted syntax is to make the creation of closures explicit via a let-expression which greatly simplifies the presentation of the abstract machine as well as the analysis presented in this paper. The syntactic restriction is by now rather standard, see for example [PJPS96,Lau93,Ses97,GS99].

## 2.2  Semantics

We will take Sestoft's abstract machine [Ses97] as the semantic basis of our work. The machine can be thought of as modelling lower-level abstract machines based on so called update markers, such as the TIM [FW87] and the STG-machine [PJ92]. A correspondence between Sestoft's machine and Launchbury's natural semantics for lazy evaluation [Lau93] has been shown in [Ses97]. For the purpose of the abstract machine we extend the set of terms to include expressions of the form $\mathtt{add}_n^\kappa\ e$, which represents an intermediate step in the computation of $n^{\kappa'} +^\kappa e$. We define a reduction relation $e \mapsto e'$ between terms:

$$(\lambda x.e)^\kappa\ y \mapsto e[x := y] \qquad n^{\kappa'} +^\kappa e \mapsto \mathtt{add}_n^\kappa\ e \qquad \mathtt{add}_{n_0}^\kappa\ n_1^{\kappa'} \mapsto \lceil n_0 + n_1 \rceil^\kappa$$

$$\begin{pmatrix} \mathtt{case}\ \mathtt{nil}^\kappa\ \mathtt{of} \\ \mathtt{nil} \Rightarrow e_0 \\ \mathtt{cons}\ x'\ y' \Rightarrow e_1 \end{pmatrix} \mapsto e_0 \qquad \begin{pmatrix} \mathtt{case}\ (\mathtt{cons}\ x\ y)^\kappa\ \mathtt{of} \\ \mathtt{nil} \Rightarrow e_0 \\ \mathtt{cons}\ x'\ y' \Rightarrow e_1 \end{pmatrix} \mapsto e_1[x' := x, y' := y]$$

$$\langle H \,;\, \texttt{let}\ \vec{b}\ \texttt{in}\ e \,;\, S \rangle \overset{\text{Let}}{\longmapsto} \langle H, \vec{b} \,;\, e \,;\, S \rangle$$

$$\langle H, x =^{\omega} e \,;\, x \,;\, S \rangle \overset{\text{Var-}\omega}{\longmapsto} \langle H \,;\, e \,;\, \#x, S \rangle$$

$$\langle H, x =^{1} e \,;\, x \,;\, S \rangle \overset{\text{Var-}1}{\longmapsto} \langle H \,;\, e \,;\, S \rangle$$

$$\langle H \,;\, R[e] \,;\, S \rangle \overset{\text{Unwind}}{\longmapsto} \langle H \,;\, e \,;\, R, S \rangle$$

$$\langle H \,;\, v^{\kappa} \,;\, R, S \rangle \overset{\text{Reduce}}{\longmapsto} \langle H \,;\, e \,;\, S \rangle \quad \text{if } R[v^{\kappa}] \mapsto e$$

$$\langle H \,;\, v^{\omega} \,;\, \#x, S \rangle \overset{\text{Marker-}\omega}{\longmapsto} \langle H, x =^{\omega} v^{\omega} \,;\, v^{\omega} \,;\, S \rangle$$

$$\langle H \,;\, v^{1} \,;\, \#x, S \rangle \overset{\text{Marker-}1}{\longmapsto} \langle H \,;\, v^{1} \,;\, S \rangle$$

**Fig. 1.** Abstract machine transition rules

Note that no reduction depends on an annotation. The annotations are instead taken into account in the abstract machine transition rules.

Configurations in the abstract machine are triples $\langle H \,;\, e \,;\, S \rangle$, where $H$ is a heap, $e$ is the term currently being evaluated and $S$ is the abstract machine stack:

| Heaps | $H ::= b_1, \dots, b_n$ |
|---|---|
| Stacks | $S ::= \epsilon \mid R, S \mid \#x, S$ |
| Reduction contexts | $R ::= [\cdot]\, x \mid [\cdot] +^{\kappa} e \mid \texttt{add}_n^{\kappa}\, [\cdot] \mid \texttt{case}\, [\cdot]\, \texttt{of}\ alts$ |

A heap consists of a sequence of bindings. The variables bound by the heap must be distinct and the order of bindings is irrelevant. Thus a heap can be considered as a partial function mapping variables to terms and we will write $\text{dom}(H)$ for the set of variables bound by $H$. We will write $H_0, H_1$ for the concatenation of $H_0$ and $H_1$. An abstract machine stack is a stack of shallow reduction contexts and update markers. The stack can be thought of as corresponding to the "surrounding derivation" in a natural semantics, where the rôle of an update marker $\#x$ is to keep track of a pending update of $x$. The update markers on the stack will be distinct, that is there will be no more than one pending update of the same variable. We will consider an update marker as a binder and we will write $\text{dom}(S)$ for the variables bound by the update markers in $S$. Consequently, we will require the variables bound by the stack to be distinct from the variables bound by the heap. We will also require that configurations are closed and we will identify configurations up to $\alpha$-conversion, that is renaming of the variables bound by the heap and the stack. We will also identify configurations up to garbage meaning that we may remove or add bindings and update markers to the heap as long as the configuration remains closed. An initial configuration is of the form $\langle \epsilon \,;\, e \,;\, \epsilon \rangle$, where $e$ is a closed expression. The transition rules of the abstract machine are given in Figure 1. The rule Let

$$\langle H \,;\, \texttt{let}\ \vec{b}\ \texttt{in}\ e \,;\, S \rangle \overset{\text{Let}}{\longmapsto} \langle H, \vec{b} \,;\, e \,;\, S \rangle$$

creates new bindings in the heap. For the rule to be applied the variables bound by $\vec{b}$ must be distinct from the variables bound by $H$ and $S$. This condition can always be met simply by $\alpha$-converting the let-expression. The rule Var-$\omega$

$$\langle H, x =^\omega e \; ; \; x \; ; \; S \rangle \overset{\text{Var-}\omega}{\longmapsto} \langle H \; ; \; e \; ; \; \#x, S \rangle$$

gives semantics to bindings annotated with $\omega$. The rule states that an update marker shall be pushed onto the stack so that the variable $x$ eventually may be updated with the result of evaluating $e$. The removal of the binding corresponds to so called black-holing: if the evaluation of $e$ to a value depends on $x$ (i.e., $x$ depends directly on itself) the computation will get stuck, since $x$ is no longer bound by the heap. Note that we still consider the configuration to be closed, since $x$ is bound by the update marker on the stack. The rule Var-1

$$\langle H, x =^1 e \; ; \; x \; ; \; S \rangle \overset{\text{Var-1}}{\longmapsto} \langle H \; ; \; e \; ; \; S \rangle$$

gives semantics to bindings annotated with 1. Such bindings may only be used once so there is no need to update the binding and thus no update marker is pushed onto the stack. Note that we require configurations to be closed so the rule does not apply unless the configuration remains closed. An example of where the rule does not apply is the configuration

$$\langle x =^1 1 +^\omega 2 \; ; \; x \; ; \; [\cdot] +^\kappa x, \epsilon \rangle$$

which cannot reduce further since there is a reference to $x$ on the stack. This restriction is important since an open configuration would correspond to dangling pointers in an implementation. If the rule does not apply the computation will go *wrong*, and we will consider the configuration and the term it originates from to be ill-annotated. The key property of the type system presented in this paper is that if a term is well-typed then it cannot go wrong. Note that, the insistence that configurations remain closed is a stronger requirement than the intuitive "used at most once" criterion, which says that it is safe to avoid updating a closure if it is used at most once. For example, according to the weaker criterion it is safe to not update $x$ in

$$\texttt{let } x = 1 + 2 \texttt{ in } x + (\lambda y.3) \, x$$

because $x$ is only used once, but according to our criterion it is not safe. Our stronger criterion is useful for two reasons. Firstly, with dangling pointers special care has to be taken so that the garbage collector does not follow them – and there is a cost associated with that. Secondly, usage annotations can be used to justify certain program transformations, such as more aggressive inlining. Gustavsson and Sands [GS99] have shown that the stronger criterion can guarantee that these transformations are time and space safe, but with the weaker "used at most once" criterion the transformations can lead to an asymptoticly worse space behaviour. The rule Unwind

$$\langle H \; ; \; R[e] \; ; \; S \rangle \overset{\text{Unwind}}{\longmapsto} \langle H \; ; \; e \; ; \; R, S \rangle$$

allows us to get to the heart of the evaluation by "unwinding" a shallow reduction context. When the term to be evaluated is a value the next transition depends on whether an update marker or a reduction context is on top of the stack. If it is a reduction context the rule Reduce

$$\langle H \ ; \ v \ ; \ R, S\rangle \overset{\text{Reduce}}{\longmapsto} \langle H \ ; \ e \ ; \ S\rangle \quad \text{if } R[v] \mapsto e$$

applies, the value is plugged into the reduction context and a reduction can take place. If the top of the stack is an update marker, what happens depends on the annotation on the value. If it is $\omega$ the value may be used several times and we apply the rule Update-$\omega$

$$\langle H \ ; \ v^{\omega} \ ; \ \#x, S\rangle \overset{\text{Marker-}\omega}{\longmapsto} \langle H, x =^{\omega} v^{\omega} \ ; \ v^{\omega} \ ; \ S\rangle$$

which takes care of the update marker and performs the update. If the value on the other hand is annotated with 1, the value may only be used once so the rule Update-1

$$\langle H \ ; \ v^{1} \ ; \ \#x, S\rangle \overset{\text{Marker-1}}{\longmapsto} \langle H \ ; \ v^{1} \ ; \ S\rangle$$

throws away the marker without performing the update. Again, note that the rule does not apply unless the configuration remains closed. So, for example,

$$\langle \epsilon \ ; \ 3^{1} \ ; \ \#x, [\cdot] +^{\kappa} x, \epsilon\rangle$$

goes wrong and we consider the configuration to be ill-annotated.

## 3   Type System

The semantics in Section 2 specifies that for a binding $x = e$ to be safely annotated with a 1 it is required that whenever the binding is used through the rule

$$\langle H, x =^{1} e \ ; \ x \ ; \ S\rangle \overset{\text{Var-1}}{\longmapsto} \langle H \ ; \ e \ ; \ S\rangle,$$

the configuration must remain closed. Thus there may only be one (non-binding) occurrence of $x$ in the configuration, namely the one that is dereferenced. Similarly, to safely annotate a value with 1 it is required that if and when the value is used and there is an update marker $\#x$ on the stack

$$\langle H \ ; \ v^{1} \ ; \ \#x, S\rangle \overset{\text{Marker-1}}{\longmapsto} \langle H \ ; \ v^{1} \ ; \ S\rangle \quad ,$$

then there is no live occurrence of $x$ in the configuration so that the configuration remains closed. Our type system (and most other type based usage analyses) is based on the following simple idea. If, when a binding $x = e$ is created, $x$ occurs only once in the configuration and $x$ never gets duplicated during the computation then $x$ will occur only once if and when it is dereferenced. [1]

---

[1]   We will strengthen this idea in an obvious but important way – when a variable occurs once in several branches of a case-expression. Then, since eventually only one branch will be taken, we may consider it as occurring only once.

## 3.1   Type Language

In order to construct a type system for the annotated language we need a corresponding annotated type language. We start by extending the annotation language from the previous section to include annotation variables.

$$\text{Annotations } \kappa ::= 1 \mid \omega \mid k \mid j$$

We will use two kinds of variables, *type annotation variables*, ranged over by $k$, and *program annotation variables*, ranged over by $j$. Type annotation variables may occur in the annotations on a type but not in the annotations on a program. Conversely, program annotation variables may occur in programs but not in types.

The structure of the type language closely follows the structure of the term language and we will have one kind of type for every syntactic category. We let $\rho$ range over *value types* which is the form of type we will assign to values.

$$\text{Type Variables } a$$
$$\text{Value Types} \quad \rho ::= a \mid \text{Int} \mid \sigma \to \tau \mid \text{List } \kappa_0 \, \kappa_1 \, \kappa_2 \, \kappa_3 \, \rho$$

Our value types contains type variables, an integer type, function types and the list type. The function types relies on a notion of *binding types*, ranged over by $\sigma$, and *expression types*, ranged over by $\tau$, which we will introduce below. Expression types are used to give types to expressions and are defined as follows.

$$\text{Expression Types } \tau ::= \rho^\kappa$$

An annotated value $v^\kappa$ will be given a type of the form $\rho^\kappa$ and a non-value $e$ will be given a type such that the annotated value of $e$ (if $e$ terminates) will have that type. Thus, for example, saying that a term has a type $\rho^\omega$ means that the value of the term may be used any number of times. Binding types which we will use to give a type to bindings are defined as follows.

$$\text{Binding Types } \sigma ::= \tau_\kappa$$

A binding $x =^\kappa e$ may be given a type of the form $\tau_\kappa$ where $\tau$ is the type of $e$. We also use binding types to give a type to a variable when we can think of the variable as a reference, for example when we pass it as an argument to a function. A type of a variable is then simply the type of the bindings it may refer to. Recall that we used expression types and binding types in the type $\sigma \to \tau$ of a function. A function of this type can be applied to a variable (remember functions can only be applied to variables due to the syntactic restriction in our language) with the binding type $\sigma$ and then it will return something of type $\tau$. We can also use binding types to logically justify our type $\text{List } \kappa_0 \, \kappa_1 \, \kappa_2 \, \kappa_3 \, \rho$ of lists. We can obtain this type simply by annotating the right hand side of the data type definition

$$\text{List } a = \text{nil} \mid \text{cons } a \, (\text{List } a)$$

such that the arguments to the constructors are binding types, as follows.

$$\texttt{List } k_0\, k_1\, k_2\, k_3\, a = \texttt{nil} \mid \texttt{cons}\; a_{k_0}^{k_1}\; (\texttt{List } k_0\, k_1\, k_2\, k_3\, a)_{k_2}^{k_3}$$

The reason for why the arguments to the constructors should be binding types is simply because constructors, due to the syntactic restriction, may be applied only to variables.

## 3.2   Subtyping

A key observation which we will use to justify our subtyping relation is that 1 operationally approximates $\omega$, i.e., if we in any term $e$ replace any occurrence of 1 with $\omega$ then the modified term will run successfully without going wrong if and when $e$ does. We define the subtyping relation on *closed* types where the ordering on annotations is the operational approximation $1 < \omega$ by the following rules.

$$\frac{\sigma' \leq \sigma \qquad \tau \leq \tau'}{\sigma \to \tau \leq \sigma' \to \tau'} \qquad \frac{\rho_{\kappa_0}^{\kappa_1} \leq \rho'^{\kappa_1'}_{\kappa_0'} \qquad \kappa_2' \leq \kappa_2 \qquad \kappa_3' \leq \kappa_3}{\texttt{List } \kappa_0\, \kappa_1\, \kappa_2\, \kappa_3\, \rho \leq \texttt{List } \kappa_0'\, \kappa_1'\, \kappa_2'\, \kappa_3'\, \rho'}$$

$$\frac{}{\texttt{Int} \leq \texttt{Int}} \qquad \frac{\rho \leq \rho' \qquad \kappa' \leq \kappa}{\rho^\kappa \leq \rho'^{\kappa'}} \qquad \frac{\tau \leq \tau' \qquad \kappa' \leq \kappa}{\tau_\kappa \leq \tau'_{\kappa'}}$$

Note that the subtype ordering is contravariant with respect to the ordering on the annotations. The rule for lists can be understood by unfolding the annotated data type definition for lists.

## 3.3   Constraints

In order to extend the subtyping relation to types with type variables and annotation variables we need the notion of constraints. To be able to represents constraints compactly we introduce a new form of constraints which may contain calls to *constraint abstractions*. A constraint abstraction is simply a function that given some annotation variables returns a constraint. We will let $\phi$ range over constraint abstractions, $l$ range over constraint abstraction variables and $\Pi$ range over constraints.

Annotation constraints $\Pi ::= \kappa_0 \leq \kappa_1 \mid \Pi_0, \Pi_1 \mid \texttt{let } \vec{\phi} \texttt{ in } \Pi \mid \exists \vec{k}.\Pi \mid l\, \vec{\kappa}$

Constraint abstractions $\phi ::= l\, \vec{k} = \Pi$

Constraint abstractions allow different substitution instances of a constraint to share the same representation. For example to represent instances of the constraints $k_0 \leq k_1$, $k_1 \leq k_2$ we can define an abstraction

$$l\, k_0\, k_1\, k_2 = k_0 \leq k_1,\ k_1 \leq k_2$$

and represent $(\kappa_0 \leq \kappa_1,\ \kappa_1 \leq \kappa_2), (\kappa_3 \leq \kappa_4,\ \kappa_4 \leq \kappa_5)$ as

$$\texttt{let } l\, k_0\, k_1\, k_2 = k_0 \leq k_1,\ k_1 \leq k_2 \texttt{ in } l\, \kappa_0\, \kappa_1\, \kappa_2,\ l\, \kappa_3\, \kappa_4\, \kappa_5.$$

Thus with constraint abstractions the size of any instance is linear in the number of free type annotation variables of the constraint but the size of the original constraint may be quadratic in the sum of the number of free type annotation variables and free program annotation variables (or even worse if it contains existential quantifiers). With constraint abstraction we can avoid the exponential explosion of constraints which can happen with a naive approach. To see why consider a program of the following form.

$$
\begin{aligned}
&\text{let } f_0 = \ldots \\
&\text{in let } f_1 = \ldots f_0 \ldots f_0 \ldots \\
&\quad \text{in let } \ldots \\
&\qquad \text{in let } f_n = \ldots f_{n-1} \ldots f_{n-1} \ldots \\
&\qquad \quad \text{in } \ldots f_n \ldots f_n \ldots
\end{aligned}
$$

The first naive algorithm, for the similar problem of flow analysis with bounded flow polymorphism, presented by Mossin [Mos97] which suffers from the exponential explosion problem would proceed as follows. It first infers the polymorphic type for $f_0$. Then to compute the type for $f_1$ it instantiates the type of $f_0$ twice and thus make two instances of the constraints contained in the type schema so the constraints for $f_1$ will be at least twice as big. This is repeated $n$ times and thus the size of the resulting constraints will be exponential in the call depth $n$. In practice the call depth typically does not grow linearly with the size of the program but the call depth does tend to increase with program size which makes this into a problem that occurs in practice. With constraint abstractions we can avoid the problem and represent the constraints as follows

$$
\begin{aligned}
&\text{let } l_0 \, \vec{k}_0 = \ldots \\
&\text{in let } l_1 \, \vec{k}_1 = \ldots l_0 \, \vec{k}_0' \ldots l_0 \, \vec{k}_0'' \ldots \\
&\quad \text{in let } \ldots \\
&\qquad \text{in let } l_n \, \vec{k}_n = \ldots l_{n-1} \, \vec{k}_{n-1}' \ldots l_{n-1} \, \vec{k}_{n-1}'' \ldots \\
&\qquad \quad \text{in } \ldots l_n \, \vec{k}_0' \ldots l_n \, \vec{k}_0'' \ldots
\end{aligned}
$$

To give semantics to constraints we will use closing substitutions from type variables to value types and annotation variables to annotations, ranged over by $\vartheta$. The meaning of a constraint $\Pi$ is given by a relation $\vartheta; \vec{\phi} \models \Pi$ (read as $\vartheta; \vec{\phi}$ models $\Pi$) defined coinductively by the following rules.

$$
\frac{\kappa_0 \vartheta \leq \kappa_1 \vartheta}{\vartheta; \vec{\phi} \models \kappa_0 \leq \kappa_1} \qquad \frac{\vartheta; \vec{\phi} \models \Pi_0 \quad \vartheta; \vec{\phi} \models \Pi_1}{\vartheta; \vec{\phi} \models \Pi_0, \Pi_1} \qquad \frac{\vartheta; \vec{\phi}, \vec{\phi}' \models \Pi}{\vartheta; \vec{\phi} \models \text{let } \vec{\phi}' \text{ in } \Pi}
$$

$$
\frac{\vartheta; \vec{\phi} \models \Pi[\vec{k} := \vec{\kappa}]}{\vartheta; \vec{\phi} \models \exists \vec{k}.\Pi} \qquad \frac{\vartheta; \vec{\phi} \models \Pi[\vec{k} := \vec{\kappa}]}{\vartheta; \vec{\phi} \models l \, \vec{\kappa}} \quad l \, \vec{k} = \Pi \in \vec{\phi}
$$

We will sometimes write $\vartheta \models \Pi$ as a shorthand for $\vartheta; \epsilon \models \Pi$. We will let $\Psi$ range over constraints concerning type variables.

$$
\text{Type variable constraints } \Psi ::= a_0 \leq a_1 \mid \Psi_0, \Psi_1 \mid \exists \vec{a}.\Psi
$$

The meaning of a constraint $\Psi$ is given by a relation $\vartheta \models \Psi$ (read as $\vartheta$ models $\Psi$). We define $\vartheta \models \Psi$ inductively by the following rules.

$$\frac{\vartheta(a_0) \leq \vartheta(a_1)}{\vartheta \models a_0 \leq a_1} \qquad \frac{\vartheta \models \Psi_0 \quad \vartheta \models \Psi_1}{\vartheta \models \Psi_0, \Psi_1} \qquad \frac{\vartheta[\vec{a} := \vec{\rho}] \models \Psi}{\vartheta \models \exists \vec{a}.\Psi}$$

We will let $\Theta$ range over pairs $\Pi; \Psi$ and we define $\vartheta \models \Theta$ as $\vartheta \models \Pi; \Psi$ iff $\vartheta \models \Pi$ and $\vartheta \models \Psi$. The whole purpose of having constraints is that they allow us to extend the subtyping relation to types with variables. We will define a relation $\Theta \models \rho_0 \leq \rho_1$ where $\rho_0$ and $\rho_1$ may be open types, which reads: $\rho_0 \leq \rho_1$ is a consequence of $\Theta$. It is defined as $\Theta \models \rho_0 \leq \rho_1$ iff for every $\vartheta$, if $\vartheta \models \Theta$ then $\rho_0 \vartheta \leq \rho_1 \vartheta$. We also define $\Theta \models \tau_0 \leq \tau_1$ and $\Theta \models \sigma_0 \leq \sigma_1$ in the same manner.

## 3.4    Type Schemas

Our type system incorporates bounded polymorphism so we need type schemas where the quantified variables are bounded by some constraints.

$$\text{Type Schemas } \chi ::= \forall \vec{k}, \vec{a}. \, \rho \mid \Theta$$

We will define a relation $\Theta \models \chi \prec \rho$ which reads as: it is a consequence of $\Theta$ that $\chi$ can be instantiated to $\rho$. It is defined as $\Theta \models (\forall \vec{k}, \vec{a}. \, \rho \mid \Theta') \prec \rho[\vec{k} := \vec{\kappa}, \vec{a} := \vec{\rho}]$ iff for every $\vartheta$, if $\vartheta \models \Theta$ then $\vartheta \circ [\vec{k} := \vec{\kappa}, \vec{a} := \vec{\rho}] \models \Theta'$. We will sometimes consider a value type $\rho$ to be a type schema with no quantified variables and no constraints.

## 3.5    Contexts

We use $\Gamma$ and $\Delta$ to range over typing contexts which are multisets of type associations of the form $x : \chi_\kappa^{\kappa'}$ (and since we may consider a value type $\rho$ as a type schema there may also be type associations of the form $x : \rho_\kappa^{\kappa'}$). As usual we will use contexts when we give a type to a term with free variables. Thus we will say that $e$ has the type $\tau$ in a context $\Gamma$ if we can give $e$ the type $\tau$ assuming that the free variables in $e$ has the types given by $\Gamma$. However the context also plays another important rôle; it records the number of times each variable occurs in the term. Thus if $x$ occurs $n$ times in $e$ it also occurs $n$ times in $\Gamma$ (with one important exception, namely if $x$ occurs in different branches of a case-expression). This may be a bit surprising at first. Consider for example the term $(\lambda y.y +^1 y)^1 \, x$ with the free variable $x$. We will be able to say that this term has the type $\text{Int}^1$ in the context $x : \text{Int}_\omega^\omega$. According to the reduction relation the term can reduce to $x +^1 x$ so we would expect to be able to give $x +^1 x$ the same type in the same context. However this will not be possible since $x$ now occurs twice in the term. Instead we can type the term in the context $x : \text{Int}_\omega^\omega, x : \text{Int}_\omega^\omega$ where $x$ occurs twice. To be able to state a relation between the contexts before and after a reduction we define a rewrite relation on contexts.

$$\Gamma, x : \chi_\omega^\omega \to \Gamma, x : \chi_\omega^\omega, x : \chi_\omega^\omega \qquad \Gamma, x : \chi_\kappa^{\kappa'} \to \Gamma$$

$$\text{Abs} \frac{\Theta; \Gamma_0, \Gamma_1 \vdash e : \tau \qquad x \notin \text{dom}(\Gamma_0)}{\Theta; \Gamma_0 \vdash \lambda x.e : \sigma \to \tau \qquad \Theta \models x : \sigma \to^* \Gamma_1}$$

$$\text{Int} \frac{}{\Theta; \emptyset \vdash n : \text{Int}} \qquad \text{Nil} \frac{}{\Theta; \emptyset \vdash \text{nil} : \text{List } \kappa_0 \; \kappa_1 \; \kappa_2 \; \kappa_3 \; \rho}$$

$$\text{Cons} \frac{}{\Theta; x : \chi_{0 \kappa_0}^{\kappa_1}, y : \chi_{1 \kappa_2}^{\kappa_3} \vdash \text{cons } x \; y : \rho'} \qquad \begin{array}{l} \rho' \equiv \text{List } \kappa_4 \; \kappa_5 \; \kappa_6 \; \kappa_7 \; \rho \\ \Theta \models \chi_0 \prec \rho_0, \; \chi_1 \prec \rho_1 \\ \Theta \models \rho_{0 \kappa_0}^{\kappa_1} \leq \rho_{\kappa_4}^{\kappa_5}, \; \rho_{1 \kappa_2}^{\kappa_3} \leq \rho'_{\kappa_6}^{\kappa_7} \end{array}$$

**Fig. 2.** Typing rules for values

We have two rewrite rules. The first says that a type association of the form $x : \chi_\omega^\omega$ may be duplicated. This is supposed to model the duplication of a variable $x$ during the computation. Note that we may not duplicate a type association of the form $x : \chi_1^1$. This reflects our intention that a variable that refers to a binding which will not be updated, must not be duplicated. The second rule simply allows us to remove a type association. This corresponds to the case when a variable is dropped during the computation (for example since it occurred in a branch of a case-expression that was not selected). These rewrite rules will play a rôle similar to the contraction and weakening rules in logic. The restricted duplication (i.e., that we may only duplicate type associations of the form $x : \chi_\omega^\omega$) corresponds to the restricted form of contraction in linear logic [Gir87]. We extend the relation to contexts with open types in the same way as with the subtyping relation by defining $\Theta \models \Gamma_0 \to^* \Gamma_1$ iff for every $\vartheta$, if $\vartheta \models \Theta$ then $\Gamma_0 \vartheta \to^* \Gamma_1 \vartheta$. Finally we will also need the relation $\Theta \models \text{if } \kappa = \omega \text{ then } \Gamma \to^* \Gamma, \Gamma$ which holds iff for every $\vartheta$, if $\vartheta \models \Theta$, and $\kappa \vartheta = \omega$ then $\Gamma \vartheta \to^* \Gamma \vartheta, \Gamma \vartheta$.

### 3.6 Typing Judgements

Typing judgements for values take the form $\Theta; \Gamma \vdash v : \rho$ and shall be read: under the constraints $\Theta$ and in the context $\Gamma$, the value $v$ can be given the value type $\rho$. Similarly we will have typing judgements for expressions, alternatives and bindings. As discussed in the previous section the context $\Gamma$ in our judgements as usual keeps track of the types of the free variables in the term but it also records the number of times each variable occurs in the term.

### 3.7 Typing Rules

The typing rules for values are in Figure 2. The key feature of the rule Abs

$$\frac{\Theta; \Gamma_0, \Gamma_1 \vdash e : \tau \qquad x \notin \text{dom}(\Gamma_0)}{\Theta; \Gamma_0 \vdash \lambda x.e : \sigma \to \tau \qquad \Theta \models x : \sigma \to^* \Gamma_1}$$

is that if $x$ occurs more than once in $e$ then the abstraction will be assigned a type of the form $\rho_{\kappa'}^\kappa \to \tau$ where $\kappa$ and $\kappa'$ are constrained to be $\omega$ indicating that a

$$\text{Value}\frac{\Theta;\Gamma\vdash v:\rho\qquad\Theta\models\text{if }\kappa'=\omega\text{ then }\Gamma\rightarrow^*\Gamma,\Gamma}{\Theta;\Gamma\vdash v^\kappa:\rho^{\kappa'}\qquad\Theta\models\kappa'\leq\kappa}$$

$$\text{Var}\frac{}{\Theta;x:\chi^{\kappa_1}_{\kappa_0}\vdash x:\tau}\quad\frac{\Theta\models\chi\prec\rho}{\Theta\models\rho^{\kappa_1}\leq\tau}\qquad\text{App}\frac{\Theta;\Gamma\vdash e:(\rho^{\kappa_0}_{\kappa_1}\rightarrow\tau)^\kappa}{\Theta;\Gamma,x:\chi^{\kappa_0}_{\kappa_1}\vdash e\,x:\tau}\quad\Theta\models\chi\prec\rho$$

$$\text{Plus}\frac{\Theta;\Gamma_0\vdash e_0:\text{Int}^{\kappa_0}\qquad\Theta;\Gamma_1\vdash e_1:\text{Int}^{\kappa_1}}{\Theta;\Gamma_0,\Gamma_1\vdash e_0+^\kappa e_1:\text{Int}^{\kappa'}}\quad\Theta\models\kappa'\leq\kappa$$

$$\text{Alts}\frac{\Theta;\Gamma_0,\Gamma_1\vdash e_0:\tau\qquad\Theta;\Gamma_0,\Gamma_2,\Gamma_3\vdash e_1:\tau}{\Theta;\Gamma_0,\Gamma_1,\Gamma_2\vdash\{\text{nil}\Rightarrow e_0;\text{cons }x\,y\Rightarrow e_1\}:\rho'\Rightarrow\tau}\quad\begin{array}{l}\rho'\equiv\text{List }\kappa_0\,\kappa_1\,\kappa_2\,\kappa_3\,\rho\\x,y\notin\text{dom}(\Gamma_0,\Gamma_2)\\\Theta\models x:\rho^{\kappa_1}_{\kappa_0},y:\rho'^{\kappa_3}_{\kappa_2}\rightarrow^*\Gamma_3\end{array}$$

$$\text{Case}\frac{\Theta;\Gamma_0\vdash e:\rho^\kappa\qquad\Theta;\Gamma_1\vdash alts:\rho\Rightarrow\tau}{\Theta;\Gamma_0,\Gamma_1\vdash\text{case }e\text{ of }alts:\tau}$$

**Fig. 3.** Typing rules for expressions

variable will be duplicated if it is passed to the abstraction. This is accomplished by first typing $e$ in a context $\Gamma_0,\Gamma_1$ where $x\notin\text{dom}(\Gamma_0)$. Then, if $x$ occurs more than once in $e$, $x$ will occur more than once in $\Gamma_1$. Now the second side condition specify that we must be able to rewrite $x:\rho^\kappa_{\kappa'}$ to $\Gamma_1$ which clearly involves duplicating $x:\rho^\kappa_{\kappa'}$ (since $x$ occurs more than once in $\Gamma_1$) which will constrain $\kappa$ and $\kappa'$ to be $\omega$. The typing rule for integers is straightforward and the rules for lists can be understood by unfolding the annotated data type definition for lists.

We have divided the typing rules for expressions into two figures. Most rules appear in Figure 3 but the rules which concern let expressions are in Figure 4. The rule Value

$$\frac{\Theta;\Gamma\vdash v:\rho\qquad\Theta\models\text{if }\kappa'=\omega\text{ then }\Gamma\rightarrow^*\Gamma,\Gamma}{\Theta;\Gamma\vdash v^\kappa:\rho^{\kappa'}\qquad\Theta\models\kappa'\leq\kappa}$$

is used to type an annotated value. Saying that an annotated value has the type $\rho^{\kappa'}$ means that if $\kappa'$ is $\omega$ the value may be used any number of times and thus it will take care of any update marker on the stack. Taking care of an update marker means updating with the value, thus duplicating any free variables of the value. The purpose of the side condition $\Theta\models\text{if }\kappa'=\omega\text{ then }\Gamma\rightarrow^*\Gamma,\Gamma$ is to ensure that these variables may safely be duplicated if $\kappa'$ is constrained to be $\omega$.

In order to type case-expressions we introduce an auxiliary form of judgements for alternatives. We give alternatives a type of the form $\rho\Rightarrow\tau$ where $\rho$ is the type of the value that is being scrutinised and $\tau$ is the type of the branches. The rule Alts

$$\text{Binding} \frac{\Pi_0; \Psi; \Gamma \vdash e : \rho^{\kappa_0}}{\Pi; \Gamma \vdash x =^\kappa e : (x : (\forall \vec{k}_1, \vec{a}_1. \rho \mid l\vec{k}_2; \exists \vec{a}_0.\Psi)^{\kappa_0}_{\kappa_1}) \text{ where } l\vec{k}_2 = \exists \vec{k}_0.\Pi_0} \quad (*)$$

$$\text{Binding group-}\epsilon \frac{}{\Pi; \epsilon \vdash \epsilon : \epsilon \text{ where } \epsilon} \quad \begin{array}{l} \vec{k}_0 \notin ftav(\Gamma, \rho^\kappa_0), \ \vec{a}_0 \notin ftv(\Gamma, \rho^\kappa_0), \\ (*)\, \vec{k}_1 \notin ftav(\Gamma, \kappa_0, l\vec{k}_2 = \exists \vec{k}_0.\Pi_0), \\ \vec{a}_1 \notin ftv(\Gamma), \ \Pi \models \kappa_1 \le \kappa \end{array}$$

$$\text{Binding group} \frac{\Pi; \Gamma_0 \vdash b : (x : \chi^{\kappa_1}_{\kappa_0}) \text{ where } \phi \qquad \Pi; \Gamma_1 \vdash \vec{b} : \Delta \text{ where } \vec{\phi}}{\Pi; \Gamma_0, \Gamma_1 \vdash b, \vec{b} : (x : \chi^{\kappa_1}_{\kappa_0}, \Delta) \text{ where } \phi, \vec{\phi}}$$

$$\text{Let} \frac{\Pi_0; \Gamma_0, \Gamma_1 \vdash \vec{b} : \Delta \text{ where } \vec{\phi} \qquad \Pi_1; \Psi; \Gamma_2, \Gamma_3 \vdash e : \tau}{\Pi; \Psi; \Gamma_1, \Gamma_3 \vdash \texttt{let } \vec{b} \texttt{ in } e : \tau} \quad \begin{array}{l} \text{dom}(\Gamma_1, \Gamma_3) \cap \text{dom}(\Delta) = \emptyset \\ \Pi \models \Delta \to^* \Gamma_0; \Gamma_2 \\ \Pi \models \Pi_0, \texttt{let } \vec{\phi} \texttt{ in } \Pi_1 \end{array}$$

**Fig. 4.** Typing rules for bindings and let expressions

$$\frac{\Theta; \Gamma_0, \Gamma_1 \vdash e_0 : \tau \qquad \Theta; \Gamma_0, \Gamma_2, \Gamma_3 \vdash e_1 : \tau}{\Theta; \Gamma_0, \Gamma_1, \Gamma_2 \vdash \{\texttt{nil} \Rightarrow e_0; \texttt{cons } x\, y \Rightarrow e_1\} : \rho' \Rightarrow \tau} \quad \begin{array}{l} \rho' \equiv \texttt{List } \kappa_0\, \kappa_1\, \kappa_2\, \kappa_3\, \rho \\ x, y \notin \text{dom}(\Gamma_0, \Gamma_2) \\ \Theta \models x : \rho^{\kappa_1}_{\kappa_0}, y : \rho'^{\kappa_3}_{\kappa_2} \to^* \Gamma_3 \end{array}$$

for alternatives contains a subtle treatment of contexts. If a variable occurs once in each branch of the case-expression and thus twice in the term it may still occur only once in the context. This is achieved by collecting the variables that occur in both branches in a common context $\Gamma_0$, thus effectively counting a variable occurring in both branches as one. Finally, the side conditions take care of the variables bound in the cons-pattern. They see to that if $x$ (and/or $y$) occurs several times in $e_1$ then $\kappa_0$ and $\kappa_1$ (and/or $\kappa_2$ and $\kappa_3$) will be constrained to be $\omega$. Thanks to the auxiliary rule for alternatives the rule for case-expressions becomes entirely straightforward.

To type let-expressions we first introduce an auxiliary form of typing judgements for bindings. We will give bindings a type of the form $x : \chi^{\vec{\kappa}_0}_{\kappa_1}$, i.e., the type of a binding includes the name of the bound variable (so it can be considered as a type association). The rules for typing bindings appears in Figure 4. To type a binding with the rule Binding

$$\frac{\Pi_0; \Psi; \Gamma \vdash e : \rho^{\kappa_0}}{\Pi; \Gamma \vdash x =^\kappa e : (x : (\forall \vec{k}_1, \vec{a}_1. \rho \mid l\vec{k}_2; \exists \vec{a}_0.\Psi)^{\kappa_0}_{\kappa_1}) \text{ where } l\vec{k}_2 = \exists \vec{k}_0.\Pi_0} \quad (*)$$

$$\begin{array}{l} \vec{k}_0 \notin ftav(\Gamma, \rho^\kappa_0), \ \vec{a}_0 \notin ftv(\Gamma, \rho^\kappa_0), \\ (*)\, \vec{k}_1 \notin ftav(\Gamma, \kappa_0, l\vec{k}_2 = \exists \vec{k}_0.\Pi_0), \\ \vec{a}_1 \notin ftv(\Gamma), \ \Pi \models \kappa_1 \le \kappa \end{array}$$

we first type the expression in the binding and yield the constraints $\Pi_0; \Psi$. We may then existentially quantify variables which appear in the constraints to obtain $\exists \vec{k}_0.\Pi_0$ and $\exists \vec{a}_0.\Psi$ providing $\vec{k}_0$ and $\vec{a}_0$ do not occur free elsewhere in the judgement. This is ensured by the first line of side conditions. We then form the type schema $\forall \vec{k}_1, \vec{a}_1. \rho \mid l\vec{k}_2; \exists \vec{a}_0.\Psi$ by universally quantifying $\vec{k}_1$ and $\vec{a}_1$. The second line of side conditions simply ensures that $\vec{k}_1$ and $\vec{a}_1$ do not occur free elsewhere in the judgement. We put $\exists \vec{a}_0.\Psi$ in the type schema but not $\exists \vec{k}_0.\Pi_0$. Instead we introduce a constraint abstraction $l\vec{k}_2 = \exists \vec{k}_0.\Pi_0$ and put a call to the constraint abstraction into the type schema. We also need a form of judgements for groups of bindings. As you would expect the type of a group of bindings is just a set of type associations (i.e., a typing context) and the typing rules just collect the type associations and the corresponding constraint abstractions. In the rule Let

$$
\frac{\Pi_0; \Gamma_0, \Gamma_1 \vdash \vec{b} : \Delta \textbf{ where } \vec{\phi} \quad \Pi_1; \Psi; \Gamma_2, \Gamma_3 \vdash e : \tau}{\Pi; \Psi; \Gamma_1, \Gamma_3 \vdash \texttt{let } \vec{b} \texttt{ in } e : \tau} \quad \begin{array}{l} \mathrm{dom}(\Gamma_1, \Gamma_3) \cap \mathrm{dom}(\Delta) = \emptyset \\ \Pi \models \Delta \to^* \Gamma_0; \Gamma_2 \\ \Pi \models \Pi_0, \texttt{let } \vec{\phi} \texttt{ in } \Pi_1 \end{array}
$$

we first type the bindings which gives a context $\Delta$ which contains the type schemas associated with each binding. The first two side conditions ensures that the type schema $\chi_{i \kappa_i}^{\kappa_i'}$ associated with each variable $x_i$ in $\Delta$ is consistent with the type of each use of $x_i$. They also ensures that if $x_i$ may be used more than once then $\kappa_i$ and $\kappa_i'$ must be constrained to $\omega$. It is achieved as follows. If $x_i$ occurs more than once in $e$ and the right hand sides of $\vec{b}$ then $x_i$ will also occur more than once in $\Gamma_0, \Gamma_2$. Thus the second side condition will ensure that $\kappa_i$ and $\kappa_i'$ is constrained to be $\omega$. The typing of the bindings also gives a group of constraint abstraction $\vec{\phi}$. With the constraint abstraction we form the constraint $\texttt{let } \vec{\phi} \texttt{ in } \Pi_1$ which by the third side condition must be a consequence of the constraints in the conclusion of the rule.

### 3.8   Soundness

The soundness of our type system simply says that a well typed program is well annotated, i.e., when we run it in the abstract machine it does not go wrong.

**Theorem 1.** *If $\Theta; \emptyset \vdash e : \tau$ and $\vartheta \models \Theta$ then $e\vartheta$ cannot go wrong.*

The result is established by extending the type system to abstract machine configurations and then proving a subject reduction result which says that typings are preserved by transitions in the abstract machine. A very similar proof for the type system in [Gus98] is presented in full detail in [Gus99].

### 3.9   Inference Algorithm

As stated the type system is undecidable since it employs type polymorphic recursion. Our inference algorithm will therefore take a term which is explicitly typed in the underlying ordinary type system and can handle type polymorphic recursion if presented to it through the type annotations. It will first compute a usage typing judgement which is principal with respect to the given typing judgement, i.e., every other usage typing judgement is an instance of the computed judgement if "stripping the annotations" from it yields the judgement in the underlying type system. The second phase of the algorithm then computes the best solution to the constraints in the principal judgement using the techniques described in a companion paper [GS01].

The time complexity of the algorithm is dominated by the cost of the constraint solving in the second phase. We can argue, as follows, that the time complexity of the second phase is $O(n^3)$ where $n$ is the size of the explicitly typed term. Let the *skeleton* of the constraints be the constraints where all occurrences of inequality constraints of the form $\kappa_0 \leq \kappa_1$ have been removed. What remains are the binding occurrences of variables and all calls to constraint abstractions. By inspecting the typing rules we can see that the size of the skeleton of the constraints required to type a program is proportional to the size of the explicitly typed program. Moreover the number of free annotation variables in the constraints are proportional to the size of the program. From these facts and theorem 2 of [GS01] we can conclude that the complexity is $O(n^3)$ where $n$ is the size of the typed program.

For a version of the analysis in this paper without usage-polymorphic recursion we have developed an algorithm based on *non-recursive* constraint abstractions with a worst case complexity of $O(n * m * t^2)$ where $n$ is the size of the untyped lambda lifted version of the program, $m$ is the size of the type of the largest set of (properly) mutually recursive definitions and $t$ is the size of the largest instantiated type [Sve00]. Since $m$ and $t$ typically grow slowly or not at all with program size we expect that algorithm to scale up well in practice.

## 4   Related Work

There is a rich literature on analyses which aims at avoiding updates. See [Gus99] for a thorough overview. This work especially lends ideas from the type based approach by Turner, Wadler and Mossin [TWM95], and its followups by Gustavsson [Gus98] and Wansbrough and Peyton Jones [WPJ99]. Bounded polymorphism was proposed by Turner, Wadler and Mossin [TWM95] and the idea to use subtyping in usage analysis originates from the work by Faxén [Fax95] (the subtyping in his flow analysis and the directed edges in the post processing achieves the same effect as the subtyping in this paper) although it was independently proposed by Gustavsson [Gus98] and Wansbrough and Peyton Jones [WPJ99].

The analysis which seems to be closest in expressive power to ours is an analysis by Faxén based on an undecidable type based flow analysis [Fax97]. Due to the undecidable nature of the analysis his inference algorithm is not complete with respect to the type system. The algorithm is parametrised by a notion of finite name supply and the larger name-supply the better the algorithm approximates the type system. The exact relationship between the different degrees of approximations computed by his algorithm and our type system is not clear to us.

The aim of this work is to make usage analysis scale up for large programs and in that respect it is most closely related to recent work by Wansbrough and Peyton Jones [WPJ00]. They have also observed that usage polymorphism is crucial for the accuracy of the analysis of large programs but they side-step the difficulties associated with bounded polymorphism. Instead they have a simple usage polymorphism where the quantified variables may not be constrained. This is achieved by an algorithm which eliminates inequality constraints prior to quantification by unifying constrained variables. The drawback of their approach is that as they refrain from using bounded polymorphism, they get an analysis which is rather inaccurate when it comes to data structures. Consider for example the following program fragment.

$$\ldots \mathrm{map\ square\ (fromto\ 1\ 100)} \ldots$$

The spine of the list produced by *fromto* is consumed linearly by *map* but a type system with their simple usage polymorphism cannot discover it. The reason being that in a system with simple usage polymorphism the usage of the spine must be unified with the usage of the elements and in this case the elements are used more than once. In our system with bounded polymorphism the usage of the spine and the elements need only to constrain each other through an inequality constraint so we can deduce that the spine is used linearly although the elements are not. We believe that this situation is common enough in practice to have a significant effect on the accuracy of the analysis.

That the number of constraints explodes is a problem also for other type based program analyses with bounded polymorphism. In that respect our work is most closely related to the work by Faxén [Fax95], Mossin [Mos97] and Rehof and Fänhdrich [RF01]. Faxén and Mossin present inference algorithms for type based flow analyses which simplifies constraint sets to smaller but equivalent constraint sets. In their recent work on type based flow analysis Rehof and Fänhdrich uses *instantiation constraints* to represent constraints compactly and thus instantiation constraints plays a rôle similar to our constraint abstractions.

## 5   Conclusions and Future Work

We have presented a powerful and accurate type system for usage analysis with bounded usage polymorphism and subtyping. A key contribution is a new expressive form of constraints which allows constraints to be represented compactly through calls to *constraint abstractions*. In a companion paper [GS01] we show how to efficiently compute a least solution to constraints with constraint abstractions and we use this technique to obtain an $O(n^3)$ inference algorithm for our usage analysis, where $n$ is the size of the explicitly typed program.

## Acknowledgements

We would like to thank David Sands and Makoto Takeyama for comments on this paper and Karl-Filip Faxén, Jakob Rehof and Keith Wansbrough for discussions on the relations to their work.

# References

BJ96.     U. Boquist and T. Johnsson. The grin project: A highly optimising back end for lazy functional languages. In *Proc. of IFL'96, Bad Godesberg, Germany.* Springer Verlag LNCS 1268, 1996.

BS96.     E. Barendsen and S. Smetsers. Uniqueness Typing for Functional Languages with Graph Rewriting Semantics. *Mathematical Structures in Computer Science*, 6:579–612, 1996.

DHM95.    D. Dussart, F. Henglein, and C. Mossin. Polymorphic recursion and subtype qualifications: Polymorphic binding-time analysis in polynomial time. In *proceedings of 2nd Static Analysis Symposium*, September 1995.

Fax95.    Karl-Filip Faxén. Optimizing lazy functional programs using flow inference. In *Proc. of SAS'95*, pages 136–153. Springer-Verlag, LNCS 983, September 1995.

Fax97.    Karl-Filip Faxén. *Analysing, Transforming and Compiling Lazy Functional Programs*. PhD thesis, Royal Institute of Technology, Sweden, June 1997.

FW87.     J. Fairbairn and S. Wray. TIM: A Simple, Lazy Abstract Machine to Execute Supercombinators. In *Proc. of FPCA'87*, pages 34–45. Springer Verlag LNCS 274, September 1987.

Gir87.    Jean-Yves Girard. Linear logic. *Theoretical Computer Science*, 50:1–102, 1987.

GS99.     J. Gustavsson and D. Sands. A foundation for space-safe transformations of call-by-need programs. In *Proc. of HOOTS'99*, volume 26 of *ENTCS*. Elsevier, 1999.

GS01.     J. Gustavsson and J. Svenningsson. Constraint abstractions. In *Proc. of Second Symposium on Programs as Data Objects*, LNCS. Springer Verlag, 2001. To Appear.

Gus98.    J. Gustavsson. A Type Based Sharing Analysis for Update Avoidance and Optimisation. In *Proc. of ICFP'98*, pages 39–50, Baltimore, Maryland, September 1998.

Gus99.    J. Gustavsson. A Type Based Sharing Analysis for Update Avoidance and Optimisation. Licentiate thesis, May 1999.

Lau93.    J. Launchbury. A Natural Semantics for Lazy Evaluation. In *Proc. of POPL'93*, Charleston, N. Carolina, 1993.

LGH+92.   J. Launchbury, A. Gill, J. Hughes, S. Marlow, S. L. Peyton Jones, and P. Wadler. Avoiding Unnecessary Updates. In J. Launchbury and P. M. Sansom, editors, *Functional Programming*, Workshops in Computing, Glasgow, 1992.

Mar93.    S. Marlow. Update Avoidance Analysis by Abstract Interpretation. In *Proc. 1993 Glasgow Workshop on Functional Programming*, Workshops in Computing. Springer–Verlag, 1993.

Mog97.    T. Mogensen. Types for 0, 1 or many uses. In *Proc. of IFL '97*, pages 112–122. Springer-Verlag, LNCS 1467, September 1997.

Mos97.    C. Mossin. *Flow Analysis of Typed Higher-Order Programs (Revised Version)*. PhD thesis, University of Copenhagen, Denmark, August 1997.

PJ92.     Simon L. Peyton Jones. Implementing lazy functional languages on stock hardware: the spineless tagless g-machine. *Journal of Functional Programming*, 2(2):127–202, July 1992.

PJPS96.   S. Peyton Jones, W. Partain, and A. Santos. Let-floating: moving bindings to give faster programs. In *Proc. of ICFP'96*, pages 1–12. ACM, May 1996.

PS00.      R. Peña and C. Segura. Non-determinism analysis in a parallel-functional
           language. In *Proceedings of the 12th International Workshop of Functional
           Languages*, LNCS, September 2000. Also in this volume.
RF01.      Jakob Rehof and Manuel Fändrich. Type-Based Flow Analysis: From Poly-
           morphic Subtyping to CFL-Reachability. In *Proceedings of 2001 Symposium
           on Principles of Programming Languages*, 2001. To appear.
Ses91.     P. Sestoft. *Analysis and Efficient Implementation of Functional Programs*.
           PhD thesis, DIKU, University of Copenhagen, Denmark, October 1991.
Ses97.     P. Sestoft. Deriving a lazy abstract machine. *Journal of Functional Pro-
           gramming*, 7(3):231–264, May 1997.
Sve00.     Josef Svenningsson. An efficient algorithm for a sharing analysis with poly-
           morphism and subtyping. Masters thesis, June 2000.
TJ94.      J.-P. Talpin and P. Jouvelot. The type and effect discipline. *Information
           and Computation*, 111(2), 1994.
TWM95.     D. N. Turner, P. Wadler, and C. Mossin. Once upon a type. In *Proc. of
           FPCA*, La Jolla, 1995.
WPJ98.     Keith Wansbrough and Simon Peyton Jones. Once Upon a Polymorphic
           Type. Technical Report TR-1998-19, Department of Computing Science,
           University of Glasgow, December 1998.
WPJ99.     Keith Wansbrough and Simon Peyton Jones. Once Upon a Polymorphic
           Type. In *Proc. of POPL'99*, January 1999.
WPJ00.     Keith Wansbrough and Simon Peyton Jones. Simple Usage Polymorphism.
           In *ACM SIGPLAN Workshop on Types in Compilation*, September 2000.

# Polygonizing Implicit Surfaces
# in a Purely Functional Way

Thorsten H.-G. Zörner, Pieter Koopman, Marko van Eekelen, and
Rinus Plasmeijer

Computing Science Institute,
University of Nijmegen,
The Netherlands
{zoerner,pieter,marko,rinus}@cs.kun.nl

**Abstract.** Implicit surfaces are defined by a real valued function. They
can easily be defined and manipulated and have therefore gained great
popularity in computer graphics. This paper presents a purely functional
implementation of a well known algorithm to polygonize implicit surfaces, based on spatial partitioning by means of octrees. While conventional implementations are laden with practical issues, our implementation in Clean is straightforward, implements the algorithm very concisely
and makes essential use of lazy evaluation.
Further we present two enhancements to this basic algorithm: Introducing a memo function greatly improves time efficiency. The appearance of
a visualized implicit surface can be greatly enhanced by providing normal vector information. For calculating normal vectors we adopt a lazy
implementation of automatic differentiation.

## 1   Introduction

An implicit surface is given by the set of zeros of the underlying function, the
so called implicit function. Implicit surfaces have many properties that make
them attractive to model geometric objects, which is an important task in areas
like computer graphics or animation. Implicit surfaces can be defined in a very
concise way, transformed and manipulated easily.

We visualize implicit surfaces by approximating the actual surface with polygons. We refer to the process of finding this approximation as generating or
polygonizing an implicit surface.

In order to find an appropriate number of zeros, we fix the domain we are
interested in and partition it regularly using an octree, which means the (recursive) partition of a cube into eight similar subcubes. Partitioning this way
is continued recursively for all cubes that intersect with the surface, till a prescribed depth is reached. Then the zeros on the edges of a cube are calculated
and connected to polygons.

We implement this algorithm in a purely functional way in the pure and
lazy functional language Clean [13]. We obtain code that is much shorter than a
comparable public domain implementation [3] in C. Due to lazy evaluation the

M. Mohnen and P. Koopman (Eds.): IFL 2000, LNCS 2011, pp. 158–175, 2001.
© Springer-Verlag Berlin Heidelberg 2001

space consumption of the program is minimal, but execution time of the Clean code is higher than that of the C code.

We claim that our program can easily be understood and be changed and demonstrate this by adding two improvements to the basic version of our Clean implementation: We improve the run time behavior dramatically by introducing a memo function. This technique avoids evaluating the implicit function more than once at the same point in space. Further we adopt a lazy implementation of automatic differentiation [7,8,9] to calculate normal vectors and add it to our code. Normal vector information can greatly enhance the appearance of objects for certain visualization tools.

The remainder of the paper is organized as follows: In the following section we briefly compare the three basic ways to define surfaces in three dimensional space and discuss their properties. Then we introduce the octree algorithm, which is followed by our Clean implementation in section four. Section five discusses efficiency issues, followed by a comparison of our implementation and the public domain C implementation. The next section sketches the concept of automatic differentiation and how it can be used for our purposes. The final section contains concluding remarks.

The source code of the Clean program is available for public use [15].

## 2   Surfaces in Three Dimensional Space

There are basically three ways to calculate a two dimensional surface in three dimensional Euclidean space: explicit, parametric and implicit. We choose the unit sphere as our example.

- Explicit: $z = \pm\sqrt{1 - x^2 - y^2}$; $x, y \in \mathbb{R}$
  This mapping defines a sphere explicitly. It is not a function, as it returns two, one or no result depending on the input. For each chosen $x \in \mathbb{R}$ and $y \in \mathbb{R}$ we calculate the $z$ coordinate(s). For $x^2 + y^2 > 1$ there is no result, for $x^2 + y^2 = 1$ we have one result $z = 0$, and for $x^2 + y^2 < 1$ we obtain two results.
- Parametric: $x = \cos\phi\sin\theta$, $y = \sin\phi\sin\theta$, $z = \cos\theta$; $\phi, \theta \in \mathbb{R}$
  A parametric definition of the sphere is given by three trigonometric functions. For each chosen $\phi, \theta \in \mathbb{R}$ we calculate $x, y$ and $z$ respectively.
- Implicit: $F(x, y, z) = x^2 + y^2 + z^2 - 1$
  Finally the unit sphere can be implicitly defined by only one function $F : \mathbb{R}^3 \to \mathbb{R}$, where the surface is the set of coordinates $x, y, z \in \mathbb{R}$, for which holds $F(x, y, z) = 0$.

The implicit definition is the most compact and uniform way to define the unit sphere. Here the explicit definition can easily be derived from the implicit one. In general this is a very difficult task.

Besides the conciseness there are many more possibilities and advantages when employing implicit functions to the area of geometric modelling [11]. Here we will only look at a particularly appealing manipulation, the blending of two or more implicit surfaces.

For example a blend of two intersecting spheres can be described very easily. We use boldface to denote a vector $\mathbf{x} := (x, y, z)$. Let $F(\mathbf{x})$ define one sphere and $G(\mathbf{x})$ another. We further assume that both $F$ and $G$ are negative at interior points of the respective spheres, which is no important restriction. Then the blend of the two is readily described by

$$H(\mathbf{x}) := \min \{ F(\mathbf{x}), G(\mathbf{x}) \}.$$

**Fig. 1.** Two blended spheres cut open in order to show, that blending is neither intersection, nor a simulation of soap films

The resulting surface is then the set of points $\mathbf{x}$ for which $H(\mathbf{x}) = 0$. The same method, which we generate implicit surfaces with for $F$ and $G$, can be applied to $H$ without any additional effort like calculating the intersection (explicit case) or adjusting parameters (parametric case).

It might be a problem that a blending function using min is no longer smooth (continuously differentiable). If smoothness is desired there exist other ways of blending surfaces that result in a continuously differentiable function. The following function, which we use in our examples, yields a smooth function, but is of course more expensive:

$$H(\mathbf{x}) := \frac{1}{2} \left( F(\mathbf{x}) + G(\mathbf{x}) - \sqrt{F(\mathbf{x})^2 + G(\mathbf{x})^2} \right)$$

## 3   The Octree Approach

In this section we will discuss an algorithm for polygonizing implicit surfaces based on spatial decomposition, as discussed by Bloomenthal [2].

The nodes building the polygons are zeros of the implicit function. We need to find an appropriate number of zeros: Not too few because they do not approximate the surface well and not too many, as they would flood any visualization tool with redundant or invisible information (think of polygons below pixel size).

The algorithm is based on the partitioning of space in cubes, which are first recursively refined in areas close to the surface and finally get polygons inscribed into. The data structure that models the partitioning is a tree structure where each parent node possesses eight child nodes. Therefore it is called octree.

We describe the basic idea in more detail: Given an implicit function $F$, we know that $F(\mathbf{x}) = 0$ holds for all points $\mathbf{x} = (x, y, z)$ on the surface. For all other points $\mathbf{z}$, $F(\mathbf{z})$ is either positive or negative, depending on what side of the surface $\mathbf{z}$ is. Let us assume two points $\mathbf{y}$ and $\mathbf{z}$ for which $F$ has different signs $F(\mathbf{y}) > 0$ and $F(\mathbf{z}) < 0$. Then on a straight line between them there is (at least) one point $\mathbf{x}$ for which $F(\mathbf{x})$ is zero. Finding this point on a straight line is a simple one dimensional problem and can be solved by means of bisection.

We have reduced the problem to finding suitable positive and negative points, close to the actual surface, and to build polygons. This is accomplished by partitioning interesting parts of the three dimensional space in a regular fashion.

We start off with a cubic domain, which contains the area that we are interested in. Edges of this and all subsequent cubes are parallel to the coordinate axes. We cut the initial cube into eight subcubes of equal size and repeat to do so recursively for interesting cubes.

Cubes are referred to as interesting when they are intersected by the surface. In order to test this we evaluate the function at all eight nodes of a cube. Interesting cubes are the ones where the sign of the function value at least at one corner node differs from the others. In other words a cube with all positive/negative nodes lies completely on one side of the surface - and is therefore uninteresting for our purposes.

This criterion is obviously not suitable to determine accurately if surface and cube in question are disjoint. There can always be a small detail in the surface, for which the checks at the corners fail. Additional checks will detect intersection in many more cases, but not all. A remedy to this shortcoming is to increase the prescribed depth of the tree.

By construction all interesting cubes at the maximal depth have the same side length. Assuming the side length of the initial cube to be $l_0$, then the side of a cube at depth $k$ has length $l_k = l_0 2^{-k}$. When this depth is reached, we calculate the zeros on the edges of the cube between nodes of opposite signs, which will be the nodes of the polygons to be drawn.

For each interesting cube at the desired depth we inscribe one or more polygons. Unfortunately there are configurations of positive and negative nodes on a cube where this task is ambiguous, as Figure 2 shows.

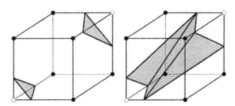

**Fig. 2.** Ambiguous node configuration on a cube. The node in the front left and the node in the back right have a different sign from the others

However it is unambiguous on a tetrahedron. All $2^4 = 16$ possible configurations of positive and negative signs on the four nodes of a tetrahedron, boil down to just three basic cases, shown in Figure 3.

**Fig. 3.** The three basic node configurations on a tetrahedron

For each tetrahedron we obtain either nothing (all four nodes of the same sign), one triangle (one node differs from the others) or one quadrilateral (two signs differ from the other two).

We cut each interesting cube into six tetrahedra. This allows for a proper visualization, as all neighboring polygons share entire edges rather than just nodes with their neighbors.

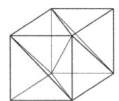

**Fig. 4.** Cube cut into six tetrahedra

## 4   The Clean Implementation

We assume basic knowledge of functional languages and in particular on the pure and lazy functional language Clean [13].

As we work in Euclidean space we base all geometric information on three dimensional vectors. We prefer an algebraic data type instead of an array, for the ease of access. There are only three elements within the vector, one for each coordinate direction, of type `Real`.

```
:: Vector3 = Vector3 !Real !Real !Real
```

Since the edges of each cube are parallel to a respective coordinate axis, two vectors in three dimensional space suffice to define it. One vector contains the minimal values of each direction, the other one the maximal values. A pair of such vectors forms a cube.

```
:: Cube := ( Vector3, Vector3)
```

We define a record to contain the tree structure of our octree and the geometric information of the current cube. Combinations of three first letters as

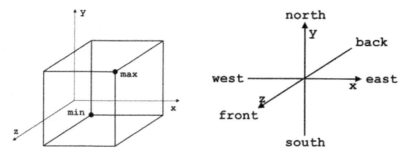

**Fig. 5.** Left hand side shows a cube being defined by two nodes. All edges are parallel to the coordinate axis. Right hand side gives the names of the six directions

field name indicate which subtree the field refers to. For instance `wnf` refers to west, north, front.

```
:: Octree =
   { cube :: Cube
   , wnf  :: Octree, enf :: Octree, wsf  :: Octree, esf :: Octree
   , wnb  :: Octree, enb :: Octree, wsb  :: Octree, esb :: Octree
   }
```

The implementation consists basically of two functions: a generating function, that generates the octree and a consuming function, that consumes the octree and produces the polygons. It exploits the fundamental advantage of functional programming as pointed out by Hughes [6]: the possibility of glueing programs together.

The generating function defines a complete and unbounded octree.

```
genOctree :: Cube -> Octree
genOctree current_cube =:
   ( min =: Vector3 west south back
   , max =: Vector3 east north front)
# (Vector3 mx my mz) = (min + max) /. 2.0
= { cube = current_cube
  , wnf = genOctree ( Vector3 west my mz, Vector3 mx north front)
  , enf = genOctree ( Vector3 mx my mz, max)
  , wsf = genOctree ( Vector3 west south mz, Vector3 mx my front)
  , esf = genOctree ( Vector3 mx south mz, Vector3 east my front)
  , wnb = genOctree ( Vector3 west my back, Vector3 mx north mz)
  , enb = genOctree ( Vector3 mx my back, Vector3 east north mz)
  , wsb = genOctree ( min, Vector3 mx my mz)
  , esb = genOctree ( Vector3 mx south back, Vector3 east my mz)}
```

Due to lazy evaluation this potentially infinite data structure is only evaluated as far as needed. We fix three global constants `depthMAX`, `depthBS`, `depthMIN`. `depthMAX` prescribes the maximal depth of the octree, `depthBS` the number of bisection steps. A minimal depth of the octree is given by `depthMIN` in order to to prevent the premature termination of the program for surfaces with many gaps.

The cubes in the octree are used as a basis to generate polygons describing the surface defined by the function. Now we define a function `f` of the type

```
f :: Vector3 -> Real
```

and a macro to check for its sign

```
F x :== f x > 0.0
```

We want to generate polygons, which we described by a list of vectors.

```
:: Polygon :== [Vector3]
```

The consuming function takes a counter for the current depth, the defined octree and a list for the output by continuation.

```
consumeOctree :: Int Octree [Polygon] -> [Polygon]
```

The function `consumeOctree` distinguishes the following cases.

- If the minimum depth has been reached, and the function has the same sign at all corner points, which means the current cube is not interesting, nothing has to be drawn inside this cube. The current cube is dropped.
- If the maximum depth is reached, the current cube is cut into six tetrahedra, in which polygons are inscribed into. This is done by the function `tetra`.
- Otherwise we apply the function `consumeOctree` to all subcubes of the current cube by continuation.

```
consumeOctree n t =: { cube =
    ( Vector3 west south back, Vector3 east north front)} cont
  | n>depthMIN && allTheSame [F nwnf, F nenf, F nwsf, F nesf
      ,F nwnb, F nenb, F nwsb, F nesb] = cont
  | n>=depthMAX =
      ( tetra nwsf nesf nwsb nwnf
      ( tetra nenf nwnf nwnb nwsb
      ( tetra nesf nenf nwsb nwnf
      ( tetra nesb nwsb nesf nenf
      ( tetra nenb nenf nwnb nesb
      ( tetra nwnb nenf nwsb nesb cont))))))
  #! n = n+1
  | otherwise =
        ( consumeOctree n t.wnf ( consumeOctree n t.enf
        ( consumeOctree n t.wsf ( consumeOctree n t.esf
        ( consumeOctree n t.wnb ( consumeOctree n t.enb
        ( consumeOctree n t.wsb ( consumeOctree n t.esb
```

```
            cont))))))))
where
    allTheSame xs = and xs || not (or xs)
    nwnf = Vector3 west north front
    nenf = Vector3 east north front
    nwsf = Vector3 west south front
    nesf = Vector3 east south front
    nwnb = Vector3 west north back
    nenb = Vector3 east north back
    nwsb = Vector3 west south back
    nesb = Vector3 east south back
```

The decision if a polygon is inscribed into a tetrahedron (and if so which polygon) is made by a case distinction on the signs of the function at the four corners of the tetrahedron.

If a polygon is inscribed into a tetrahedron the nodes spanning this polygon are the zeros of the implicit function on according edges of the tetrahedron. The zeros of the function on these edges are approximated using a simple bisection algorithm along the edge. For some visualization tools the orientation of the nodes of a polygon matters in which they are connected, so we maintain a right handed system.

```
tetra :: Vector3 Vector3 Vector3 Vector3 [Polygon] -> [Polygon]
tetra v1 v2 v3 v4 cont
| p1 | p2 | p3 | p4 = cont
                    = [[ zero14, zero34, zero24] : cont]
            | p4 = [[ zero13, zero23, zero34] : cont]
                    = [[ zero14, zero13, zero23, zero24] : cont]
        | p3 | p4 = [[ zero12, zero24, zero23] : cont]
                    = [[ zero12, zero14, zero34, zero23] : cont]
            | p4 = [[ zero12, zero24, zero34, zero13] : cont]
                    = [[ zero12, zero14, zero13] : cont]
    | p2 | p3 | p4 = [[ zero12, zero13, zero14] : cont]
                    = [[ zero12, zero13, zero34, zero24] : cont]
            | p4 = [[ zero12, zero23, zero34, zero14] : cont]
                    = [[ zero12, zero23, zero24] : cont]
        | p3 | p4 = [[ zero14, zero24, zero23, zero13] : cont]
                    = [[ zero13, zero34, zero23] : cont]
            | p4 = [[ zero14, zero24, zero34] : cont]
                    = cont
where
    p1 = F v1
    p2 = F v2
    p3 = F v3
    p4 = F v4
    zero12 = bisection depthBS v1 v2
```

```
zero13 = bisection depthBS v1 v3
zero14 = bisection depthBS v1 v4
zero23 = bisection depthBS v2 v3
zero24 = bisection depthBS v2 v4
zero34 = bisection depthBS v3 v4
```

```
bisection :: Vector3 Vector3 -> Vector3
bisection depth r l
    | depth == 0   = mid
    | f l == f mid = bisection (depth-1) mid r
    | otherwise    = bisection (depth-1) l mid
where
    mid = (l + r) /. 2.0
```

This is all we need to determine polygons in interesting cubes. It remains the task of visualization.

We have chosen VRML [1] to draw the polygons, which stands for Virtual Reality Modelling Language. VRML has a number of advantages: It is a standardized description language for three dimensional objects. There exist VRML browsers on many platforms, some are plug-ins to common web browsers. Some VRML browsers let the user fly through the depicted three dimensional object, allowing him to explore them well. Normal vector information can be added to get a smoother picture of the object, a feature that we will exploit in section six.

## 5    Efficiency Issues

We will now discuss the time and space efficiency of the Clean implementation. The implementation above only uses a couple of kilobytes for execution and runs pretty fast. We begin with some fairly simple optimizations. Later on we discuss how once computed values of the implicit function can be reused. At the end of this section we will measure the effects of these optimizations.

### Simple Optimizations

Some small changes are introduced to enhance the efficiency. The representation of the cube is changed to a record that contains all eight corners.

```
:: Cube =
    { enf :: Real, wnf :: Real, esf :: Real, wsf :: Real
    , enb :: Real, wnb :: Real, esb :: Real, wsb :: Real
    }
```

This is convenient since all corners of the cube are eventually needed. The generation of octrees is updated accordingly.

Some superfluous packing and unpacking of values in data types is prevented by passing three coordinates separately to the implicit function instead of packed into a single vector. The type of the implicit function becomes:

```
f :: !Real !Real !Real -> Real
```

instead of:

```
f :: Vector3 -> Real
```

## Memoization

The implicit function is repeatedly calculated for a large number of points. The point in the middle of a cube for instance is a corner point of its eight subcubes. Moreover it is a corner of one of the subcubes of each subcube, and so on. It seems worthwhile to share this computation using some form of memoization [5,12]. We could further try to share the approximated zeros on neighboring edges of a tetrahedron, but we will not consider this here. Clean has no built-in memoization mechanism. So sharing computation has to be indicated explicitly. There are two problems concerning sharing.

Firstly there is a very large number of potential points where this function can be evaluated. For an octree depth of $n$, the potential number of points is $2^n$ for each dimension. That means that the total amount of possible evaluations is $(2^n)^3$. Even for a moderate depth of an octree, say 4 or 5, storing function values in an array of this size is not feasible. It simply consumes too much space. Moreover, the value of the implicit function is computed only for a small fraction of all possible points of an octree. The shape of the implicit surface determines at which points the function has to be evaluated.

The second problem is that the arguments of the implicit function are of type `Real`. Real numbers however are only approximated on ordinary computer hardware, and therefore rounding errors will occur. We have to make sure that the coordinates of a shared point are always the same, regardless which cube refers to it.

Nevertheless it is possible to implement an elegant and easy to use memoization mechanism for this situation. There are two key ideas which we need to construct the memoization function: rational numbers and a tailor-made data structure.

## Rational Numbers

First we use rational numbers like $\frac{3}{4}$ instead of the corresponding real numbers. Our rational numbers are based on integers and do not incur troubles with rounding errors. All points inside the outermost cube are addressed by rational numbers between zero and one. The maximum depth of evaluation of the octree is `depthMAX+depthBS+1`. This implies that $2^{\texttt{depthMAX+depthBS+1}}$ can be used as the (fixed) denominator of the rational numbers used. On standard hardware `depthMAX+depthBS` is limited to 30 in this representation, which is certainly sufficient for practical applications.

```
:: Rat     :== Int
:: RatVec = Vector3 !Rat !Rat !Rat

den :: Int
den =: 1 << (depthMAX+depthBS+1)     // bitshift instead of
                                     // 2^(depthMAX+depthBS+1)
```

We do not want to change the definition of the implicit function, which accepts a vector as argument. Hence we need to define a conversion from the rational numbers used inside the octree to a vector expected by the implicit function:

```
RatToReal :: !Rat -> Real
RatToReal num = toReal num/toReal den

toRealx x :== 2.0 * RatToReal x - 1.0
toRealy y :== 2.0 * RatToReal y - 1.0
toRealz z :== 2.0 * RatToReal z - 1.0
```

The generation of polygons has to be changed slightly. The type `Vector3` in the octree is replaced by `RatVec` and the function `f` is altered to:

```
F :: !Rat !Rat !Rat -> Real
F x y z = f (toRealx x) (toRealy y) (toRealz z)
```

## Binary Trees to Implement Memoization

The second idea for memoization is the fact that the implicit function is not evaluated at random points. The evaluation will follow the octree. The implicit function is not evaluated at all points of the octree, but all points where the function is evaluated are part of the octree. The data type used for the memoization reflects the octree approach. The outermost cube is treated specially. All inner points are stored in a, potentially infinite, binary tree.

In order to address the points in the cube uniquely we will use nested one-dimensional trees rather than a straight three dimensional tree.

```
:: Memo t  = { zero :: t, btwn :: MemoT t, one :: t}

:: MemoT t = { smll :: MemoT t, half :: t, grtr :: MemoT t}
```

We use lazy evaluation again to construct only the necessary parts of these trees. The following function generates memo trees for a given function and will find a needed value in such a tree.

```
genMemo :: (Rat -> t) -> Memo t
genMemo f = {  zero    = f 0
            ,  btwn    = genMemoT f (den>>1) (den>>2)
```

```
        ,   one       = f den
        }


genMemoT :: (Rat -> t) Int Int -> MemoT t
genMemoT f n d
    #! d2    = d>>1  //  d2  = d/2
    =   {   smll      = genMemoT f (n-d) d2
        ,   half      = f n
        ,   grtr      = genMemoT f (n+d) d2
        }


lookup :: !(Memo t) !Rat -> t
lookup memo num
    | num==0      = memo.zero
    | num==den    = memo.one
    | num<den     = lookupT memo.btwn num (den>>1)


lookupT :: !(MemoT t) !Rat !Int -> t
lookupT memot num d
    | num<d       = lookupT memot.smll num (d>>1)
    | num==d      = memot.half
                  = lookupT memot.grtr (num-d) (d>>1)
```

We have to change the function F again to implement memoization. A shared local data structure of type Memo (Memo (Memo Bool)) is defined, which contains the required values. If a function value is needed, it is retrieved from this data structure.

```
F :: !RatVec -> Bool
F (Vector3 x y z) = lookup (lookup (lookup memo_f x) y) z

memo_f :: Memo (Memo (Memo Bool))
memo_f =: genMemo (\x -> genMemo (\y -> genMemo (\z ->
           isPos (fig0 (toRealx x) (toRealy y) (toRealz z)))))
```

## Measurements

In order to determine the effect of these optimizations we compare the execution time of four different versions of the program. The first version is the original implementation outlined in section four. The second version incorporates the simple optimizations of the first subsection. In the third version we have replaced the type Real by Rat to compute the corner points of the cubes in the octree. The final version uses the data structure Memo for the memoization of values of the implicit function.

We compare the execution time for three different examples: The first example is a blend of two spheres, as shown in Figure 1 and 7. The second example of medium complexity is a blend of three tori and three cylinders, shown in Figure 8. The third and most complicated example is a blend of 27 cylinders and a sphere and is depicted in Figure 6.

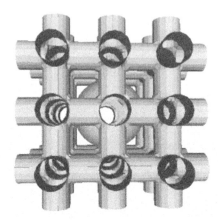

**Fig. 6.** Complicated example: blend of 27 cylinders and a sphere, depth = 5

Table 1 lists the run-time behavior of the Clean code. We chose `depthMAX=4` and `depthBS=4`. The listed execution time includes writing the generated polygons to a file, but excludes the generating of VRML output. All measurements were done on a 266MHz PC running Windows 95. The programs had 40MB of heap and 1MB of stack. The executable was generated by version 1.3.3 of the Clean Compiler.

**Table 1.** Run-time behavior of the Clean implementation: Execution time (ex), garbage collection time (gc), total execution time (tot) all given in seconds

| Figure | Polygons | Original | | | Improved | | | Using **Rat** | | | **Rat** and Memo | | |
|--------|----------|------|------|------|------|------|------|------|------|------|------|------|------|
|        |          | ex | gc | tot | ex | gc | tot | ex | gc | tot | ex | gc | tot |
| simple  | 2952  | 1.49 | 0.17 | 1.66 | 0.24 | 0.02 | 0.26 | 0.22 | 0.02 | 0.24 | 0.37 | 0.16 | 0.53 |
| medium  | 5572  | 9.54 | 1.54 | 11.1 | 1.04 | 0.04 | 1.08 | 0.82 | 0.03 | 0.85 | 0.70 | 0.17 | 0.87 |
| complex | 12025 | 100  | 20.8 | 121  | 17.1 | 2.84 | 19.9 | 13.4 | 2.51 | 15.9 | 3.08 | 1.27 | 4.35 |

From these figures we conclude that the simple modification that prevent packing and unpacking `Reals` in a `Vector3` speeds up the program by almost an order of magnitude. This is not surprising since the implicit function is evaluated very often.

The introduction of rational numbers within the octree incurs some overhead, i. e. the rational numbers must be transformed to `Real` before the implicit function can be applied. Apparently this overhead is outweighed by the more efficient handling of integers. The execution time decreases in spite of the overhead.

The introduction of memoization exhibits a more subtle behavior. For the simplest implicit function the execution time doubles. Apparently it is more efficient to recompute such a simple function than looking up the function values in the Memo data structure. For the medium example (three cylinders and three tori) there is almost no difference between recomputing the function and memoization. For the most complex implicit function memoization increases the efficiency by a factor four. For simple implicit functions the introduction of memoization increases the execution time slightly, but for complex implicit functions memoization reduces the execution time significantly. Hence, we consider the introduction of memoization an improvement.

In order to get an impression of the absolute speed of our implementation we compare it with the public domain implementation of a related algorithm in C [3]. The comparison gives only an indication of the relative speed since there are a number of significant differences. The C implementation requires a small cube near the surface of the implicit function as starting point. From this starting point a set of equal sized cubes containing the surface is generated. There are no octrees involved. For each of these cubes polygons are generated by dividing the cube into six tetrahedra. The C implementation generates two triangles instead of a quadrilateral. Moreover, the C implementation also reuses computed zeros on the edges shared by neighboring tetrahedra. For the medium example, the C program generates 8028 triangles in 0.7 seconds. Despite all differences this corresponds very well to the execution time of our Clean implementation (0.8 seconds, see Table 1). We conclude that our program performs pretty well.

## 6   Adding Normal Vector Information

Polygonizing an implicit surface yields polygons, that are spanned by nodes on the surface. The edges of these polygons are most likely disjoint with the surface, as they just approximate it, which may result in artificially sharp features of the surface.

A remedy to that is offered by many graphical engines, if the user can provide normal vectors on nodes. While shading the surface, the engine uses normal vectors to interpolate the area around edges to give the visual impression of a smooth surface. As mentioned earlier we chose VRML as output format, as it also supports normal vector information.

For implicit surfaces the normal vector at a given point on the surface is just the gradient at this very point. The gradient is the column vector built by all first partial derivatives. Let $F$ define an implicit surface, then the normal vector $n$ at $(x, y, z)$ is

$$n(x, y, z) = \nabla F(x, y, z) = \begin{bmatrix} F_x(x, y, z) \\ F_y(x, y, z) \\ F_z(x, y, z) \end{bmatrix}.$$

There are basically three ways to compute derivatives of a function, i. e. numerically, symbolically, and automatically.

Numerical differentiation usually approximates the derivative using the definition of the differential quotient with a step size in the denominator. The smaller the step size the more accurate the result will get. However a step size, which is chosen too small might lead to huge roundoff errors and meaningless results. The C implementation accompanying [3] calculates normal vectors numerically.

By symbolical differentiation one usually obtains a function, which can then be evaluated at the points needed. However symbolic differentiation can be a very intricate task. Numerical and automatic differentiation only yield the derivative at a single point, but are much easier to calculate.

For the Clean implementation we have adopted automatic differentiation, which has already been employed successfully in a functional context [7,8]. The method calculates the derivative at a given point at machine precision. For an introduction to automatic differentiation we refer to Rall, Corliss [14], for a comprehensive treatment to Griewank [4].

Automatic differentiation can be coded very elegantly in a pure functional language using operator overloading and lazy evaluation.

In order to automatically differentiate a given function, we shift the function from the real domain to a differential domain. This is done by replacing each subexpression $p$ by an infinite sequence that contains the subexpression and all its derivatives. We refer to it as a differential object: $[p, p', p'', p''', ...]$. For a constant subexpression $c$ the differential object contains almost all zeros $[c, 0, 0, 0, ...]$, as the derivative of a constant is zero.

We model the differential objects by the algebraic data type `Diff`.

```
:: Diff a = Zero | D a (Diff a)
```

If the tail of a differential object contains only zeros, we abbreviate it by using the `Zero` constructor. For instance a constant $c$ is modeled by `D c Zero`. For a simple variable $x$, the first derivative is one and all subsequent derivatives are zero. The representation is therefore `D x (D one Zero)`.

All overloaded operators that appear in the implicit function are instantiated for differential objects. These instances contain all the necessary information of differential calculus. Addition and multiplication on differential objects becomes:

```
instance + (Diff a) | + a
where
    (+) Zero      g         = g
    (+) f         Zero      = f
    (+) (D x xs) (D y ys) = D (x+y) (xs+ys)


instance * (Diff a) | *, + a
where
    (*) Zero                   _ = Zero
    (*) _                   Zero = Zero
    (*) f=:(D x xs) g=:(D y ys) = D (x*y) (xs*g + f*ys)
```

As an example we evaluate the function h x = x * x at $x = 3$. The latter is modelled by (D 3.0 (D 1.0 Zero)). The application of h to (D 3.0 (D 1.0 Zero)) yields D 9.0 (D 6.0 (D 2.0 Zero)), which corresponds to the value of h and its first, and second derivative at $x = 3$.

Due to lazy evaluation we only calculate the derivatives really needed. For the first derivative we have to look no further than the second element of the resulting differential object.

After the polygon generation we apply automatic differentiation to all the generated nodes. The overhead to calculate normal vectors is thus proportional to the number of nodes generated. We lift a node to the differential domain and apply an instance Diff Real of the implicit function to it. Finally the required normal vector is extracted from the differential object.

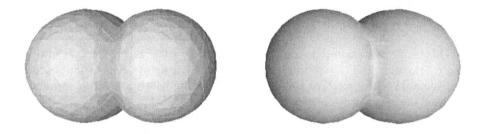

**Fig. 7.** Simple example: blend of two spheres, depth = 5. Right hand side with normal vectors

# 7  Related Work

There are two papers directly related our work: Karczmarczuk [9] advocates the use and advantages of implicit surfaces in general and in a functional setting, however without octrees.

O'Donnel [10] also gives a functional formulation of a traditionally imperative algorithm from computer graphics. A framework of the hierarchical radiosity algorithm (a two dimensional problem) is coded in Haskell, utilizing a forest of quadtrees of unbounded depth, while low level calculation is done in C.

# 8  Conclusion

Implicit functions are a convenient way to specify and manipulate surfaces in computer graphics. The octree approach, which determines the set of polygons that approximates the surface of an implicit function, can be implemented very concisely in a lazy functional programming language.

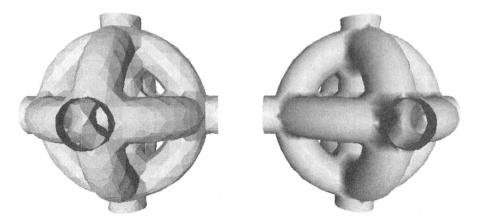

**Fig. 8.** Medium example: blend of three tori and three cylinders, depth = 5. Right hand side with normal vectors

This implementation relies on the use of infinite data structures, lazy evaluation, overloading and the composition of program fragments. Due to the succinct implementation of the octree approach the algorithm becomes easily comprehensible and encourages optimization and extensions.

In this paper we have demonstrated this by introducing memoization to improve efficiency. Through this optimization the resulting functional implementation is almost as efficient as related algorithms implemented in C.

The second extension of the algorithm is automatic differentiation. Using automatic differentiation we calculate normal vectors at the nodes of the polygons approximating the implicit surface. This information is used by visualization tools to let the surface appear much smoother.

Our paper shows that a lazy functional programming language like Clean is an outstanding tool for the implementation of this algorithm. Due to typical properties of lazy functional programming languages like infinite date structures, lazy evaluation pattern matching and the composition of program fragments the implementation is clear and flexible. It appears to be a suitable starting point for further research. The runtime penalty, which is often used as an argument against functional programming languages, is very low.

## Acknowledgements

The first author wishes to thank Jerzy Karczmarczuk for the inspiration to work on this topic.

## References

1. Andrea L. Ames, David R. Nadeau, John L. Moreland. *VRML 2.0 Sourcebook.* New York, NY, 1996

2. Jules Bloomenthal. *Polygonization of Implicit Surfaces.* Computer Aided Geometric Design, vol. 5, no. 4, 1988, pp. 341-355
3. Jules Bloomenthal. *An Implicit Surface Polygonizer.* In Paul Heckbert, editor. *Graphics Gems IV.* New York, NY, 1994
4. Andreas Griewank. *Evaluating Derivatives: Principles and Techniques of Algorithmic Differentiation.* SIAM, Philadelphia, PA, 2000
5. John Hughes. *Lazy Memo-functions.* In Jean-Pierre Jouannaud: *Functional Programming Languages and Computer Architecture.* LNCS 201, Nancy, France, 1985
6. John Hughes. *Why functional programming matters.* The Computer Journal, vol. 32, no. 2, 1989
7. Jerzy Karczmarczuk. *Functional Differentiation of Computer Programs.* Proc. Third International Summer School on Advanced Functional Programming, Baltimore, MD, 1998, pp. 195-203
8. Jerzy Karczmarczuk. *Functional Coding of Differential Forms.* Proc. First Scottish Workshop on Functional Programming, Stirling, Scotland, 1999
9. Jerzy Karczmarczuk. *Geometric Modelling in Functional Style.* Proc. Third Latin-American Conference on Functional Programming, Recife, Brazil, 1999
10. John O'Donnel, Gudula Rünger. *A Coordination Level Functional Implementation of the Hierarchical Radiosity Algorithm.* Draft proc. Glasgow Workshop on Functional Programming, Ullapool, Scotland, 1997
11. Alexander Pasko, Valery Adzhiev, Alexei Sourin, Vladimir Savchenko. *Function Representation in Geometric Modeling: Concepts, Implementation and Applications.* The Visual Computer, vol. 11, no. 8, 1995, pp. 429-446
12. Simon Peyton Jones, Simon Marlow, Conal Elliott. *Stretching the storage Manager: Weak Pointers and Stable Names in Haskell.* In Pieter Koopman, Chris Clack: *Implementation of Functional Languages.* LNCS 1868, Lochem, The Netherlands, 1999
13. Rinus Plasmeijer, Marko van Eekelen. *Concurrent Clean Language Report - version 1.3.* Technical Report CSI-R9816, Computing Science Institute, University of Nijmegen, The Netherlands, 1998
14. Louis B. Rall, George F. Corliss. *An Introduction to Automatic Differentiation.* In Martin Berz, Christian Bischof, George Corliss, Andreas Griewank, Editors. *Computational Differentiation: Techniques, Applications, and Tools* SIAM, Philadelphia, PA, 1996
15. Thorsten H.-G. Zörner. `http://www.cs.kun.nl/~zoerner/implicit.html`, 2000

# Freja, Hat and Hood – A Comparative Evaluation of Three Systems for Tracing and Debugging Lazy Functional Programs

Olaf Chitil, Colin Runciman, and Malcolm Wallace

University of York, UK
{olaf,colin,malcolm}@cs.york.ac.uk

**Abstract.** In this paper we compare three systems for tracing and debugging Haskell programs: Freja, Hat and Hood. We evaluate their usefulness in practice by applying them to a number of moderately complex programs in which errors had deliberately been introduced. We identify the strengths and weaknesses of each system and then form ideas on how the systems can be improved further.

## 1   Introduction

The lack of tools for tracing and debugging has deterred software developers from using functional languages [13]. Conventional debuggers for imperative languages give the user access to otherwise invisible information about a computation by allowing the user to step through the program computation, stop at given points and examine variable contents. This tracing method is unsuitable for lazy functional languages, because their evaluation order is complex, function arguments are usually unwieldy large unevaluated expressions and generally computation details do not match the user's high-level view of functions mapping values to values.

In the middle of the 1980's a wave of research into tracing methods for lazy functional languages started and has been increasing since. In this paper we compare the tracing systems that (a) cover a large subset of a standard lazy functional language, namely Haskell 98 [9], (b) are publicly available and (c) are still actively developed. Freja[1] [7,5] is a system that creates an evaluation dependency tree as trace, a structure based on the idea of declarative/algorithmic debugging from the logic programming community. Hat[2] [12,11] creates a trace that shows the relationships between the redexes (mostly function applications) reduced by the computation. The most recent system, Hood[3] [2], enables the programmer to observe the data structures at given program points. It can basically be used like **print** statements in imperative languages, but the lazy evaluation order is not affected and functions can be observed as well.

---

[1] http://www.ida.liu.se/~henni
[2] http://www.cs.york.ac.uk/fp/ART
[3] http://www.haskell.org/hood

M. Mohnen and P. Koopman (Eds.): IFL 2000, LNCS 2011, pp. 176–193, 2001.

In this paper we compare Freja 1.1, Hat 1.0 and Hood July 2000 release. We evaluate the systems in practice by applying them to a number of moderately complex programs in which errors are deliberately introduced. Tracing systems are interactively used tools. In this paper we concentrate on the usefulness of the systems for the programmer. Runtime and space usage measurements are reported in other papers [5,6,11]. We do not aim for a quantitative comparison to crown a winner. Only with a large number of programmers could we have obtained statistically valid data about, for example, how long it takes to locate a specific error with a specific system. Even these data depend for example on how well the programmers are trained for a system, especially because the systems are rather different. Our aim is to explore the design space of tracers and gain insights for the future development of tracing and debugging systems. Our experiments highlight and sometimes even uncover previously unnoticed similarities and distinguishing features of the three systems. The experiments enable us to evaluate the usefulness of system features and lead us to new ideas for how the current systems can be improved or even be combined.

The paper is structured as follows. Section 2 gives a short introduction to each of the three systems. Section 3 compares the systems with respect to their approach to tracing, design and implementation. Section 4 reports on our practical experiments and the insights they gave us into the systems' distinguishing properties and their usefulness. Section 5 briefly describes other systems for tracing and debugging. Section 6 concludes.

## 2   Learn Three Systems in Three Minutes

To give an idea about what the three tracing systems provide and how they are used we give a short introduction here. Because all three systems are still under rapid development we try to avoid details that may change soon.

We demonstrate the use of each system with the following example program[4].

```
main = let xs = [4*2, 3+6] :: [Int]
           in (head xs, last xs)

head (x:xs) = x

last (x:xs) = last xs
last [x]    = x
```

Note that the evaluation in Section 4 is based on experiments with far larger programs.

---

[4] Freja actually expects **main** to be of type **String** and the other two systems expect it to be of type **IO** (). Here we abstract from the details of input/output.

## 2.1   Freja

Freja is a compiler for a subset of Haskell 98. A debugging session consists of the user answering a sequence of questions. Each question concerns a reduction of a redex – that is, a function application – to a value. The user has to answer *yes*, if the reduction is correct with respect to his intentions, and *no* otherwise. In the end the debugger states which reduction is the cause of the observed faulty behaviour – that is, which function definition is incorrect.

The first question always asks if the reduction of the function `main` to the result value of the program is correct. If the question about the reduction of a function application is answered with *no*, then the next question concerns a reduction for evaluating the right-hand-side of the definition of this function. Freja can be used rather similarly to a conventional debugger. The input *no* means "step into current function call" and the input *yes* means "go on to next function call". If the reduction of a function application is incorrect but all reductions for the evaluation of the function's right-hand-side are correct, then the definition of this function must be incorrect for the given arguments.

The following is a debugging session with Freja for our example program. The symbol $\perp$ represents an error and the symbol ? represents an expression that has never been evaluated and whose value hence cannot have influenced the computation.

```
main ⇒ (8,⊥)      no
4*2 ⇒ 8           yes
head [8,?] ⇒ 8    yes
last [8,?] ⇒ ⊥    no
last [?] ⇒ ⊥      no
last [] ⇒ ⊥       yes
Bug located! Erroneous reduction: last [?] ⇒ ⊥
```

## 2.2   Hat

Hat consists of a modified version of the nhc98 Haskell compiler[5] and a separate browser program. A program compiled for tracing executes as usual except that alongside the normal computation it builds a redex trail in heap and instead·of terminating at the end it waits for the browser to connect to it. The browser shows the output of the program. The user selects a part of it and asks the browser for its parent redex. The parent redex of an expression is the redex that through its own reduction created the expression. Each part of the redex has again a parent redex which the browser shows on demand. A trail ends at the function (redex) `main`, which has no parent. Debugging with Hat works by going from a faulty output or error message *backwards* until the error is located.

The browser has a graphical user interface which we do not discuss here. Basically the system is used as follows to locate the error in our example program. The program aborts with an error message and the browser directly shows its

---

[5] http://www.cs.york.ac.uk/fp/nhc98

parent redex: `last []`. The user is surprised that the function `last` is ever called with an empty list as argument and asks the browser for the parent redex of `last []`. The answer, `last (3+6:[])`, makes clear that the definition of `last` is not correct for a single element list. The browser presents the redex trail as shown in the following figure. To demonstrate how the parent of a subexpression is presented (`4*2` is the parent of `8`), more of the redex trail is shown than is needed for locating the error.

```
• last []
│ last (3+6:[])
│ last (8:3+6:[])
│  ▽ 4*2
⊥ main
```

The browser can also show where in the program text for example `last` is called with the argument `[]` in the equation for `last (x:xs)`.

## 2.3   Hood

Hood currently is simply a Haskell library. A user annotates some expressions in a program with the combinator `observe`, which is defined in the library. While the program is running, information about the values of the annotated expressions is recorded. After program termination the user can view for each annotation the observed values.

We annotate the argument of `last` in our example program:

```
main = let xs = [4*2, 3+6]
           in (head xs, last (observe "last arg" xs))
```

When the modified program terminates it gives us the following information:

```
-- last arg
  _ : _ : []
```

The symbol `_` represents an unevaluated expression. Note that the first element of the list `xs` is evaluated by the program, but not by the function `last`.

To gain more insight into how the program works we observe the function `last`, including all its recursive calls:

```
last = observe "last" last'

last' (x:xs) = last xs
last' [x]    = x
```

The value of the function is shown as a finite mapping of arguments to results:

```
-- last
  { \ (_ : _ : []) -> throw <Exception>
  , \ (_ : []))    -> throw <Exception>
  , \ []  -> throw <Exception>
  }
```

So `last` is called with an empty list. We draw the conclusion that `last` applied to the one element list caused this erroneous call, but strictly the information provided by Hood does not imply this.

# 3   Comparison in Principle

At first sight the three systems do not seem to have anything in common except the goal of aiding debugging. However, all three systems take a two phase approach: while the program is running, information about the computation process is collected. After termination of the program the collected information is viewed in some kind of browser. In Freja, the browser is the part that asks the questions, in Hat the program that lets the user view parents and in Hood the part that prints the observations. This approach should not be confused with classical post-mortem debugging where only the final state of the computation can be viewed. Having a trace that describes aspects of a full computation enables new forms of exploring program behaviour and locating errors which should make these systems also interesting for strict functional languages or even non-functional languages.

All three systems are suitable for programs that show any of the three kinds of possible faulty observable behaviour: wrong output, abortion with error message, non-termination. In the latter case the program can be interrupted and subsequently the trace can be viewed.

## 3.1   Values and Evaluation

All three systems are source-level tracers. They mostly show Haskell-like expressions which are built from functions, data constructors and constants of the program. To improve comprehensibility, all three systems show values instead of arbitrary expressions as far as possible. Hood only shows values anyway. Both Freja and Hat show an argument in a redex not as it was passed in the actual computation but as a value. Only (a part of) an argument that was never evaluated is shown as an unevaluated redex in Hat (3+6 in the previous example) whereas Freja and Hood represent it by a special symbol (? in Freja and _ in Hood). Freja and Hat show an expression only up to a given depth (for example `map succ (0 : succ 0 : □)` in Hat; □ represents the elided subexpression). A subexpression beyond that depth is only shown on demand. None of the systems changes the usual observable behaviour of a program. In particular, they do not force the evaluation of expressions that are not needed by the program.

However, the systems differ in that Hood shows values as far evaluated as they are *demanded in the context* of the observation position whereas both Freja and Hat show how far values are evaluated in the whole computation, including the effect of sharing. Hence in the previous example Freja and Hat show the first element of the list argument in the first call of `last` as 8 whereas Hood only represents that element by _.

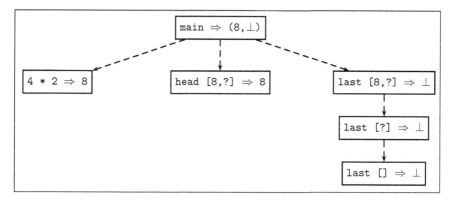

**Fig. 1.** Evaluation dependency tree

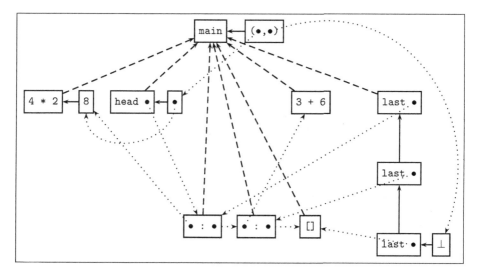

**Fig. 2.** Redex trail

## 3.2 Trace Structures

In Hood a trace is a set of observations. These observations are shown in full to
the user. In contrast, each of Freja and Hat create a single large trace structure
for a program run. It is impossible to show such a trace in full to the user. The
browser of each system permits the programmer to walk through the structure,
always seeing only a small local part of the whole trace.

Freja creates an Evaluation Dependency Tree (EDT) as trace. Each node
of the tree is a reduction as shown in the browser. The tree is basically the
derivation/proof tree for a call-by-value reduction with miraculous stops where
expressions are not needed for the result. The call-by-value structure ensures
that the tree structure reflects the program structure and that arguments are

maximally evaluated. Figure 1 shows the EDT for our example program of Section 2. The symbol $\perp$ represents the value of the error message.

Hat creates a redex trail as trace. A redex trail is a directed graph of value nodes and redex nodes. Each node, except the node for `main`, has an arrow to its parent redex node. Because subexpressions of a redex may have different parents or may be shared, redex nodes may contain arrows to nodes of their subexpressions. Figure 2 shows the redex trail for our example program of Section 2. Dotted arrows point to subexpressions. Both dashed and solid arrows denote the parent relationship. $(8, \perp)$ is the result value of the computation. As in Freja, $\perp$ represents the value of the error message.

The graphs of the two trace structures are laid out to stress their similarity. All arrows of the EDT are also present in the redex trail but point in the opposite direction. If the redex trail held information about which parent relations correspond to reductions (these are shown as solid arrows), then the EDT could be constructed from the redex trail (however, see also the next paragraph and Section 4.1 about free variables). In contrast, the redex trail contains more information than the EDT, because it additionally links every value with its parent redex and describes how expressions are shared.

The redex trail shown in Figure 2 is a simplified version of the one that is really created by Hat. The real redex trail has an additional node `xs` with parent `main` and children $4 * 2$, $3 + 6$, the two $\bullet : \bullet$ nodes and `[]`. That is, the redex trail also records the reduction of the `let` expression. The whole `let` expression is a redex, but in the redex trail it is represented by the defined variable `xs`. Similarly a node `xs` $\Rightarrow$ `[8,?]` that records the reduction of the `let` expression could be added to the EDT. So recording a `let` reduction is an option for both the EDT and the redex trail and the implementors of Freja and Hat made different decisions with respect to this option. On the one hand recording `let` reductions leads to larger traces with an unusual kind of redex. On the other hand it enables more fine grained tracing (cf. Section 4.3).

Because Hood observations contain values as they are demanded in a given context, whereas both the EDT and the redex trail contain values in their most evaluated form, it is not possible to gain Hood observations from either the EDT or the redex trail. Conversely, even observing every subexpression of a program with Hood would not enable us to construct an EDT or redex trail, because there is no information about the relations between the observations.

### 3.3   Implementation and Portablility

Each system consists of two parts, the browser and a part for the generation of the trace. We will discuss the browsers in Section 4.

The developers of the three systems made different choices about the level at which they implemented the creation of the trace. In Freja the trace is created in the heap directly by modified instructions of the abstract graph reduction machine. Hat transforms the original Haskell program into another Haskell program. Running the compiled transformed program yields the redex trail in addition to the normal result. Finally, in Hood the trace is created as a side effect by the combinator `observe`, which is defined in a Haskell library.

The level of implementation has direct effects on the portability to different Haskell systems. Hood can be used with different Haskell systems, because the library only requires a few non-standard functions such as `unsafePerformIO` which are provided by every Haskell system[6]. The transformation of Hat is currently integrated into the nhc98 compiler but could be separated. A transformed program uses a few non-standard unsafe functions to improve performance. Furthermore, some extensions of the Haskell run-time system are required to retain access to the result after termination or interruption and to connect to the browser. Finally, Freja is a Haskell system of its own. Adding its low-level trace creation mechanism to any other Haskell system would require a major rewriting of this system.

## 3.4   Reduction of Trace Size

In Hood the trace consists only of the observations of annotated expressions. Hence its size can be controlled by the choice of annotations[7]. In contrast, both Freja and Hat construct traces of the complete computation in the heap.

To reduce the size of the trace, both Freja and Hat enable marking of functions or whole modules as trusted. The reduction of a trusted function itself is recorded in the trace, but not the reductions performed to evaluate the right-hand-side of its definition. The details of the trusting mechanisms of both systems are non-trivial, because the evaluation of untrusted functions which are passed to trusted higher-order functions have to be recorded in the trace. Usually at least the Haskell Prelude is trusted.

To further reduce the space consumption, both Freja and Hat support the construction of partial traces. In Freja, first only an upper part of the EDT may be constructed during program execution. When the user reaches the edge of the constructed part of the EDT in the browser, this part is deleted and the whole program is re-executed, this time constructing the part of the EDT that can be reached next by the questions. So, except for the time delay caused by re-execution, the user has the impression that the whole EDT is present.

Hat can produce partial traces by limiting the length of the redex trails. Because a redex trail is browsed backwards, the system prunes away those redexes that are further than a certain length away from the live program data or output. Hat does not provide any mechanism like re-execution in Freja to recreate a pruned part of the redex trail.

---

[6] The version of Hood which can handle not only terminating programs but also those that abort with an error message or do not terminate requires the non-standard exception library supplied with the Glasgow Haskell compiler.

[7] A variant of Hood allows the annotated running program to write observed events directly to a file, so that the trace does not need to be kept in primary memory. However, to obtain observations, the events in the file need to be sorted. Hence the browser for displaying observations reads the complete file and thus has problems with large observations.

Requiring less heap space may reduce garbage collection time, but Hat still spends the time for constructing the whole trace whereas Freja does not need to spend time on trace construction after construction of an upper part of an EDT.

## 4    Evaluation of the Systems

Differences between the systems directly raise several questions. Is it desirable to add a feature of one system to another system? Does an alternative design decision make sense? How far is a distinguishing feature inherent to a system, possibly determined by its implementation method or its tracing model? Because the design space for a tracer is huge, it is sensible to evaluate system features in practice early. We applied the three systems to a number of programs in which errors had deliberately been introduced. The errors caused all three kinds of faulty observable behaviour mentioned earlier: wrong output, abortion with error message and non-termination.

Our evaluation experiments use the following protocol: At least two programmers are involved. First the author of a correctly working program explains how the program works. Then one programmer secretly introduces several deliberate errors into the program, of a kind undetected by the compiler. Given the faulty program, the other programmers use a tracing system to locate and fix all the errors, thinking aloud and taking notes as they do so.

All the participants are experienced Haskell programmers.

The programs used in the experiments are of moderate complexity. The largest program, PsaCompiler, a compiler for a toy language, consists of 900 lines in 13 modules and performs 20,000 reductions for the input we provided. The longest running program, Adjoxo, an adjudicator for noughts and crosses (tic tac toe), consists of only 100 lines but performs up to 830,000 reductions for our inputs. In our choice of programs we were restricted by the subset of Haskell that Freja supports. For example, Freja does not implement classes and unfortunately not even every Freja program is a valid Haskell program. Freja had been applied to a mini compiler with 16 million reductions [6] and Hat had been applied to a version of nhc98 with 14,000 lines and 5.2 million reductions and a chess end-game program with 20 million reductions [11]. These papers give performance figures but do not indicate how easy debugging programs of this size is. We cannot make such statements either, but our programs are definitely beyond toy examples and of a size often occurring in practise. Our programs also do not perform monadic input/output. Freja does not implement it and Hat only supports a few operations. It would be interesting to see if Hood's ability to show the return value of an executed input/output action is sufficient in practice.

### 4.1    Readability of Expressions

In contrast to our preliminary fears that the expressions shown by the browsers – reductions, redexes and values – would be too large to be comprehensible, for our programs they are mostly of moderate size and easily readable.

As we will discuss in Section 4.2 the user of a tracing system not only views the trace but also the program. Nonetheless in Freja and Hat informative variable (function) names, that convey the semantics of the variable well, substantially reduce the need for viewing the program and thus increase the speed of the debugging process substantially.

**Unevaluated Expressions.** Freja shows unevaluated expressions as ? and the undefined value as ⊥. This property makes expressions even shorter and more readable. This also holds for Hood. Only in some cases more information would be desirable for better orientation. In Hat the display of the unevaluated redexes in full sometimes obscures higher level properties, for example the length of a list. All in all our observations suggest that unevaluated expressions should be collapsed into a symbol by default but should be viewable on demand.

Hood shows even less of a value than Freja, because it only shows the part demanded in a given context. Note that this amount of information would suffice for answering the questions of Freja. Because Hat is not based on questions, it is less clear if showing only demanded values would be suitable for it. Finally, the fact that Freja and Hat show values to the extent to which they are evaluated in the whole computation whereas Hood shows them to the extent to which they are demanded is closely linked to the respective implementations of the systems and thus not easily changeable.

**Functions.** In Haskell, functions are first-class citizens and hence function values may appear for example as arguments in redexes or inside data structures.

For the representation of function values, Hood deviates from the principle of showing Haskell-like expressions. It shows function values as finite mappings from arguments to results. Because the mapping contains only expressions that were demanded during the computation, the representation is short in most cases. However, for functions that are called often and especially for higher-order functions the representation is unwieldy. The representation requires some time to get used to. In return, it permits a rather abstract, denotational view of program semantics which is useful for determining the correctness of part of a program.

In Freja and Hat a function value is shown as a function name, a $\lambda$-abstraction, or as a partial application of a function name or a $\lambda$-abstraction. Function names and their partial applications are easily readable but $\lambda$-abstractions are not. Both systems do not show a $\lambda$-abstraction as it is written in the program but represent it by a new symbol: `<lambda#`$n$`>` for a number $n$ in Freja and `(\)` in Hat. Both systems can show the full $\lambda$-abstraction on demand. However, because of the necessary additional step and because $\lambda$-abstractions are often large expressions, reading expressions involving $\lambda$-abstractions is hard. We conjecture that with Freja or Hat debugging programs that make substantial use of $\lambda$-abstractions, as commonly done for stylised abstractions such as continuation passing, higher-order combinators and monads, is rather difficult. Our programs hardly use stylised abstractions. In fact, PsaCompiler uses only named functions, even in the definitions of its parser combinators, where most Haskell programmers would use λ-abstractions. During tracing, Freja and Hat show very readable expressions for PsaCompiler.

**Free Variables.** Both λ-abstractions and the definition bodies of locally defined functions often contain free variables. To answer a question in Freja the values of such free variables must be known. Hence Freja shows this information in a `where` clause. The following question from an evaluation experiment demonstrates that this information usually adds to the comprehensibility of a question considerably:

```
tableRead
  "y"
  (TableImp
    (newTableFunction
      where
        newIndex = "x",
        newEntry = 1,
        oldTableFunction = implTableEmpty))
=>
Just 1
```

The correct answer is obviously *no*.

Hat does not show the values of free variables. This information can be obtained only indirectly by following the chain of parent redexes of such a function. To realise that a function has free variables and to see the corresponding arguments of parent redexes it is necessary to follow links to the program source.

In Hood an observation of a locally defined function can be misleading. The observation is really for a family of different functions, with different values for free variables. In our experiments one observation of a local function `moveval` is presented as follows

```
-- moveval
{ ... , \ 8 -> Draw, ... }
{ ... , \ 8 -> Win, ... }
```

### 4.2   Locating an Error

With all three systems we successfully locate all errors in our programs. For locating an error in our largest program we answer between 10 and 30 questions in Freja, look at 0 to 6 parents in Hat and add `observe` up to 3 times for Hood. The relation between these numbers is typical. However, the numbers cannot be compared directly to determine speed of use, because the counted operations are completely different. A major difference between the systems is the time the user has to spend thinking about what to do next, and the effort required to do it. For example, the time required in Hood for deciding where to add `observe` annotations, modifying the program (discussed further in

Section 4.4), recompiling the program and reexecuting it is substantially higher than answering a question or selecting an expression for viewing its parent. Furthermore, the amount of data produced by a single observe annotation is usually substantial.

**Guidance and Strategies.** Freja asks questions which the user has to answer whereas in both other systems the user also has to ask the right questions. Freja guides the user towards the error.

Hat at least starts with the program output, an error message or the last evaluated redex in an interrupted program and the main operation is to choose a subexpression and ask for its parent. There are usually many subexpressions to choose from and the system never states that an error has been located at a given position in the program. Wrong parts in the output or wrong arguments in redexes are candidates for further enquiry. Nonetheless, for the less experienced user it is easy to get lost examining an irrelevant region of the redex trail.

Hood gives the complete freedom to observe any value in the program. The initial choice of what to observe is difficult and often seems arbitrary. In general Hood users apply a top-down strategy in their placement of observe combinators, if the faulty behaviour does not point to any program location, for example when the program does not terminate. Then the questions the Hood users asks are similar to those asked by Freja. If, on the other hand, the position where the observable fault is caused can be identified, for example when the program aborts with an error message occurring only once in the program, then a Hood user tries to apply a bottom-up strategy reminiscent of Hat.

Our programs contain several errors. Users of Hat and Hood locate the errors in the same order, because they always locate the error that causes the observed faulty behaviour. In contrast, the questions of Freja sometimes lead to the location of a different error. It is possible to tackle a specific faulty behaviour by answering some questions incorrectly, but that requires care. One may easily steer into irrelevant regions of the EDT.

**General Usability.** Hat with its complex browser has the steepest learning curve for a new user. In contrast, the principle of questions and answers of Freja is easy to grasp and Hood has the advantage of using the idea of print statements, which are well-known from imperative languages. Hence a mode that would hide some features from the beginner seems desirable for Hat.

**Information Used.** A Hood user has to modify the program and hence look at it. Sometimes just the process of searching for a good placement of observe reveals the error. Users of Freja and Hat, especially the former, tend to neglect the program. As long as the user knows the intended meaning of functions he can use Freja without ever looking at the program. This does however imply that the user does not try to follow Freja's reasoning and to understand how the finally located error actually caused the observed faulty behaviour. Redexes as shown by Hat are not intended to be the only source of information for locating an error. Viewing the program part where a redex is created gives valuable context information and at the end the program is needed to locate the error. Both Freja and Hat provide quick access to the part of the program relating to the current question or redex. Nonetheless, it seems worthwhile to test if automatically showing the relevant part of the program when a new question or parent is shown would improve usability.

In contrast to the other two systems Hat also gives information about which expressions are shared. This information is useful in some cases, usually when expressions are shared unexpectedly.

A trace of Hood is a set of observations. The trace unfortunately contains no information about the relations between these observations. Hence, with a few exceptions, we observe functions to obtain at least a relation between arguments and result. In particular, the representation of an observed function shows clearly which (part of an) argument is *not* demanded by the function for determining its result. This feature is helpful for locating errors.

**Wrong Subexpressions.** Often, in the questions posed by Freja, a specific subexpression of a result is wrong. For example in the following program the *1* in the second list element should be a *2*. But there is no way to give Freja this information. We can only confirm or refute the reduction as a whole.

```
translateStatement
  (TableImp
    (newTableFunction
      where
        newIndex = "y",
        newEntry = 2,
        oldTableFunction = newTableFunction
                            where
                              newIndex = "x",
                              newEntry = 1,
                              oldTableFunction = implTableEmpty))
    ?
    (Assignment "x" (Compound (Var "x") Minus (Var "y")))
  =>
  _Tuple_2 [Lod 1,Lod 1 ,Sb,Sto 1] 4
```

In contrast, the redex trail contains the parent of every subexpression. A Hat user seldom asks for the parent of a complete expression but usually for the parent of some subexpression. We believe that this is the major reason why we look at far less parents with Hat than we answer questions of Freja for locating the same error. A Hood user obviously also tries to use information about wrong subexpressions but it is not easy to decide where to place the next observe combinator.

**Reduction of Information.** In Hood, the user determines the size of the trace by the placement of `observe` combinators. It is, however, sometimes not easy to foresee how large an observation will be. The trusting mechanisms in Freja and Hat not only save space but also reduce the amount of information presented to the user. The ability of the Freja browser to dynamically trust a function and thus avoid further questions about it is useful. For Hat a corresponding feature seems desirable. In Freja, sometimes a question is repeated, because the same reduction is performed again. Hence memoisation of questions and their answers is desirable. It would also be useful to be able to generalise an answer, to avoid a series of very similar questions all requiring the same answer.

**Runtime Overhead.** With respect to the time overhead caused by the creation of traces the low-level implementation of Freja pays off. The overhead is not noticeable. In contrast, in Hat traced computations are more than ten times slower. For some inputs adjoxo seems to be non-terminating but it is only slow! We experience the same with Hood when we observe at positions that are computed very often and that lead to large observations. So in Hood the time overhead is considerable but it is only proportional to the amount of observed data.

**Compiler Messages.** A helpful error message from a compiler can reduce the need for a tracer. If a function is called with an argument for which no matching equation exists, then the aborting program gives the function name if it was compiled with the Glasgow Haskell compiler[8], but not if it was compiled with Freja or nhc98. However, in that case Hat directly shows the function with its arguments whereas Freja requires the answers to numerous questions before locating the error.

### 4.3   Redexes and Language Constructs

A computation does not only consist of reductions of function applications. We noted already in Section 3.2 for `let` expressions that there are other kinds of redexes. This aspect only concerns Freja and Hat, because Hood only shows values.

**CAFs.** A constant applicative form (CAF) is a top-level variable of arity zero, in other words a top-level function without arguments. Its value is computed on demand and shared by its users. Both Freja and Hat take the view that a CAF has no parent. Hence the trace of a program in Freja is generally not a single EDT but a set of EDTs, an EDT for each CAF including `main`. These EDTs are sorted so that a CAF only uses those CAFs about which questions have already been asked and which are hence known to be free of errors. Unfortunately one of our experiment programs contains 35 CAFs. We have to confirm the correctness of evaluation for all CAFs before reaching the question about `main`, although

---

[8] http://www.haskell.org/ghc

none of these CAFs are related to any of the errors. Freja can be instructed to start with the question about `main`. However, that implies stating that the evaluation of all CAFs is correct, which may not be the case and thus lead Freja to give a wrong error location. An alternative definition of the EDT could imply that all users of a CAF are its parents. Then a question about a CAF would be asked only if it were relevant and memoisation of the question and its answer could avoid asking the same question when another reduction using the CAF were investigated.

For Hat a corresponding modification without losing sharing of CAFs seems to be more difficult, because the redex trail is browsed by going backwards from an expression to its unique parent. In our experiments the fact that a CAF has no parent in a redex trail is not noticeable, because none of the introduced errors concerns CAFs. However, programs can be constructed where this lack of information hinders locating an error:

```
nats :: [Int]
nats = 0 : map succ nats

main = print (last nats)
```

The computation of this program does not terminate. When the programmer interrupts the computation, Hat may show `map succ (0 : succ 0 : □)` as next redex to be evaluated. The parent of this redex is `nats`, which has no parent. The error may well be that the programmer intended to call another function than `last` in the definition of `main`, but unfortunately the redex `last nats` is unreachable.

We stated in Section 3.2 that Hat has a special kind of redex for locally defined variables of arity zero (defined in `let` expressions and `where` clauses). The parent of such a variable redex is the redex that created the definition and not – as for function application redexes – the redex that created the application. So as for CAFs redexes may become unreachable.

**Guards, `cases` and `ifs`.** In Haskell the selection of an equation of a definition may not only be determined by pattern matching but may also depend on the value of a guard:

```
test :: (a -> Bool) -> a -> Maybe a

test p x | p x       = Just x
         | otherwise = Nothing
```

In Freja the reduction of a guard (`p x`) is a child of the reduction of the function (`test`). Redex trails are, however, traversed backwards from the result value (`Just` $x$ or `Nothing`). To hold the information about the reduction of a guard, redex trails have an additional sort of redexes. In the example, if the first equation were chosen, then the value `Just` $x$ would have the parent | `True` $\lhd$ `test` $p$ $x$, and if the second equation were chosen, then the value `Nothing` would have the parent | True ◁ | False ◁ test $p$ $x$. By asking for the parents of the truth values True and False in the redexes, the user can obtain information about the evaluation of the guards.

Similarly, Hat uses special redexes for case and if expressions. On the one hand, these special redexes complicate the system. On the other hand, they are useful for large function definitions. The special redexes enable more fine grained tracing up to the level of guards, cases and ifs, whereas Freja only identifies a whole function reduction as faulty. Similar to the situation for locally defined variables it is possible to extend the definition of Freja's EDT by special nodes for guard, case and if reductions. For Hat, special redexes for these reductions are important to make parts of the redex trail reachable by backward traversal that otherwise would be unreachable.

### 4.4   Modification of the Program

Whereas Freja and Hat are applied to the original program, requiring only special compilation, Hood is based on modifying the program. Sometimes the introduction of the observe combinator requires modifications which are non-trivial, if an operator is observed (because of its infix position) or if not a specific call but all calls of a function are observed as in our example in Section 2.3. Furthermore, the main function has to be modified and the library has to be imported in every program module that uses its entities. Most importantly, a data type can only be observed if it is an instance of a class Observable. Some of our experiment programs define many data types; because we want to observe most of them, we have to write many instance definitions. Writing these instance definitions is easy but time consuming. Additionally, all these modifications potentially introduce new errors in the program and also make the program less readable.

On the other hand it might be useful to leave the modifications for Hood in the program. They could be en-/disabled during compilation by a preprocessor flag for a debug mode. Then most modifications, especially writing instances of the class Observable, require only a one-time effort. The observe combinator may even be placed to observe the main data structures of the program. Thus debugging is integrated more closely into program development. In contrast, Freja and Hat cannot save any information from a tracing session for future versions of the program.

## 5   Other Tracers and Debuggers

Buddha [4,10] is a tracing system which like Freja constructs an EDT. Its implementation is based on a source-to-source transformation, but unlike the transformation of Hat this transformation is not purely syntax-directed but requires type information. Buddha is still actively developed.

Booth and Jones [3,1] sketch a system which creates a trace quite similar to an EDT. The main difference is that a parent node is only connected directly to one child. All sibling nodes are connected with each other according to the structure of the definition body of the parent node. Thus the trace has the nice property that all connecting arrows denote equality, unlike the arrows in an EDT or a redex trail. The authors describe a browser which gives more freedom in traversing the trace than the questions of Freja.

There also exist several systems for showing the actual computation sequence of a lazy functional program. Section 2.2 of [14], Chapter 11 of [5] and Chapter 2 and Section 7.5 of [8] review a large number of tracing and debugging systems for lazy functional languages.

We could not include any of these systems in our experiments, because there are only limited prototypes, not publicly available.

## 6   Summary and Conclusions

We have compared and evaluated the tracing and debugging systems Freja, Hat and Hood by applying them to a number of programs.

Tracing and debugging systems for lazy functional languages have made considerable progress in recent years: all three systems prove to be effective tools for debugging our programs. Though none of our programs is very large, some of them are large enough to show that the scope of application for the tools goes well beyond easy exercises. Unfortunately the practical usability of Hat and especially Freja is currently limited by the fact that they do not support full Haskell 98.

Each of the tracing tools takes a unique approach with specific strengths. In particular, Freja has a systematic fault-finding procedure; Hat starts at the observed error and enables exploring backwards the history of every subexpression; Hood observes the data flow at specific program points by need.

Based on our experiments we identify in Section 4 the strengths but also the weaknesses of each system. For some weaknesses we already suggest improvements, often based on the convincing solutions of the problems in other systems. Other weaknesses are linked either to the tracing method or the implementation, which we discuss in Section 3. Hence they are more difficult to address and require further research. For example, Freja cannot take advantage of the common case that only a subexpression of a reduction is wrong, Hat is slow and Hood gives almost no indication of how values are related. We claim that an integration of Freja into Hat is feasible whereas Hood's approach is rather different from the approaches of the other two systems.

Finally, good tools are not sufficient for debugging. The user needs advice on how to effectively use each system; a strategy needs to be developed for Hat and especially for Hood, but even Freja would benefit from advice on how to employ its advanced features. Also a strategy for using several systems together, taking advantage of their respective strengths, is desirable.

# Acknowledgments

We thank Henrik Nilsson and Jan Sparud for taking part in the evaluation experiments and making valuable observations.

# References

1. Simon P Booth and Simon B Jones. Walk backwards to happiness – debugging by time travel. Technical Report Technical Report CSM-143, Department of Computer Science and Mathematics, University of Stirling, 1997. This paper was presented at the 3rd International Workshop on Automated Debugging (AADEBUG'97), hosted by the Department of Computer and Information Science, Linköping University, Sweden, May 1997.
2. Andy Gill. Debugging Haskell by observing intermediate data structures. In *Proceedings of the 4th Haskell Workshop*, 2000. Technical report of the University of Nottingham.
3. Simon B. Jones and Simon P. Booth. Towards a purely functional debugger for functional programs. In *Proceedings Glasgow Workshop on Functional Programming 1995*, Ullapool, Scotland, July 1995.
4. Lee Naish and Tim Barbour. Towards a portable lazy functional declarative debugger. In *Proc. 19th Australasian Computer Science Conference*, January 1996.
5. Henrik Nilsson. *Declarative Debugging for Lazy Functional Languages*. PhD thesis, Linköping, Sweden, May 1998.
6. Henrik Nilsson. Tracing piece by piece: affordable debugging for lazy functional languages. In *Proceedings of the 1999 ACM SIGPLAN International Conference on Functional Programming*, pages 36–47. ACM Press, 1999.
7. Henrik Nilsson and Jan Sparud. The evaluation dependence tree as a basis for lazy functional debugging. *Automated Software Engineering: An International Journal*, 4(2):121–150, April 1997.
8. Alastair Penney. *Augmenting Trace-based Functional Debugging*. PhD thesis, Department of Computer Science, University of Bristol, September 1999.
9. Simon L. Peyton Jones, John Hughes, et al. Haskell 98: A non-strict, purely functional language. http://www.haskell.org, February 1999.
10. Bernard Pope. Buddha: A declarative debugger for Haskell. Technical report, Dept. of Computer Science, University of Melbourne, Australia, June 1998. Honours Thesis.
11. Jan Sparud and Colin Runciman. Complete and partial redex trails of functional computations. In C. Clack, K. Hammond, and T. Davie, editors, *Selected papers from 9th Intl. Workshop on the Implementation of Functional Languages (IFL'97)*, pages 160–177. Springer LNCS Vol. 1467, September 1997.
12. Jan Sparud and Colin Runciman. Tracing lazy functional computations using redex trails. In H. Glaser, P. Hartel, and H. Kuchen, editors, *Proc. 9th Intl. Symposium on Programming Languages, Implementations, Logics and Programs (PLILP'97)*, pages 291–308. Springer LNCS Vol. 1292, September 1997.
13. Philip Wadler. Functional programming: Why no one uses functional languages. *SIGPLAN Notices*, 33(8):23–27, August 1998. Functional programming column.
14. R. D. Watson. *Tracing Lazy Evaluation by Program Transformation*. PhD thesis, Southern Cross, Australia, October 1996.

# Porting the Clean Object I/O Library to Haskell

Peter Achten[1] and Simon Peyton Jones[2]

[1] Computing Science Department, University of Nijmegen, 1 Toernooiveld, 6525 ED,
Nijmegen, The Netherlands
peter88@cs.kun.nl
[2] Microsoft Research Cambridge, St. George House, 1 Guildhall street, Cambridge,
CB2 3 NH, UK
simonpj@microsoft.com

**Abstract.** Pure, functional programming languages offer several solutions to construct Graphical User Interfaces (GUIs). In this paper we
report on a project in which we port the Clean Object I/O library to
Haskell. The Clean Object I/O library uses an explicit environment passing scheme, based on the uniqueness type system of Clean. It supports
many standard GUI features such as windows, dialogues, controls, and
menus. Applications can have timing behaviour. In addition, there is support for interactive processes and message passing. The standard functional programming language Haskell uses a monadic framework for I/O.
We discuss how the Object I/O library can be put in a monadic framework without loosing its essential features. We give an implementation
of an essential fragment of the Object I/O library to demonstrate the
feasibility. We take especial consideration for the relevant design choices.
One particular design choice, how to handle state, results in two versions.

## 1 Introduction

The pure, lazy, functional programming language *Clean* [9,17,21] offers a sophisticated library for programmers to construct Graphical User Interfaces (GUI) on
a high level of abstraction, the *Object I/O library*. The *uniqueness type system*
[24,7] of Clean is the fundamental tool to allow safe and efficient Input/Output.
This has been taken advantage of in the Object I/O library, which employs
an *explicit multiple environment passing style* (a less precise but more concise
term is *"world as value"*). From the outset on [1,2] one of the key features of the
Clean I/O project has been the explicit handling of *state*, and the specification of
graphical user interfaces at a high level of abstraction. The approach has proven
to be successful and flexible, allowing the model to be extended with interactive
processes (on an interleaving and concurrent basis [3]), message passing (synchronous and asynchronous), and local state resulting in an object oriented style
[4,5]. The library provides a rather complete set of GUI objects for real-world
applications and produces efficient code. This has been demonstrated by writing
a complete integrated development environment, the *CleanIDE*.

In Clean the uniqueness type system is used to support I/O in an explicit
multiple environment passing style. Two other styles of solutions have been proposed to handle I/O in a purely-functional setting: *stream based* and *monad*

M. Mohnen and P. Koopman (Eds.): IFL 2000, LNCS 2011, pp. 194–213, 2001.
© Springer-Verlag Berlin Heidelberg 2001

*based* [27,18]. The standard functional programming language *Haskell* [15,20] initially adopted a stream based solution up to version 1.2. From version 1.3 on monads were firmly integrated in the language. Many interesting experimental frameworks have been proposed to handle GUI programming in both styles ([10,16,23,25] to name a few). For a broad overview see Section 7.

In this paper we report on a project in which we ported a core subset of this I/O system to Haskell. There are several motives to embark on such a project.

- Monads are considered to be a standard way of handling I/O in pure functional languages. In this project we demonstrate that it is possible to transfer the concepts of the Object I/O system to a monadic framework.
- Designing a solution to functional GUI programming is one thing, but it is a truly large effort to maintain, extend and improve such a system. The Clean Object I/O library has proven itself in practice. It is efficient and in a fairly stable state. Porting this library to Haskell is a relatively small effort.
- When comparing programming languages and the applications written in them, it is crucial to share identical libraries. Especially for the important application domain of interactive applications, the lack of these libraries makes it hard to do serious comparative studies.
- The development of the Object I/O system and the Clean language have mutually influenced each other beneficially. One can expect similar effects between library and language when porting the system to Haskell.
- The Haskell compiler that we use in this project is the Glasgow Haskell Compiler 4.08.1. It extends Haskell 98 with several features that are required by the Object I/O system (*existential types* and a *foreign function interface*). In addition to these features it supports a variety of useful extensions such as *rank-2 polymorphism*, *thread creation*, and *communication/synchronisation* primitives. In this project we show how we have used these extensions to simplify the implementation of interactive processes and message passing.

One might wonder if this project is bound to fail in advance, because Clean and Haskell use different basic techniques to bring pure functional programming and I/O into close harmony. The answer is no because even though the Object I/O system uses the world as value paradigm, it does not essentially rely on it. The key idea of the system is that GUI objects are described by algebraic data types. The *behaviour* of a GUI object is defined by a set of *callbacks*. A callback is essentially a piece of code that must be executed in well-defined circumstances (usually called *events*). In a world as value paradigm one can simply model these callbacks as *functions* of type `(state,*World) -> (state,*World)`. In a monadic framework these callbacks can be modeled as *monadic actions* of type `state -> IO state`, or even just `IO ()`.

A closely related question is whether it is possible to handle *local state* in a monadic framework in a way that reflects the philosophy of the Object I/O library. We show that it is possible to provide a translation to Haskell that (except for the obvious difference in callbacks) is exactly identical to the Clean version. However, we also explored an alternative design, in which state is held in mutable variables, an approach that turns out to give a considerably simpler type structure. Because the local state version of the Object I/O library has been discussed at length elsewhere [4,6], we will discuss the alternative mutable variable based design in full detail in this paper, and compare it with the local state version in Section 3.

The Clean Object I/O library is **big**. Version 1.2.1 consists of 145 modules that provide an *application programmer's interface* (API) of 43 modules giving access to roughly 500 functions and 125 data types. For a feasibility study this is obviously a bit to much to port, so we have restricted ourselves to a fragment of the API that contains the essential features. This subset, the *mini Haskell Object I/O library*, is sufficiently expressive to create as a test case target a *concurrent talk* application (see Figure 1(a)). In the mini Haskell Object I/O library you can open and close arbitrarily many *interactive processes* (two in the test case). Each interactive process can open and close arbitrarily many *dialogues* (one in each interactive process). Each dialogue can contain arbitrarily many *text-, edit-,* and *button controls* (in the test case the dialogues contain two edit controls, one for input, one for output). In addition we have ported *asynchronous message passing* (text typed in the upper edit control is sent to the receiver of the other interactive process which displays the text in the lower edit control).

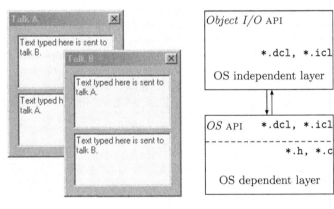

**Fig. 1. (a)** Concurrent talk     **(b)** Layered architecture

Another means of reducing the porting effort to Haskell is by making use of the layered architecture of the Clean Object I/O library (see Figure 1(b)). The Object I/O library basically consists of two layers: at the bottom we have a layer that implements the actual interface with the underlying operating system. This is the OS *dependendent layer*. It defines an interface that is used by the top layer, which is therefore OS *independent*. The OS independent layer is written entirely in Clean. The OS dependent layer has been designed in such a way that it is relatively easy to implement on most kinds of GUI toolkits. For this we

have drawn on our experience of porting earlier versions of Clean I/O libraries
to platforms as Microsoft Windows, Macintosh, and X Windows.

The remainder of this paper is structured as follows. We start with a detailed
discussion of the mutable variable based version of the mini Haskell Object I/O
library API in Section 2. We then compare this new approach with a one-to-one
translation of the Clean Object I/O library to Haskell in Section 3. The implementation of the OS independent layer (Section 4) and the OS dependent layer
(Section 5) are basically the same for both versions. Porting the Clean Object
I/O library to Haskell is a good opportunity to compare the two languages, libraries, and tools. This is done in Section 6. We present related work in Section 7
and conclude in Section 8.

## 2  The Mini Haskell Object I/O API

As our first step, we present the design of the mini Haskell Object I/O system,
as seen by the programmer. The version presented in this section handles state
by means of mutable variables. The design rationale is basically the same as the
local state version of the Object I/O library, so we will not discuss these. Instead
we content ourselves with a brief overview based on examples.

As has been argued briefly in the introduction, the only true language independent difference between the two libraries is the way callbacks are represented.
We give the monadic approach in Section 2.1. Then we illustrate the way local
state is handled in Section 2.2. The remaining essential GUI components that
are required for the concurrent talk test case are handled in Section 2.3.

### 2.1  A Monad for State Transitions

The principal concept to grasp about the Object I/O library is that it is a *state
transition system*. The behaviour of every GUI object that can be defined in
the library is a *callback* that, when it needs to be evaluated, is applied to the
'current' *process state* and returns a new process state. The new process state
is the next 'current' process state. The programmer only needs to define initial
state values and the GUI objects that contain the behaviour functions. The
Object I/O system takes care of all GUI event handling and ensures that the
proper functions are applied to the proper state.

In the Clean Object I/O library, the process state is handed to the programmer explicitly as environment value of abstract type IOSt (called the *I/O state*).
This environment is managed entirely by the Object I/O system. Every callback
is forced by the uniqueness type system of Clean to return a unique I/O state.
As the I/O state is an abstract value, and there are no denotations available to
the programmer we can ensure that all GUI operations can be performed safely.

In Haskell, instead of passing the I/O state around explicitly, we encapsulate
it in a monad, in the standard way:

```
data GUI a = GUI (IOSt -> IO (a,IOSt))}

instance Monad GUI where
    (>>=)  = bindGUI
    return = returnGUI

bindGUI :: GUI a -> (a -> GUI b) -> GUI b
bindGUI (GUI fA) to_ioB ioSt
  = GUI (\ioSt -> do { (a,ioSt1) <- fA ioSt ;
                       case to_ioB a of
                         GUI fB -> fB ioSt })

returnGUI :: a -> GUI a
returnGUI a = GUI (\ioSt -> return (a,ioSt))
```

Defining the GUI monad to be an *enhanced* IO monad allows us to combine existing Haskell I/O code with the Object I/O code. For this purpose one can *lift* any IO action to a GUI action:

```
liftIO :: IO a -> GUI a
liftIO m = GUI (\ioSt -> m >>= \a -> return (a,ioSt))
```

## 2.2   A Simple Example

Let us write a GUI application that displays an up-down counter: a displayed number, together with a button to increment it and another to decrement it:

One writes a program with a graphical user interface by defining a value of type GUI () and then "running" it by applying startGUI:

```
main :: IO ()
main = startGUI upDownGUI

upDownGUI :: GUI ()
upDownGUI = do { counter <- newCounter
              ; openDialog (Dialog "Counter" counter []) }

newCounter::GUI(TupLS TextControl (TupLS ButtonControl ButtonControl))
newCounter = ...to be defined shortly...
```

Here, newCounter creates one instance of our up-down counter, while open-Dialog opens a window in which the up-down counter is wrapped:

```
startGUI      :: GUI () -> IO ()
class Dialogs d where
    openDialog :: d -> GUI ()
```

The function openDialog opens a dialogue window (Dialog ...) whose contents can include all manner of things, which is why it is overloaded. Indeed, as you can see, the type of `newCounter` expresses the fact that it returns a component composed of three sub-components.

The next thing we must do is to define `newCounter`. A new feature of the mini Haskell Object I/O library, when compared with the Clean Object I/O library is the way local state is handled. We have chosen to use mutable variables [19] to handle local *and* public state. In this approach local state can still be encapsulated in the object, and hidden from the context in which it is used, thus supporting reusable GUI objects. Here, then, is how we define `newCounter`:

```
newCounter::GUI(TupLS TextControl (TupLS ButtonControl ButtonControl))
newCounter = do { c_state <- newMVar 0
                ; disp_id <- openId

                ; let display :: TextControl
                      display = TextControl "0" [ControlId disp_id]

                      dec, inc :: ButtonControl
                      dec = ButtonControl "-" [ControlFunction down]
                      inc = ButtonControl "+" [ControlFunction up]

                      up,down :: GUI ()
                      up   = update disp_id c_state (+ 1)
                      down = update disp_id c_state (- 1)

                ; return (display :+: dec :+: inc) }

update :: Id -> MVar Int -> (Int->Int) -> GUI ()
-- Update the MVar, and display new value in control identified by Id
update d m f = do { v <- takeMVar m
                  ; let new_v = f v
                  ; putMVar m new_v
                  ; setControlText d (show new_v) }
```

`newCounter` uses the GUI monad to create (a) a mutable cell, `c_state`, that will contain the state of the counter, and (b) a unique identifier, `disp_id`, used to name the display. Then it constructs the three sub-components, `display`, `dec`, and `inc`, composes them together using `(:+:)`, and returns the result.

To achieve all this, we used the following library functions and data types:

```
newMVar  :: a -> GUI (MVar a)
takeMVar :: MVar a -> GUI (MVar a)
putMVar  :: MVar a -> a -> GUI ()

openId   :: GUI Id
setControlText :: Id -> String -> GUI ()

infixr 9 :+:
data TupLS a b      = a :+: b
data ButtonControl  = ButtonControl String [ControlAttribute]
data TextControl    = TextControl   String [ControlAttribute]
data ControlAttribute = ControlId Id
```

```
| ControlFunction (GUI ())
| ControlKeyboard (...) (...)
                    (KeyboardState -> GUI ())
| ...
```

The MVar family allow you to create and modify a mutable cell; these operations are described in detail in [19].

For every GUI object an algebraic data type is provided that describes what that object looks like and how it behaves. Every type has a small number of mandatory arguments and a list of optional attributes — see the definitions for ButtonControl and TextControl given above. The TupLS type allows you to compose two controls to make a larger one. Notice, though, that the entire GUI component is simply a data value describing the construction of the component.

The component can be given a behaviour by embedding callbacks in the attributes of the component. In particular, the ControlFunction attribute of the inc and dec controls is a callback that updates the counter. This call-back is run whenever the button is clicked; simply calls update. The latter updates the state of the counter, and uses setControlText to update the display.

In order to change GUI components we need to *identify* them. That is what disp_id :: Id is doing. It is used by the callbacks up and down to identify the GUI component (disp) they want to side-effect. Indeed, MVars and Ids play a very similar role: an MVar identifies a mutable location, while an Id identifies a mutable GUI component. Fresh, unique Id values are created by openId.

It is very useful to be able to create Id and MVar values at any place in the program (see Section 2.3). For this reason, it is convenient to overload these functions so they can be used in either the IO or GUI monad:

```
class Ids m where
    newMVar  :: a -> m (MVar a)
    takeMVar :: MVar a -> m (MVar a)
    putMVar  :: MVar a -> a -> m ()

    openId :: m Id
    ... Ids also has other methods ...
instance Ids IO
instance Ids GUI
```

## 2.3   Concurrent Talk

As a second example we take the concurrent "talk" program, depicted in Figure 1(a). Text typed into the upper panel of either window should be echoed in the lower panel of the other window.

**Receivers.** This application involves two concurrent "processes", and we require a channel of communication going in each direction. The following functions manipulate channels:

```
class Ids m where ...
    openRId  :: m (RId a)
asyncSend    :: RId msg -> msg -> GUI SendReport

class Receivers rdef where
    openReceiver :: rdef -> GUI ()
instance Receivers (Receiver msg)

data Receiver msg
  = Receiver (RId msg) (msg -> GUI ()) [ReceiverAttribute]
```

A new channel is created by `openRId`, which is overloaded like `openId`, and returns a typed receiver name of type `RId`. You can send a message to a receiver using `asyncSend`. That triggers a callback in a (non-displayed) component of type `Receiver`. The latter contains its identifier together with the callback to be run when the message is received.

**Interactive Processes.** So the main program looks like this:

```
main :: IO ()
main = do { a      <- openRId
          ; b      <- openRId
          ; let talkA = talk "A" (a,b)
                talkB = talk "B" (b,a)
          ; startProcesses [talkA,talkB] }

talk :: String -> (RId TalkMsg, RId TalkMsg) -> Process
talk str (me,you) = Process (...) (talkGuts str (me,you))
                                [ProcessClose (quit you)]

talkGuts :: String -> (RId TalkMsg, RId TalkMsg) -> GUI ()
talkGuts = ...to be defined...

quit :: RId TalkMsg -> GUI ()
quit = ... to be defined ...
```

The overloaded function `startProcesses` takes an interactive process definition[1] and evaluates them until all child processes have terminated. The two talk processes are identical except for their (string) name and receiver identification. This is expressed conveniently by parameterisation of the `talk` function.

We consider an *interactive process* to be a collection of GUI objects that share some common user interface. A process performs no independent computational activity other than the callback mechanism. Interactive processes are specified in the same way as all other GUI objects by means of an algebraic type constructor, which is defined in the library as follows:

```
data Process = Process (...) (GUI ()) [ProcessAttribute]
startProcesses :: [Process] -> IO ()
closeProcess   :: GUI ()
```

---

[1] or, in the real library, a (nested) list of them

Process has two mandatory arguments (we ignore the first) and a list of optional attributes. The (GUI ()) argument is the *initialisation action* of an interactive process: it is the first action of the interactive process, and is run when the process is started by startProcesses. We will consider only one process attribute, ProcessClose, which is analogous to the WindowClose attribute discussed above: the callback associated with this attribute is evaluated whenever the user dismisses the interactive process.

In this example, the initialisation action is defined by talkGuts:

```
talkGuts :: String -> (RId TalkMsg, RId TalkMsg) -> GUI ()
talkGuts str (me,you)
 = do { outId <- openId
      ; inId  <- openId
      ; let talkdialog :: Dialog (TupLS EditControl EditControl)
            talkdialog = mkTalkDialog you inId outId

            receiver :: Receiver TalkMsg
            receiver  = Receiver me (receive outId) []
      ; openDialog talkdialog
      ; openReceiver receiver }

mkTalkDialog :: RId TalkMsg -> Id -> Id
                           -> Dialog (TupLS EditControl EditControl)
mkTalkDialog you inId outId
 = Dialog ("Talk "++name) (infield:+:outfield) [WindowClose(quit you)]
   where
      infield  = EditControl "" (ContentWidth "mmmmmmmmmm") 5
                 [ ControlId inId, ControlKeyboard (...) (...) input ]
      outfield = EditControl "" (ContentWidth "mmmmmmmmmm") 5
                 [ ControlId outId, ControlPos (Below inId,zero) ]

input :: KeyboardState -> GUI ()
input = ...to be defined...
```

This code creates two new Ids to identify the two panels of the window, constructs the dialogue and receiver, and then opens them. The receiver is straightforward — we defined Receiver in the previous section — and is passed the callback (receive outId). The dialogue is built in a very similar way that we built the counter earlier, except that it uses editable-text panels (EditControl) instead of buttons. The ControlKeyboard attribute of the infield takes a callback, input, which tells the control how to respond to user input.

**Message Passing.** The remaining pieces of the puzzle are those that send messages. First we need to define the type of messages that flow between the two processes. As specified informally in the introduction, keyboard input in the input field of the talk dialogue of one interactive process should be sent to the other interactive process (and displayed in the output field). In addition, if the user dismisses either dialogue, the other one should also be notified as terminated. This is arranged by the following simple message type:

```
data Message = NewLine String | Quit.
```

The receiver callback action straightforwardly implements the informal specification above: the response to a (NewLine text) message should be to change the content of the output field to text (using the library function setControlText), and the response to a Quit message should be to terminate its parent process (using the library function closeProcess):

```
receive :: Message -> GUI ()
receive (NewLine text) = setControlText outId text
receive Quit           = closeProcess
```

The behaviour of the input callback is to read the current content of the input control and send it to the other interactive process. (The library function getParentWindow returns an abstract value that represent the current state of the complete dialogue. The function getControlText retrieves the content of any text related control. Their types are included below.)

```
input :: KeyboardState -> GUI ()
input _
    = do { Just window <- getParentWindow inId
         ; let text     = fromJust (snd (getControlText inId window))
         ; error        <- asyncSend you (NewLine text)
         ; return () }
-- Library types:
getParentWindow :: Id -> GUI (Maybe WState)
getControlText  :: Id -> WState -> (Bool,Maybe String)
```

Finally, the quit callback closes its own process, and sends a Quit message to the other process:

```
quit :: RId TalkMsg -> GUI ()
quit you = do { asyncSend you Quit;  closeProcess }
```

It should be observed that it is not possible in the Object I/O library for one interactive process to terminate other interactive processes. The closeProcess function has no process identification, but always terminates the interactive process of the GUI component which callback evaluates this function. This is also the case for all other actions: one interactive process can not directly create or close a window in another interactive process. The only interaction between interactive processes is message passing or via the external world.

## 3    The Pros and Cons of MVars

The mini Haskell Object I/O API discussed so far relies on mutable variables to keep track of the state of an interactive program. This is different from the way state is handled in the Clean Object I/O library. We will not discuss this system in detail, because this has been done extensively elsewhere [4,6]. Briefly, the Clean Object I/O system keeps track of all state. Type security is obtained by parameterisation of all GUI type constructors with the types of the local and public state. Specialised type constructor combinators are required to obtain the proper state encapsulation. Both approaches to handle state have been implemented in the mini Haskell Object I/O port. In this section we analyse the features of the two approaches.

Handling state with mutable variables has a number of advantages when compared with the Clean scheme.

Firstly, the set of type constructors is *simpler* (no state type variables) and *smaller* (local state type constructor combinators are superfluous). In our experience these elements of the Object I/O library cause a steep learning curve to novice GUI programmers. Despite the reduction of complexity, GUI definitions are identical to the local state version (which is identical to the Clean version). This allows to easily convert code between these versions.

The second advantage is *increased flexibility*: GUI components can share state in a more complex way than is possible in the local state version. It is unclear if it is possible to extend the local state version with more powerful state combinators, but even so this will increase the complexity of the system.

Thirdly, even though mutable variables are globally accessible, the fact that one requires its reference gives the programmer fine grained control over the actual access to the data. This is in fact analogous to the current situation with identification values: we can use the same lexical scoping techniques to control access to GUI objects as well as state objects (and get similar 'preambles' as discussed at the end of Section 2.3).

The major disadvantage of handling state with mutable variables is that it is *less declarative*. The burden of state management is shifted from the library implementer to the application programmer. To illustrate this case, here is the local state version of the up-down counter (Section 2.2):

```
newCounter
  = do { disp_id <- openId
       ; let ... control definitions are identical ...
             up   = update disp_id (+ 1)
             down = update disp_id (- 1)
       ; return (NewLS 0 (display :+: dec :+: inc)) }

update :: Id -> (Int->Int) (Int,ps) -> GUI ps (Int,ps)
update d f (v,state) = do { let new_v = f v
                          ; setControlText d (show new_v)
                          ; return (new_v,state) }
```

Instead of retrieving and storing the current count explicitly from a mutable variable, **update** has direct access to the local state, and is required by the type system to return a new value. The relation between the initial local state value 0 and the counter is determined by the **NewLS** type constructor combinator.

We need more experience to decide which of the approaches to handle state is the best choice.

# 4   The OS Independent Layer

The only crucial difference between the Clean and Haskell version of the Object I/O libary is the way callbacks are handled (*functions* versus *actions*). The Clean Object I/O library is a sequential implementation that encodes the interactive process scheduling mechanism and message passing. This implies that it is in principle sufficient to reimplement only the callback evaluation mechanism, and simply translate the other parts from Clean to Haskell.

In the introduction we have stated that we were going to use GHC (for issues related to other Haskell compilers we refer to Section 8). The major motivation is that the Object I/O library (in fact, some of its predecessor versions [3]) has been designed with concurrency in mind: it should, in principle, be possible to implement interactive processes as *concurrent* evaluation processes, and even to create *distributed* interactive applications. These are things that are well supported by GHC, and the combination with other required features fixed the choice for this particular compiler technology.

We are not going to discuss every detail of the implementation of the OS independent layer. Instead we focus on the following aspects of its implementation: in Section 4.1 we discuss how monadic callbacks with local state can be evaluated, in Section 4.2 we show how interactive processes are mapped to concurrent threads, and in Section 4.3 how message passing is handled.

## 4.1   Evaluation of Monads with Local State

Computing state transitions is straightforward in the mini Haskell Object I/O system based on mutable variables: whenever a callback action must be evaluated, the run-time system only needs to locate the proper action and apply it. All state handling is done by the callback action. In the local state version things are more complicated: the run-time system not only needs to locate the proper action, but also construct the proper state argument to apply the action to. The thus computed new state must then be restored in the administration.

The Clean Object I/O implementation uses an elegant solution to compute and store local state [5]. It relies on *lazy evaluation* to create references to local state values that will eventually be computed by callback functions (ensured by the type system). These references are stored in the internal administration (the IOSt environment) which is passed as the argument to the callback function. Because the involved environments are explicitly available in the Clean Object I/O library, it is rather intuitive to 'connect' these forward references. In the local state version of the mini Haskell Object I/O library we have been able to copy this strategy, using the monadic extension fixIO. Due to lack of space we omit a detailed presentation. Here the key idea is that fixIO also allows us to manipulate results that are not yet computed, but lazily available.

## 4.2   Interactive Processes

The concurrent talk test case spawns two interactive processes. Interactive processes have been designed with concurrent evaluation in mind. They should behave as if they were independent applications running in a pre-emptive OS. We have implemented interactive processes using the Concurrent Haskell primitives [19] forkIO (for thread creation), MVars (for sharing context information), and Channels (for abstract event dispatching). Because the Microsoft Windows OS expects a single event loop driven application, we can't implement each of these processes as independent loops fetching and dispatching OS events. The architecture of the concurrent implementation is sketched in Figure 2.

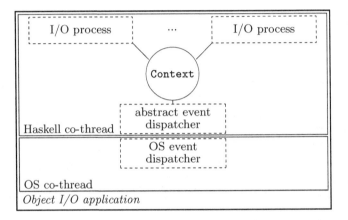

**Fig. 2.** Concurrent implementation of interactive processes

The co-thread architecture is a legacy from the Clean implementation. We can't call Clean from C. This is necessary on the Microsoft Windows platform, because some OS calls require further callbacks to be evaluated before the call is finished (for instance, when creating a window several dozens of callbacks are triggered). Instead of calling Clean from C directly, this communication is done indirectly via two OS threads that run as co-routines. Information is passed via a small globally accessible buffer. It should be noted that in Haskell one can call Haskell from C [12], so we should be able to eliminate these co-threads. Because of the preliminary nature of this project, we have not changed the code of the OS co-thread nor the architecture.

The Haskell co-thread is basically a reorder of existing pieces of functional code in the scheduling module of the Clean implementation. Because we use the forkIO primitive, the scheduling code disappears. Each interactive process (I/O process) runs in a Haskell thread. They are driven by an event loop that handles only abstract events. The closeProcess function terminates the loop, and the I/O process gets garbage collected. Abstract events are generated by an additional Haskell thread, the *abstract event dispatcher*, that maps OS events to abstract events and dispatches them to the proper I/O processes. Recall that interactive programs are created with the startProcesses library function. This function creates the initial Haskell threads.

The only information required by the abstract event dispatcher is which I/O processes are currently present in order to dispatch the proper abstract events. This is stored in the globally accessible `Context`, stored conveniently in a `MVar`. Every I/O process maintains an OS event filter function in this `Context`. After every callback evaluation, it updates this entry, and in the act of termination it removes it from the administration. The abstract event dispatcher terminates when this list is empty, resulting in the required behaviour of `startProcesses`.

The major advantage of this architecture is that it is scaleable: it is easy to create and destroy interactive processes. It is also very suitable for a *distributed environment*: if ever Object I/O applications distribute themselves over a network almost everything we need to do is to create a new remote initial context, an event dispatcher, and an initial I/O process thread.

### 4.3   Message Passing

In the concurrent implementation as described above `Channels` are the obvious Concurrent Haskell medium to implement message passing. Recall that a receiver that handles messages of some type `msg` is unambiguously identified by a receiver identification value of type (`RId msg`) (Section 1). Its implementation is

```
data RId msg = RId { rid::Int, ridIn::(Chan msg) }
```

The `rid` field is a fresh value to uniquely identify the receiver (inherited from the original implementation). The `ridIn` field is new. It is a `Channel` that implements the message queue.

Messages are sent with the function `asyncSend :: RId msg -> msg -> GUI SendReport`. After the usual correctness checks it places the message in the message queue using `writeChan`. The receiver is notified that a message is available in the message queue by inserting a pseudo OS event in the abstract event stream environment (which is part of the shared `Context`). This pseudo OS event is mapped to an abstract event which is dispatched to the parent I/O process of the receiver. The receiver will eventually remove the message from its message queue (using `readChan`) and handle the appropriate callback action.

## 5   The OS Dependent Layer

In this project we have reused the existing C code completely. So we have integrated these C modules into the Haskell implementation. For Haskell 98 the *Foreign Function Interface* [11] has been proposed to be able to write down Haskell code that calls upon foreign functionality. We illustrate how this has been done by means of the following C procedure, defined in the module `cpicture.c`:

```
extern void WinGetStringWidth
            (CLEAN_STRING,CLEAN_STRING,int,int,int,HDC,OS,int*,OS*)
```

`CLEAN_STRING`s point to structs of a length field (`int`) and a buffer of `chars` of the given length. The types `HDC` and `OS` are also `integers`. If a Clean function returns a tuple of results, then these are passed by the C procedure by means of pointer values (int* and OS* respectively). The C procedure returns void. If a Clean function returns one value then the C procedure also returns that value. The Clean code looks as follows (module pictCCall_12.icl):

```
WinGetStringWidth :: !{#Char} !Fnt !Int !HDC !*OS -> (!Int,!*OS)
WinGetStringWidth _ _ _ _ _
= code { .inline WinGetStringWidth
              ccall WinGetStringWidth "SSIIIII-II"
          .end
      }
```

In the Haskell implementation we need to add marshalling code to convert the Haskell arguments to the arguments as required by the C procedures. For all functions we follow the same scheme. Here is the Haskell code:

```
winGetStringWidth :: String -> Fnt -> Int -> HDC -> IO Int
winGetStringWidth a1 (a2,a3,a4) a5 a6
    = do s1 <- createCLEAN_STRING a1
         s2 <- createCLEAN_STRING a2
         o1 <- malloc 4
         o2 <- malloc 4
         cWinGetStringWidth s1 s2 a3 a4 a5 a6 osNewToolbox o1 o2
         mapM_ freeCLEAN_STRING [s1,s2]
         r1 <- fpeek o1
         r2 <- free o2
         return r1
foreign import stdcall "cpicture" "WinGetStringWidth"
    cWinGetStringWidth :: Addr -> Addr -> Int -> Int -> Int -> HDC -> Int
                        -> Addr -> Addr -> IO ()
```

Haskell Strings are lists of characters. These are converted to CLEAN_STRINGs using the function createCLEAN_STRING. This function has been implemented in Haskell, using the GHC language extensions modules Addr, Bits, and Storable. For all output arguments memory is allocated, using malloc. This is probably extremely inefficient but at the time of writing our prior interest was correctness.

When all arguments have been created the C procedure can be called. The connection is made with the foreign import statement which identifies the C module and procedure name. As you can see, the type of the function closely follows that of the C procedure given above. After evaluation, the necessary results need to be freed. This is done by freeCLEAN_STRING for strings, and fpeek which before freeing its argument peeks it and returns the value.

## 6   Experience

This project was carried out by an experienced Clean programmer and an experienced Haskell programmer. This was a good occasion to compare the two languages. Clean and Haskell are clearly cousins. Proficient Clean (Haskell) programmers can master Haskell (Clean) easily. Still, the two languages have their advantages when compared with each other. Clean languages advantages are:

**Records:** Haskell field labels are fairly equivalent to Clean records. Haskell field labels automatically convert to field selector *functions*. Therefore one can't existentially quantify these fields because the field selector functions become ill-typed. In Clean, a record is basically an algebraic data type with one data constructor. The fields identify the arguments of the constructor. The normal type rules apply, including those for existential types. Finally, Clean allows the same record field name to occur in several record types. These expressions can always be disambiguated by either a unique combination of field names or by adding the type constructor name inside the record notation. As an illustration, the following definitions are valid Clean (in Haskell syntax – note the absence of a data constructor):

```
data R1 = {a::Int, b::Bool}
data R2 = {a::Bool,c::Real}
                        -- Inferred types:
f1 {a,b}    = (a,b)  -- f1 :: R1 -> (Int,Bool)
f2 {a,c}    = (a,c)  -- f2 :: R2 -> (Bool,Real)
f3 {R1 | a} = a      -- f3 :: R1 -> Int
f4 {R2 | a} = a      -- f4 :: R2 -> Bool
```

**Macros:** although in GHC one can use the C preprocessor, one can not export macros which limits their use. Constant functions don't help because you can't use them in pattern-matches.

**Strictness annotations.** Strictness is a well-established concept in Clean. One annotates data types, function argument types, and local definitions strictly. This gives Clean programmers fine grained control over evaluation order.

**Type constructor operators.** In Clean and Haskell type and data constructors have separate name spaces. In Clean these spaces contain the same range of symbols. This allows us to give all Clean Object I/O library GUI type definitions (including :+:) to have identical type and data constructor names everywhere.

**Module structure.** The Clean module system distinguishes *implementation* and *definition* modules. This basically means that Clean programmers write their .hi files. Definition modules are not allowed to be cyclicly dependent, but implementation modules are. Compiling a project therefore involves compiling a tree of modules.

Haskell language advantages are:

**Field labels** are also selector functions. As a programmer you do not have to write your own access functions. This results in elegant code.

**Derived instances** help programmers avoid writing code that can be derived by the compiler.

**Rank 2 polymorphism.** Clean and GHC Haskell support existential types. However, the GHC makes this language feature complete by extending the type system with *rank-2 polymorphism*. This extension allows one to write higher order functions on existentially quantified data structures.

**Cyclic modules.** Because Haskell modules consist of one file with an interface header (the export list), modules must be allowed to be cyclicly dependent. This increases expressiveness when compared with Clean. It has allowed us to parameterise all GUI types uniformly with respect to the state arguments. (Unfortunately, the GHC can't deal with cyclic Haskell modules without help from the programmer who is forced to write .hi-boot files.)

**Monads and do-notation** handle the environment passing part of interactive programs. The resulting code is less cluttered with environments when compared to equivalent Clean code.

The mini Haskell Object I/O library implements only a part of the Clean Object I/O library, see the left table below. The table to its right shows this for the Haskell mini Object I/O library with local state (*LS*) and mutable variables (*MVAR*). Note that because we have used a straightforward translation from Clean to Haskell this results in virtually identical sizes of the OS independent layers. Clean does not support rank 2 polymorphism which leads to significant duplication of code that handles existentially quantified data structures. The Haskell version could take advantage of this. The Haskell OS dependent layer is about twice the size of the Clean version due to marshalling (Section 5). The shared C implementation consists of 39 *.c, *.h modules, and 13132 loc.

| Clean | #mod. (%total) | #loc (%total) |
|-------|---------------|---------------|
| OS indep. | 50 (45.9%) | 8956 (30.5%) |
| OS dep. | 20 (54.0%) | 3961 (53.9%) |

| Haskell | #mod. | #loc *LS* | #loc *MVAR* |
|---------|-------|-----------|-------------|
| OS indep. | 54 | 8583 | 8202 |
| OS dep. | 21 | 6393 | 6393 |

When writing large applications or libraries it becomes increasingly important to have dedicated development tools. From the very start Clean versions have been released together with integrated compiler/editor environments. In contrast, the GHC is a command-line based, Unix oriented system. It does not come with any development environment. Instead, one is supposed to use make files. For programmers being used to GUI based IDEs this is a rude awakening.

A final important factor with increased application sizes is the quality of the compiler. GHC's error messages are more informative than Clean's, especially when concerned with the type system. The Clean compiler is significantly faster than GHC. Compilation time measurements conducted on the Object I/O libraries indicate that Clean compiles 10 to 20 times as fast as GHC.

## 7 Related Work

The main purpose of this project was to study the relationship between the Clean Object I/O library and Haskell, and to see if and how it can be implemented in a monadic framework. Except for the new approach (from a Clean point of view) to handle (local) state using MVars, the Object I/O library has not changed. This is the reason why we give only a very brief comparison with related work. ([5] discusses related work with respect to the 'original' Object I/O library.)

We have shown how the Object I/O library can be simplified using mutable variables. Mutable variables are used in several functional GUI systems

(*TkGofer*, *pidgets*, *tclHaskell* – [26,23,22] respectively –). FUDGETS and *gadgets* ([10,16]) use stream communication to model *global* state, and recursive functions for *local* state. The latter technique is used in *Opal*[13] to model *global* state. Even if (local) state is handled by means of mutable variables, the Object I/O library differs because of its emphasis on defining GUI objects by means of algebraic data structures. This allows one to define functions that pass around GUI specifications that can be manipulated and changed before they are actually created. In all other systems GUI objects can only be created, using actions.

We have demonstrated that it is possible to have a concurrent implementation of a functional GUI system without sacrificing the deterministic semantics of interactive processes. The use of Concurrent Haskell primitives results in a simpler and shorter implementation of the library, without changing its semantic properties. This contrasts strongly with the general opinion that one has to use a concurrent functional language to construct GUI programs flexibly [23,13].

# 8    Conclusions and Future Work

In this project we have successfully ported an essential subset[2] of the Clean Object I/O libary to Haskell. We have argued that the Object I/O library is really independent of the underlying paradigm to integrate side effects in pure functional languages. Callbacks are modeled in Clean using explicit environment passing functions, while they are represented as monads in Haskell. In this way we preserve the best properties in both languages.

The mini Object I/O library covers 42% of the whole Object I/O library. We have focussed on the 'hard bits'. All crucial design and implementation issues have been solved. Due to lack of resources we have not been able to check uni- and bi-direction synchronous message passing and the construction of a drawing monad (which should encapsulate a `Picture` environment). Except for these parts, porting the rest of the code should not prove to be difficult.

We have used the GHC 4.08.1. It implements Haskell 98 and extends it with several language and library features. This raises the question if this project has become a GHC project rather than a Haskell 98 project. The Object I/O library can not be implemented straight away in Haskell 98. To implement the 'pure' Object I/O library one needs to extend Haskell 98 with existential types. The rest of the library can be obtained by translation from Clean to Haskell. To implement the `MVar` state version existential types are not required. The only extensions needed are `MVars`. These can be added to any Haskell compiler as a separate library, though they also require significant runtime support.

We think that it is worthwhile for the Haskell and Clean community to complete this project for several reasons: *(a)* the Haskell community will obtain a GUI library that has proven itself in practice, *(b)* the library can, because of its internal architecture, be easily ported to more traditional Haskell platforms, *(c)* it will encourage code sharing between Haskell and Clean. The existence

---

[2] Available in the GHC CVS repository at `fptools/hslibs/object-io`

of a GUI library that is both easily portable and language independent will strengthen the position of functional languages on the long term.

## Acknowledgements

Peter would like to thank Simon Marlow, Julian Seward, and Reuben Thomas for their advice and help on Haskell and the GHC compiler, Andrei Serjantov for showing him around in Cambridge, and the people at Microsoft Research Cambridge for providing a stimulating working environment.

## References

1. Achten, P.M., van Groningen, J.H.G., and Plasmeijer, M.J. High Level Specification of I/O in Functional Languages. In Launchbury, J., Sansom, P. eds., *Proceedings Glasgow Workshop on Functional Programming*, Ayr, Scotland, 6-8 July 1992. Workshops in Computing, Springer-Verlag, Berlin, 1993, pp. 1-17.
2. Achten, P.M. and Plasmeijer, M.J. The ins and outs of Clean I/O. In *Journal of Functional Programming* **5**(1) - January 1995, Cambridge University Press, pp. 81-110.
3. Achten, P.M. and Plasmeijer, M.J. Concurrent Interactive Processes in a Pure Functional Language. In Vliet, J.C. van, ed., *Proceedings Computing Science in the Netherlands, CSN'95*, Jaarbeurs Utrecht, The Netherlands, November 27-28, Stichting Mathematisch Centrum, Amsterdam, 1995, pp. 10-21.
4. Achten, P.M. and Plasmeijer, M.J. Interactive Functional Objects in Clean. In Clack, C., Hammond, K. and Davie, T. eds., *Proceedings 9th International Workshop Implementation of Functional Languages, IFL'97*, St. Andrews, Scotland, UK, September 1997, selected papers, LNCS **1467**, Springer, pp. 304-321.
5. Achten, P.M. and Plasmeijer, M.J. The implementation of interactive local state transition systems in Clean. In Koopman, P., Clack, C. eds., *Proceedings 11th International Workshop Implementation of Functional Languages, IFL'99*, Lochem, The Netherlands, September 1999, selected papers, LNCS **1868**, Springer, pp. 115-130.
6. Achten, P.M. and Wierich, M. A Tutorial to the Clean Object I/O Library - version 1.2. *Technical Report CSI-R0003*, February 2, 2000, Computing Science Institute, Faculty of Mathematics and Informatics, University of Nijmegen, The Netherlands.
7. Barendsen, E. and Smetsers, J.E.W. Uniqueness Type Inference. In [14], 189-206.
8. Bjørner, D., Broy, M., Pottosin, I.V. eds. *Perspectives of System Informatics, Second International Andrei Ershov Memorial Conference Akademgorodok*, Novosibirsk, Russia, June 25-28, 1996, Proceedings, LNCS **1181**, Springer.
9. Brus, T., Eekelen, M.C.J.D. van, Leer, M.O. van, and Plasmeijer, M.J. Clean: A Language for Functional Graph Rewriting. In Kahn. G. ed. *Proceedings of the Third International Conference on Functional Programming Languages and Computer Architecture*, Portland, Oregon, USA, LNCS **274**, Springer-Verlag, pp. 364-384.
10. Carlsson, M. and Hallgren, Th. FUDGETS - A Graphical User Interface in a Lazy Functional Language. In *Proceedings of Conference on Functional Programming Languages and Computer Architecture*, Copenhagen, Denmark, 9-11 June 1993, ACM Press, pp. 321-330.

11. Finne, S. A Haskell foreign function interface. Available as GHC extension, see: http://www.haskell.org/ghc/docs/latest/set/sec-foreign.html.

12. Finne, S., Leijen, D., Meijer, E., and Peyton Jones, S. Calling hell from heaven and heaven from hell. In *ACM SIGPLAN International Conference on Functional Programming (ICFP'99)*, Paris, ACM Press, pp. 114-125.

13. Frauenstein, Th., Grieskamp, W., Pepper, P., and Südholt. Communicating Functional Agents and Their Application to Graphical User Interfaces. In [8], pp. 386-397.

14. Hermenegildo, M. and Swierstra, S.D. eds. *Proceedings of Seventh International Symposium on Programming Languages: Implementations, Logics and Programs*, Utrecht, The Netherlands, 20-22 September 1995, LNCS **982**, Springer-Verlag.

15. Hudak, P., Peyton Jones, S., Wadler, Ph., Boutel, B., Fairbairn, J., Fasel, J., Hammond, K., Hughes, J., Johnsson, Th., Kieburtz, D., Nikhil, R., Partain, W., Peterson, J. Report on the programming language Haskell, In *ACM SigPlan Notices*, **27** (5): 1-164.

16. Noble, R. and Runciman, C. Gadgets: Lazy Functional Components for Graphical User Interfaces. In [14], pp. 321-340.

17. Nöcker, E.G.J.M.H., Smetsers, J.E.W., Eekelen, M.C.J.D. van, and Plasmeijer, M.J. Concurrent Clean. In Aarts, E.H.L., Leeuwen, J. van, Rem, M., eds., *Proceedings of Parallel Architectures and Languages Europe*, June, Eindhoven, The Netherlands. LNCS **506**, Springer-Verlag, pp. 202-219.

18. Peyton Jones, S.L. and Wadler, Ph. Imperative Functional Programming. In *Proceedings of the 20th Annual ACM SIGACT-SIGPLAN Symposium on Principles of Programming Languages*, Charleston, South Carolina, January 10-13, 1993, 71-84.

19. Peyton Jones, S., Gordon, A., Finne, S. Concurrent Haskell. In *23rd ACM Symposium on Principles of Programming Languages (POPL'96)*, January 1996, St.Petersburg Beach, Florida, ACM, pp. 295-308.

20. Peyton Jones, S. and Hughes, J. eds. *Report on the Programming Language Haskell 98 – A Non-strict, Purely Functional Language*, 1 February 1999.

21. Plasmeijer, M.J. and van Eekelen, M.C.J.D. *Functional Programming and Parallel Graph Rewriting*. Addison-Wesley Publishing Company 1993.

22. Sage, M. *TclHaskell*. http://www.dcs.gla.ac.uk/~meurig/TclHaskell/.

23. Scholz, E. PIDGETS - Unifying Pictures and Widgets in a Constraint-Based Framework for Concurrent GUI Programming. In Kuchen, H., Swierstra, S.D. eds. *Proceedings of eighth International Symposium on Programming Languages: Implementations, Logics, and Programs*, Aachen, Germany, September 1996, LNCS **1140**, Springer, pp. 363-377.

24. Smetsers, J.E.W., Barendsen, E., Eekelen, M.C.J.D. van, and Plasmeijer, M.J. Guaranteeing Safe Destructive Updates through a Type System with Uniqueness Information for Graphs. In Schneider, H.J., Ehrig, H. eds. *Proceedings Workshop Graph Transformations in Computer Science*, Dagstuhl Castle, Germany, January 4-8, 1993, LNCS **776**, Springer-Verlag, Berlin, pp. 358-379.

25. Vullinghs, T., Schulte, W., and Schwinn, Th. The Design of a Functional GUI Library Using Constructor Classes. In [8], pp. 398-408.

26. Vullinghs, T., Tuijnman, D., and Schulte, W. Lightweight GUIs for Functional Programming. In [14], pp. 341-356.

27. Wadler, Ph. Comprehending monads. In *Proceedings of the ACM Conference on Lisp and Functional Programming*, Nice, 1990, ACM Press, pp. 61-78.

# Organizing Speculative Computations
# in Functional Systems

Raimund Schroeder and Werner Kluge

Department of Computer Science,
University of Kiel,
D-24098 Kiel, Germany
wk@informatik.uni-kiel.de

**Abstract.** Speculative evaluation relates to computing several (alternative) threads of control of large programs concurrently without knowing in advance which of them contribute to which extent to final results. This approach may be used to advantage to compute, at the expense of deploying considerable processing power, solutions of $np$–hard search problems on average a lot faster than sequentially.
This paper addresses the organizational measures necessary to perform speculative computations concurrently in a distributed memory multi-processor system. They primarily concern task management and scheduling, a fairness regulation scheme which ensures progress of all speculative tasks at about the same pace, and the conflict between fairness and bounded numbers of speculative tasks. Though these measures are discussed in the context of functional languages and systems, they are in principle applicable in the imperative world as well.

## 1  Introduction

Programs of functional languages are known to be perfectly suited for concurrent processing. Conceptually, program execution is a process of meaning–preserving program transformations based on a set of rewrite rules which for all semantically meaningful programs eventually terminates with a result which is itself a program. Since all rewrite rules perform context–free substitutions of equals by equals, creating no side effects elsewhere in the program, they may be applied in any order without affecting the determinacy of results.

Of the various concepts of executing functional (or function–based) programs concurrently, speculative evaluation is the most challenging one from an organizational point of view. However, at the expense of committing considerable resources, it may also be the least rewarding one in terms of performance gains. The idea is to evaluate several sub–terms of a functional program concurrently without having, at the time the respective tasks or threads of control are being created, sufficient information at hand to decide which of them may contribute to which extent to the normal form of the entire program eventually.

Under a lazy regime, speculative evaluation is often employed to evaluate some or all function arguments in advance and possibly beyond the point actually

M. Mohnen and P. Koopman (Eds.): IFL 2000, LNCS 2011, pp. 214–230, 2001.

needed, provided sufficient processing power can be made available that would otherwise be idling (though this so–called **eager–beaver** approach runs somewhat counter to the idea of laziness since more than absolutely necessary is usually done to compute normal forms) [Jon87, Par91, Mat93, Che94].

This paper is on the speculative evaluation of sets of rewrite rules, specified as pattern matching clauses embedded in **case** (or switch) constructs. Pattern matching, generally speaking, is to abstract specific (sub–)terms from given structural contexts (the argument terms to which the **cases** are applied) and to substitute them into specific syntactical positions of other contexts (the body terms of the matching clauses). As several patterns of a **case** may be overlapping, they may produce as many matches on given arguments. Under a purely functional interpretation, the patterns are applied in the order in which they are specified in the **case**, and the first matching clause is the one that is being picked as the result of the entire **case** application. In compliance with this execution order, the clauses are usually arranged so that the patterns covering special argument features precede those that cover the more general (structural) features.

However, rule based applications such as term rewriting (logic reasoning) or many search problems are typically of a nature where several clauses feature overlapping patterns which can not be given a unique ordering. If more than one of these patterns matches a particular argument, the respective clauses may have to be evaluated speculatively since sufficient information as to which of them will lead to some desired result (problem solution) eventually may become available only further down the road as more pattern clauses (rules) are being applied. Unfortunately, such trial–and–error computations generally feature an exponential complexity which renders them intractable for large problem sizes, particularly when doing them sequentially. However, evaluating all matching clauses of **case** applications concurrently on a speculative basis may considerably improve the chances of computing solutions of such problems decidedly faster, a generous supply of processing power provided.

Of primary concern in this paper are the organizational measures necessary to support in some orderly form this kind of speculative concurrency in a multiprocessor system both effectively and efficiently. To do so, the system must

- distinguish between vital tasks (or threads of control) whose results are bound to contribute to problem solutions and speculative tasks (threads) whose results may or may not be required;
- treat all vital tasks with higher priority than speculative tasks, and possibly distinguish several priority levels among the latter, to prevent the monopolization of the system with computations of which most are known to be superfluous;
- abort speculative tasks or lift their status to vital as soon as decisions to this effect can be made;
- apply a fair scheduling discipline to all speculative tasks originating from the same **case** application to ensure that all of them proceed at about the same pace as long as no clues are available as to which of them have the best

chances of succeeding; otherwise too many resources may be committed to just the wrong computations while those that produce useful solutions are left starving;

– strike an acceptable compromize between limitation of resources, specifically processing power, on the one hand and fair progress of potentially unbounded numbers of speculative tasks on the other hand.

The paper discusses conceptual solutions for these organizational problems which have been successfully implemented as extensions of an existing concurrent graph reduction system $\pi$-RED [Klu83, BHK94, GK96]. This implementation has been extensively tested and validated by means of a parameterizable program which simulates searches of a spider for exits in a maze.

The paper is organized as follows: the next section introduces some essential language constructs, Section 3 outlines the basic principles of organizing speculative computations, Section 4 describes the measures that sustain reasonable fairness while limiting the number of speculative tasks, Section 5 reports on some performance results, and Section 6 discusses some related work.

## 2   The Language

For the purpose of this paper it suffices to consider a simple dynamically typed and strict functional kernel language with a reduction semantics [Berk75, Klu94], i.e., program execution is governed by a set of term rewrite rules. The program terms are recursively constructed as follows:

$$
\begin{aligned}
e = \ & const \mid var \mid prim\_fun \\
& \mid (e\_0\,e\_1 \ldots e\_n) \\
& \mid \text{IF } e\_0 \text{ THEN } e\_1 \text{ ELSE } e\_2 \\
& \mid \text{LET } u\_1 = e\_1 \ldots u\_n = e\_n \text{ IN } e\_0 \\
& \mid < e\_1, \ldots, e\_n > \\
& \mid \text{DEFINE } \ldots, f\,u\_1 \ldots u\_n = e\_f, \ldots \text{ IN } e\_0 \ . \\
& \mid \text{CASE } pat\_1 \to e\_1, \ldots, pat\_i \to e\_i, \ldots, pat\_n \to e\_n \text{ END\_CASE} \\
pat = \ & const \mid var \mid \_ * pat\_* \mid < \ldots, pat\_k, \ldots >
\end{aligned}
$$

These terms denote, from top to bottom, constant values, variables, primitive functions such as $+$, $-$, $\ldots gt$, $le$ ... etc., applications of terms $e\_0$ in function position to $n$ argument terms $e\_1, \ldots, e\_n$, IF\_THEN\_ELSE clauses, LET terms, $n-$ tuples ($n$–ary lists) of terms, and sets of mutually recursive function definitions, with $f, u\_1, \ldots, u\_n$ and $e\_f$ respectively denoting a function identifier, the formal parameters of the function, and the function body term (which computes the function value). The term $e\_0$, which may call upon any of the functions defined, computes the value of the entire DEFINE construct.

The terms of primary interest in this paper are CASE–constructs of some $n$ pattern matching clauses $pat\_i \to e_i$ which may be used to define sets of rewrite rules for tuple terms. The patterns may be composed of constants, variables, wild card patterns (denotes as _ * *pat* * _), and tuples of these items, including recursively tuples as tuple components.

A tuple pattern *pat* is said to match an argument term if it has an identical tuple structure, each pattern constant literally equals a constant value in an identical tuple position of the argument, and each pattern variable matches a (sub–)structure in an identical argument position[1]. This being the case, each occurrence of a pattern variable in the body term $e\_i$ is substituted by the respective argument component, and the term thus instantiated is evaluated.

The entire CASE–construct in fact specifies a complex unary function. When applied to an argument value, a strictly functional interpretation requires that all clauses be tried in the order from left to right, and the value of the first clause whose pattern matches be returned as function value. This evaluation order guarantees determinacy of results even in the presence of several (potentially) matching patterns.

If none of the patterns matches, the CASE application may simply return itself as its own value since it can obviously not be re-written into anything else Alternatively, the application may be considered undefined and be replaced by the bottom symbol $\perp$.

Thus, the meaning (or the semantics) of a CASE application may be defined by an evaluator function EVAL as:

$$\text{EVAL}\big[\,(\,\text{CASE}\,\ldots,\,pat\_i \to e\_i,\ldots\,\text{END\_CASE}\,e\_a\,)\,\big]$$

$$= \begin{cases} \text{EVAL}\big[\,e\_i[\Leftarrow]\,\big] \text{ if MATCH } (pat\_i,\ e\_a) = \text{SUCC} \\ \qquad \text{and } (\forall\, j \in \{1,\ldots,n\})\ \text{MATCH } (pat\_j,\ e\_a) = \text{FAIL} \\[2ex] (\,\text{CASE}\,\ldots,\,pat\_i \to e\_i,\ldots\,\text{END\_CASE}\,e\_a\,) \\ (\text{or } \perp)\ \text{otherwise} \end{cases}$$

where MATCH($pat\_i$, $e\_a$) returns SUCC (for succeed) if $pat\_i$ matches the argument term $e\_a$, and FAIL otherwise[2]; $e\_i[\Leftarrow]$ denotes the instantiation of occurrences of the pattern variables in the body term $e\_i$ by the (sub-)terms extracted from the matching positions of the argument term $e\_a$.

However, there are many interesting applications, specifically search problems, where clauses (rewrite rules) with overlapping patterns cannot be given a unique ordering with respect to a best possible choice of a solution. There may be several promising alternatives to pursue, and the choice may have to be made further down the road as more information to this effect becomes available, say

---

[1] Trivial constant patterns match identical constant arguments, and trivial variable patterns match all legitimate argument terms. Wild card patterns _ * *pat* * _ may only occur as components of tuple patterns. They match sequences of $geq1$ tuple components in the arguments, of which one must match the pattern *pat*. If the wild card _ preceding or succeeding *pat* is missing, then *pat* must match the first or the last component, respectively, of the matching sequence.

[2] Note that both SUCC and FAIL are not elements of the functional language proper but are values of the function MATCH used by the evaluator EVAL.

by repeated application of the same or other CASEs, and some of the alternatives can safely be discarded (e.g., those that produce a FAIL). Until such choices can be made, evaluating matching clauses remains inevitably speculative as it is not a priori known which of them will fail or succeed eventually. However, to speed things up, several or all matching clauses may be computed concurrently since, in a functional setting, they do not inflict side effects on each other.

Denoting a CASE construct as S_CASE if it is to be evaluated speculatively, the meaning of an S_CASE application may be defined as:

$$\text{EVAL}\big[\,(\,\text{S\_CASE}\,\ldots,\,pat\_i \to e\_i,\ldots\,\text{END\_CASE}\,e\_a\,)\,\big]$$

$$= \begin{cases} (\,\text{S\_CASE}\,\ldots,\,pat\_i \to e\_i,\ldots\,\text{END\_CASE}\,e\_a\,) \quad (\text{or } \bot\,) \\ \quad \text{if } \forall\,i \in \{1,\ldots,\,n\}\,\text{MATCH}\,(pat\_i,\,e\_a) = \text{FAIL} \\[2mm] \{\,\text{EVAL}\,[\,e\_i[\Leftarrow]\,]\,\}\mid \text{MATCH}\,(pat\_i,\,e\_a) = \text{SUCC}\,\} \quad \text{otherwise} \end{cases}$$

i.e., the value of such an application, again, is the application itself (or the bottom symbol $\bot$) if none of the patterns matches, and the set of values of the instantiated body terms of all clauses whose patterns match the argument value $e\_a$ otherwise.

Based in this definition, it may be further qualified what a (best possible) problem solution (result) that is to be chosen from this set should be. There are basically three options available:

- One could be content with just one of possibly several results, e.g., the one returned first. However, as such result may depend on execution orders chosen by the underlying system, it is generally non–determinate and thus violates the functional semantics.
- To guarantee determinacy, the criterion for selecting a single out of several possible results has to be made dependent upon an algorithmic or application–specific property. Such a criterion could be the least number of rule applications performed to arrive at a result, and if there is more than one result that meets it, then one could pick the leftmost of the particular S_CASE.
- Another alternative would be to ask for the full set of solutions. Unfortunately, it cannot generally be decided by the system whether this set can be computed at all since the computation may not terminate in all branches. However, the user could specify an upper bound on the number of rule applications to be executed in each speculative branch, and accept as a solution the subset of results that can be computed within this limit.

Selecting one of these options may be specified by means of distinct key words N_CASE (for non–determinate single solutions) D_CASE (for determinate single solutions) and M_CASE (for multiple solutions) which control appropriate interpretation or compilation to machine code.

The need to count rule applications in the latter two cases goes hand in hand with the need to halt in some orderly form runaway computations effected, say, by recursive function calls that fail to meet termination conditions. This may be accomplished by a system-supported count variable which prior to each program run is initialized with some user-specified integer value. Upon each application of a rewrite rule this count value is decremented by one. The computation is halted either if the program term has reached normal form or if the count value is down to zero, whichever occurs first [Berk75, GK96].

This count variable may be smoothly integrated into the definition of the evaluator EVAL, which for S_CASEs then takes the form

$$\text{EVAL}\big[\ (\ \text{S\_CASE}\ \ldots,\ pat\_i \to e\_i,\ldots\ \text{END\_CASE}\ e\_a\ )\ |\ k\ \big]$$

$$= \begin{cases} (\ \text{S\_CASE}\ \ldots,\ pat\_i \to e\_i,\ldots\ \text{END\_CASE}\ e\_a\ )\ |\ k \quad (\text{or}\ \bot\ ) \\ \quad \text{if } \forall\ i \in \{1,\ldots,\ n\}\ \text{MATCH}\ (pat\_i,\ e\_a) = \text{FAIL} \\ \quad \text{or if}\ k = 0; \\ \\ \{\ \text{EVAL}\ [\ e\_i[\Leftarrow]\ |\ k - 1\ ]\ |\ \text{MATCH}\ (pat\_i,\ e\_a) = \text{SUCC}\ \}\ \ \text{otherwise} \end{cases}$$

Assuming that the count variable has value $k$ upon entering the evaluation of an S_CASE application, it remains unchanged (or is replaced by the bottom symbol $\bot^3$) if none of the patterns matches the argument or $k$ is down to zero at this point, but is decremented by one if at least one pattern matches, whereupon the body terms of all matching clauses continue computing with their own copies of the count value $k - 1$.

Using these count values, the value (or normal form) of

- a D_CASE application can be defined as the value of the clause selected by a successful pattern match whose associated count variable $k$ has the largest remaining value (and thus evaluated the least number of applications);
- an M_CASE application can be defined as the set values of those clauses selected by successful pattern matches whose associated count variables have values $k > 0$.

## 3   Controlling Speculative Soncurrent Computations

Executing functional programs concurrently is usually based on a simple divide–and–conquer scheme which recursively spawns new tasks for program terms whose values are bound to contribute to results. The tasks at the leaves of the emerging task tree may be scheduled for processing in any order and non–preemptively since all of them are vital (or mandatory). There are also fairly simple measures at hand to prevent the creation of tasks far beyond the number of processing sites [Klu83].

Things become decidedly more complicated when speculative tasks enter the game. To commit processing capacity with top priority to useful computations,

---

[3] Note that the bottom symbol is used in the actual system implementation to easily identify speculoative computations that have failed to produce a (partial) problem solution and therefore can be aborted.

vital tasks must be given preference over speculative tasks, i.e., no speculative task may be scheduled for processing as long as there are vital tasks ready to run. Moreover, vital tasks, once running, may yield processing sites only if they terminate or suspend themselves. Scheduling speculative tasks on the processing sites that are left over must be preemptive to prevent the monopolization of the systems resources with computations that may turn out to be useless. Processing sites may have to be turned over as soon as possible to newly emerging vital tasks, and all speculative tasks ought to be moved ahead at about the same pace as long as it cannot be decided which of them are going to succeed. If there are more speculative tasks than processing sites they can run on, they must inevitably be scheduled in a round robin fashion similar to time slicing to enforce fair progress (which in fact realizes a breadth–first evaluation strategy).

A suitable fairness regulation mechanism may be based on the notion of synchronic distances as introduced in Petri net theory [GLT80], in combination with some loose form of barrier synchronization. Synchronic distances, roughly speaking, define upper bounds on the number of operational steps by which one of several competing tasks (or threads of control) can at most get ahead of the others before they must catch up. These steps can easily be counted in terms of rewrite rules performed, which nicely blends in with the count variable $k$ introduced in the preceding section as part of the definition of the evaluator EVAL, whose primary purpose is to halt runaway computations.

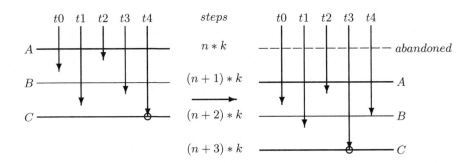

**Fig. 1.** Fairness regulation scheme with three–barrier synchronization

The fairness mechanism which, after experimenting with several alternative solutions, has emerged as the most effective one for supporting speculative computations in a distributed implementation of $\pi$-RED involves three successive barriers $A$, $B$ and $C$ which are synchronic distances of some $k$ rewrite steps away from each other (see Fig. 1). Assuming that some $n$ speculative tasks (there are five named $t0 \ldots t4$ shown in the figure) participating in the race have just managed to cross barrier $A$, they are supplied with a fuel of some $k$ rewrite steps to reach barrier $B$. Tasks arriving at barrier $B$ (and thus having exhausted their fuel) may cross and be refueled with another $k$ rewrite steps to move on towards barrier $C$. There they are blocked until all $n$ tasks have crossed barrier $B$ (the left of Fig. 1). This being the case, the three barriers are moved $k$ steps ahead, i.e., the current barrier $A$ is abandoned, barriers $B$ and $C$ become the new barriers $A$ and $B$, respectively, and a new barrier $C$ is set up $k$ steps down the road from the current one (the right of Fig. 1), and so on.

This three–barrier mechanism keeps many of the tasks alive and computing most of the time, particularly if the number of tasks only marginally exceeds the number of available processing sites. As it must exercise control over all speculative tasks across all processing sites of a distributed system, it may be realized as an attachment to the root task of the program, which for this purpose must be kept vital and running in some unique site. The root task maintains a data structure which contains pointers to the context blocks of all speculative tasks participating in the fairness regulation. This structure is updated upon receiving control messages pertaining to the spawning of new speculative tasks and to tasks changing their status from speculative to vital, terminated or aborted. Information about barriers reached (and possibly blocked) or crossed by individual tasks is held in the respective context blocks and updated whenever signals to this effect arrive.

Another sophisticated mechanism concerns the creation of speculative tasks, their registration as new parties of the fairness mechanism, and actually starting them. A vital or speculative task that executes, say, a CASE–application may become a parent task that creates a speculative child task for every matching clause, generally in some other processing site, whereupon the parent usually suspends itself since there may be little else to do but to wait for results returned by the children. The children, in turn, have to be registered with the fairness regulation mechanism and supplied with fuel to start running. The communications necessary to do so are depicted in Fig. 2. After having created in sequence speculative tasks for all matching clauses (two in the example), the parent continues until it receives acknowledge messages from the new children, together with their identities. The children are then immediately suspended until further notice. The parent registers the new children with the fairness regulation mechanism and suspends itself[4]. The fairness regulation, in turn, confirms the registration and sends out start signals, together with the fuel left by the parent to reach the next barrier.

This rather complex scheme is necessary to catch asynchronous messages which may interleave with these communications. For instance, while the parent is in the process of spawning children or registering them with the fairness regulation, an incoming message might signal the parent that the next barrier has been opened and more fuel is available, which may be immediately passed on to the children.

Termination or abortion of speculative tasks depends to some extent on the type of the desired result. As mentioned in Section 2 this could be just any one of possibly several problem solutions, e.g., the one the system returns first, a unique

---

[4] If the parent is a speculative task itself, it temporarily resigns from the fairness regulation as well.

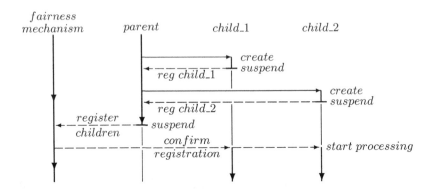

**Fig. 2.** Spawning new speculative tasks

single solution, say, the one that requires the least number of rewrite steps to arrive at, or all possible solutions requiring less than some pre–specified number of rewrite steps – the total fuel – to compute[5]. In both of the latter cases, the computations would produce determinate results irrespective of actual execution orders. In the former case, the result would be non–determinate, or dependent on actual task scheduling.

A speculative task may be aborted if

- by some criteria, typically a CASE–application with no matching clauses, it produces the bot symbol ⊥ which indicates failure of the particular clause to produce a problem solution (compare Section 2);
- it receives a signal that a solution has been produced somewhere else and the task has thus become irrelevant.

In either case the task immediately resigns from the fairness regulation, detaches itself from its parent, and releases its context block.

A task terminates regularly if it produces a solution. All other tasks

- may be aborted if just any one solution is required;
- that have already consumed more rewrite steps are signaled to abort at the next barrier if the desired solution must have consumed the least number of rewrite steps;

When computing all solutions up to the point of exhausting the total fuel, all tasks that are still alive at this point must be aborted.

However, as results must be returned to the root task, the tasks that are on the path from a terminating task to the root must, of course, in all three cases stay alive until the results have been passed through.

---

[5] Without such an upper bound the computation could get trapped in endless recursions and thus never terminate.

# 4    Fairness Versus Limited Resources

There is a fundamental conflict of interest between the demand for fair progress of all speculative tasks on the one hand and finite resources on the other hand.

With no information at hand to set priorities, all opportunities for speculative evaluation ought to be treated on an equal basis, i.e., driven ahead at about the same pace, as otherwise too much processing power might be wasted on just the wrong computations. Given a recursively unfolding search problem, a breadth–first search would require spawning unbounded numbers of speculative tasks as there is generally no upper limit on the size of the search space. However, spawning tasks far beyond the number of processing sites would not only create considerable management overhead without any further performance gains but also consume decidedly more memory for runtime structures and heap space than, say, a strictly sequential search at the other extreme.

To overcome this problem, a compromize must be made between unbounded demands for resources on the one hand and enforcing strict fairness among speculative computations as outlined in the preceding section on the other hand. The idea is to provide a pool of concessions (or tokens) – in a distributed system evenly spread out over its processing sites – to spawn new tasks [Klu83]. Whenever such an opportunity arises, the (local) pool is checked for the availability of a concession, and if so, the concession is taken and a new task is created; otherwise this opportunity is ignored and the sub–term that was to be evaluated by the new task is instead processed sequentially by the calling task. A terminating task recycles to the (same local) pool the concession it has taken, which may be immediately picked up to create another task. Thus, at any time there are at most as many tasks alive in the system as there were initially concession tokens in the pool.

Ignoring opportunities to spawn new tasks in fact implies switching from a breadth–first to a depth–first execution mode. If this approach would be applied to speculative tasks, fairness would clearly be violated: several matching clauses of a CASE application could only be evaluated in sequence, say from left to right, and depth–first, i.e., further CASE applications deeper down would recursively be treated in the same way.

The way out of this dilemma consists in placing, on the way down, into a task–specific $FIFO$–queue all matching clauses of a CASE application that for the time being must be left pending, as indicated in Fig. 3 for a recursive nesting of three CASEs that produce just two matches each. Whenever a task produces a bottom symbol $\perp$ in the leftmost branchs, indicating that the search for a solution has failed, e.g., at a CASE application with no matching pattern, it continues with the first alternative at the front–end of the queue which is the one highest up in the unfolding computational tree. Likewise, if concessions to spawn new tasks become available again later on, the queues of all existing tasks are inspected and the pending clauses highest up across all tasks residing in a particular site are chosen for the creation of new tasks.

Since a task, after having produced a bottom symbol in its leftmost branch, is supposed to backtrack to the topmost alternative clause and this clause is to

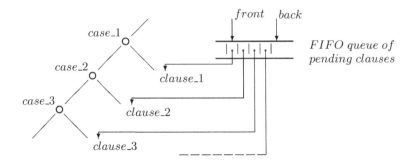

**Fig. 3.** Building a FIFO queue of pending clauses

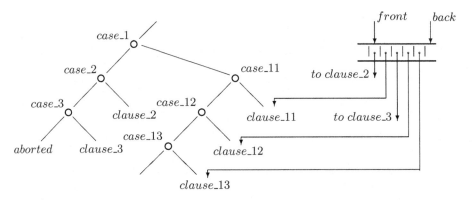

**Fig. 4.** Keeping pending clauses in the queue in descending order

be taken from the front–end of the queue, the queue cannot strictly be operated in $FIFO$ order. As illustrated in Fig. 4, the pending clauses of the new branch must be sorted into the existing queue so that clauses of higher levels always precede clauses of lower levels of the computational tree to keep the computation breadth–first as much as possible.

This strategy does depth–first evaluation whenever, after exhaustion of all concessions to spawn speculative tasks, there is no alternative left, but gives preference to breadth–first evaluation as soon as concessions are (or become again) available, i.e., it is reasonably fair without involving elaborate priority schemes, given the constraints of limited numbers of tasks.

## 5    Some Performance Experiments with a Search Problem

The concepts described in the preceding sections have been implemented as extensions of a concurrent graph reduction system $\pi$–RED [GK96, BHK94]. This system interprets abstract machine code to which high–level programs of the functional language KIR [Klu94] (whose syntax closely resembles the one given in Section 2 ) are compiled. Other than identifying S_ CASE–constructs as candidates for speculative evaluation, these programs do not contain any annotations pertaining to concurrent execution. $\pi$–RED is installed on an nCUBE/2 distributed multiprocessor system of 32 processing sites which can be configured to form sub–cubes of some $2^k \mid k \leq 5$ sites. Each site runs a micro kernel nCX which supports a single $\pi$–RED process. This process in fact realizes a small kernel of its own which handles $\pi$–RED–specific task management and communication, including signals and messages from and to the fairness mechanism.

Program code is downloaded from some front–end workstation into each nCUBE/2 processing site; program execution starts with a single task at a unique initial site (which also runs the fairness mechanism) from where it recursively spreads out over all sites of the particular configuration. The initial task in that site eventually also assembles the result of the computation and returns it to the front–end. As of now, the system interprets compiled abstract machine code as it was easier at this level to implement, modify and experiment with the pieces of code that control the creation, synchronization and termination of speculative tasks, communicate with the fairness regulation mechanism, effects status changes, etc.. For programs which heavily use pattern matching, code interpretation is about three times slower than compiled target machine code.

To systematically investigate performance enhancements due to speculative evaluation relative to sequential program execution, we have chosen a program which searches for exits in a maze. Though this problem can be elegantly and efficiently solved by encoding the maze into a set of higher–order functions, of which an application of the function that represents the starting point produces the desired result, we have deliberately chosen a decidedly more primitive algorithm. It has the advantage of creating by relatively simple means and in a controlled way sufficient computational complexity and opportunities for speculative computations.

The search is simulated by a spider walking step by step through the maze, represented as a matrix which marks walls as 1s and the aisles in between as 0s, and checking at each position, by means of pattern matches, how many alternatives are available to make a next step. If there is more than one direction to follow, the computation splits up into as many speculative searches. The search along a particular path succeeds if an exit can be reached and fails if, at a particular position, there is no alternative left but to move backward. Each search path is kept track of by generating a list (tuple) of coordinate pairs (positions) where the spider changed directions or branched out into two or three different directions. The paths that led to exits are returned as output and those that led into dead ends are discarded. The program can be parameterized with respect to size and layout (complexity) of the maze, number and positions of exits, starting position and width of the steps taken by the spider.

The program basically centers around a function *explore* as shown in Fig. 5 which, given a certain position of the spider in the maze in terms of its coordinates $x$, $y$, moves one step ahead in the direction specified by the parameter $h$

```
explore x y h =
    LET xx = (new_x x h),
        yy = (new_y y h),
    IN IF(is_exit xx yy)
        THEN << xx, yy >>
        ELSE LET hs = (scan xx yy h)
        IN ...
        ( S_CASE
            < _* 'east' _* > → (path < xx, yy > (explore xx yy 'east'))
            < _* 'west' _* > → (path < xx, yy > (explore xx yy 'west'))
            < _* 'north' _* > → (path < xx, yy > (explore xx yy 'north'))
            < _* 'south' _* > → (path < xx, yy > (explore xx yy 'south'))
        END_CASE hs )
```

**Fig. 5.** Code for the function *explore* that controls the movement of the spider

(which may assume one of the values *'east'*, *'west'*, *'north'*, *'south'*) and finds out where to move next from there.

From top to bottom, this function computes, by means of the functions $new\_x$ and $new\_y$, the new pair of coordinates $xx$, $yy$, checks whether this new position is an exit (in which case the function terminates by returning the pair of coordinates), and, if not, computes by means of the function *scan* the directions in which the spider may move next, and collects these directions in a tuple returned as function value which instantiates the LET bound variable $hs$. This tuple is then taken as an argument of an S_CASE function whose patterns[6] check it for occurrences of the four possible directions. In case of a match (of which there may be up to three since the spider is not allowed to move backward), the coordinate pair $< xx, yy >$ is appended to the list(s) of travel positions computed so far and prepended to the list of positions still to be computed by the recursive application of the function *explore* to these coordinates and to the direction identified by the pattern match.

The first problem investigated was the search for a single exit in a maze featuring the regular shape of a balanced binary tree of 128 leaves at the base (the left of Fig. 6 shows a tree of eight leaves). The search starts at the root of the tree, and terminates successfully at a leaf which is selected as the single exit. This exit position is moved from left to right along the leaves. The program execution times on the right of this figure confirm what can be expected: when doing a depth–first and left–to–right sequential search on a single processing site, the runtimes increase linearly from the exit being in the leftmost to being in the rightmost position. With speculative searches, runtimes drop considerably with increasing numbers of processing sites and become invariant against changing exit positions as the tree is well balanced. The speculative search on 16 processing sites clearly outperforms the sequential search for all but the 8 leftmost of the 128

---

[6] The patterns are specified by means of wild cards since the particular direction may be in any of at most three tuple positions.

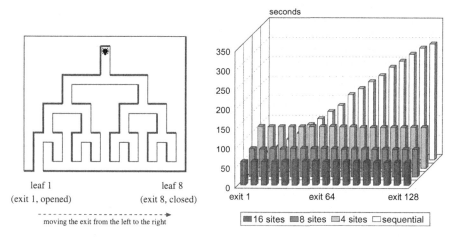

**Fig. 6.** Searching for an exit in a maze shaped as a binary tree

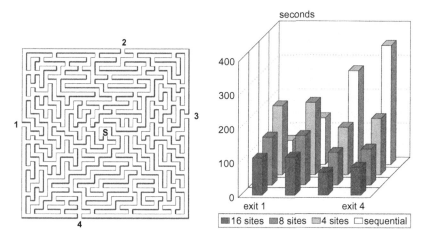

**Fig. 7.** Searching for exits in an arbitrary maze

possible exit positions. Thus, at the expense of involving considerable processing capacity, one may win in some (most) situations but lose in others.

Similar experiments have been conducted with several square–shaped mazes of highly irregular internal structures of aisles and walls, with exits placed on each of the four borders, and with different lengths of the search paths leading to these exits. A typical such maze is shown on the left of Fig. 7. The searches were done with only one of the four or with all exits open, and with the paths to one or all four exits as results. Though performance figures to some extent depend on the particularities of the maze structure and also on the machine configuration (e.g., on the chosen synchronic distance of the fairness mechanism or on upper bounds on the number of speculative tasks), it again turned out that for all mazes and system parameters investigated the speculative searches on 16 processing sites did decidedly better than all but the best case sequential searches, and that with 8 or 4 processing sites the speculative searches outperformed at least the worst case sequential searches. Representative for these results are the execution times on the right of Fig. 7.

An interesting question concerns the overhead inflicted by the organizational measures necessary to support speculative evaluation as described. This question is difficult to answer quantitatively since it would require appropriate instrumentation of the runtime system and profiling of several application programs with different system configurations (numbers of processing sites, number of concessions to spawn speculative tasks, synchronice distances of the fairness mechanism, etc.), which we simply did not have the resources to do. Comparing wallclock execution times with speculative evaluation activated and de-activated would not be very conclusive as they relate to different modes of program execution with completely different dynamic program behavior. However, looking at the performance diagrams of Figs. 6 and 7, which compare speculative evaluation of the same program on different numbers of processing sites, it can at least be concluded that the overhead must be quite substantial (i.e., in the order of 30% to 50%): doubling the number of processing sites (from 4 to 8 and then to 16) reduces program execution times merely by about a factor of 2/3.

Conclusive wallclock measurements were only possible with respect to the effect on program execution times of varying synchronic distances enforced by the fairness regulation mechanism. Representative are the data collected from a maze program that takes roughly 350.000 rule applications to find a single exit. It was run on a system configuration with 8 processing sites and unbounded numbers of speculative tasks. Changing the synchronic distance from 5000 to 50.000 rule applications (in increments of 5000) led to a nearly linear reduction of control messages from some 260 to 24 (i.e., by about an order of magnitude) and of the program runtime by about 10%.

# 6   Related Work

In the functional domain, speculative evaluation primarily relates to non–strict arguments under a lazy regime, with HASKELL as the language of choice [Par91, Mat93]. In [Che94] are described several priority schemes for speculative tasks, up– and down–grading, and both explicit and implicit abortion of tasks that have become irrelevant. This work also addresses the problem of non–determinacy and suggests introducing the notion of bags in which solutions are collected without any ordering to maintain a functional semantics.

Another interesting approach based on the speculative evaluation of LISP programs is reported in [Osb90]. It introduces a rather elaborate priority scheme based on a so–called sponsor model which favors the execution of speculative tasks with the best chances of succeeding. Sponsorships and, hence, priorities are dynamically adjusted as computations proceed and more information about possible outcomes become available. The sponsor model implicitly also gets around the fairness vs. limited resources problem.

In logic programming, the concepts closest to our approach relate to the exploitation of the so–called $OR$–parallelism in PROLOG–programs [Sha89], for which scheduling strategies are described in [Bea91]. Interestingly enough, speculative evaluation in PROLOG relates to computations that may be cut off by pruning operations such as the famous cut. Detecting this kind of speculative work is discussed in [Hau89].

Representative for related work on term–rewrite systems is [VK96]. It describes an interactive theorem prover called LARCH which allows the user to launch several speculative attempts to prove conjectures; unsuccessful attempts must be cleaned up by hand. Both $AND$– and $OR$ parallelism are supported, and the number of competing tasks or the depth of the recursive expansion can be restricted.

# 7  Conclusion

The system concept described in this paper merely supports the measures that are considered absolutely essential to organize speculative computations in some orderly form. They mainly concern a reasonably efficient usage of resources (by giving mandatory tasks scheduling priority over speculative tasks and by throttling the number of speculative tasks that may participate in a computation), ensuring fair progress among all speculative tasks, and earliest possible status changes of speculative tasks either to aborted or to vital. The emphasis of this work was primarily on feasibility studies of various alternative solutions to these problems, less so on absolute performance figures (hence interpretation of abstract machine code which facilitated experimental implementations considerably). No attempts have been made to speculate, e.g., by means of more or less elaborate priority schemes, on the likely behavior of the program at hand, and to have task scheduling governed by these priorities, as for instance in the approaches reported in [Che94] and in [Osb90]. Concentrating on the essentials has nevertheless yielded encouraging results in terms of noticeable performance gains vs. sequential execution.

Further work primarily concerns more refined scheduling strategies for speculative tasks which take into account several dynamically changing priority levels, improved mechanisms for passing control messages up and down hierarchies of speculative tasks, and compilation to target machine code.

# References

[Bea91]   A. Beaumont. Scheduling Strategies and Speculative Work. In Anthony Beaumont and Gopal Gupta, editors, *Proceedings of Parallel Execution of Logic Programs (ICLP '91)*, volume 569 of *LNCS*, pages 120–131, Berlin, Germany, June 1991. Springer.

[Berk75]  K.J. Berkling  Reduction Languages for Reduction Machines  *Proceedings 2nd Annual International Symposium on Computer Architecture*, ACM/IEEE 75CH0916-7C 1975, pages 133–140,

[BHK94]  T. Bülck and A. Held and W.E. Kluge and S. Pantke and C. Rathsack and S.-B. Scholz and R. Schröder. Experience with the Implementation of a Concurrent Graph Reduction System on an nCUBE/2 Platform. In B. Buchberger and j. Volkert, editors, *Proceedings of CONPAR 94 - VAPP IV* volume 854 of *LNCS*, Springer 1994, pages 497 – 508,

[BK92]  H. Bloedorn and W.E. Kluge. Organizing Speculative Computations in the Reduction System $\pi$-RED$^*$. In *Proc. Workshop Parallel–Algorithmen und Rechnerstrukturen*, pages 138–152. Mitteilungen der GI ISSN 0177–0454, 1992.

[Che94]  Iain G. Checkland. *Speculative Concurrent Evaluation in a Lazy Functional Language*. PhD thesis, University of York, Department of Computer Science, 1994.

[GK96]  D. Gärtner and W.E. Kluge. $\pi$-RED$^+$—An Interactive Compiling Graph Reduction System for an Applied $\lambda$-Calculus. *Journal of Functional Programming*, 6(5):723–756, 1996.

[GLT80]  H.J. Genrich and K. Lautenbach and P.S. Thiagarajan. Elements of General Net Theory In *Net Theory and Applications*, volume 84 of *LNCS*, Springer 1980, pages 21–163,

[Hau89]  B. Hausman. Pruning and Scheduling Speculative Work in OR-Parallel Prolog. In E. Odijk, M. Rem, and J.-C. Syre, editors, *Proceedings of the Conference on Parallel Architectures and Languages Europe : Vol. 2*, volume 366 of *LNCS*, Springer 1989, pages 133–150

[Jon87]  S. L. Peyton Jones. *The Implementation of Functional Programming Languages*. Computer Science. Prentice-Hall, 1987.

[Klu83]  W.E. Kluge. Cooperating Reduction Machines. *IEEE Transactions on Computers*, C-32:1002–1012, 1983.

[Klu94]  W.E. Kluge. A User's Guide for the Reduction System $\pi$-RED . Technical Report 9419, Institut für Informatik und praktische Mathematik, Universität Kiel, December 1994.

[Mat93]  J. S. Mattson. *An Effective Speculative Evaluation Technique for Parallel Supercombinator Graph Reduction*. PhD thesis, Department of Computer Science and Engineering, University of California, San Diego, February 93.

[Osb90]  Osborne. Speculative Computation in Multilisp. Technical Report DEC-CRL-90-1, Digital Equipment Corporation, Cambridge Research Lab, 90.

[Par91]  A. Partridge. *Speculative Evaluation in Parallel Implementations of Lazy Functional Languages*. PhD thesis, Dept. of Computer Science, University of Tasmania, 1991.

[Sha89]  Ehud Shapiro. The Family of Concurrent Logic Programming Languages. *ACM Computing Surveys*, 21(3):413–510, September 1989.

[VK96]  M. T. Vandevoorde and D. Kapur. Distributed Larch Prover (DLP): An Experiment in Parallelizing a Rewrite-Rule Based Prover. volume 1103 of *LNCS*, Springer 1996, pages 420–423,

# Improving Cache Effectiveness through Array Data Layout Manipulation in SAC

Clemens Grelck

University of Kiel,
Department of Computer Science and Applied Mathematics,
24098 Kiel, Germany
cg@informatik.uni-kiel.de

**Abstract.** SAC is a functional array processing language particularly designed with numerical applications in mind. In this field the runtime performance of programs critically depends on the efficient utilization of the memory hierarchy. Cache conflicts due to limited set associativity are one relevant source of inefficiency. This paper describes the realization of an optimization technique which aims at eliminating cache conflicts by adjusting the data layout of arrays to specific access patterns and cache configurations. Its effect on cache utilization and runtime performance is demonstrated by investigations on the PDE1 benchmark.

## 1 Introduction

SAC is a functional array processing language, which tries to combine generic, high-level program specifications with efficient runtime behaviour [20,21]. Particularly in the field of numerical applications, the efficient utilization of the memory hierarchy plays a key role in achieving good performance [14]. However, for many numerical application programs it can be observed that small variations in problem sizes may have a significant impact on runtime performance. This is due to systematic cache conflicts which may occur for unfavourable combinations of array access patterns and array data layout in the presence of limited cache associativity [2].

Assuming the runtime performance of a program is poor for one problem size, but turns out to be significantly better for a marginally larger problem size, it is a rather straightforward idea to mimick the data layout associated with the larger problem size when actually dealing with the smaller one. In doing so, the originally dense representation of arrays is manipulated by the introduction of dummy elements in one or another dimension, so-called array padding [1]. The array padding optimization implemented in SAC basically consists of three steps. First, SAC code within WITH-loops, the predominant SAC language construct for the specification of aggregate array operations [7], is thoroughly analysed for array accesses, and the arrays involved are associated with accurate access patterns. Second, an inference heuristic estimates the cache utilization and identifies an appropriate amount of padding where necessary. Cache phenomena

M. Mohnen and P. Koopman (Eds.): IFL 2000, LNCS 2011, pp. 231–248, 2001.
© Springer-Verlag Berlin Heidelberg 2001

such as spatial and temporal reuse are taken into account. Third, the data layout modification proposed by the inference heuristic is realized as a high-level transformation on intermediate SAC code.

The remainder of this paper is organized as follows. After a more detailed problem identification in Section 2, Sections 3, 4, and 5 describe the three steps of the implementation. Their effect on runtime performance is demonstrated by means of the PDE1 benchmark in Section 6. Section 7 sketches some related work while Section 8 concludes.

## 2   Problem Identification

We have chosen the benchmark PDE1 as an example in order to investigate and quantify the potential impact of the problem size on runtime performance. PDE1 implements red/black successive over-relaxation on 3-dimensional grids. The benchmark itself as well as various implementation opportunities for SAC are discussed in [8]. In our experiments we have systematically varied the size of the 3-dimensional grid from $16^3$ until $528^3$ in uniform steps of 16 elements in each dimension. With double precision floating point numbers, this involves array sizes between 32KB and 1.1GB. All experiments have been done on a SUN Ultra Enterprise 4000 system. Figure 1 shows the average times required to recompute the value of a single inner grid element. It can be observed that these times significantly vary for the problem sizes investigated. While 155nsec are sufficient to update an inner element of a grid of size $16^3$, it takes up to 866nsec to complete the same operation in a grid of size $256^3$. Although exactly the same sequence of instructions is executed for each inner grid element regardless of the problem size, the time required to do so varies by a factor of 5.6.

Such extreme variations in runtime performance can only be attributed to different degrees of cache utilization caused by varying data layouts introduced by different problem sizes. In order to substantiate claims like this, the SAC compiler and runtime system are equipped with a tailor-made cache simulation feature. On demand, a trace of all array accesses during program execution is generated. This allows for a complete simulation of the cache behaviour, yielding statistical information regarding the effectiveness of cache utilization. Each processor of the SUN Ultra Enterprise 4000 multiprocessor system is equipped with a 16KB L1 data cache and a 1MB L2 unified cache. Both are direct-mapped and use cache lines of 32 and 64 bytes, respectively. Figure 2 shows the percentage of L1 cache hits for the various problem sizes investigated as well as the percentage of memory requests satisfied by any of the two cache levels. It actually turns out that the extreme performance variations observed in Fig. 1 largely coincide with similar variations in simulated cache hit rates.

The design of cache memories is essentially based on two assumptions: temporal locality and spatial locality [9]. A program exhibits temporal locality if it is likely that once a memory address is referenced in the code, it will be referenced again soon. Therefore, data is loaded into the fast cache memory in order to satisfy subsequent requests without slow main memory interaction. Spatial locality

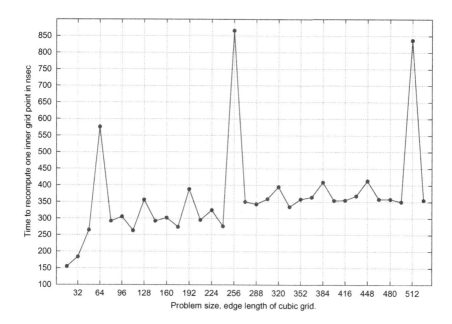

**Fig. 1.** PDE1: average time required to re-compute a single grid element

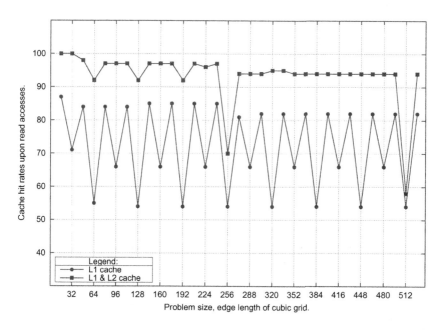

**Fig. 2.** PDE1: simulated cache performance

means that once a memory address is referenced, adjacent addresses are likely to be referenced soon. For this reason, caches are internally organized in so-called *cache lines*, which typically comprise between 16 and 128 bytes of contiguous memory. All data transfers between main memory and cache involve entire cache lines rather than single bytes or words of memory. Application programs do only benefit from caches to the extent to which they exhibit spatial and temporal locality.

However, spatial and temporal locality are mainly characteristics of a given program, and hence, do not explain the observed performance variations. In fact, it is a limitation in cache memory hardware that is responsible for this: very limited set associativity. In order to efficiently distinguish cache hits from cache misses, any given memory address can only be mapped to one of very few locations in the cache, which are directly derived from the memory address itself. Today's caches usually provide set associativities between one and four. As a consequence, data may be flushed from the cache before potential reuse is actually exploited, although the cache is sufficiently large to allow the reuse in principle. These so-called *conflict misses* may seriously limit cache utilization, as can be seen in Figs. 1 and 2. Since concrete memory addresses decide over cache conflicts, they are extremely sensitive against memory layout variations, in particular, whenever regularly structured data is accessed in regular patterns, which is typical for numerical codes involving large arrays.

Various different cache effects have been identified [22], e.g., a *spatial reuse conflict* occurs whenever not all array elements referenced in a single iteration of an inner loop can simultaneously be held in the cache. The number of different array elements which are mapped to the same cache set exceeds the cache's set associativity and, hence, cache lines are flushed from the cache before potential reuse can be realized in the following iteration. A *temporal reuse conflict* occurs when potential reuse between two references to the same array element cannot be exploited because another array reference interferes and causes the first one to be flushed from the cache before the potential reuse actually occurs. Conflicts are classified as either arising from references to the same array, so-called *self-interference* conflicts, or to different arrays, so-called *cross-interference* conflicts.

Thorough elimination of cache conflicts is crucial for keeping the runtime performance consistent over a range of problem sizes [13]. This can be achieved by a well-aimed manipulation of the data layout of arrays. Self-interference conflicts can be eliminated by modifying the internal representation of arrays, cross-interference conflicts by adjusting array base addresses. The latter approach is very difficult to realize in a language like SAC, which allocates and de-allocates all data structures dynamically. Therefore, we concentrate on self-interference conflicts in the following. One way to manipulate the internal representation of arrays is *array padding*, a well-known optimization technique that adds dummy elements to an array in one or another inner dimension [1]. For example, an array whose original shape is [100,100] may be transformed into an array of shape [100,102] by adding two columns of dummy elements. Padding an array alters the memory addresses of different elements in different ways and, hence, allows to indirectly manipulate their associated relative cache locations.

However, applying array padding manually has some serious drawbacks. It requires both a lot of effort and expert knowledge by programmers, who in this case are solely responsible to identify where which amount of padding might have a positive impact on runtime performance. Moreover, explicit array padding increases program complexity and makes programs less readable and more error-prone. Last but not least, array padding renders program specifications machine-dependent because each combination of problem size, access pattern, and cache configuration typically requires a different amount of padding.

In contrast, array padding as a compiler optimization may be well-suited to achieve more consistent performance over a wide range of problem sizes and cache configurations. However, things are not as simple in low-level languages such as C or FORTRAN. Since these languages' semantics guarantee a certain (unpadded) data layout, thorough program analysis is required in order to prove that padding does not alter the meaning of a program. Here, the design of high-level languages like SAC pays off. Since they completely abstract from any concrete data layout, language implementations are free to exploit the benefits of varying data layouts as an additional optimization technique.

## 3    Array Access Analysis

Accurate analysis of array access patterns is one of the prerequisites for reasoning about cache conflicts. Severe cache conflicts typically arise from regular array references within loops, i.e., two or more references systematically conflict with each other in every iteration of the loop. Therefore, the analysis described in this section focusses on regular array references in WITH-loops. The WITH-loop is a SAC-specific language construct for the specification of aggregate multi-dimensional array operations; a thorough description may, for instance, be found in [7]. An array reference is considered being regular if and only if it can be written in the form

$$\text{val} = \text{Array} \ [\ s * i + d\ ] \ ;$$

where $s$ denotes a constant stride vector, $d$ a constant offset vector, and $i$ the WITH-loop's index variable. Note that $*$ here denotes the element-wise product of two vectors. In other words, locations of regular array references are defined by dimension-wise affine functions of the WITH-loop's index variable. Figure 3 shows an example WITH-loop featuring a few different regular array references. All array references that cannot be converted to this affine pattern, are considered irregular. They are likely not to conflict in a systematic way with other references, irregular or regular. Therefore, they are just ignored in the sequel.

All array references in the example shown in Fig. 3 are regular with respect to the above definition. This can be inferred during a rather simple bottom-up traversal of the WITH-loop body. Compact array access information is accumulated, as outlined in Fig. 4. The array access pattern $\mathcal{AP}$ is a set of triples;

```
int[100,100] A;
int[200,150] B;
int[120,120] C;
...
A = with ([1,1] <= iv < [100,100])
    {
        a   = B[ iv - 1];
        b   = C[ iv];
        c   = B[ iv + 2];
        d   = C[ [42, 42]];
        e   = B[ [2, 1] * iv];
        tmp = iv + [1, 1];
        f   = B[ [2, 1] * tmp];
        val = a + b + c + d + e + f;
    }
    genarray([100,100], val);
```

**Fig. 3.** Examples of regular array references in a WITH-loop

```
AP = { < B,  [ 1,  1],  [-1,-1] > ,
       < C,  [ 1,  1],  [ 0,  0] > ,
       < B,  [ 1,  1],  [ 2,  2] > ,
       < C,  [ 0,  0],  [42,42] > ,
       < B,  [ 2,  1],  [ 0,  0] > ,
       < B,  [ 2,  1],  [ 2,  1] > }
```

**Fig. 4.** Array access pattern derived from example WITH-loop in Fig. 3

each triple represents exactly one regular array reference found in the WITH-loop body. The access triples themselves consist of the name of the referenced array, the stride vector $s$ and the offset vector $d$.

As already pointed out, the technique presented in this paper focusses on self-interference cache conflicts, i.e. conflicts between references to the same array. References to different arrays, although occurring in a single WITH-loop, may be handled separately. Furthermore, only array references which are characterized by identical stride vectors $s$ may actually interfere with each other in a systematic and, hence, expensive manner. These considerations lead to the division of an access pattern into disjoint so-called *conflict groups*. Each conflict group then contains exactly one subset of array references which are likely to systematically interfere with each other.

The example access pattern $AP$ in Fig. 4 results in the introduction of four conflict groups, as outlined in Fig. 5. Each conflict group is represented by a pair consisting of the type of the referenced array and a sequence of offset vectors. The stride vectors are no longer needed. Whether or not two references of the same conflict group cause a cache conflict solely depends on their relative distance in memory, which is invariant against their strides. Last but not least, no cache

$$\begin{array}{l} \mathcal{CG}_1 = <\texttt{int[200,150]}, <\ [\texttt{-1,-1]}, \ [\ \texttt{2, 2]} >> \\ \mathcal{CG}_2 = <\texttt{int[120,120]}, <\ [\ \texttt{0, 0]} >> \\ \mathcal{CG}_3 = <\texttt{int[120,120]}, <\ [\texttt{42,42]} >> \\ \mathcal{CG}_4 = <\texttt{int[200,150]}, <\ [\ \texttt{0, 0]}, \ [\ \texttt{2, 1]} >> \end{array}$$

**Fig. 5.** Conflict groups derived from access pattern $\mathcal{AP}$ in Fig. 4

conflicts may occur in conflict groups consisting of a single array reference only. As a consequence, all such conflict groups, e.g. $\mathcal{CG}_2$ and $\mathcal{CG}_3$ in Fig. 5, are simply ignored. The number of conflict groups can further be reduced by the elimination of multiple occurrences of identical ones and of those that are subsets of others.

## 4  Padding Inference Heuristic

This section presents the central padding inference algorithm. It associates each array type occurring in a SAC program or module with a padding recommendation appropriate for avoiding spatial and temporal self-interference cache conflicts. The basic idea is to pad all arrays of a given type (consisting of base type and shape) in a uniform way if at all. This helps to avoid costly transformations between unpadded and padded or even differently padded representations of arrays which originally had identical types and, hence, data layouts. Such transformations are limited to module boundaries, providing programmers with some means of control over array padding.

In addition to the conflict groups implicitly derived from SAC code, as described in Section 3, the inference scheme presented here is based on the specification of a cache configuration, which must explicitly be stated at compile time. It consists of the cache size and the cache line size, both in bytes, as well as the cache's set associativity. Furthermore, an upper limit must be set on memory consumption overhead caused by array padding.

When focussing on a single array type, which consists of a scalar base type and an original shape $SHP$, we may easily compute the cache size $CS$ and the cache line size $CLS$ in array elements. These figures, rather than the external specifications in bytes, are used by the inference scheme. Moreover, we compute the number of cache sets, $NSET := CS/(CLS * CA)$ where $CA$ denotes the cache's set associativity. With this internal cache specification at hand, all conflict groups associated with the array type under consideration are then successively analysed with respect to potential cache conflicts. Padding recommendations are accumulated in a vector $PAD$, which is initially set to $\mathbf{0}$, i.e., we start out with recommending no padding at all.

First, spatial reuse conflicts are addressed. Let us consider a conflict group $\mathcal{CG}$ representing array references $R_1, \ldots, R_n$. For each reference $R_i$, the offset vector $D_i$ is converted into a scalar offset with respect to the array shape $SHP$ extended by the padding vector $PAD$ recommended so far:

$$\forall\, i \in \{1, \ldots, n\} \quad : \quad OFFSET_i := ADDR(\ D_i\ ,\ SHP + PAD)\quad ,$$

where $ADDR(vec, shp)$ is a function that computes the offset of $vec$ in the row-major unrolling of an array with shape $shp$, i.e.

$$ADDR(vec, shp) := \sum_{k=0}^{|shp|} \left(vec_k * \prod_{m=k+1}^{|shp|} shp_m\right) \quad .$$

For reasons of simplicity it is desirable to avoid negative offsets. Since our interest is also limited to relative distances of cache locations, computed offsets can easily be shifted by a constant value. The easiest way to avoid negative offsets is to generally arrange the elements of a conflict group in ascending lexicographical order with respect to their offset vectors, and to subtract $OFFSET_0$ from each scalar offset, i.e.

$$\forall\, i \in \{1, \ldots, n\} \quad : \quad OFFSET_i := OFFSET_i - OFFSET_0 \quad .$$

With the shifted offsets at hand, we now determine the respective cache sets

$$\forall\, i \in \{1, \ldots, n\} \quad : \quad SET_i := (OFFSET_i/CLS) \bmod \mathrm{NSET} \quad .$$

For each reference $R_i$, we compute the number $NPSC_i$ of potential spatial reuse conflicts with other references. Two references $R_i$ and $R_j$ potentially conflict with each other if and only if

$$((|SET_i - SET_j| < 2 \quad \vee \quad (|SET_i - SET_j| = NSET - 1))$$

$$\wedge \quad (|OFFSET_i - OFFSET_j| > 2 * CLS) \quad ,$$

i.e., they reference non-adjacent memory addresses which are mapped to identical or directly adjacent cache sets. The latter serves as an additional buffer that allows to completely abstract from relative placements of references within cache lines. In a direct-mapped cache $(CA = 1)$, any potential conflict actually is a real conflict. However, in general, a conflict occurs whenever the number of potential conflicts equals or exceeds the cache's set associativity $CA$, i.e., the number of spatial reuse conflicts associated with each array reference is defined as

$$\forall\, i \in \{1, \ldots, n\} \quad : \quad NSC_i := \max(0,\ NPSC_i - CA + 1) \quad ;$$

the total number of spatial reuse conflicts within the conflict group is defined as

$$NSC := \sum_{i=0}^{n} NSC_i \quad .$$

If there are no conflicts, i.e., $NSC = 0$, we are done and $PAD$ is the recommended padding for this conflict group with respect to spatial reuse. If the number of conflicts is reduced relative to the best padding found so far, the current padding and the number of spatial reuse conflicts associated with it are stored as new currently best solution. As long as there are still conflicts, we try to solve them with additional padding, i.e., the padding vector $PAD$ is to be updated. For this purpose, we first identify dimensions that are eligible for padding.

Assigning the index 0 to the outermost dimension and counting upwards, the minimum padding dimension is determined as $MINPADDIM := d + 1$, where $d$ is the outermost dimension with $D_i[d] \neq D_j[d]$ for any pair of conflicting array references $R_i$ and $R_j$. The maximum padding dimension is simply chosen as $MAXPADDIM := |SHP| - 1$. Among all eligible dimensions the outermost one is chosen, where $(SHP + PAD)[d]$ is maximal. This choice of $PADDIM$ guarantees that padding overhead grows in minimal steps. Padding is preferably applied to outer dimensions in order to reduce the negative impact of the loop overhead introduced by it.

The padding vector $PAD$ is incremented by 1 in dimension $PADDIM$ and, assuming this additional padding does not exceed the given limit on memory consumption overhead, the cache behaviour is re-evaluated with this new padding vector as described so far. Otherwise, $SHP$ is reset to 0 in dimension $MINPADDIM$ and, provided that $MINPADDIM ¡ MAXPADDIM$, padding in the next dimension is increased by 1. The entire process is repeated until either all spatial reuse conflicts are eliminated or all padding vectors eligible with respect to the memory consumption overhead limit have been investigated. In the latter case, the best padding found during the process is stored as recommended padding.

With spatial reuse conflicts eliminated as far as possible, we may now focus on temporal reuse conflicts. As a first step, we determine for each reference $R_i$ if there is a chance for temporal reuse from reference $R_{i+1}$ in the presence of simple cache capacity constraints. This is the case if and only if

$$OFFSET_{i+1} - OFFSET_i \quad < \quad (NSET - 2) * CLS \quad .$$

Note here that all references are sorted with increasing offsets. For each pair of adjacent references $R_i$ and $R_{i+1}$ which may benefit from temporal reuse, we then compute the number of potential temporal reuse conflicts $NPTC$. An array reference $R_j$, $j \neq i \wedge j \neq i + 1$ represents a potential temporal reuse conflict if it is mapped to a cache set "in between" those associated with $R_i$ and $R_{i+1}$, i.e.

$$(SET_i \leq SET_j) \wedge (SET_j \leq SET_{i+1}) \iff SET_i \leq SET_{i+1} \quad ,$$
$$(SET_i \leq SET_j) \vee (SET_j \leq SET_{i+1}) \iff SET_i > SET_{i+1} \quad .$$

In analogy to spatial reuse conflicts, the term "potential" is to be understood with respect to set associativity, i.e., the number of actual temporal reuse conflicts $NTC$ is defined as

$$\forall\, i \in \{1, \ldots, n\} \quad : \quad NTC_i := \max(0,\ NPTC_i - CA + 1)$$

for each reference and in total as

$$NTC := \sum_{i=0}^{n} NTC_i \quad .$$

Whenever the current padding fails to eliminate all temporal reuse conflicts, a new padding vector candidate is determined in a similar way as for resolving spatial reuse conflicts. However, eligible padding dimensions are restricted in a slightly different way. The minimum eligible padding dimension is defined as $MINPADDIM := d + 1$, where $d$ denotes the outermost dimension with $D_i[d] \neq D_j[d] \neq D_{i+1}[d]$ for any triple of conflicting array references $R_i$, $R_j$, and $R_{i+1}$. The maximum eligible padding dimension $MAXPADDIM$ is given as the outermost dimension $d$ where $D_i[d] \neq D_{i+1}[d]$ holds for the same references $R_i$ and $R_{i+1}$ as above. The basic idea behind these choices for $MINPADDIM$ and $MAXPADDIM$ is to select a padding dimension which, on the one hand, is sufficiently large so that the relative cache locations of adjacent references with potential temporal reuse remain untouched, but, on the other hand, is sufficiently small, so that padding actually alters the relative cache locations between these adjacent references and the conflicting reference in between.

In contrast to the choice of a padding dimension for the elimination of spatial reuse conflicts, an eligible padding dimension to avoid temporal reuse conflicts not necessarily exists. In this case, array padding does not resolve this conflict, and the inference heuristic stops at this point. Otherwise, a new padding vector candidate is chosen exactly as in the context of solving spatial reuse conflicts and temporal reuse conflicts are re-evaluated iteratively until either all are eliminated or the padding overhead constraint is exhausted.

An alternative implementation different from the above inference heuristic is to evaluate all potential padding vectors eligible with respect to the given constraint on additional memory consumption. For each such padding vector, the number of spatial and temporal reuse conflicts as well as the associated overhead are computed. Afterwards, the padding vector which causes the minimal number of conflicts is selected. If there are several equally suitable padding vectors, the one which causes the least overhead is chosen. If there are still multiple candidates, the one which incurs the least padding in inner dimensions is taken eventually. While this alternative implementation is guaranteed to find the most suitable padding with respect to the number of cache conflicts, memory consumption overhead, and loop overhead, it generally requires considerably more computational effort. However, since this effort is made at compile time rather than at runtime, it may be tolerable in many situations.

## 5    Padding Transformation

The padding inference algorithm described in the previous section results in the definition of a function $\mathcal{P}ad\mathcal{T}ype$, which for each array type found in the program or module under consideration yields the recommended padded type. Types for which a manipulation of the internal data layout is not recommended are simply returned by $\mathcal{P}ad\mathcal{T}ype$ as they are. This section focusses on the actual realization of the padding recommendation, which in the sequel will be formalized by means of a transformation scheme $\mathcal{APT}$. It defines a high-level source-to-source transformation on simplified and type-annotated intermediate SAC code. The former means that nested expressions are lifted to separate assignments to temporary variables; the latter provides a function $\mathcal{T}ype$, which associates each

$\mathcal{APT}[\![\ rettypes\ fun\ (\ args\ )\ \{\ vardecs\ instrs\ \}\ Rest\ ]\!]$
$\Longrightarrow\quad \mathcal{APT}[\![\ rettypes\ ]\!]\ fun\ (\ \mathcal{APT}[\![\ args\ ]\!]\ )\ \{$
$\qquad\qquad \mathcal{R}ep\mathcal{A}rgs[\![\ args\ ]\!]\quad \mathcal{APT}[\![\ vardecs\ ]\!]$
$\qquad\qquad \mathcal{APT}[\![\ instrs\ ]\!]$
$\qquad\ \}\quad \mathcal{APT}[\![\ Rest\ ]\!]$

$\mathcal{APT}[\![\ type\ ,\ Rest\ ]\!]$
$\Longrightarrow\quad \mathcal{P}ad\mathcal{T}ype[\![\ type\ ]\!]\ ,\ \mathcal{APT}[\![\ Rest\ ]\!]$

$\mathcal{APT}[\![\ type\ argname\ ,\ Rest\ ]\!]$
$\Longrightarrow\quad \mathcal{P}ad\mathcal{T}ype[\![\ type\ ]\!]\ argname\ ,\ \mathcal{APT}[\![\ Rest\ ]\!]$

$\mathcal{R}ep\mathcal{A}rgs[\![\ type\ argname\ ,\ Rest\ ]\!]$
$\Longrightarrow\quad type\ \_argname\ ;\ \mathcal{R}ep\mathcal{A}rgs[\![\ Rest\ ]\!]\qquad —\quad \mathcal{T}o\mathcal{B}e\mathcal{P}added[\![\ type\ ]\!]$
$\Longrightarrow\quad \mathcal{R}ep\mathcal{A}rgs[\![\ Rest\ ]\!]\qquad\qquad\qquad\quad —\quad otherwise$

$\mathcal{APT}[\![\ type\ varname\ ;\ Rest\ ]\!]$
$\Longrightarrow\quad \mathcal{P}ad\mathcal{T}ype[\![\ type\ ]\!]\ varname\ ;\qquad\qquad —\quad \mathcal{T}o\mathcal{B}e\mathcal{P}added[\![\ type\ ]\!]$
$\qquad\quad type\ \_varname\ ;\ \mathcal{APT}[\![\ Rest\ ]\!]$
$\Longrightarrow\quad type\ varname\ ;\ \mathcal{APT}[\![\ Rest\ ]\!]\qquad —\quad otherwise$

**Fig. 6.** Transformation scheme $\mathcal{APT}$ on function definitions

variable with a SAC data type. The transformation scheme $\mathcal{APT}$ is based on two additional auxiliary functions: $\mathcal{S}hape[\![\ type\ ]\!]$ yields the shape part of an array data type $type$ as a vector, and $\mathcal{T}o\mathcal{B}e\mathcal{P}added[\![\ type\ ]\!]$ decides whether or not a padding is recommended for a given type, i.e.

$$\mathcal{T}o\mathcal{B}e\mathcal{P}added[\![\ type\ ]\!]\ :=\ \mathcal{P}ad\mathcal{T}ype[\![\ type\ ]\!]\ \neq\ type\quad .$$

Figure 6 shows the effect of the compilation scheme $\mathcal{APT}$ on function definitions. The formal parameters of a function are traversed, and whenever padding is recommended for a return or argument type, the original type specification is replaced by the respective padded type. A similar transformation is applied to the local variable declarations. As already pointed out in Section 4, the transformation of a padded array into its unpadded representation is necessary in certain situations, e.g. at module boundaries. Since we do not have any a priori knowledge as to whether or not such a transformation will actually be required, additional variable declarations are introduced for each padded original local variable[1]. The same is done for padded formal parameters by means of the auxiliary compilation scheme $\mathcal{R}ep\mathcal{A}rgs$.

The effect of $\mathcal{APT}$ on applications of user-defined and of built-in functions is defined in Fig. 7. Whereas nothing is to be done in the case of locally defined functions, the application of an imported function may require a change in the representations of argument as well as of result arrays. This is described by the three auxiliary compilation schemes $\mathcal{R}ename$, $\mathcal{P}ad$, and $\mathcal{U}n\mathcal{P}ad$ defined in Fig. 8.

---

[1] Superfluous variable declarations are eliminated by subsequent optimization steps.

$\mathcal{APT}[\![\ vars = fun\ (\ args\ );\ Rest\ ]\!]$
$\implies$    $vars = fun\ (\ args\ );\ \mathcal{APT}[\![\ Rest\ ]\!]$

$\mathcal{APT}[\![\ vars = module{:}fun\ (\ args\ );\ Rest\ ]\!]$
$\implies$    $\mathcal{UnPad}[\![\ args\ ]\!]$
       $\mathcal{Rename}[\![\ vars\ ]\!] = module{:}fun\ (\ \mathcal{Rename}[\![\ args\ ]\!]\ );$
       $\mathcal{Pad}[\![\ vars\ ]\!]\ \mathcal{APT}[\![\ Rest\ ]\!]$

$\mathcal{APT}[\![\ var = \mathbf{dim}(\ array\ );\ Rest\ ]\!]$
$\implies$    $var = \mathbf{dim}(\ array\ );\ \mathcal{APT}[\![\ Rest\ ]\!]$

$\mathcal{APT}[\![\ var = \mathbf{shape}(\ array\ );\ Rest\ ]\!]$
$\implies$    $var = \mathcal{Shape}[\![\ \mathcal{Type}[\![\ array\ ]\!]\ ]\!]\ ;$       — $\mathcal{ToBePadded}[\![\ \mathcal{Type}[\![\ array\ ]\!]\ ]\!]$
       $\mathcal{APT}[\![\ Rest\ ]\!]$
$\implies$    $var = \mathbf{shape}(\ array\ );\ \mathcal{APT}[\![\ Rest$       — $otherwise$
       $]\!]$

$\mathcal{APT}[\![\ var = \mathbf{psi}(\ array\ ,\ vec\ );\ Rest\ ]\!]$
$\implies$    $var = \mathbf{psi}(\ array\ ,\ vec\ );\ \mathcal{APT}[\![\ Rest\ ]\!]$

$\mathcal{APT}[\![\ var = \mathbf{modarray}(\ array\ ,\ vec\ ,\ val\ );\ Rest\ ]\!]$
$\implies$    $var = \mathbf{modarray}(\ array\ ,\ vec\ ,\ val\ );\ \mathcal{APT}[\![\ Rest\ ]\!]$

$\mathcal{APT}[\![\ var = \mathbf{reshape}(\ vec\ ,\ array\ );\ Rest\ ]\!]$
$\implies$    $\mathcal{UnPad}[\![\ array\ ]\!]$
       $\mathcal{Rename}[\![\ var\ ]\!] = \mathbf{reshape}(\ vec\ ,\ \mathcal{Rename}[\![\ array\ ]\!]\ );$
       $\mathcal{Pad}[\![\ var\ ]\!]\ \mathcal{APT}[\![\ Rest\ ]\!]$

**Fig. 7.** Transformation scheme $\mathcal{APT}$ on function applications

$\mathcal{Rename}[\![\ var\ ,\ Rest\ ]\!]$
$\implies$    $\_var\ ,\ \mathcal{Rename}[\![\ Rest\ ]\!]$       — $\mathcal{ToBePadded}[\![\ \mathcal{Type}[\![\ var\ ]\!]\ ]\!]$
$\implies$    $var\ ,\ \mathcal{Rename}[\![\ Rest\ ]\!]$       — $otherwise$

$\mathcal{Rename}[\![\ const\ ,\ Rest\ ]\!]$
$\implies$    $const\ ,\ \mathcal{Rename}[\![\ Rest\ ]\!]$

$\mathcal{Pad}[\![\ var\ ,\ Rest\ ]\!]$
$\implies$    $var = \mathtt{Pad}(\ \_var\ );\ \mathcal{Pad}[\![\ Rest\ ]\!]$       — $\mathcal{ToBePadded}[\![\ \mathcal{Type}[\![\ var\ ]\!]\ ]\!]$
$\implies$    $\mathcal{Pad}[\![\ Rest\ ]\!]$       — $otherwise$

$\mathcal{UnPad}[\![\ var\ ,\ Rest\ ]\!]$
$\implies$    $\_var = \mathtt{UnPad}(\ var\ );\ \mathcal{Pad}[\![\ Rest\ ]\!]$       — $\mathcal{ToBePadded}[\![\ \mathcal{Type}[\![\ var\ ]\!]\ ]\!]$
$\implies$    $\mathcal{Pad}[\![\ Rest\ ]\!]$       — $otherwise$

$\mathcal{UnPad}[\![\ const\ ,\ Rest\ ]\!]$
$\implies$    $\mathcal{Pad}[\![\ Rest\ ]\!]$

**Fig. 8.** Auxiliary schemes $\mathcal{Rename}$, $\mathcal{Pad}$, and $\mathcal{UnPad}$

SAC supports only a very limited number of built-in operations on arrays. For instance, **dim** and **shape** retrieve an array's dimensionality and shape, respectively. Since padding has no effect on dimensionality, any application of **dim** may simply remain as it is. In contrast, an application of **shape** must be replaced by the shape corresponding to the original type of the argument array. The function **psi** selects the element of *array* specified by the index vector *vec*. The offset in memory specified by *vec* is computed using the function $ADDR(vec, shp)$ defined in Section 4. However, this function also computes the correct offset of an array element in a padded array representation when providing the padded shape as second argument. Hence, no code transformation is required for the selection of elements regardless of whether or not an array is padded. The built-in function **modarray** yields an array that is identical to its first argument except for the element denoted by the second argument, which is replaced by the third argument. Since $\mathcal{T}ype[\![ var ]\!] = \mathcal{T}ype[\![ array ]\!]$ and hence

$$\mathcal{P}ad\mathcal{T}ype[\![ \mathcal{T}ype[\![ var ]\!] ]\!] = \mathcal{P}ad\mathcal{T}ype[\![ \mathcal{T}ype[\![ array ]\!] ]\!] \, ,$$

**modarray** can be applied to padded arrays without additional measures. The last remaining built-in function is **reshape**, which creates an array that consists of the same elements as the argument *array*, but is associated with the new shape defined by the argument *vec*. Applications of **reshape** are restricted to arguments where the given array's original shape and the new shape are compatible, i.e., they refer to arrays with the same number of elements. However, as soon as one of the two shapes is padded, this restriction is violated. Even if both shapes are padded, it is rather unlikely that the padded shapes comply with the compatibility restriction. As a way out, both the argument array as well as the result array have to be converted between padded and unpadded representations.

The transformation of an array from a padded into an unpadded representation or vice versa is subject to the three auxiliary compilation schemes $\mathcal{R}ename$, $\mathcal{P}ad$, and $\mathcal{U}n\mathcal{P}ad$ defined in Fig. 8. Whenever a padded array is encountered where an unpadded representation is required, it is transformed by means of a predefined generic function **UnPad**. In a similar way, arrays which are created in an unpadded representation for some reason, but whose types are recommended to be padded according to $\mathcal{P}ad\mathcal{T}ype$, are transformed into the corresponding padded representation using the predefined generic function **Pad**.

Aggregate array operations are defined in one way or another by means of WITH-loops in SAC itself. The effect of the compilation scheme $\mathcal{APT}$ on WITH-loops is described in Fig. 9. Apart from recursively applying $\mathcal{APT}$ to the instructions within the body of a WITH-loop, only a single code transformation is actually required. The expression that defines the shape of the result array in a **genarray**-WITH-loop is replaced by the corresponding padded shape.

Assuming a generator depends in one way or another on the shape of a padded array, all applications of the built-in function **shape** would have been abstracted out of the generator itself. These applications are then replaced by the original shapes of the arrays they refer to (see Fig. 7). As a consequence, array padding does not alter the generators of WITH-loops in any way. Should padding apply to the result array of a **genarray**-WITH-loop or **modarray**-WITH-

$\mathcal{APT}[\![$ *var* = with ( *generator* ) { *instrs* } genarray( *shp* , *val* ); *Rest* $]\!]$
$\implies$    *var* = with ( *generator* ) { $\mathcal{APT}[\![$ *instrs* $]\!]$ }
         genarray( $\mathcal{S}hape[\![$ $\mathcal{T}ype[\![$ *var* $]\!]$ $]\!]$ , *val* );    $\mathcal{APT}[\![$ *Rest* $]\!]$

$\mathcal{APT}[\![$ *var* = with ( *generator* ) { *instrs* } modarray( *old* , *iv* , *val* ); Rest $]\!]$
$\implies$    *var* = with ( *generator* ) { $\mathcal{APT}[\![$ *instrs* $]\!]$ }
         modarray( *old* , *iv* , *val* );    $\mathcal{APT}[\![$ *Rest* $]\!]$

$\mathcal{APT}[\![$ *var* = with ( *generator* ) { *instrs* } fold( *fun* , *neutral* , *val* ); *Rest* $]\!]$
$\implies$    *var* = with ( *generator* ) { $\mathcal{APT}[\![$ *instrs* $]\!]$ }
         fold( *fun* , *neutral* , *val* );    $\mathcal{APT}[\![$ *Rest* $]\!]$

Fig. 9. Transformation scheme $\mathcal{APT}$ on WITH-loops

loop, the additional dummy elements are automatically initialized according to the default rule of the WITH-loop without any additional measures required.

While the padding transformation of WITH-loops, as outlined in Fig. 9, is simple and elegant on a conceptual level, it unfortunately introduces superfluous and avoidable runtime overhead. Initializing dummy array elements according to the WITH-loop's default rule leads to additional memory accesses that, by definition, do not contribute to the program result. This observation gives way to an additional optimization which distinguishes between dummy and regular array elements in the intermediate representation of WITH-loops. The internal format of multi-generator WITH-loops, as described in [7], provides a suitable framework for this purpose.

# 6    Performance Evaluation

Figure 10 shows the effect of applying the array padding optimization outlined in Sections 3, 4, and 5 to the PDE1 benchmark. Given the same problem sizes as in the initial investigations described in Section 2 and the upper limit on memory consumption overhead set to 10%, the padding inference heuristic decides to pad 25 out of the total of 33 problem sizes under consideration. In 16 cases, it recommends a padding of [0,1,0] ($32^3$, $96^3$, $160^3$, $224^3$, $272^3$, $288^3$, $304^3$, $336^3$, $368^3$, $400^3$, $416^3$, $432^3$, $464^3$, $480^3$, $496^3$, $528^3$) and in 7 cases a padding of [0,2,0] ($64^3$, $128^3$, $192^3$, $256^3$, $320^3$, $384^3$, $448^3$). For the problem size $352^3$ a padding of [0,22,0] and for $512^3$ a padding of [0,5,1] is chosen. Figure 10 shows the effect of array padding on the simulated cache performance of the PDE1 benchmark. In fact, array padding succeeds in keeping the L1 cache hit rate on a consistently high level between 84% and 88% across all problem sizes. It also manages to avoid the sharp drops in the overall cache hit rate, which can be observed for the problem sizes $256^3$ and $512^3$ in the original figures.

Figure 11 shows the effect of array padding on the runtime performance of the PDE1 benchmark. First of all, it can be observed that for none of the problem sizes the padding heuristic yields a performance degradation. In contrast, improvements can be observed whenever the padding transformation actually is applied, some of them being quite considerable. In particular, for the problem

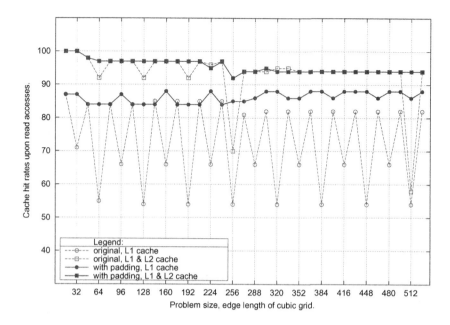

**Fig. 10.** PDE1: simulated cache performance with and without array padding

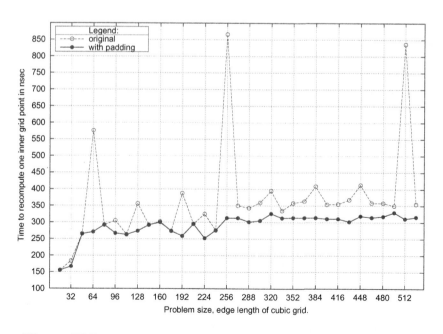

**Fig. 11.** PDE1: average time required to re-compute a single grid element

sizes $64^3$, $256^3$, and $512^3$ the average time needed to re-compute a single grid element can be reduced by 53%, 64%, and 63%, respectively. Also, the variance in runtimes is significantly decreased. With array padding consistent runtimes are achieved over the whole range of problem sizes investigated.

## 7    Related Work

In most functional programming languages, lists rather than arrays are the predominantly used data structure. The most prominent exception is the language SISAL. However, SISAL represents arrays as vectors of vectors rather than as contiguous data, and this storage format renders optimizations like array padding obsolete. So, we are not aware of any similar optimization technique in the area of functional languages.

In high-performance computing based on imperative languages, still predominantly FORTRAN, data locality has long been identified as an important issue [23]. Much research has been focussed on program transformations that reorder the sequence in which single iterations within a nesting of loops are actually executed [5,19,12]. Loop transformations such as permutation, reversal, or interchange, are used to adjust the iteration order to a given array data layout in order to achieve unit stride memory accesses in inner loops and, hence, to exploit spatial locality. Loop tiling, also called loop blocking, is a combination of loop skewing and subsequent loop permutation. It seeks to improve temporal locality in loop nestings by reducing the iteration distance between subsequent accesses to the same array element [10,4,18]. Moreover, loop fusion allows to exploit locality of reference across multiple adjacent loop nestings [11].

Often, superior cache performance can be achieved if both the iteration order as well as the memory layout are subject to compiler transformations. Examples are the combination of array transposition with loop permutation [3] or that of array padding with tiling in order to increase tile sizes and, thus, to reduce the additional loop overhead inflicted by tiled code [15]. Whereas these approaches mostly focus on capacity misses, conflict misses due to limited set associativity have been identified as another important source of performance degradation [22]. Their quantification has been achieved by so-called *cache miss equations*, i.e. linear Diophantine equations, that specify the cache line to which an array reference in a loop will be mapped [6]. Due to the complexity and expense of such accurate investigations, simpler heuristics that address both self-interference as well as cross-interference cache conflicts in FORTRAN loop nestings, have been proposed recently [16,17].

## 8    Conclusion

This paper presents an algorithm that successfully eliminates spatial and temporal reuse conflicts in SAC programs by implicitly adjusting array data layouts to access patterns and cache configurations. Cache simulation as well as runtime performance investigations on the PDE1 benchmark show that this optimization technique allows for substantial reductions in program runtimes for certain problem sizes and, moreover, achieves a decidedly more consistent runtime performance over a wide range of problem sizes.

# References

1. D.F. Bacon, S.L. Graham, and O.J. Sharp. Compiler Transformations for High-Performance Computing. *ACM Computing Surveys*, vol. 26(4), pp. 345–420, 1994.
2. B. Bershad, D. Lee, T. Romer, and B. Chen. Avoiding Conflict Misses in Large Direct-Mapped Caches. In *Proceedings of the 6th International Conference on Architectural Support for Programming Languages and Operating Systems (ASPLOS-VI), San José, California, USA*, 1994.
3. M. Cierniak and W. Li. Unifying Data and Control Transformations for Distributed Shared-Memory Machines. In *Proceedings of the ACM SIGPLAN Conference on Programming Design and Implementation (PLDI'95), La Jolla, California, USA*, 1995.
4. S. Coleman and K. McKinley. Tile Size Selection Using Cache Organization and Data Layout. In *Proceedings of the ACM SIGPLAN Conference on Programming Language Design and Implementation (PLDI'95), La Jolla, California, USA*, pp. 279–290, 1995.
5. D. Gannon, W. Jalby, and K. Gallivan. Strategies for Cache and Local Memory Management by Global Program Transformation. *Journal of Parallel and Distributed Computing*, vol. 5(5), pp. 587–616, 1988.
6. S. Ghosh, M. Martonosi, and S. Malik. Cache Miss Equations: A Compiler Framework for Analyzing and Tuning Memory Behavior. *ACM Transactions on Programming Languages and Systems*, vol. 21(4), pp. 703–746, 1999.
7. C. Grelck, D. Kreye, and S.-B. Scholz. On Code Generation for Multi-Generator WITH-Loops in SAC. In P. Koopman and C. Clack, editors, *Proceedings of the 11th International Workshop on Implementation of Functional Languages (IFL'99), Lochem, The Netherlands, selected papers, Lecture Notes in Computer Science*, vol. 1868, pp. 77–94. Springer-Verlag, 2000.
8. C. Grelck and S.-B. Scholz. HPF vs. SAC — A Case Study. In A. Bode, T. Ludwig, W. Karl, and R. Wismüller, editors, *Proceedings of the 6th International Euro-Par Conference on Parallel Processing (Euro-Par'00), Munich, Germany, Lecture Notes in Computer Science*, vol. 1900, pp. 620–624. Springer-Verlag, 2000.
9. J. L. Hennessy and D. A. Patterson. *Computer Architecture: A Quantitative Approach, Second Edition*. Morgan Kaufmann, 1995.
10. M.S. Lam, E.E. Rothberg, and M.E. Wolf. The Cache Performance of Blocked Algorithms. In *Proceedings of the 4th International Conference on Architectural Support for Programming Languages and Operating Systems (ASPLOS-IV), Palo Alto, California, USA*, pp. 63–74, 1991.
11. N. Manjikian and T.S. Abdelrahman. Fusion of Loops for Parallelism and Locality. *IEEE Transactions on Parallel and Distributed Systems*, vol. 8(2), pp. 193–209, 1997.
12. K. McKinley, S. Carr, and C.-W. Tseng. Improving Data Locality with Loop Transformations. *ACM Transactions on Programming Languages and Systems*, vol. 18(4), pp. 424–453, 1996.

13. K. McKinley and O. Temam. A Quantative Analysis of Loop Nest Locality. In *Proceedings of the 8th International Conference on Architectural Support for Programming Languages and Operating Systems (ASPLOS-VIII), Boston, Massachusetts, USA*, 1996.

14. T. Mowry, M. Lam, and A. Gupta. Design and Evaluation of a Compiler Algorithm for Prefetching. In *Proceedings of the 5th International Conference on Architectural Support for Programming Languages and Operating Systems (ASPLOS-V), Boston, Massachusetts, USA*, pp. 62–73, 1992.

15. P.R. Panda, H. Nakamura, N.D. Dutt, and A.Nicolau. A Data Alignment Technique for Improving Cache Performance. In *Proceedings of the International Conference on Computer Design VLSI in Computers and Processors, Austin, Texas, USA*, pp. 587–592. IEEE Computer Society Press, 1997.

16. G. Rivera and C.-W. Tseng. Data Transformations for Eliminating Conflict Misses. In *Proceedings of the ACM SIGPLAN International Conference on Programming Language Design and Implementation (PLDI'98), Montréal, Canada, ACM SIGPLAN Notices*, vol. 33(5), pp. 38–49. ACM Press, 1998.

17. G. Rivera and C.-W. Tseng. Eliminating Conflict Misses for High Performance Architectures. In *Proceedings of the ACM International Conference on Supercomputing (ICS'98), Melbourne, Australia*. ACM Press, 1998.

18. G. Rivera and C.-W. Tseng. A Comparison of Compiler Tiling Algorithms. In *Proceedings of the 8th International Conference on Compiler Construction (CC'99), Amsterdam, The Netherlands, Lecture Notes in Computer Science*, vol. 1575, pp. 168–182. Springer-Verlag, 1999.

19. V. Sarkar and R. Thekkath. A General Framework for Iteration-Reordering Loop Transformations. In *Proceedings of the ACM SIGPLAN Conference on Programming Language Design and Implementation (PLDI'92), San Francisco, California, USA*, pp. 175–187, 1992.

20. S.-B. Scholz. On Defining Application-Specific High-Level Array Operations by Means of Shape-Invariant Programming Facilities. In S. Picchi and M. Micocci, editors, *Proceedings of the International Conference on Array Processing Languages (APL'98), Rome, Italy*, pp. 40–45. ACM Press, 1998.

21. S.-B. Scholz. A Case Study: Effects of WITH-Loop Folding on the NAS Benchmark MG in SAC. In K. Hammond, T. Davie, and C. Clack, editors, *Proceedings of the 10th International Workshop on Implementation of Functional Languages (IFL'98), London, UK, selected papers, Lecture Notes in Computer Science*, vol. 1595, pp. 216–228. Springer-Verlag, 1999.

22. O. Temam, C. Fricker, and W. Jalby. Cache Interference Phenomena. In *Proceedings of the ACM SIGMETRICS Conference on Measurement and Modeling of Computer Systems, Nashville, Tennessee, USA*, pp. 261–271. ACM Press, 1994.

23. M. E. Wolf and M. S. Lam. A Data Locality Optimizing Algorithm. In *Proceedings of the ACM SIGPLAN Conference on Programming Language Design and Implementation (PLDI'91)*, pp. 30–44, 1991.

# The Collective Semantics
# in Functional SPMD Programming

John O'Donnell

Computing Science Department, University of Glasgow,
Glasgow G12 8QQ, UK
jtod@dcs.gla.ac.uk
http://www.dcs.gla.ac.uk/~jtod/

**Abstract.** SPMD programs are usually written from the perspective of
a single processor, yet the intended behaviour is an aggregate computation comprising many processors running the same program on local
data. Combinators, such as map, fold, scan and multibroadcast, provide
a flexible way to express SPMD programs more naturally and more abstractly at the collective level. A good SPMD programming methodology
begins with a specification at the collective level, where many significant transformations and optimisations can be introduced. Eventually,
however, this collective level program must be transformed to the individual level in order to make it executable on an SPMD system. This
paper introduces a technique needed to make the transformation possible within a formal framework: a special collective semantics for the
individual level program is required in order to justify a transformation
from the collective level to the individual level. The collective semantics
defines the meanings of the collective communication operations, and it
allows equational reasoning to be used for deriving and implementing
SPMD programs.

## 1 Introduction

Two popular methods for writing parallel programs are *expressing parallelism
using combinators* (such as map and scan), and *SPMD programming* (which is
commonly supported by commercially available parallel systems). These methods, which will be described shortly, offer complementary advantages.

It would be helpful to be able to use both styles in constructing parallel
applications. The programmer could specify an algorithm at a high level using
parallel combinators, and a variety of effective methods exist for improving such
algorithms via program transformation. In order to make it executable on a
real parallel machine, the program could then be transformed to the lower level
SPMD style. This transformation might be performed either by a compiler or
by the programmer, using formal equational reasoning.

This paper identifies a difficulty, called the *collective/individual equivalence
problem*, which arises while transforming a parallel combinator program into
an SPMD program, and it sketches an approach for solving the problem. The

M. Mohnen and P. Koopman (Eds.): IFL 2000, LNCS 2011, pp. 249–265, 2001.
© Springer-Verlag Berlin Heidelberg 2001

difficulty, in a nutshell, is that part of the meaning of the SPMD program is defined implicitly by a nonstandard semantics, and this must be taken into account in order to establish the equivalence of the high and low level versions of the algorithm. The purpose of the paper is to point out the problem and an approach to solving it, but a complete and precise implementation of the proposed solution remains as future work.

In Section 2, the parallel combinator and SPMD programming styles are described, and the collective/individual equivalence problem is discussed. Section 3 then introduces a solution to the problem, using a restricted setting (purely local computation) to keep things simple. In Section 4 we consider communications operations and a more realistic monadic coordination language, and Section 5 concludes.

# 2    Two Styles of Parallel Programming

Parallel programming languages, for both the parallel combinator style and the SPMD style, consist of two parts:

- A set of *parallel operations*. For high level programming with parallel combinators, every parallel operation is expressed directly as a combinator. For SPMD programming, different mechanisms are used, depending on whether the parallel operation is purely local or uses interprocessor communication.
- A *coordination language*, which expresses the algorithm as a sequence of parallel operations. For a functional language with parallel combinators, the coordination language could comprise the entire functional language (e.g. Haskell), but it could also be restricted to functions written in a particular form. For conventional SPMD programming, the coordination language is C or Fortran.

We will first describe the combinator and SPMD styles in more detailed, and then discuss the collective/individual equivalence problem.

## 2.1    Parallel Combinators

The combinator method for expressing parallelism is well suited for abstract, high level specifications of algorithms. A family of functions, such as map, fold and scan, is used to express parallel computations. For example, a set of parallel local computations using the same function f can be expressed as pmap f xs, where the data structure xs is distributed among the memories of the parallel processors, and the individual function applications f xi, where xi is one of the elements of xs, are executed simultaneously in different processors. This style of programming is convenient for many applications. There is a rich set of mathematical laws relating the combinators, making this approach well suited for formal reasoning as well as a variety of optimisations and program transformations.

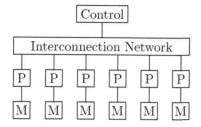

**Fig. 1.** Distributed memory machine

## 2.2 SPMD Programs

SPMD (single program, multiple data) is another popular model for programming parallel computers [1,6]. Many commercially available parallel systems support the SPMD style, and it offers relatively good program portability. The idea behind SPMD is simply that the programmer writes a program that will run on one processor, but the parallel operating system executes the program by loading a copy into all the processors, which then execute it concurrently. The term SPMD is apt because the processors all use the same program, but they normally have different data in their local memories.

SPMD programs are usually written in an imperative language, such as C or Fortran, using a standard communications library, such as MPI [8,7]. The resulting language is often referred to as C+MPI. The most characteristic attribute of conventional SPMD programming style is that the program is written from the viewpoint of a single processor, yet the programmer must bear in mind that there are actually many. For example, suppose that the aim is to perform a computation on each element of a vector, expressed as a sequential iteration:

```
for (i=0; i<n; i++)
  { y[i] = sqrt (x[i]); }
```

This program fragment requires x and y to be declared as arrays, and it would be executed sequentially. To introduce SPMD parallelism, we can distribute the arrays across the processors, so that each processor $P_i$ computes $y[i]$ using the value of $x[i]$ in its local memory. To express this, however, we don't use arrays at all; instead, x and y are declared as singletons, and the parallel iteration is expressed using an ordinary assignment statement:

```
y = sqrt (x);
```

Interprocessor communication is generally achieved through collective communication operations, which are defined in a library such as MPI. Typical examples are *fold* (also called *reduce*) and *scan* (also called multiprefix). Conceptually, collective communication operations make sense only at the collective level, since they inherently require information from all the processors. In a C+MPI program, however, they must be expressed at the individual level.

Therefore a collective communication operation is performed by arranging for each processor to call the same system library procedure, providing a local singleton argument. The parallel computer's interconnection network (Figure 1) hardware and software perform the operation, and they return a singleton value to each processor.

SPMD programs can be written in a functional language as well as in C, by treating the program as a sequence of operations. The standard MPI procedures can be called directly from a Haskell program, using a foreign language interface [9].

## 2.3    Compilation via Program Transformation

One way to proceed would be to define the collective communication operations as parallel functions, perhaps using Glasgow Parallel Haskell and algorithmic strategies [2]. However, that does not lead to an SPMD program. The aim here is different: we want to specify the program abstractly with combinators at the collective level, and then to transform it down to the individual level for parallel execution.

Most people who use SPMD systems simply write the final code in C+MPI. The drawback of SPMD programming at the individual level is that it hinders reasoning about programs. Methodologies for deriving high performance programs, such as TwoL [5] and Abstract Parallel Machines [4], require the ability to express algorithms abstractly and to transform them. The programmer needs to think at the collective level, not the individual level. Furthermore, there is a rich algebra for the standard collective communication operations, particularly the family of map, fold and scan functions, which have proven effective for a variety of program transformations and optimisations. These algebraic laws operate at the collective level, and unfortunately cannot be applied to conventional SPMD programs at the individual level. Merely expressing the low level program in Haskell rather than C is not enough; we need a way of writing collective level programs and transforming them down to the individual level.

Compilation is the transformation of a program written in a high level notation into an executable low level form. This is usually viewed as a completely automatic "black box" process. An alternative view—compilation as a sequence of program transformations—offers a range of potential benefits. The ghc compiler for Haskell consists of a sequence of program transformations, using typed intermediate languages. This organisation makes it easier to incorporate program analysis and optimisation techniques, which are often expressed as transformations. It also reduces the gap between the structure of a compiler and the framework that would be needed to carry out a correctness proof. Even without doing such a detailed proof, it is arguably better to organise a large software project in a way that links more strongly with semantics.

Fully automatic compilers are limited to optimisations that can be discovered and proved correct by algorithms. Yet many useful optimisations can be discovered by clever programmers, but are too subtle for compilers to find. This may be one reason for the continued popularity of low level languages like Fortran for applications that require high performance: the more abstract languages cannot offer equally good performance, because their compilers are not always able to find the most efficient way to implement the algorithm.

A potential solution to these problems is to combine the programmer's insight into how an algorithm could run efficiently with the ability of software tools to support straightforward transformations. In effect, this approach would lead to compilers even more open than ghc, where the results obtained by automatic compilation could be used when they are good enough, and they could be improved by the programmer when he or she has an idea for an effective optimisation and the extra work seems justified by the need for better performance.

### 2.4   The Equivalence Problem

A serious technical problem arises when transforming a parallel combinator program into its SPMD equivalent. The difficulty is that the two versions of the algorithm are *essentially* the same—they will yield the same results—yet mathematically they are not at all the same! For example, the parallel computation expressed by `pmap f xs` would be transformed into `f x` in the SPMD version, yet the equivalence equation

`pmap f xs = f x`

is simply untrue.

The essence of the problem is that the collective level program defines the behaviour explicitly, while an SPMD program leaves part of the behaviour implicit. Consequently there is no way to transform a program from the collective level to the individual level, using correctness preserving transformations and equational reasoning.

We propose a solution to the problem, comprising three components:

1. A special combinator-to-SPMD transformation rule is introduced. This rule is used exactly one time when transforming the high level algorithm to the target executable program, and that step is the one where the algorithm changes its view from the collective level to the individual level.
2. A new nonstandard *collective semantics* is introduced; this gives the meaning that an SPMD program will have when run in the intended way, on an SPMD system. For example it defines the meaning of a singleton computation $f\,x$ to be *map f xs*, provided that $x$ is a component of an aggregate $xs$ that is distributed across the processors.
3. The soundness of the combinator-to-SPMD transformation is established formally, through equational reasoning, using both the standard and the nonstandard semantics. The soundness theorem states that the collective semantics applied to the SPMD program gives the same function as the standard semantics applied to the combinator program.

The remainder of this paper sketches how these components work, but full definitions of the transformation rule and the collective semantics, and a proof of the soundness theorem, remain as future work.

It is worth noting that the problem identified here results from combining the techniques of combinator parallelism, SPMD programming, and formal program transformation via equational reasoning. A programming methodology that omits any of these elements will not run into the difficulty at all:

- Parallel applications are often written directly in C+MPI. A good long term aim for parallel functional programming researchers would be to give convincing evidence that better results can be obtained by starting with combinator parallelism. One way to show that would be to compile the parallel combinator program to SPMD form automatically, thus saving the programmer's time. Another way would be to improve the application's efficiency using program transformations at the combinator level.
- Formalisms such as algorithmic skeletons and BMF are unable to express SPMD algorithms in the first place, so issues about transforming skeleton/BMF programs into SPMD do not arise. The only way to run a skeleton/BSP program on an SPMD system is to translate it to machine code in a black box compiler, while the purpose of this paper is to show how such programs can be transformed into the machine code in a sequence of steps justified by equational reasoning.

Semantic definitions provide the formal justification for program transformations. Ordinarily, we use the standard semantics $\mathbb{S}$, where $\mathbb{S} [\![ P ]\!]$ gives the meaning of the program P. One program can be transformed to another if they both have the same meaning under the standard semantics:

**Definition 1.** *If* $\mathbb{S} [\![ P_1 ]\!] = \mathbb{S} [\![ P_2 ]\!]$, *then* $P_1$ *is transformable to* $P_2$ *under the standard semantics. This is written as* $P_1 \rightsquigarrow P_2$.

A transformation from a program $P_1$ expressed at the collective level to the corresponding program $P_2$ expressed at the individual level must be treated differently, since $\mathbb{S} [\![ P_1 ]\!] \neq \mathbb{S} [\![ P_2 ]\!]$. First we introduce a nonstandard collective semantics $\mathbb{C}$ that gives the "real" meaning of the SPMD program. That is, $\mathbb{C} [\![ P ]\!]$ is the function computed by the entire SPMD system when each of its processors is executing a copy of P. Note that $\mathbb{S} [\![ P ]\!]$ is the behaviour of an individual processor. Now we can introduce a special transformation that enables us to move from the collective level to the individual level:

**Definition 2.** *If* $\mathbb{S} [\![ P_1 ]\!] = \mathbb{C} [\![ P_2 ]\!]$ *then* $P_1$ *is transformable to* $P_2$ *under the collective semantics. This is written as* $P_1 \overset{\mathbb{C}}{\rightsquigarrow} P_2$.

In a formal methodology for deriving parallel programs, we would start with an abstract specification at the collective level, and perform a sequence of ordinary transformations using $\rightsquigarrow$. Such transformations could improve performance, introduce decisions about how to organise the computation, bring the program closer to a low level implementation, and so on. When we need to make the jump to the individual level, we use $\overset{\mathbb{C}}{\rightsquigarrow}$, which can be used only one time in a derivation. Further ordinary $\rightsquigarrow$ transformations can then be applied to the individual level program, perhaps to introduce low-level optimisations.

# 3   Local Computation with Compositional Coordination

In this section we consider the simplest case, where the only parallel operation is local computation, corresponding to parallel map, and the coordination language is pure function composition. This simplification is unrealistic for most applications, but it clarifies the distinction between parallel combinators and SPMD, and is simple enough for a fully detailed presentation here.

Let $a$ be the type of the state of an individual processor. The state of the entire system is modelled by a value of type $[a]$. This is not an arbitrary Haskell list; the list must have exactly one element for each processor, and there is no concept of sharing of lists elements. Strictly speaking, we should use a special finite sequence data type, but it is convenient to use lists so that standard functions like map can be applied. It is *not* intended that the list will be represented using the standard box and pointer data structure, and many of the properties of Haskell lists, such as sharing and infinite lists, will also be avoided.

The only parallel operation allowed is one where every processor applies the same function $f$ to its state, resulting in a new state. The behaviour of the entire system is then *map f xs*, where *xs* is the list of processor states.

The coordination language is the simplest possible, pure function composition. The parallel program thus consists of a sequence of state transition functions to be executed. Such a program is expressed as the forwards composition of the operations. The program will look more natural when expressed with the forward composition operator $(\odot)$:

$$(\odot) \;::\; (a \to b) \to (b \to c) \to a \to c$$
$$(f \odot g)\, x \;=\; g\,(f\,x)$$

In general, the type of the state could change with each operation, but let us assume here that each processor has the same state type $a$, and that each operation leaves the state type unchanged.

We call this level of abstraction, where the program specifies the computation of the entire aggregate, the *collective level*. Consider a parallel program $pc$, expressed at the collective level, which specifies that all the processors apply $f_1$ to their states in parallel, followed by parallel applications of $f_2$ and $f_3$. This program has the form:

$$pc \;::\; [a] \to [a]$$
$$pc \;=\; map\ f_1 \ \odot\ map\ f_2 \ \odot\ \ map\ f_3$$

A program that describes what one individual processor does is said to be expressed at the *individual level*. The actual code that runs on the parallel computer must be expressed at the individual level, and the aim of our transformational methodology is to translate the abstract specification (collective level) into this executable form (individual level). The program $pc$ corresponds to the individual level program $pi$:

$$pi \;::\; a \to a$$
$$pi \;=\; f_1 \ \odot\ f_2 \ \odot\ f_3$$

Thus for programs that perform purely local computations, the only difference between the collective and individual levels is a map that expresses the fact that many processors are doing the same thing.

## 3.1    Transformation

As the previous example suggests, all we have to do in translating the program is to remove the maps. (Naturally, the translation is more complex when communication operations are introduced, or when the coordination language is enhanced.) The program transformation $\overset{\mathbb{C}}{\leadsto}$ is defined as follows:

**Definition 3.** *Let $P$ be a program expressed at the collective level, within the pure function composition coordination language. Then the collective to individual transformation $\mathbb{T}[\![\,P\,]\!]$ is defined by*

$$\begin{aligned}
\mathbb{T}\,[\![\,f_1 \odot f_2\,]\!] &= \mathbb{T}\,[\![\,f_1\,]\!] \,\circledcirc\, \mathbb{T}\,[\![\,f_2\,]\!] \\
\mathbb{T}\,[\![\,\mathtt{map}\ f\,]\!] &= f
\end{aligned}$$

*If $\mathbb{T}\,[\![\,P_1\,]\!] = P_2$, we write $P_1 \overset{\mathbb{C}}{\leadsto} P_2$.*

## 3.2    Collective Semantics

The meaning of the collective level program is just given by its standard semantics. If it is written in Haskell, we can just compile it and the compiler will produce code that computes the right value. However, the meaning of the individual level program $P$ running on an SPMD system is *not* given by the standard semantics. Therefore we need to define a special collective semantics $\mathbb{C}$ that gives the real (collective) meaning of $P$. This is defined as follows:

**Definition 4.** *Let $P$ be a program expressed at the individual level, within the pure function composition coordination language. Then the collective semantics $\mathbb{C}\,[\![\,P\,]\!]$ is defined by*

$$\begin{aligned}
\mathbb{C}\,[\![\,f_1 \odot f_2\,]\!] &= \mathbb{C}\,[\![\,f_1\,]\!] \,\circledcirc\, \mathbb{C}\,[\![\,f_2\,]\!] \\
\mathbb{C}\,[\![\,\mathtt{f}\,]\!] &= map\ (\mathbb{S}[f])
\end{aligned}$$

Again, the simplicity of this definition results from the lack of communication operations. Note that if $P :: a \to a$, then $\mathbb{C}\,[\![\,P\,]\!] :: [a] \to [a]$.

## 3.3    Soundness

Clearly a collective level program $pc$ and its individual level translation $pi$ represent different mathematical functions, and they have different types. However, when $pi$ is executed on the processors of an SPMD system, it behaves just the same as $pc$. The collective to individual transformation is said to be *sound* if the individual level program has—on an SPMD system—the same behaviour as the collective level program using the standard semantics. The following straightforward theorem states that $\mathbb{T}$, as defined above for the pure composition coordination language, is sound.

**Theorem 1.** *Let*

$$f_1, \ldots, f_n \; :: \; a \to a$$
$$pc \; = \; map \; f_1 \; \textcircled{\scriptsize o} \; \cdots \; \textcircled{\scriptsize o} \; map \; f_n$$

*such that pc is well typed. Then*

$$\mathbb{C} \, [\![ \, \mathbb{T}[\![ \, pc \, ]\!] \, ]\!] \; = \; \mathbb{S} \, [\![ \, pc \, ]\!].$$

*Proof.* Structural induction over the program text. For the base case, let f be a piece of program text denoting a basic function; then

$$\mathbb{C} \, [\![ \, \mathbb{T}[\![ \, \mathtt{map \; f} \, ]\!] \, ]\!]$$
$$= \; \mathbb{C} \, [\![ \, \mathtt{f} \, ]\!]$$
$$= \; map \, (\mathbb{S} \, [\![ \, \mathtt{f} \, ]\!])$$
$$= \; \mathbb{S} \, [\![ \, \mathtt{map \; f} \, ]\!]$$

In the inductive case, assume the theorem holds for f and g. Then

$$\mathbb{C} \, [\![ \, \mathbb{T}[\![ \, \mathtt{f} \; \textcircled{\scriptsize o} \; \mathtt{g} \, ]\!] \, ]\!]$$
$$= \; \mathbb{C} \, [\![ \, \mathbb{T}[\![ \, \mathtt{f} \, ]\!] \odot \mathbb{T}[\![ \, \mathtt{g} \, ]\!] \, ]\!]$$
$$= \; \mathbb{C} \, [\![ \, \mathbb{T}[\![ \, \mathtt{f} \, ]\!] \, ]\!] \odot \mathbb{C} \, [\![ \, \mathbb{T}[\![ \, \mathtt{g} \, ]\!] \, ]\!]$$
$$= \; \mathbb{S} \, [\![ \, \mathtt{f} \, ]\!] \odot \mathbb{S} \, [\![ \, \mathtt{g} \, ]\!]$$
$$= \; \mathbb{S} \, [\![ \, \mathtt{f} \; \textcircled{\scriptsize o} \; \mathtt{g} \, ]\!]$$

What this theorem gives us is a formal justification for performing the collective to individual level transformation. Without the theorem, it is impossible to use ordinary equational reasoning to make that step.

## 4   Collective Communications and Monadic Coordination

Although the language presented in the previous section is suitable for a few simple pipelining problems, it is inadequate for nearly all practical parallel programming. A crucial limitation is that there is no provision for interprocessor communication, and a less severe problem is that pure function composition is inconvenient as a coordination language. Both of those problems are addressed in this section: collective communication operations are incorporated, and a monadic coordination language is provided. Again, we need a transformation from the collective to the individual level, a collective semantics for the individual level, and a soundness theorem. These will only be sketched in this paper, and a complete specification and proof are left for future work.

### 4.1   Collective Communication Operations

A collective communication operation involves all the processors in the system. A typical example is a scatter operation, in which one processors produces a vector of values $[x_0, x_1, \ldots, x_{P-1}]$, where there are $P$ processors; the result of the scatter operation is that processor $P_i$ receives $x_i$. A similar (but opposite) operation is gather, where one processor builds a vector in its local memory, where the $i$th element is provided by processor $i$.

The essential point about collective communications is that all the processors must participate in it at the same time, and they must all agree on what operation is being performed. This is quite different from random point-to-point message passing, where each processor can do what it likes, when it likes. Collective communications fit well with SPMD programming, since the constraint that every processor is running the same program makes it feasible to ensure that the processors stay synchronised sufficiently to ensure that they all agree about what communications operation to perform next. SIMD systems also provide collective communications, since the hardware requires every processor to be executing the same instruction as all the others. However, the SPMD style allows the simplicity of the data parallel programming model, while still allowing the processors to execute different instructions.

A particularly interesting class of collective communications involve computation as well as communication. For example, the fold (or reduce) operation requires every processor to send a data value into the network, which must then use a binary operator $f$ to combine pairs of values, eventually producing a singleton result.

In this section we consider just three collective communication operations, which are sufficient to illustrate how the collective to individual transformation works in the presence of communications. These operations are `pfold`, `piscanl`, and `piscanr`.

The parallel fold function `pfold` combines the elements of a list using a function `f`. In order to allow a log time parallel implementation, `f` is assumed to be associative; for this reason its type is $(a \to a \to a)$ rather than the more general types permitted for sequential folds.

```
pfold :: (a->a->a) -> [a] -> a
```

The intention is that a parallel system will implement `pfold` in log time using a tree-structured computation. One way to achieve this is to write a conventional compiler that translates a `pfold` application into the necessary machine code.

Our purpose here, however, is to investigate how to transform the high level program into a low level SPMD program *expressed in the same functional language*. At the high level, we *specify* the semantics of `pfold` using the standard `foldl1` function; this suffices for rapid prototyping as well as formal reasoning. Thus the abstract definition of `pfold` should be viewed as a mathematical definition, which enables the high level program to be executed directly.

```
pfold = foldl1
```

Scan is a generalisation of fold: when `f` is scanned over a list, `pfold` gives the final result and `scan` produces a list of all the intermediate results. Again, the function `f` is assumed to be associative. A list can be scanned from the left in parallel (`piscanl`, giving the intermediate results of `foldl`) or from the right `piscanr`, giving the intermediate results of `foldr`). These are both *inclusive* scans; i.e. the first element of their result includes the first element of the argument, and there is no singleton accumulator argument.

```
piscanl, piscanr :: (a->a->a) -> [a] -> [a]
piscanl f xs
  = [foldl1 f (take (i+1) xs)
       | i <- [0.. length xs - 1]]
piscanr f xs
  = [foldr1 f (drop i xs)
       | i <- [0 .. length xs - 1]]
```

The mathematical specifications of these functions are expressed with list comprehensions, since experience has shown this to give a clear and direct specification suitable for equational reasoning. The specifications are also executable, so they can be used for rapid prototyping. However, they are inefficient, as they require $O(n^2)$ time to scan a list of length $n$, while there are sequential accumulator-style definitions that require only $O(n)$ time, and the parallel implementation is $O(\log n)$. However, efficiency is less important than clarity for semantic specifications.

## 4.2   A Monadic Coordination Language

Practical parallel programs use many variables, and the collective communication operations will typically access and update just a few of these. It is possible, but awkward, to express such programs using function composition to coordinate the operations. To do this, we would need to define two helper functions for every variable, one to access the processor state and fetch the variable's value, and the other to update the state with a new value for that variable.

A much more convenient approach is to use a monadic coordination language. This enables us to bind a name to the result returned by an operation, it can handle the state transitions, and it can also provide Input/Output operations. Monadic collective communication operations for the `fold`, `piscanl` and `piscanr` functions can be defined as IO operations that return the result specified by the corresponding function:

```
opfold :: (a->a->a) -> [a] -> IO a
opfold f xs = return (pfold f xs)
opiscanl, opiscanr :: (a->a->a) -> [a] -> IO [a]
opiscanl f xs = return (piscanl f xs)
opiscanr f xs = return (piscanr f xs)
```

## 4.3   Example: Maximum Segment Sum (MSS)

The standard Maximum Segment Sum problem will be used to illustrate the programming style at the collective and individual levels. The problem is to find the largest possible sum of a sequence of contiguous numbers within a list of numbers. One could derive a solution to the problem from first principles, using a sequence of standard $\rightsquigarrow$ transformations, but that is not the point of this paper. Readers interested in how MSS works are referred to [1,3]. The algorithm mss can be expressed at the collective level, with monadic coordination, as follows:

```
mss :: [Int] -> IO ()
mss xs =
  do ss <- opiscanl (+) xs
     ms <- opiscanr max ss
     let bs = [m-s+x | (m,s,x) <- zip3 ms ss xs]
     r <- opfold max bs
     putStr ("result = " ++ show r ++ "\n")
     return ()
```

For example, running

```
test1 = mss [2,3,-50,20,30,-100,20,-19,21,22,23,-100,60]
```

produces 67, since the largest segment sum is $20 + -19 + 21 + 22 + 23$: extending the segment either to the left or right will make the result smaller, because of the big negative numbers, but it's worth including the -19 in order to include also the 20. The intermediate lists computed for this example are:

```
ss = [2,5,-45,-25,5,-95,-75,-94,-73,-51,-28,-128,-68]
ms = [5,5,5,5,5,-28,-28,-28,-28,-28,-28,-68,-68]
bs = [5,3,0,50,30,-33,67,47,66,45,23,-40,60]
result = 67
```

## 4.4  Transformation

We must now transform the collective level program mss into the individual level, where the collective communication operations are performed in three steps:

1. The processor sends a *request* to the interconnection network, specifying which collective communication operation is to be performed, and supplying the data values contributed from the processor's local memory.
2. The interconnection network synchronises; that is, it waits until all processors have made a request. It checks that all processors have requested the *same* operation; if not a fatal error has occurred. Otherwise, the network performs the operation, which in general involves both communication and computation. In the case of scan, for example, the network is responsible for arranging the necessary applications of $f$; it is immaterial where the actual work is performed physically—the network could execute the applications, or it could have the processors do that work.
3. Finally, the interconnection network packages the results of the operation into a set of *replies*, one for each processor. The processors receive their replies, which will normally contain data values, at which point they can resume their computations.

The transformation to the individual level is straightforward. The type of the program has changed from `[Int] -> IO ()` to `Int -> IO ()`, and each collective communications operation is replaced by an operation with a similar name which requests the operation. The local computation that was expressed by a list comprehension (essentially, by a map) becomes just a local singleton computation, expressed as `let b = m-s+x`.

```
mss_ind :: Int -> IO ()
mss_ind x =
  do s <- req_opiscanl Plus x
     m <- req_opiscanr Max s
     let b = m-s+x
     r <- req_opfold Max b
     putStr ("result = " ++ show r ++ "\n")
     return ()
```

A request to perform a collective communication operation contains a tag specifying which operation is being performed, and all necessary arguments. All of the collective communications requests are produced by a generic ouput operation putReq, which takes the operands of the operation, packages them into a data structure representing the request, and outputs it to the network. From the viewpoint of the individual processor, putReq is simply on I/O operation.

```
req_opiscanl, req_opiscanr, req_opfold :: FunRep -> Int -> IO Int
req_opiscanl f x = putReq Req_opiscanl f x
req_opiscanr f x = putReq Req_opiscanr f x
req_opfold f x    = putReq Req_opfold   f x
```

A tag of type Request indicates which operation is to be performed. Naturally, the system supports a fixed set of operations, so it is convenient to represent them with an enumerated type:

```
data Request
  = Req_opiscanr | Req_opiscanl | Req_opfold
    deriving Show
```

The functional argument f to the fold and scan functions must also be included in the request. Several different approaches have been taken on real parallel systems for representing functional arguments. Some systems, such as the programming languages for the Connection Machine, restrict such functional arguments to a fixed set. This restriction is appropriate when the function applications will be performed by dedicated hardware within the interconnection network, and that hardware is limited to a small fixed set of functions. In such systems, it is natural to represent the function to be represented as another enumerated type:

```
data FunRep
  = Plus | Times | Max | Min
    deriving Show
```

However, this Draconian restriction prevents many useful programs from being expressed. A better alternative is to provide actual executable code as the function representation, but this raises several further problems: for instance, some computers use special hardware in the interconnection network to perform the function applications needed by fold and scan, and ordinary compiled functions won't run in the network nodes. Allowing an arbitrary function $f$ to be specified is more complicated to implement, but it greatly enhances the system's flexibility. In the remainder of this paper we take the simpler approach, where functions must be represented by `FunRep`.

In order to make the individual level program executable on an ordinary workstation, `putReq` can be defined simply to output a string to the standard output channel, and to return a value parsed from a string that is read in. The definition below can be used for testing the individual level program, but the parallel system will provide its own IO channel for collective communication requests, and will have its own binary format for representing the requests and responses.

```
putReq :: Request -> FunRep -> Int -> IO Int
putReq r f x =
  do putStr (show r ++ " " ++ show f ++ " " ++ show x ++ "\n")
     y <- getInt
     return y
```

Now we can outline the transformation $\overset{C}{\leadsto}$, which changes a program from the collective to the individual level. The transformation has to replace each collective communication combinator operation with the request to perform that operation. In doing so, the functional argument `f` is replaced by its representation of type `FunRep`; this is performed by the $\mathbb{F}$ transformation. Furthermore, the type of the program is changed, to reflect the aggregate input. Parallel maps are replaced by singleton computations, and this must be done for list comprehensions as well as direct applications of map. A sketch of the definition of $\overset{C}{\leadsto}$ is given below, but there are a number of details that are omitted here.

$$
\begin{array}{lll}
\texttt{pc :: [a] -> IO ()} & \overset{C}{\leadsto} & \texttt{pi :: a -> IO ()} \\
\texttt{let ys = map f xs} & \overset{C}{\leadsto} & \texttt{let y = f x} \\
\texttt{ys <- opiscanl f xs} & \overset{C}{\leadsto} & \texttt{y <- req\_opiscanl} \left(\mathbb{F}[\![\,\texttt{f}\,]\!]\right) \texttt{x} \\
\texttt{ys <- opiscanr f xs} & \overset{C}{\leadsto} & \texttt{y <- req\_opiscanr} \left(\mathbb{F}[\![\,\texttt{f}\,]\!]\right) \texttt{x} \\
\texttt{ys <- opfold f xs} & \overset{C}{\leadsto} & \texttt{y <- req\_fold} \left(\mathbb{F}[\![\,\texttt{f}\,]\!]\right) \texttt{x} \\
\end{array}
$$

There is one subtle point to note about the parallel fold operation, `opfold`. Ordinarily, fold functions return a singleton result, while scan functions return a list. Data parallel programs usually follow the same convention, and there is a unique control processor that receives the singleton result of operations like fold. In SPMD programming, however, there is no special control processor, so there is no obvious unique place to send the result of a fold. One approach would be to choose one particular processor to be the recipient of the result (just as one processor is chosen to receive the results of a gather operation). Here, we take a different approach: the fold operation produces a singleton result, which is broadcast by the network to every processor. Thus the fold and scan functions have the same type: both produce aggregate (e.g. list) results, and the only difference is that with fold, all the elements of the list are the same.

## 4.5   Collective Semantics

The individual level program can be expressed in Haskell, and it has a standard semantics provided by the Haskell compiler. This can be executed directly on the system hardware; thus we can transform a program from a high level collective specification all the way down to executable parallel code, using formally justified transformations throughout. The final individual level program is definitely sequential, but instead of performing normal Input/Output operations to ordinary peripherals, it does its I/O to the interconnection network, "outputting" requests for collective communications, and "inputting" the results. From the point of view of the hardware, it is just an ordinary sequential imperative program.

The nonstandard collective semantics must model the behaviours of all the processors, as well as the interconnection network. Recall that in Section 3.2 we used a collective semantics that modelled the set of processors with the *map* function. Since there was no communication, nothing had to be done about the interconnection network. Now, however, the collective semantics needs to perform a full simulation of the parallel system in order to define the meaning of an individual level request for collective communications.

The simulation can be done in several ways; one approach is sketched here. Consider how we can define the collective meaning of

```
y <- req_opiscanl f x
```

The simulation is defined monadically, as a collective operation that performs the following sequence of steps:

1. Each processor is executed in turn, and its request operation is redefined so that it saves the data provided by the processor into an aggregate structure.
2. Now that all the inputs to the interconnection network are known, the behaviour of the network is simulated using the appropriate combinator (for example, `piscanl`). This will produce a list of responses.
3. Each response in the list is made available to the corresponding processor, as the result of its operation.

It is interesting to consider exactly where each part of the computation takes place. A program written at the collective level contains both the function definitions of the parallel combinators (although these may be gathered in a separate library) and the full algorithm, expressed in the coordination language. For example, the complete program `mss` from Section 4.3 contains the definition of `piscanl` and its use. (It makes no difference in principle if the combinator is loaded from a standard library; it could be defined by the programmer, just like any other function.)

When the program is expressed at the individual level, there is no definition of the combinators. These are, in effect, magic operations provided by the interconnection network. The actual user code contains only the coordination algorithm; the combinators correspond to whatever combination of hardware and software the manufacturer used to implement the MPI library on its parallel system.

Occasionally, manufacturers of parallel systems provide software tools that simulate the full system, but which run on ordinary workstations. This is intended to allow programmers to develop and debug their code on their own machines, saving expensive time on the parallel machine. The collective semantics is exactly like such a software tool; it allows the individual level program to be executed in Haskell, on an ordinary workstation, in order to find out what result the program will have on the parallel system.

### 4.6   Soundness

To support our transformational programming methodology, we need a soundness theorem for the monadic coordination language with the full complement of collective communication operations. A precise statement of the theorem, and its proof, will not be given here.

A program $P^c$ written at the collective level (with normal scans and folds, for example) has just one meaning $\mathbb{S}[\![P^c]\!]$, delivered by the standard semantics $\mathbb{S}$ and implemented by the Haskell compiler. A program $P^i$ written at the individual level has two distinct meanings:

- If we have compiled $P^i$ into C+MPI and are running it on a real parallel system, the program treats collective communication operations like Input/Output operations, with the interconnection network acting as a special I/O port.
- The collective semantics gives the program $P^i$ a meaning in the functional world by simulating the parallel system hardware, including all the processors and the interconnection network.

## 5   Conclusion

It is conventional to write SPMD programs at the individual level, but it it is clearer to write high level specifications more abstractly, at the collective level. In order to exploit transformational programming in the SPMD model, we need a special transformation rule that converts a collective level operation into a corresponding request at the individual level. In order to provide a formal justification for this collective-to-individual transformation, we provide a nonstandard collective semantics, and a soundness theorem.

This paper has taken only the first step; much further work remains. The next step is to formalise the transformation for a practical, complete SPMD programming language and to prove the soundness theorem. We could choose a reasonable subset of MPI as the set of collective communication operations; the approach proposed here would then make it possible to compile a high level combinator program almost all the way down to an executable C+MPI program, using formally justified transformations throughout the entire process.

# References

1. S. G. Akl. *Parallel Computation—Models and Methods*. Prentice Hall, 1997.
2. K. Hammond and G. Michaelson, editors. *Research Directions in Parallel Functional Programming*. Springer Verlag, 1999.
3. John O'Donnell. *Research Directions in Parallel Functional Programming*, chapter Data Parallelism. Springer Verlag, 1999.
4. John O'Donnell and Gudula Rünger. Abstract parallel machines. *Computers and Artificial Intelligence (continued as Computing and Informatics)*, 19(2):105–129, 2000.
5. Thomas Rauber and Gudula Rünger. Deriving structured parallel implementations for numerical methods. *Microprocessing and Microprogramming*, 41:589–608, 1996.
6. D. Skillicorn and D. Talia. Models and languages for parallel computation. *ACM Computing Surveys*, 30(2):123–169, 1998.
7. M. Snir, S. W. Otto, S. Huss-Lederman, D. Walker, and J. Dongarra. *MPI—The Complete Reference*. MIT Press, 1995.
8. D. Walker. The design of a standard message-passing interface for distributed memory concurrent computers. *Parallel Computing*, 20(4):657–673, April 1994.
9. Michael Weber. hMPI, a Haskell binding for MPI. http://www-i2.informatik.rwth-aachen.de/Software/Haskell/libs, 2000.

# Author Index

# Lecture Notes in Computer Science

For information about Vols. 1–1944
please contact your bookseller or Springer-Verlag

Vol. 1983: K.S. Leung, L.-W. Chan, H. Meng (Eds.), Intelligent Data Engineering and Automated Learning – IDEAL 2000. Proceedings, 2000. XVI, 573 pages. 2000.

Vol. 1984: J. Marks (Ed.), Graph Drawing. Proceedings, 2001. XII, 419 pages. 2001.

Vol. 1985: J. Davidson, S.L. Min (Eds.), Languages, Compilers, and Tools for Embedded Systems. Proceedings, 2000. VIII, 221 pages. 2001.

Vol. 1987: K.-L. Tan, M.J. Franklin, J. C.-S. Lui (Eds.), Mobile Data Management. Proceedings, 2001. XIII, 289 pages. 2001.

Vol. 1988: L. Vulkov, J. Waśniewski, P. Yalamov (Eds.), Numerical Analysis and Its Applications. Proceedings, 2000. XIII, 782 pages. 2001.

Vol. 1989: M. Ajmone Marsan, A. Bianco (Eds.), Quality of Service in Multiservice IP Networks. Proceedings, 2001. XII, 440 pages. 2001.

Vol. 1990: I.V. Ramakrishnan (Ed.), Practical Aspects of Declarative Languages. Proceedings, 2001. VIII, 353 pages. 2001.

Vol. 1991: F. Dignum, C. Sierra (Eds.), Agent Mediated Electronic Commerce. VIII, 241 pages. 2001. (Subseries LNAI).

Vol. 1992: K. Kim (Ed.), Public Key Cryptography. Proceedings, 2001. XI, 423 pages. 2001.

Vol. 1993: E. Zitzler, K. Deb, L. Thiele, C.A.Coello Coello, D. Corne (Eds.), Evolutionary Multi-Criterion Optimization. Proceedings, 2001. XIII, 712 pages. 2001.

Vol. 1995: M. Sloman, J. Lobo, E.C. Lupu (Eds.), Policies for Distributed Systems and Networks. Proceedings, 2001. X, 263 pages. 2001.

Vol. 1997: D. Suciu, G. Vossen (Eds.), The World Wide Web and Databases. Proceedings, 2000. XII, 275 pages. 2001.

Vol. 1998: R. Klette, S. Peleg, G. Sommer (Eds.), Robot Vision. Proceedings, 2001. IX, 285 pages. 2001.

Vol. 1999: W. Emmerich, S. Tai (Eds.), Engineering Distributed Objects. Proceedings, 2000. VIII, 271 pages. 2001.

Vol. 2000: R. Wilhelm (Ed.), Informatics: 10 Years Back, 10 Years Ahead. IX, 369 pages. 2001.

Vol. 2001: G.A. Agha, F. De Cindio, G. Rozenberg (Eds.), Concurrent Object-Oriented Programming and Petri Nets. VIII, 539 pages. 2001.

Vol. 2002: H. Comon, C. Marché, R. Treinen (Eds.), Constraints in Computational Logics. Proceedings, 1999. XII, 309 pages. 2001.

Vol. 2003: F. Dignum, U. Cortés (Eds.), Agent Mediated Electronic Commerce III. XII, 193 pages. 2001. (Subseries LNAI).

Vol. 2004: A. Gelbukh (Ed.), Computational Linguistics and Intelligent Text Processing. Proceedings, 2001. XII, 528 pages. 2001.

Vol. 2006: R. Dunke, A. Abran (Eds.), New Approaches in Software Measurement. Proceedings, 2000. VIII, 245 pages. 2001.

Vol. 2007: J.F. Roddick, K. Hornsby (Eds.), Temporal, Spatial, and Spatio-Temporal Data Mining. Proceedings, 2000. VII, 165 pages. 2001. (Subseries LNAI).

Vol. 2009: H. Federrath (Ed.), Designing Privacy Enhancing Technologies. Proceedings, 2000. X, 231 pages. 2001.

Vol. 2010: A. Ferreira, H. Reichel (Eds.), STACS 2001. Proceedings, 2001. XV, 576 pages. 2001.

Vol. 2011: M. Mohnen, P. Koopman (Eds.), Implementation of Functional Languages. Proceedings, 2000. VIII, 267 pages. 2001.

Vol. 2013: S. Singh, N. Murshed, W. Kropatsch (Eds.), Advances in Pattern Recognition – ICAPR 2001. Proceedings, 2001. XIV, 476 pages. 2001.

Vol. 2015: D. Won (Ed.), Information Security and Cryptology – ICISC 2000. Proceedings, 2000. X, 261 pages. 2001.

Vol. 2018: M. Pollefeys, L. Van Gool, A. Zisserman, A. Fitzgibbon (Eds.), 3D Structure from Images – SMILE 2000. Proceedings, 2000. X, 243 pages. 2001.

Vol. 2020: D. Naccache (Ed.), Topics in Cryptology – CT-RSA 2001. Proceedings, 2001. XII, 473 pages. 2001

Vol. 2021: J. N. Oliveira, P. Zave (Eds.), FME 2001: Formal Methods for Increasing Software Productivity. Proceedings, 2001. XIII, 629 pages. 2001.

Vol. 2022: A. Romanovsky, C. Dony, J. Lindskov Knudsen, A. Tripathi (Eds.), Advances in Exception Handling Techniques. XII, 289 pages. 2001

Vol. 2024: H. Kuchen, K. Ueda (Eds.), Functional and Logic Programming. Proceedings, 2001. X, 391 pages. 2001.

Vol. 2026: F. Müller (Ed.), High-Level Parallel Programming Models and Supportive Environments. Proceedings, 2001. IX, 137 pages. 2001.

Vol. 2027: R. Wilhelm (Ed.), Compiler Construction. Proceedings, 2001. XI, 371 pages. 2001.

Vol. 2028: D. Sands (Ed.), Programming Languages and Systems. Proceedings, 2001. XIII, 433 pages. 2001.

Vol. 2029: H. Hussmann (Ed.), Fundamental Approaches to Software Engineering. Proceedings, 2001. XIII, 349 pages. 2001.

Vol. 2030: F. Honsell, M. Miculan (Eds.), Foundations of Software Science and Computation Structures. Proceedings, 2001. XII, 413 pages. 2001.

Vol. 2031: T. Margaria, W. Yi (Eds.), Tools and Algorithms for the Construction and Analysis of Systems. Proceedings, 2001. XIV, 588 pages. 2001.

Vol. 2034: M.D. Di Benedetto, A. Sangiovanni-Vincentelli (Eds.), Hybrid Systems: Computation and Control. Proceedings, 2001. XIV, 516 pages. 2001.

Vol. 2035: D. Cheung, G.J. Williams, Q. Li (Eds.), Advances in Knowledge Discovery and Data Mining – PAKDD 2001. Proceedings, 2001. XVIII, 596 pages. 2001. (Subseries LNAI).

Vol. 2037: E.J.W. Boers et al. (Eds.), Applications of Evolutionary Computing. Proceedings, 2001. XIII, 516 pages. 2001.

Vol. 2038: J. Miller, M. Tomassini, P.L. Lanzi, C. Ryan, A.G.B. Tettamanzi, W.B. Langdon (Eds.), Genetic Programming. Proceedings, 2001. XI, 384 pages. 2001.

Vol. 2040: W. Kou, Y. Yesha, C.J. Tan (Eds.), Electronic Commerce Technologies. Proceedings, 2001. X, 187 pages. 2001.